PASSION PARTNERS

Passion Partners

THE PIETY OF
George Mackay Brown
&
Gerard Manley Hopkins

ALISON GRAY

Angelico Press

First published in the USA
by Angelico Press 2024
Copyright © Alison Gray 2024

All rights reserved:
No part of this book may be reproduced or transmitted,
in any form or by any means, without permission

For information, address:
Angelico Press, Ltd.
169 Monitor St.
Brooklyn, NY 11222
www.angelicopress.com

ppr 979-8-89280-024-2
cloth 979-8-89280-025-9

Book and cover design
by Michael Schrauzer

STABAT MATER

"Grant that I may carry within me the death of Christ, make me a partner in his Passion, let me relive his wounds."

(a liturgical fragment from Analecta Hymnica Medii Aevi)[1]

---

[1] Duffy, *The Stripping of the Altars* (Yale University Press, 1992), 259.

CONTENTS

CITATIONS X

ACKNOWLEDGMENTS XI

INTRODUCTION 1

CHAPTER ONE
The Greenfields Kirk 31

CHAPTER TWO
A Thousand Candles of Gorse 61

CHAPTER THREE
Fetching Out Inscape and Instress 99

CHAPTER FOUR
Stalling and Stemming with Stars and Stations 136

CHAPTER FIVE
Hurrahing in the Harvests 175

CHAPTER SIX
Immortalizing Storms and Shipwrecks 210

CHAPTER SEVEN
Theological Blades 244

CONCLUSION 280

APPENDIX 295

WORKS CITED 297

INDEX 305

CITATIONS

All citations are in a single footnote for each paragraph or series of related paragraphs, listing citations in sequence.

The following abbreviations are used:
- MS   Manuscript
- TS   Typescript
- EWM   Ernest Walker Marwick Collection
- NLS   National Library of Scotland
- OLA   Orkney Library Archive

The National Library of Scotland George Mackay Brown Collection is cited throughout in the fullest form in order to elevate its ranking in the reader's mind as the central concern of this study. The intention is to give the strongest sense possible of the materiality of the *Essays and Notebooks* and thus Mackay Brown's development and the workings of his spirituality and intellect during this Edinburgh period. Equally "Mackay Brown" is used throughout as opposed to "Brown" because this was his pen name chosen specifically to give the fullest sense of his literary identity.

ACKNOWLEDGMENTS

I would like to thank all those who have helped and supported me in my research especially in granting permission to reproduce copyright materials.

George Mackay Brown Literary Estate

Jenny Brown Associates

National Library of Scotland

Edinburgh University Special Collections

Ernest Walker Marwick Estate

Gunni Moberg Estate

Lucy Gibbon Orkney Library Archive

Herald Printshop

William S. Peterson, George Mackay Brown Online Bibliography

Right Rev Hugh Gilbert OSB, Bishop of Aberdeen

Pluscarden Abbey

John Radford London

Sarah Drever Kirkwall

Inga Croy Kirkwall

Mark & Geraldine Ferguson Orkney

INTRODUCTION

"WHEN I LANDED IN THE REPUBLIC OF CONscience it was so noiseless when the engines stopped, I could hear a curlew high above the runway."[1] Seamus Heaney was in the mind of Orkney when he remembered the silence—and then the call of the curlew—the first time he landed in the islands in June 1982 for the St. Magnus Festival.[2] As the dancing metrics of the curlew birdsong entranced him, he truly landed in the shared poetical mind of George Mackay Brown and Gerard Manley Hopkins. The haunting birdsong of the curlew with its under- and overtones, its silence, twitter, and trill, called up and marked out the dancing metrics of shape, pattern and sound that Heaney identified as "the republic of conscience."[3] Strong writers, strong poets, cluster together in a canon, mostly defined by the language and culture wherein they express themselves. The literary critic Harold Bloom argued that in their perceived strength they feel the need to clear imaginative space for themselves because their predecessors intimidate and inhibit the poet's creative processes. He argued this can create a strong driving impetus towards literary achievement. But clearly this was not how it worked for the Orcadian poet George Mackay Brown or Gerard Manley Hopkins. These two amazing poets heard

---

1 Heaney, in his introduction to a series of writings put together by Amnesty International Irish Section and published by the Irish Times to mark the 60th anniversary of the Universal Declaration of Human Rights, said about his poem "From the Republic of Conscience" published in *The Haw Lantern* in 1985: "I took it that Conscience would be a republic, a silent, solitary place where a person would find it hard to avoid self-awareness and self-examination; and this made me think of Orkney. I remembered the silence the first time I landed there. When I got off the small propeller plane and started walking across the grass to a little arrivals hut, I heard the cry of a curlew. And as soon as that image came to me, I was up and away, able to proceed with a fiction that felt workable yet unconstrained, a made-up thing that might be hung in the scale as a counterweight to the given actuality of the world." Heaney gifted a signed copy to Mackay Brown From the Republic of Conscience. See Peterson [Mackay Brown's LIBRARY].
2 The St Magnus International Festival is an annual arts festival which takes place at midsummer on the islands of Orkney, off the north coast of mainland Scotland. It was founded in 1977 by a group including the composer Sir Peter Maxwell Davies, who was a resident of Orkney, and George Mackay Brown.
3 Heaney, "From the Republic of Conscience" in *The Haw Lantern*.

1

that "sweet clear spirit,"[4] the call of Christ, in the call from the curlew, and worked within its dancing metrics of patterns and shapes, of sight and sound and what they understood to be its source. In a letter to Jeanette Marwick in 1962 Mackay Brown wrote, "I know I have none of the qualities of a scholar—so look for no monumental tomes on Hopkins, with copious footnotes, etc. If he infects me with some of his sweet clear spirit, that is all I ask."[5] Mackay Brown's postgraduate *Essays and Notes* on Hopkins from his time at Edinburgh University in the 1960s harbors the marks of that "infection" and much else besides. That "sweet clear spirit" that flowed through Hopkins to Mackay Brown was Christ. They carried within themselves His death, His passion, His wounds, and they unmistakably wrote about it from beginning to end in their literary projects.

That "sweet clear spirit" held within it the piety of Mackay Brown and Hopkins, *Passion Partners* from first to last. Their literary achievements shared in a settled disposition of textual and existential character where a loyalty and duty towards the native tradition was deeply invested in a use of language that was at once tender, gentle, and compassionate as it was piercing, forceful and classically heroic. Their minds received through the senses a dynamic flow of images and impressions of what they experienced and came to understand as truth revealing itself. These were pre-theologic poetic materials in all their diverse strands that formed in them a real and permanent inward knowledge, the sort of place Heaney described as "the republic of conscience." This place was Catholic to its core: a core where the mind and heart converged, and assented to, a distinctive and particular epistemology. The inner processes of these poets aligned with John Henry Newman's principles and arguments (perception, apprehension, assent and inference, conscience, certitude, and illative sense) examined at length in *An Essay in Aid of a Grammar of Assent*.[6] These poetic materials are what the twentieth century theologian Hans Urs von Balthasar ascribed as pre-theologic.[7]

---

4 Mackay Brown, Letter to Jeanette Marwick (wife of Ernest Marwick), 12 October 1962. OLA. EWM Collection.   5 Ibid.
6 Newman, *An Essay in Aid of a Grammar of Assent*.
7 Balthasar, *The Glory of the Lord. A Theological Aesthetics. I: Seeing the Form*, 32-3.

Introduction

In my earlier book, *George Mackay Brown: No Separation*, I give considerable attention to Mackay Brown and his pre-theologic workspace that he contextualized according to his own principled perceptions that had more in common with Newman, Hopkins, and Balthasar who each in their turn had worked on the frontiers of theology, poetry, and all things literary from a dynamic Catholic angle of vision. It is simply not enough to link Mackay Brown to pluralistic theologians or sociologists such as Richard McBrien,[8] David Tracey,[9] Andrew Greely,[10] or Marina Warner.[11] Sabine Schmid's *Keeping the Sources Pure: The Making of George Mackay Brown*[12] and Linden Bicket's *George Mackay Brown and the Scottish Catholic Imagination*[13] open considerable literary commentary, but neither of these studies considers exactly where Mackay Brown situated himself to be able to manage the multiple contexts that his life was deeply embedded in. Their literary method puts commentary first and then bolts on a choice of generalized theologians in support. To avoid a compromised understanding of Mackay Brown's Catholicism and spirituality, this book takes up his own writings, published and unpublished, as central to his self-understanding and exactly where he positioned himself.

Both Schmid and Bicket draw on Newman as formative for Mackay Brown, but their reading of his *Essay in Aid of a Grammar of Assent* (which Mackay Brown never read) does not appreciate that Newman stepped away from Romanticism when he became a Catholic. Newman's understanding of the imagination was a factor in his own conversion, but as it turned out it was not the critical construct for the inner processes (cognitive and emotional) that led him to his conversion. He sought certainty in how the human person came to the faith position, and although the high intensity of the Romantics did much to uncover an earlier pre-Reformation world view, Newman, Hopkins and then Mackay Brown found personal certainty guided as they were by the ethos of the Oxford Movement. Epistemically, they were then drawn into an extraordinarily rich Catholic intellectual tradition

---

8 McBrien, *Catholicism*.
9 Tracey, *The Analogical Imagination*.
10 Greely, *The Catholic Imagination*.
11 Warner, *Alone of All Her Sex*.
12 Schmid, *Keeping the Sources Pure*.
13 Bicket, *George Mackay Brown and the Scottish Catholic Imagination*.

where they could question, wonder, and experiment with their writing.¹⁴ Conversion was that point of reference that reached certainty by the multi-faceted pathways of the illative sense, rather than being ruled by poetic materials in an unbridled imagination. The serenity that came from certainty was defined as that calm that ensued from the interpenetration and later adjudication of the imagination by reason. Newman articulated this serenity as the action of the illative sense.¹⁵

This book, therefore, takes up Mackay Brown and Hopkins as *Passion Partners* in their respective literary projects crafted according to their own Stabat Mater: "grant that I may carry within me the death of Christ, make me a partner in his Passion, let me relive his wounds."¹⁶ Their literary craft was their piety absorbed as it was in "a concentrated meditation on the Passion of Christ that was so popular in the primers of the late medieval period (used by the laity)."¹⁷ This path re-opened the pre-Reformation worldview and took them forward as they crafted texts in their discordant times aligned with a theological aesthetics very much Balthasarian. This was the rich intellectual tradition of a Catholicism that is not daunted by skepticism and empiricism. Hopkins specifically unleashed in the realm of poetical language a strong form of empiricism, absorbed as he was in the natural world and the philosophical position of Duns Scotus. Newman's systems approach in the *Grammar* had given Hopkins license to be a kind of "I will show you how" poet with his giftedness to use language in such a reinvigorated way that was true to nature and the human person able to see Christ in all things. Doubt and experimental evidence were never inhibitors. Because of them, Hopkins enhanced his use of language as he articulated

---

14 Newman, *Apologia Pro Vita Sua*, 116–18. "I became excited at the view thus opened upon me.... After a while, I got calm. And at length the vivid impression upon my imagination faded away.... I had to determine its logical value, and its bearing upon my duty.... It was clear I had a good deal to learn... and that perhaps some new light was coming upon me. I determined to be guided, not by my imagination, but by my reason... that new conception of things should only so far influence me, as it had a logical claim to do so. If it came from above, it would come again,—so I trusted—and with more definite outlines and greater cogency and consistency of proof."
15 Newman, *An Essay in Aid of a Grammar of Assent*. See Chapter Two.
16 *Stabat Mater* (a liturgical fragment from *Analecta Hymnica Medii Aevi*). Cited in Duffy, *The Stripping of the Altars*, 259.
17 Gray, *George Mackay Brown: No Separation*, 69.

the intelligent design of the natural world and the human person through inscape and the creative force of the instress.

Heaney's "call of the curlew" is an inscape of sound experienced as a dynamic form of moral obligation. The birdsong of the curlew, the inscape of the sound, is intimate in its reverberations and echoes. The subjective nature of Heaney's experience functions as a voice, or echo of a voice, to the poet, under the shifting shapes and colors and sounds of a very tangible natural world. This is Newman's moral argument for the existence of God at work. It was a particular experience of it for Heaney, yet it had a pressing universality in the world of facts as they "swarmed" in the minds of the poets. There they found discernment of the conscience at work as a connecting principle between the creature and his Creator. The experience of that sense of moral obligation in the curlew birdsong is also a glimpse of what is not heard and not seen. The poets detected and discerned the hiddenness of the supernatural in the natural world that led them to trace what is unseen and unheard with the inner processes of how the human person is mentally constituted in the first place.

Newman's principles of assent formed a dialectic that moved him and others from the world of the Church Fathers through the Oxford Movement into Catholicism and an objective order that is absolute, never pluralistic or deconstructed with relativism. It is precisely these pre-theologic poetic materials that gave rise to the craft of Hopkins and then Mackay Brown in accord with univocity[18] rather than the convention of analogy. As passion partners they carried within themselves and their literary craft the pre-Reformation experience of the wounds of Christ in ways that embrace the deep sense of loss in language as well as adding to it by seamlessly resonating with Christ's timeless words in John's Gospel (14:9): "Anyone who has seen me has seen the Father." Hopkins restored, reinvigorated, and renewed linguistic symmetry by overturning the literary conventions of his times. He made his own existential irregularity a means to reclaim an understanding of the inbuilt shapes and forms of beauty that are the world. Mackay Brown was

---

18 Univocity of being is the idea that words describing the properties of God mean the same thing as when they apply to people or things, even if God is vastly different in kind. It is associated with the doctrines of the Scholastic theologian John Duns Scotus.

also walking the path reordering the sacred and the profane of his native tradition that so intrigued and baffled his audience all at once and is so marked in the literary criticism that has come his way. His distinctive fusion of the ancient and modern holds within his text what seems an effortless soft fascination and numinous radiance. Little do his readers know that this is released into language because of the poet's engagement with a primal patterning intelligence that is the Logos.

Mackay Brown's published and unpublished materials give evidence of his own distinctive principles that he chose to work within. Like Hopkins, he was increasingly clear about them as he fiercely fought for his sanity and his literary credibility throughout his life. It is important for me in this book to be as clear as one can about Mackay Brown's complex poetic vision according to what he wrote about it and what his plethora of texts and lexica reveal it to be. Mackay Brown's postgraduate *Essays and Notes* on Hopkins is an important part of the evidence that reveals Mackay Brown to be far removed from those literary studies that are more serial and linear than inter-disciplinary, more deconstructive than contextual, more content with surface than depth. Hopkins and Mackay Brown bring a philosophical method and allegiance to the native tradition that converged in a swarm of pre-theologic materials so convincing of their radical piety and craft. They bring to their poetry an artistic sense driven by majestic materials to go beyond the boundaries of language into the whole sensory sphere that is subordinate to the spiritual sense.[19] Furthermore, Hopkins and Mackay Brown forge words "freighted with a content that exceeds even the load placed on the relation of the expression"[20] and the back-and-forth movement of their dancing metrics was the textual journey between the universal and the essence in existence. They keep close to the mystery that God is. The conceptual links that are made by analogical language were superseded by a vibrant poetic language that can do just that—keep mystery close. These were poets who experienced the act of writing as bi-directional in the circling movement that thought is constrained to perform. The poets' journey was a constant circulation between essence and appearance; and within this procession of sources, they word-gamed in the epistemic forge

---

19 Balthasar, *Theo-Logic I: The Truth of the World*, 159-60.   20 Ibid.

Introduction

of the sensory and the conceptual. This was a moral imperative to them, and they could do no other. Their poetic thought was an experience of an intense, intimate reciprocity in the mystery between essence and appearance, universality and particularity, the evidence for this being the texts that emerged with the "sense-laden and harmonious"[21] presence of the mystery itself.

The critical point this book keeps foremost in mind is that Hopkins and Mackay Brown followed in the steps of Newman through the ethos of the nineteenth century Oxford movement into the Catholic Church by means of faith and reason leaving behind a resonating Romanticism that had enthralled their emotions. They sought with great diligence a life of balance within their own frailties. To do justice to their experience of life and to be able to express it meant their craft took on a passion and a piety that was well-structured to give voice to harmony and discord all in one, seamlessly, as they aligned their expression with a vision of majestic beauty. To use the word "seamless" (and Mackay Brown used it often) is to articulate a process that is smooth and continuous, with no apparent gaps or spaces between one part and the next: as poetry dances metrically to record not only the call of the curlew but all aspects of the natural and supernatural worlds, interwoven as they are in a vibrant state "on the quiver"[22] and "in oscillation"[23] at "trembling stations."[24] To be a Romantic poet calls up the descriptor, the imagination, but Mackay Brown and Hopkins were working in tune with what Newman discerned as the illative sense, a forerunner of what we may be more familiar with now in terms of the medical and psychological language of neural pathways and their levels of interacting plasticity.

They moved out of the ethos of the Oxford Movement into a Catholic epistemology that held fast to faith and reason in unison. This was what made their craft so distinctive and makes them difficult to categorize by pluralistic literary studies. This book gives prominence to the Mackay Brown voice, in unison with Hopkins's, forsaking the terms and language of pluralistic studies so mixed up with their own controversies that lead away from

---

21 Ibid., 158.
22 Hopkins, *The Letters of Gerard Manley Hopkins to Robert Bridges*, 188.
23 Balthasar, *Theo-Drama: Theological Dramatic Theory III*, 297.
24 Mackay Brown, "Everyman." Unpublished MS OLA, EWM Collection.

poetic texts so alive with primary sources, to the point that the original integrity of the text disappears. Hopkins and Mackay Brown, in circular movement between the sensory and the concept, emerged with the multiple use of descriptors such as on the quiver, trembling stations, seamless and dancing metrics because of the dynamic world they inhabited where they found Christ. Whereas Schmid gives prominence to the crafted linguistics of Mackay Brown and Hopkins converging in a sacramental view of the universe, and Bicket champions Mackay Brown's analogical use of language, this book puts before the reader Mackay Brown's and Hopkins's passion partnership forged within a *univocal*[25] use of language that took them beyond the usual literary conventions to embrace the particular and the universal in unison. Their poetic craft reinvigorated a use of language that was able to hold within its grasp difference-in-unity and unity-in-difference, what Balthasar articulates as the katalogical[26] perspective.

Readers who find Mackay Brown difficult[27] often remark on his use of time and they have not the patience to follow the narrative. Mackay Brown and Hopkins make their readers work hard—there is no doubt about that. The bi-directional katalogical perspective works downward from Creator to creation in addition to the one-directional upward movement of the analogical perspective. The back-and-forth processional movement is well suited to do so with Newman's multi-pathway illative sense that held within itself the tensions of difference and unity. Hopkins and Mackay Brown's language traces the natural world inscape by inscape within their respective centuries by means of how the human person is constituted in the first place. They craft their language by means of set forms, to master the flux of tensions and dimensions, through enigmatic signs and symbols as they swarm and pulsate because they saw and experienced this world in the way they did. Their craft carries within itself the past, present, and future. This book presents an articulation of this craft, at times moving from tense to tense to be true to

---

25 Univocal—admitting of no doubt or misunderstanding; having only one meaning or interpretation and leading to only one conclusion.
26 Schumacher, *A Trinitarian Anthropology*, 30-1.
27 Germaine Greer was a notable critic who in the Booker Prize (1994) adjudication expressed her displeasure over Mackay Brown's *Beside the Ocean of Time*. See fuller discussion in Fergusson's *George Mackay Brown: The Life*, 283-84.

Introduction

the dynamic systems approach initiated by Newman, poetically licensed by Hopkins and absorbed into the twentieth century theological Balthasarian project, *The Glory of the Lord*.

Mackay Brown was working within this theological stream, consciously and unconsciously, where a symphonic array of the particular and the universal were at play in the pre-theologic world of poetry. The evidence for this is the accumulated documentary survival of the published and unpublished collections as a whole and the historical reality of Mackay Brown's twentieth century context. This was his position and the place where he discovered lines of development expanding them into a frontier, an Orkney poetics. Mackay Brown's postgraduate *Essays and Notes* are that uncharted territory of his work on Hopkins. In this key set of papers, a literary trajectory was crystallized and consolidated in a powerful working process that opened onto a narrow path. There Mackay Brown's voice is elevated above all others to be true to his privacy. That ultimate defensive wall concealed important levels of erudition, a resounding passion and piety, a religious experience marked with a deep sense of mea culpa, but tempered with the "sweet clear spirit" he loved so dearly in Hopkins, in Orkney, in the world, in Christ. Mackay Brown and Hopkins as passion partners exhibit difference in unity and unity in difference, in their personhood and in their literary craft.

Drawing on primary and secondary sources follows a pattern throughout this book to substantiate the inner processes (using Newman's system approach of how the human person is mentally constituted in the first place) of the poet Mackay Brown and to measure the influence of Hopkins on Mackay Brown. Prominence is given to Mackay Brown, primarily in the light of his published and unpublished materials on Hopkins. My research is an extraction from a temporarily diverse and not necessarily linear or chronologically regular array of sources; however, chronological sequence is attempted, but not confined by, a superimposed "pre-Edinburgh period, an Edinburgh period, and a post-Edinburgh period." The Hopkins materials are at the heart of this book. These manuscript materials are difficult to fully understand "on their own" or by extracting "a few nuggets."[28] They need to be

---

28 Fergusson, "The Praise Singers: Poets George Mackay Brown and Gerard Manley Hopkins," *The Tablet*. "I slipped into the manuscripts room to look

absorbed into a fuller engagement with Mackay Brown's literary texts to fathom his complex poetic vision. They are quoted to give prominence to the voice of Mackay Brown, to let him speak for himself and, where relevant, to examine the cultural period, the philosophical and literary tradition within which he chose to write, the literary criticism that came his way, and my own interactions with Mackay Brown in conversation and correspondence.

I am conscious of the overlap between Schmid's book and my own, but I would see my book as going further theologically into the relationship between Mackay Brown and Hopkins and the emergence of their craft. This means getting beyond the generalization of "a sacramental view of the universe" and positioning Mackay Brown and Hopkins within the depths and stream of the Balthasarian project, *The Glory of the Lord*. I am also conscious of Bicket's approach and construct of "the Scottish Catholic Imagination" with which my book takes issue. There is a conscious effort to try and position Mackay Brown into certain contemporary constructs of an ethos stranded with national, political, and religious concerns and trends; whereas this book is aligning itself with Mackay Brown texts at source alongside those of Hopkins. One also takes heed of a spirituality, a religious sense, and a political sense that emerges; but, in keeping with both Hopkins and Mackay Brown, this book is weighted towards the artistic sense that they both agreed was the ultimate criteria by which their work might be judged. The weight of this artistic sense does not in any way diminish or separate itself from the piety of their Catholicism; but there is no doubt that readers can engage with their craft without giving assent to their chosen religion.

So it was, with this "sweet clear spirit" in mind, I went to view the Mackay Brown manuscripts at the National Library of Scotland in Edinburgh. I also held in my mind his own words from his autobiography *For the Islands I Sing*,[29] "From time to time someone will say, what happened to your work on Gerard Manley Hopkins?"[30] knowing that I was one of those persons.[31] He would give the nod, gesturing to their existence

---

through rough jottings made by George in a handful of buff-covered exercise books in the 1960s. Here are just a few of the nuggets I found."
29 Mackay Brown, *For the Islands I Sing*, 158.   30 Ibid.
31 See *George Mackay Brown: No Separation*, and *Circle of Light: The Catholic Church in Orkney Since 1560*, which include extracts of our correspondence.

Introduction

up the stairs. He goes on to say a few lines later, "I'm sure no publisher would give those fugitive essays a second glance. Nor would I want them read by others."[32] However, there I was at the NLS to read them, knowing only full well the love he had for Hopkins's poetry and the discussions we had in the last years of his life. I remember vividly a deep exchange about the Hopkins poem "Inversnaid" in 1995. I wanted to be true to his eagerness "to know how he [Hopkins] forged and hammered those resounding marvels.... No English poet ever fell upon the language with such skill, sweetness and boisterous daring."[33]

I found them to consist of *Essays* and preparatory *Notes*[34] from the poet's post graduate days in Edinburgh University in the 1962–64, plus three student notebooks.[35] I also chose to look closely at twenty-three loose leaves from 1947–48 that were acquired by the NLS coming from the same source at the same time.[36] There had been intriguing glimpses of this collection of loose leaves described as "Brown's Commonplace Book" in the first serious study of the Mackay Brown literary writings, contextualized alongside the development of his life.[37] My intentions are to take strong account of these unpublished materials and weld them together to give prominence to the inner processes of the poets George Mackay Brown and Gerard Manley Hopkins that reveal the "sweet clear spirit"[38] at its source.

The first thing that struck me was that Mackay Brown drank at the fountain of priest poet, Gerard Manley Hopkins, but was still his own man. He recognized the astonishing independence of Hopkins when he gave prominence to a quote[39] from an 1888 letter to Hopkins's friend and fellow poet, Robert Bridges: "the effect of studying masterpieces is to make me admire and do otherwise."[40] This letter citation was often quoted through

---

32 Mackay Brown, *For the Islands I Sing*, 158.   33 Ibid., 150.
34 Mackay Brown, *Essays and Notebooks. Unpublished manuscripts, 1962–64 NLS.*
35 Ibid.
36 Murray, Literary Executor George Mackay Brown Estate. Jenny Brown Associates. 31 Marchmont Rd. Edinburgh EH9 1HU.
37 Murray R and B, *Interrogation of Silence: The Writings of George Mackay Brown*, 20–21. This is a fine book and an essential starting point for a strong "feeling" for the reality of the poet and the world he lived in.
38 Mackay Brown, Letter to Jeanette Marwick, 12 October 1962. OLA, EWM Collection.   39 Mackay Brown, *Notebook One, NLS*.
40 Hopkins, *The Letters of Gerard Manley Hopkins to Robert Bridges*, 291.

time by the literary critics[41] of Hopkins, who all recognized a poet quite different from his predecessors and contemporaries and could not categorize him according to their received literary notions. Mackay Brown, already cognizant of his own poetical gift, was in what Bloom described as a "clear imaginative space"[42] where he also defied his readers and critics who struggled with the problem of assigning him his place in the literary canon.

W. H. Gardner authored an article in 1937 "The Religious Problem in G. M. Hopkins."[43] Was Catholicism, so decisively chosen by both Hopkins and Mackay Brown, a problem in being able to understand, appreciate and give judgment on their poetical greatness? This book takes the view that being Catholic does not make you a great poet. The greatness of poets comes from a judgment of how far up or down the scale they are embedded in their sources and can give expression to their artistry by means of a seamless integration between form and content.[44] This stance, that of the bard, is a forecourt, a space that is pre-theological, and pre-political, and its vision is not narrow. It is a place that has its own imperative but does not sit quietly in a definitive literary "project," whether it be a "fictional, imaginary, and sometimes idealized" offshoot of developments in "nation theory,"[45] the "Scottish Catholic Imagination,"[46] or "The Literary Politics of Scottish Devolution."[47] It is not that these "projects" are without merit and don't have powerful arguments, but the artistry of Hopkins and Mackay Brown arises from what the poet and Mackay Brown mentor, Edwin Muir, called "some other place."[48] Nevertheless, these strands of Scottish literary culture are touched upon here to set the scene for the sorts of

---

41 Roberts, *Gerard Manley Hopkins: The Critical Heritage*.
42 Bloom, *The Anxiety of Influence*, 5.
43 Gardner, "The Religious Problem in G. M. Hopkins," in Roberts, *Gerard Manley Hopkins: The Critical Heritage*, 373–83.
44 Gray, *George Mackay Brown: No Separation*.
45 Hall, *The History of Orkney Literature*, 7.
46 Bicket, *George Mackay Brown and the Scottish Catholic Imagination*, 7.
47 Hames, *The Literary Politics of Scottish Devolution: Voice, Class, Nation*. This book charts the interplay between Scottish literary culture and the national movement during the 20th century. The exclusive relationship between Scottish nationalism and Scottish literary culture has found it difficult to include Mackay Brown within the politicized literary elites that they champion.
48 Muir, *An Autobiography*, 71. See also an exploration of *George Mackay Brown: No Separation*, 6.

Introduction

pressures Mackay Brown had to withstand when he was alive. Now, after his death, his life and work are in the process of being reconstructed according to the issues and concerns that so mark literary culture going forward.

I hold Newman's view, that literary greatness is assigned to those of great creative and technical ability, giving life and form to writing in the English language within their times. "They have formed its limbs and developed its strength; they have endowed it with vigor, exercised in suppleness and dexterity, and taught it grace. They have made it rich, harmonious, various and precise. They have furnished it with a variety of styles, which from their individuality may almost be called dialects, and are monuments both of the powers of language and the genius of its cultivators."[49] It may appear to be idiosyncratic to draw upon the nineteenth century Newman, but he was a critical influence for Hopkins and Mackay Brown, as well as for the theological richness in Balthasar's vast project *The Glory of the Lord*, not to mention this book. Newman defined the literature of a nation and its language as a living voice that seizes upon the public mind and cannot be destroyed or reversed.[50] "We must take things as they are, if we take them at all";[51] with this realism in mind (so characteristic of Newman), we must likewise acknowledge the secular space (or public mind) that the literary texts of Hopkins and Mackay Brown occupied alongside their literary neighbors.

Newman's nineteenth century standpoint identified the literature written in the English language as having a markedly Protestant character whose "past cannot be undone."[52] Indeed, this would not be appropriate within his understanding of the real and the concrete experience of life. Such a literature is a great work of the human person. Newman went further with the colorful insight of a National Literature as being "the untutored movements of the reason, imagination, passions and affections of the natural man [or person], the leapings and friskings, the plungings and snortings, the sportings and the buffoonings, the clumsy play and aimless toil, of the noble lawless savage of God's intellectual creation."[53] This colorful insight caught the ferment of his times but also can be applied to Mackay Brown

---

[49] Newman, "English Catholic Literature" in *The Idea of a University*, 188.
[50] Ibid., 188-89. [51] Ibid., 186. [52] Ibid., 192. [53] Ibid., 191.

studies as one surveys the available interpretations. Mackay Brown responded to the constraints placed upon him with his lifelong fiercely maintained privacy for all things that involved "work." This privacy protected his complex poetic vision and the spiritual and intellectual greatness to be found across his writings, published and unpublished.

Newman had presided over the nineteenth century Oxford Movement[54] which drew upon the philosophical, theological, and political quest of those times. This quest channeled Hopkins in the nineteenth century and then Mackay Brown in the twentieth towards, and into, Catholicism so convincingly by means of the inner processes that formed them. It is precisely those inner workings of heart, soul, and mind that propelled them simultaneously into Catholicism and the canon of English language and literature.[55] Both poets contended with the ferments of their country and their times that led them to swim against convention as the moral imperative to go with poetical counter-currents within led them to linguistically reclaim, restore, and

---

54 The Oxford Movement as an intersection of events, ideas, personalities constituted a pattern of religious crisis marked by growth and decline in nineteenth century British society. From Newman's point of view, it began upon his return from his European travels to the sermon on "National apostasy" by John Keble July 14, 1833. Tractarianism came to the forefront of the religious movement through a series of pamphlets by Newman, Keble and Pusey which sought to purify Anglicanism of its Protestant elements. Newman embarked for his part in the Movement on a quest to rediscover an ecclesiology that had for its sources the primal sources and tradition of Christianity. He entered from an evangelical-come-High-Church position in the Church of England and emerged a Roman Catholic. His writings took him on a journey of discovery through *Tracts for the Times* (1833), *The Arians of the Fourth Century* (1833), *Lecture on the Prophetical Office of the Church* (1836), *Lectures on the doctrine of Justification* (1838), *The Tamworth Reading Room* and *Tract 90* (1841). These publications had an oral dimension in the lectures and sermons he delivered as Vicar of St Mary's Oxford. His writings, lectures, and sermons are marked by a preoccupation with the reality of the person of Christ and his ability to communicate a powerful realization of Christ as a living being. This realization touched the minds and hearts of many. His conversion and reception into the Roman Catholic Church in 1845 followed a withdrawal into a monastic life in Littlemore where he had immersed himself in Patristic studies. He had configured a path to conversion for himself and others, including Gerard Manley Hopkins and George Mackay Brown. St. John Henry Newman was canonized on October 13, 2019. Other important writings: *An Essay in Aid of a Grammar of Assent* (1845). *Idea of a University* (1852) *Apologia pro Vita Sua* (1864).
55 Hall, *The History of Orkney Literature*, 193. "As well as being receptive to outside and cultural and literary influences, Orkney identity has always absorbed, and will continue to absorb, new languages, new ethnicities... resulting in a rich literary and linguistic mix."

Introduction

re-invigorate rather than undo a past and a present by means of their poetic vision. The details of Newman's life and work were important to both poets, and it would be an untruth to extract his formative influence from an understanding of their work.

Newman set the bar for the classics of a national literature as being those literary works that were outstanding examples of a particular style and have lasting worth with a timeless quality. The creators of these classics according to Newman were in a line of succession, "a type of a generation or the interpreter of a crisis." They are each in their turn made for their day and their day made for them.[56] If we believe that and recognize the legitimacy of such a view, we are compelled to look for those literary patterns where language develops according to the incessant demand for a "succession of skillful artists." This artistic succession ensures that the language is worked "up to its proper perfection."[57] The evidence for this is those artists, "of a peculiar talent," who arise one after the other, according to the circumstances of their times. They can give the language its flexibility in expression of a variety of thoughts and feelings accompanied by a penetrating discernment, a clarity of vision or intellect that provides a deep understanding and insight. Vocabulary is added and a grace and harmony underpin the lexicon. The style of each artist "henceforth becomes a property of the language itself that hitherto did not exist," gradually passing into the conversation and the composition of the educated.[58] The complex cultural mix that Hopkins and Mackay Brown worked within in their respective centuries created a body of evidence for the unique durability of their literary achievement in terms of artistic technicalities of thought, feeling, discernment, intellect, vision, and vocabulary interwoven and elegantly shaped for survival.

So, Newman, in this obscure and not well-known essay,[59] "Catholic Literature in the English Tongue, 1854-8"[60] gave an incisive and realistic insight into those literary patterns that formed the "making" of the English language[61] fully recognizing

---

[56] Newman, "English Catholic Literature" in *The Idea of a University*, 187.
[57] Ibid., 193.   [58] Ibid., 193-94.
[59] Ker, *The Catholic Revival in English Literature*, 1.
[60] Newman, "English Catholic Literature" in *The Idea of a University*.
[61] Davis, *The Early English Settlement of Orkney and Shetland*, x. "In its structures the language [Norn] shows faint echoes of Anglo Saxon, heavily

the "vast English-speaking world-wide-race."⁶² He applauded those authors such as Milton and others, who have breathed hatred against the Catholic Church. He recognized their giftedness and place in the artistic succession because he knew the critical importance of that secular space, that mind of the public, where literature must operate as convincingly as it can, to inject itself out into the commercial world of publishing in all its forms. Newman described English literature as a literature marked with a strong Protestant character, going on to pithily argue that we should not only take things as they are, but enter the literary marketplace and give literary credit where it is due regardless of creeds and persuasions with which we may, or may not, agree.

When Sir Robert Peel championed libraries and reading rooms at Tamworth in 1841, several months before he was re-elected prime minister, he suggested that reading would not only lead people to appreciate the wonders of creation, but also make them good and virtuous citizens. Peel was implicitly replacing religion with secular knowledge when he asserted the primacy of usefulness that should promote and govern education. Peel quoted Newman: "It is the parent of virtue, the nurse of religion; it exalts man to his highest perfection and is the sufficient scope of his most earnest exertions." Newman, writing to *The Times*, counters Peel: "If virtue be a mastery over the mind, if its end be action, if its perfection be inward order, harmony, and peace, we must seek it in graver and holier places than in Libraries and Reading-rooms."⁶³ Newman recognized his times and the Protestant character stemming from the principle of private judgment that drove the Reformation and detached a prior world view from its firmament. Newman foresaw what lay ahead as he detached himself from Protestantism, seeking the fullness of Christianity in Catholicism. Having identified the national literature as strongly marked by Protestantism, he could see it was well established in its trajectory of taking up a markedly secular character in the years to come. Hopkins understood this well, and so did Mackay Brown. When his time came, Mackay Brown wrote of Hopkins:

---

overlaid by later Viking influences. Orkney and Shetland Norn are not merely a dialect of the Old Norse language with local modifications (as usually assumed), but rather a predominantly Old Norse language with certain embedded Anglo-Saxon features."   62 Ibid., 185.
63 Newman, "The Tamworth Reading Room," letters to *The Times*, 1841.

Introduction

"It was a heroic lonely attempt to put [meaning] back into a language grown thin and washed-out. Somewhere literature had left the high road and smithy and marketplace for the salon and the university and grown anaemic."[64]

But writers who are Catholic "should do as their neighbors," at best seeking out their way within the secular discipline of literature and its language (such as it was in Newman's time and now) "striving to create a current in the direction of Catholic truth."[65] A singly classical writer must be able enough to swim in the succession of artists, rising above mediocrity in terms of thought and technique and contending with the nationalism of the times and the processes of corruption that stem from "the admixture of foreign elements."[66] Hopkins and Mackay Brown contended with their times and beyond, never seeking to reverse the disassembling forces of history, but working towards a reintegration of created reality, taking things as they experienced them, according to their peculiar and singly artistic vision. There was an emphatic artistic, intellectual, and spiritual convergence between them as they drew upon principles that revealed a strongly understood theory of knowledge, an epistemology that powered their literature and language.

Their lives ran counter to the usual sociological strands that are expected to compose a family, a community, a country, being inheritors and practitioners that defied the incoherencies and disjointed biographical details in the assessments that have been made of these poets. Their poetic craft seamlessly revealed something other and a deep palpable encounter with their vision of the how and why of existence that was music to the heart, mind, and soul of their public. A comparison quickly emerges: their conversion to Catholicism and their association with the Oxford Movement and St. John Henry Newman. They both went through successive stages of isolation and difference from family, community, and country. Soul-searching and faith mattered to both. They loved the arts and were profuse letter-writers. They both speak from an extensive build-up of materials, diaries and notebooks and unpublished manuscripts that have surfaced over

---

64 Mackay Brown, *For the Islands I Sing*, 150.
65 Newman, "English Catholic Literature" in *The Idea of a University*, 185.
66 Ibid., 98.

time. They shouldered emotional distress and physical illness, but it can be firmly said that "sickness did not break them." They were both men of conscience to their core, a defining characteristic. Heaney made the point well in his conceptualization of the conscience where *the call of the curlew* was to the moral impetus to finely tune and stabilize the poetic vision. Hopkins and Mackay Brown did just that because as original poets working with primary sources, they were highly disciplined and driven to align their craft with nature and the human person by expressing this originality through univocity of language.

What came from the Mackay Brown pen was compellingly and serenely driven by a particular individual vision and craft. There is much evidence that shows Hopkins had influenced him and steered him onward with his call to things literary and spiritual. Mackay Brown is not in tune with his supervisor in the conventional academic manner. One gets a strong sense of Mackay Brown's immersion in Hopkins's poems as one reads the manuscript. Then suddenly turning a page, Mackay Brown the student becomes poet and dramatist with notes on the a draft of his play *A Spell for Green Corn*.[67] Here also is the mysterious blind fiddler, known to have frequented his imagination often, plus a piece on St Magnus wrapped up in the *Orkneyinga Saga*.[68] Mackay Brown's admiration for Hopkins does not interfere with his concurrent preoccupation with an Orkney poetics. Mackay Brown is in tune with Hopkins, whose influence will stay with him in a very distinctive way. According to a note Mackay Brown wrote in 1947, he was deeply rooted in an Orkney poetic, in fact it defined him: "I want my poetry to be a pattern of the true images of this world—or rather Orkney. The small part of it I know...."[69] His vision and craft were well underway, set to mature and blossom. The "flourish of pleasing prose," the "counterpart" that flowed through Mackay Brown to his readers, roots down deep into its sources, as Hopkins would say: "their knowledge leaves their minds swinging; poised, but on the quiver."[70]

---

67 Mackay Brown, *A Spell for Green Corn*.
68 Pálsson & Edwards (eds), *The Orkneyinga Saga*.
69 Mackay Brown, *The Commonplace Book* "23 pages of notes 1947–48" MS Leaf 49. December 1947, NLS.
70 Hopkins, *The Letters of Gerard Manley Hopkins to Robert Bridges*, 188.

Introduction

This stance takes careful note of a conversation with Mackay Brown's Orcadian mentor Ernest Marwick: "My stories are only 'Orkney' stories in that they are set in an Orkney landscape, or in Orkney history. There is no such thing as an Orkney man or an Orkney woman. The characters are just human beings who happen to live in Hoy or Stromness or Sandwick. They are conditioned a little by their environment, and by their occupations. Their humanity—the fact of their being human beings—is what really interests me. To see people exclusively as Orcadians, or people in Thrums or Buchan, is to see a bunch of pawky, sentimental rustics, caricatures."[71] Mackay Brown was primarily the poet, then the journalist, short story writer, novelist, and dramatist. He never rested in the DNA of being Orcadian. Orkney was a window through which he saw the manifestation of human life that found its completion in the fixed destination, somewhere other, namely Eternity.

Mackay Brown had a firm allegiance to origins and ends, as did Hopkins. The Orkney fable and firmament, crystallized by Edwin Muir, heralded a long and calm storytelling in Mackay Brown. Muir articulated the decline not only of the novel, but also the trajectory that prompted the conversion of Hopkins and Mackay Brown. A modern literature or "post-modern ecriture"[72] that had a grasp of origins but not of ends, and sees "existence, like our works, is an unfinished sentence"[73] was not a place for these poets, who could not live with an incompleteness in thought and belief. Hopkins and Mackay Brown sought a reintegration of created reality, taking things within time as they experienced them, but rising to a higher reality beyond time in the patterns of the natural world. They powered their perceptions of inscape and instress, and technically expressed them as evidence of a higher reality.

---

71 Mackay Brown in conversation with EW Marwick. *An Orkney Anthology: Selected Works of Ernest Walker Marwick. Vol. 2,* 239.

72 Derrida, *Of Grammatology*. 1967. His argument "there is nothing outside context" critiques Western philosophy and its metaphorical depth models that govern its conception of language and consciousness. This preference has led to "metaphysics of presence" and "logocentrism" creating a hierarchy of binary oppositions that influence everything from our conception of speech's relation to writing to our understanding of racial difference. "Deconstruction" is an attempt to expose and undermine such "metaphysics."

73 Muir, "The Decline of the Novel" *in Essays on Literature and Society*, 144.

Mackay Brown's curious mind with its predilections was at work in his postgraduate work on Hopkins at Edinburgh University in the 1960s: (*Essays and Notes*)[74] plus 23 pages of notes (1947–48)[75] that includes a piece of writing about the nature of the Roman Catholic Church. They are given pride of place for their common ground with Hopkins in the enduringly crafted visionary sensation of their poetry. Mackay Brown's absorption in sight and sound, light and the dark shadows, echoing memories and dancing metrics, evidenced in the *Essays and Notes* are also explored within an Orkney poetics swarming with symbols and wordplay in affinity with Hopkins's bold experimental work. Using this core collection of sources, Mackay Brown takes us on his journey to a deeper understanding and appreciation of the Orkney heritage, sharing his knowledge of art, music, and literary and spiritual readings.

As Mackay Brown said himself, "... intricate word games appeal to me enormously... the mere sound of words is intoxicating."[76] The intellectual and spiritual richness that he shared with Hopkins informed all his work. As Hopkins wrote in 1879 "A poet is a public in himself,"[77] and to understand these amazing poets, this book looks to the principles they used to compose their poetry. The technicalities of their experimental word games are examined closely: both Hopkins and Mackay Brown asked their readers to pay attention to the senses and to respect the power and purpose of memory. Their mutually shared intellectual rigor and spirituality came from a theory of knowledge, an epistemology unashamedly moored in the stronghold of antiquity and what Edwin Muir called the "other place."[78]

Newman is an important thinker for Hopkins and then Mackay Brown because he could see the cartography of modernism and postmodernism[79] on the horizons from the nine-

---

74 Mackay Brown, *Essays and Notes*, NLS.
75 Mackay Brown, *23 pages of notes (1947–48)*, NLS.
76 Mackay Brown, "Good Morning, Scotland" (1 January 1974) BBC transcript, preparatory comment for recording, dated 24 December 1973, OLA, EWM Collection.
77 Hopkins, Letter to RB, January 19, 1879. *The Letters of Gerard Manley Hopkins to Robert Bridges*, 59.
78 Muir, *An Autobiography*, 35.
79 Mitchell, *Cartographic Strategies of Postmodernity*. The later twentieth century can be understood as a space from which emerged a self-conscious

teenth century. Traditional literary borders would be blurred with new interpretations where a completely secular view of things would renegotiate the universal as global and culture as local. Literature would be a composite of that array of views inherent in the principle of private judgment that can reconstruct and realign according to the politics of the day. Hopkins and then Mackay Brown wanted to get clear of such trends as they had an experience of poetic vision that had more in common with the pre-Reformation world view that had the type of primary sources and linguistic plasticity they resonated with. The interwoven and seamless energy of the sacred and the profane was exciting for them and gave them huge scope. Such constructs as a "Scottish Catholic Imagination" or "Literary Politics of Scottish Devolution" were just the sort of thing they wanted to cut free from to be the poets they felt called to be. They had a moral imperative, an inner voice of their own that this book endeavors to be specific about and demonstrate exactly how it formed in them a theory of knowledge, an epistemology that drew their artistry to new levels of achievement.

Hopkins, with his mantra, "A poet is a public in himself,"[80] injected the sweet clear spirit of his dancing metrics into the Orcadian poet Mackay Brown, their apparent "oddity" disappearing as they worked "in the spirit of the living English language,"[81] drawing on its roots and currencies, coining and expanding its range, depth, and connectivity.[82] Hopkins began the project of creating new lines for an older firmament. For his part, Mackay Brown, equally independent and certain, was not afraid to embrace the subconscious world of desire and myth, fable and folktale, its various interchanging linguistics and moving boundaries[83] and creating a realization of the "Greenfields Kirk." The moral struggle of these poets contended and

---

"cartographic" writing, a writing in which traditional borders have been blurred or even obliterated. A new space is opened that is at once global and local. From this process has emerged not only the phenomenon of geographically aware poststructuralist theories, but also that of a postmodernist "world literature." This literature, with its ties to postmodernist fiction, is explicitly concerned with articulating the late twentieth century's renegotiation of global and local spaces and cultures.
80 Manley Hopkins, Letter to Robert Bridges, January 19, 1879. *The Letters of Gerard Manley Hopkins to Robert Bridges*, 59.
81 Leavis, "Doughty and Hopkins," *Scrutiny*, 316–17.   82 Ibid.
83 See Gray, *George Mackay Brown No Separation*.

contested the trajectory of the anthropological interpretations of the human person within a type of social structure ever moving on a course of betterment and development,[84] with the univocity of their dancing metrics. The clear sweet spirit, the call of the curlew, are echoes of another story that resonated with Christ himself when he said, "Anyone who has seen me has seen the Father."[85] As early as 1947, Mackay Brown had put his intellectual, spiritual, and epistemic credentials on the record in a letter to fellow Orcadian and early mentor Ernest Marwick, "Have you ever read John Henry Newman's *Apologia Pro Vita Sua*? I have just finished it; it has shaken me to the core. There is a magnificent devastating logic about it."[86] What exactly did he mean by "magnificent devastating logic?" Mackay Brown was in the pre-theologic workspace of the poet where he experimented with language as Hopkins had done. He traded in images and impressions according to literary convention. He had used analogy bejeweled with a swarm of symbols to significant effect. But, like Hopkins, he moved where this "magnificent devastating logic" took him. The images and impressions that were so vibrant in the Romantic movement were overtaken in Newman's *Apologia* and *Grammar of Assent*, where he laid out the processes and discipline of Catholic epistemology so acutely aware of those polyvalent and multi-pathways of how the human person is constituted. Coming to faith was an adventure, but it was not a romantic flight of fancy.

Mackay Brown followed Hopkins's responsive reinvigoration of the pre-Reformation firmament in spiritual and literary

---

[84] John Henry Newman articulated a cartography in the 19th century in *An Essay in Aid of a Grammar of Assent* within which he "catalogues" the "data" of his times. His very public debate in *The Times* over the incapacity of reading rooms and libraries to singly "better and develop" the human person stands as testimony to the insights of Edwin Muir. A trajectory emerges and is acted upon in the Oxford Movement. Hopkins offered to write an accompanying account of the *GA*, which Newman declined. Hopkins went on to complete his conversion, strike out on his own Jesuit priestly path, steered by the Oxford Movement to expand the classical intellectual tradition, and engage deeply with a reconfiguration of a new firmament against the forces of the ever-encroaching secularism. Edwin Muir, keenly sensitive to the literary patterns of his time, articulated a substantial body of poetry and reflective intellectual insights to challenge the decay in thought and belief. Mackay Brown was keenly aware of this intellectual and spiritual succession, and from an Orkney poetics, worked within it. [85] John 14:9.
[86] Mackay Brown, Letter to Ernest Marwick, 1947. OLA, EWM Collection.

Introduction

terms with its decisive forms of inscape and instress. Literary convention had usefully employed a one-directional analogical approach to language, explaining and clarifying meaning in an upward or ascending movement from the known to the unknown. Describing God as good is done so analogously, arguing from comparison, correspondence, or partial similarity. This approach worked well for literary devices and for the process that created innovative words and inflections based on irregularity. Hopkins found that approach constraining and he pursued irregularity in language under the influence of Newman, Duns Scotus and Ignatian formation following his own poetic path into *univocity* and its bi-directional katalogical perspective. Here he could be precise with difference-in-unity and unity-in-difference because univocity liberated language to align itself more exactly with the reality of nature and the human person. If God is good, so is the human person. The word good means the same thing. The difference between the goodness of God and the goodness of the human person is a matter of degree rather than of kind. Analogic comparison is overtaken by univocity with the one voice of the Real Presence. It was expressed through Hopkins's new linguistic charter particularly and universally all-in-one.

Newman had given Hopkins and Mackay Brown the confidence and courage of their convictions. The "magnificent devastating logic"[87] that Mackay Brown experienced in Newman led him decisively to the classical tradition both in theological and literary terms through the reconnection with the Church Fathers. Mackay Brown consciously located himself within a theological stream of thought that was biblical, patristic, deeply connected to Newman, Hopkins, and Duns Scotus who were all absorbed into the work of von Balthasar and his vast theological project *The Glory of the Lord*. There is much in Mackay Brown's writings and his own discussion of his life and work that puts him into the realm of the Catholic literary elites that have quietly worked behind the scenes in "the application of Christian learning, especially biblical typology and symbolic thought."[88] He did say to me once that he could not be held responsible

---

[87] Ibid.
[88] Antonsson, "Salvation and Early Saga Writing in Iceland," in *Viking, and Medieval Scandinavia*, 130.

for how people interpreted his work (and it was quite a tense conversation).[89] But it can also be said with great certainty he has left his own ideas, thoughts, feelings, views across his published and unpublished writings. This book aims to give that sense of the man himself and his complex poetic vision by letting him speak from those writings as fully as copyright will allow and it is not my intention to reconstruct him in a way that goes against the written evidence.

This book, therefore, is ordered to that moral imperative and, chapter by chapter, Mackay Brown himself, his voice, his writings, his person, is foregrounded from first to last. Chapter One, "The Greenfields Kirk," begins with the contextualization of the Mackay Brown poetic vision in the intelligent design of Creation where Christ is that Creation. This was the argument for the existence of God in the minds of Hopkins and Mackay Brown. Why start here? The Greenfields Kirk was Mackay Brown's starting point for a lifelong development of the strands and seeds that were hidden from view but were conceptualized in a stable poetic expression of what had been instilled in him by a many-layered Orkney. This was his ultimate challenge that developed his Catholic mind and heart with an epistemology that found profound convergence within Hopkins's view of things. The Greenfields Kirk set context and tone for his assimilation of Hopkins's intelligent design as his fabric and firmament. Mackay Brown acted increasingly on his own particular, that purposefully distinctive "taste of myself," as he put it. He found his voice to express a specific angle of Hopkins's sacramental view of things universal and particular and its innovative language that aligned with the action of Christ univocally. This was his craft to weave and interweave, stitch by stitch, in and out, over and over, to the point of what was and is for some an archaic monotony, for others a radiant polyphonic song of praise resplendent in its fibers as they quiver and tremble, strand by strand. This was the craft of tapestry to make the firmament that is Creation, the Greenfields Kirk, a tangible reality. Consequently, the expression of an

---

89 In this specific instance we were talking about his writing that was influenced by Japanese and Chinese literature. Misinterpretation obviously pained him. At the time I understood that he was likely to be referring to local reception in Orkney and how he was perceived in certain negative ways.

analogic sacramentality of the universe radiated Christ liturgically through sign and symbol in the seven sacraments giving way to pre-theologic poetic language grounded in the natural world and the human person freighted with atmosphere and energy, not metaphorically but really. The Orcadian version, in its native tradition, spoke particularly and universally in unison, with the one voice of Christ through Mackay Brown's experience of the natural world inscape by inscape stemmed in the Divine *instress*.

Chapter Two, "A Thousand Candles of Gorse," explores the eucharistic Christ as the ultimate "set form" that was and is the central core of the universe, the central core of the Greenfields Kirk and the Mackay Brown and Hopkins texts. It was not enough for Hopkins and Mackay Brown to fall headlong into an uncontrolled disordered experience of Creation. They saw the hand of its Creator in the intelligent design of its patterns. Mackay Brown's development is explored through his set forms that emerged ever more definitively. His love of literary litanies reclaimed from the suppression of the Reformation legacy, increased in him his Catholic heart and mind enabled to infuse his language with the majesty and sweetness of his experience of Christ. It was the Eucharist more than anything else that gave his texts a set form that was as liturgical as it was pre-theologically poetic, giving the public face to his private vision so defended from view across his life-long project. This was a leitourgia, his work for the people that was ceremonial and processional, and it was a joyous project patterned with a consistent repertoire of ideas, phrases, or observances. The Mackay Brown view of things, his vision, is presented through his experience of Hopkins, in a way that does not obscure his own work to the point that its distinctiveness vanished from sight.

Chapter Three, "Fetching Out Inscape and Instress," examines the poetical craft where Christ is the instressed-inscape, not metaphorically but really. Holding fast to the roots of language, Hopkins unleashed the inscape and instress into an unsuspecting and uncomprehending literary world that found him difficult. Mackay Brown thrived in his own levels of difficulty as he unmistakably flushed out his determination to work univocally with method and system, in a swarm of micro-set forms of particularities. With his vivid apprehension of Christ's presence in the universe, he held fast to the roots of language as he came to a stable realization of an epistemology, a theory of knowledge that worked for him, as it had for Hopkins. They gave to their public the world of bluebells and daffodils not only in their botanic form but as lexical and metrical vehicles that burst forth into the other place in a timeless voyage building a consciousness beyond the boundaries of language and glittering surfaces of images. This other place takes us into the Mackay Brown vision beyond the sort of shopfront of his writing: into the art of using language to pattern out the swarm of symbols in his crafted mastery. Univocally, not analogically, words became stars of light as they draw his reader into his work through liturgical set forms that engaged and unknowingly deepened their relationship with his own inner piety. Hopkins's world of Christ-birds became Mackay Brown's redemption, and that of his public. Tracing the ever-flowing tides of the force field that was the Mackay Brown Greenfields Kirk led to its eucharistic center and source. Words, phrases, poems functioned as electromagnetic oscillations that for Hopkins and Mackay Brown were sightings of the eucharistic Christ ablaze with the instressed-inscapes of a "thousand candles of gorse." The fetching out of bright yellow flowers shimmering on the altar was the elemental level of the tapestry of Mackay Brown's dynamic poetic craft.

Chapter Four, "Stalling and Stemming Stars and Stations: Elements of Verse," traces the sprung rhythm that was Christ, according to the specification of how a disciplined univocity energized these passion poets. They use language with a particular elemental precision of number, meter, music, and sound curvature. This craft is never a closed system of static, serialized, or episodic images that move in a parallel of literary devices beside a procession of facts. This is a poetical craft instressed deeply, word by word, in the absolute nature of the Creator, not by analogical language but by univocity where Christ was and is that one voice of unambiguous meaning and definition. To do so reveals the sprung rhythm of a Christian illumination, patterned according to Pythagorean number theory, where the irregularity of life becomes a new form of symmetry, a sort of "putty in their hands." The sacramental firmament, with its warp and weave of multitudinous instressed-inscapes, radiates in the sprung rhythm of elements of verse to appear as intelligent design around a central eucharistic core. By asserting the native tradition, what had been a dark foreboding world, becomes center stage for the human person as poetic subject.

Chapter Five, "Hurrahing in the Harvests," analyzes the conceptualization of the human person with which Mackay Brown and Hopkins worked. Christ is the form of the human person, and this is their conceptualization. They address human flaws and frailties that exist in a dark shadowy world of sin. At an auspicious point in their own personal crisis, they elevate not only themselves but also their characterization of persons through their experience of the incarnational Christ. The path of Redemption through a dark foreboding world is for these poets a personal act of atonement with a moral imperative. The level of precision of this experience becomes the carefully controlled elements of verse that radiate with sainted portrayals: Hopkins's Harry, Tom, Felix, Alphonsus, and Mackay Brown's Magnus, the Everyman, Thorfinn, Ikey, Rognvald, Peter, Ally, Gudrun and Mhairi to name but a few as they form a spiral of poetic subjects. Mackay Brown's world of tinker, saint, crofter, tramp, lifeboatman, fisherman, doctor, librarian, and tailor is his encryption of the archetypal Creator in a glory of praise. The human person may sin and fall, be stricken down with frailties, but is haloed with grace and hallowed in Christ, where the human person emerges as a poetic subject. One by one persons rose from the shadows of the dark foreboding world to become "Caged Skylarks" in the "Redeeming Waves" impassioned in poetry, not metaphorically but really.

Chapter Six, "Immortalizing Storms and Shipwrecks," looks specifically at storms and shipwrecks as "annunciations of terror," otherwise known as the Dark Night of the Soul. The depression known to have inhabited Hopkins and Mackay Brown so formatively, univocally bursts forth in a fulsome expression of their artistic sense. Mackay Brown's overarching liturgical frame was a collaborative fusion and radical witness to a convincing linguistic reality that was able to speak the truth of the human person through a restored and reinvigorated Christian illumination. The liturgical frame that Mackay Brown wraps around his maritime tribe presses towards the Real Presence that is Christ. He flushes out the Passion and Resurrection in terms not unlike

Hopkins's, but the difference resides in his own levels of linguistic vibrancy with the heptahedron, his distinctive algorithmic harp. Hopkins and Mackay Brown through their piety and passion show difference-in-unity and unity in-difference that requires patient decryption of the seamless interaction of their elements of verse. Their poetic vision rests in unity and celebrates difference.

Chapter Seven, "Theological Blades," finally gives way to the dazzling, complex and bewildering intensities of the poetical vision with its spiral of bi-directional katology attributed to Balthasar. This katology is influenced by Newman, and Hopkins's Scotian conceptualization. This book does not shrink back from the discoveries of Hopkins and Mackay Brown. It heightens their voices from published and unpublished materials through the lens of this manuscript collection. Their uneasy complex vision re-worked the world of facts using *univocity* as the way forward not only to defy the concerns and literary conventions of the nineteenth century but also those of the twentieth, with its modernism and its post-modern legacies. This Chapter extracts the all-consuming theological trends that pulsated under the textual surface. Those theological blades prove to be deft oar-strokes that led Mackay Brown to attempt an ambitious project to encompass the study of Hopkins's poems within the eucharistic liturgy in each and all its phases. This project or mapping of Hopkins's poems was tried but lies incomplete in these manuscripts; nevertheless, patterns of the seamless movement of the sacred and the profane and the credibility of spiritual combat give voice to what Mackay Brown discerned as a new dark strength.

Mackay Brown himself, his voice, his writings, his person drive this book from first to last. He is not reconfigured according to the perceptions of the times. His prolific literary texts evidence the man and poet with a lengthy period of development seriously weighted towards the artistic sense. He fired up his texts as an act of praise in a blazing and bewildering world of facts made sensually intelligible by his insight into the other world: the higher reality that he experienced day in and day out in the theophany of the Orkney islands. Accompanied by selections of poetry across his full collection, the argument of his journey is univocity. This was his forge, as it was for Hopkins. These selections are not exhaustive and are biased towards his

Introduction

own preoccupation with the artistic sense as the critical factor in any assessment of literary merit. Each choice from word, phrase, parts of poems, to complete poems, is to give the Mackay Brown voice, that taste of himself, and not weaken its original strength. Each segment is an integral part of the greater whole, the tapestry seamlessly woven as the Mackay Brown North Atlantic Fornaldarsǫgur of his native tradition.

Chapter titles, subtitles, and quotes that underlie each Chapter heading guide the reader through the text that is everything. They are chosen because they form a pattern of development. Because of the cryptic, private intricacies that some would call an obsessive pursuit of language with its integration of sight, sound, taste, touch, smell, the poetic vision of pre-theologic materials is complex and complicated. It is never linear, static, or episodic. Therefore, the discussion and analysis of the poetic vision bears that intricacy and complexity. That is the task of the poet: to master the symbols, go beyond the boundaries of language using each element of it to open a higher reality. That was their genius—to express the firmament, its Creator, the intelligent design that became a univocal rather than analogical expression. This was their passion and piety and, yes, it has an elevated level of difficulty if the reader stays at surface level of images and cannot embrace the streaming oscillation of the bi-directional katalogical perspective. This was the Catholic intellectual tradition wherein Mackay Brown found himself. Like Hopkins, Mackay Brown had his own lexicon, hence this book's reliance upon it. Where analysis may fail, the text can prevail in its swarm of symbols and trembling stations and even such a critic as Alan Bold recognized literary greatness, despite much that irked him, and saw that it was "beautifully shaped for survival. It is like a vast ocean over which shine starlike images and symbols. He takes us on a timeless voyage on the ocean and makes us aware of the profound depths beneath the glittering surface."[90]

This book, therefore, is different in certain specific ways. It puts forward Mackay Brown, his voice, in the various pathways of the cumulative body of textual evidence to argue from its polyvalent and multi-pathways. The plasticity of Newman's thought ran through Hopkins and Mackay Brown with its illative sense

---

90 Bold, *George Mackay Brown*, 113.

that absorbed the imagination into its workings. The poetic materials are complex because the vision is complex. Mackay Brown was interpersonally private about it but cumulatively public about it in his written materials. An analogical perspective may help to process these materials, but it is a univocal perspective at work in Hopkins and Mackay Brown that unleashed the suppression inflicted on language and literature at the Reformation. In the realism of taking things as they are, they took a literary path that expanded in the face of a diminished human person detached from the sacramental universe by the Reformation. Hopkins moved language into the realms of univocity, reinstating the sacramental universe in literary terms. Mackay Brown crystallized the Greenfields Kirk, not metaphorically but really, as it reconnected his language with its source to the point of no separation.

Their inscaped-instressed language stepped away from the Romantic movement and dispensed with the fractured and fragmented modernism and the empty void of post-modernism. Once again, the majestic nature of Creation could be experienced as the force-field of the Real Presence. The Creator and Redeemer could draw the human person into a consciousness of the Kingdom of God that is very near through language that could plummet the dark night of the soul in its depressive forms, but equally give rise to the expression of the majestic world of grace. The Jesuit historiography and ethos played its part for Hopkins and Mackay Brown in real terms. Their passion and piety in all things poetic were lived and loved in the theophany of their native tradition, leaving a corpus of texts published and unpublished but spoken of in unison to give the strongest sense of their persons on that poetic journey to the triumph of their artistry. As Mackay Brown experienced Newman's *Apologia* in 1947, "there is a magnificent devastating logic about it."[91] This book takes that same sentiment to heart in the study that lies ahead of the artistry and vision of these passion poets.

---

91 Mackay Brown, Letter to Ernest Marwick, 1947. OLA, EWM Collection.

CHAPTER ONE

The Greenfields Kirk

> "Nature the dazzling garment of the Garment of God. He did well to praise it; that for him was one kind of holy living; the pool he haunted was lonely, but it was beautiful with the rare beauty of God."[1]

MACKAY BROWN'S GREENFIELDS KIRK IS that enchanted constellation of form, shape and patterns of the natural world, God's creation, illumined and tranced. This was Mackay Brown's territory, his native tradition that underwent a lifelong literary development composed of many strands and seeds. He crafted them into a stable poetic conceptualization instilled with a distinctive fusion of natural beauty and vanished communities. This was his ultimate challenge and the Catholic mind and heart that emerged within him found profound convergence within Hopkins's view of things. This chapter examines the Greenfields Kirk as Mackay Brown's context and tone for his poetic vision. What may appear to be a disjointed selection of Mackay Brown's writings because of the differences across his literary timeline is in fact a central concern of this study. This chapter traces the historical, literary, philosophical, and theological strands that evidence Mackay Brown's understanding of Hopkins's intelligent design that became his own particular fabric and firmament, his Orkney tapestry. Each selection of a text is a key moment from the points of time across Mackay Brown's range of materials both published and unpublished. Mackay Brown's voice is elevated above all others to give the fullest insight into the intricacies of his poetic vision.

Hopkins's "that taste of myself"[2] so purposefully distinctive enabled Mackay Brown to find his voice to express a specific angle of vision. This was his craft to weave and interweave, in

---

1 Mackay Brown, *Notebook Three*. NLS.
2 Hopkins, "Comments on the Spiritual Exercises of Ignatius Loyola," in *Gerard Manley Hopkins Poems and Prose*, 145.

and out, over and over again to the point of what became for some an archaic monotony, for others a radiant polyphonic song of praise resplendent in its fibers as they quiver and tremble, strand by strand. This was his craft of tapestry to make the firmament of the creation story of the Greenfields Kirk a tangible reality, univocally. The Orcadian version, in its native tradition, speaks particularly and universally in unison bearing the Hopkins signature in an experience of the natural world inscape by inscape stemmed in the divine instress. Mackay Brown was at work with his poetic needle drawing the threads through the text, not metaphorically but really.

Mackay Brown evidenced this process early in 1949 on a Sabbath journey to Rackwick, "In Search of a Green Valley." Mackay Brown was well able to sense and write the vision, "The early dawn broke cloudless and clear. The birds woke to a new summer day. Whispers of wind went over the sea and rustled in the heavy grasses."[3] He captured the Hoy narrative, "But Nature has worked out a subtle drama here. For it is not the mountains, the high glens and the crags that conquer after all. At the extreme west of this lofty and wild terrain, hemmed in by the hills, a valley lovelier than any other in Orkney slopes down to the sea. Here are the white sands and singing larks; here in Rackwick is a patchwork of fields, and a burn where the music is sweeter because of the surrounding hostility and desolation."[4] Mackay Brown wrote in 1951 as he looked down from Brinkies Brae above Stromness across the form, shape and patterns of Orkney: "from the point of view of worship it is almost as good as having been in church."[5] Decades later in 1993 he wrote in the poem "Sunday in Selskay Isle"[6] that Mr. Frame the schoolmaster, not an atheist, found "the divine" everywhere in Nature filtered with books and music. "Clever" Mr. Frame worships in the "Greenfields Kirk"[7] and takes no part in church attendance.

The sweet clear spirit, the call of the curlew, was the luminous echo of the moral imperative that for Mackay Brown reverberated in the natural world of the Greenfields Kirk. Here the presence

---

3 Mackay Brown, *Northern Lights: A Poet's Sources*, 87. Also, in *The Collected Poems of George Mackay Brown*, 413-15.
4 Ibid., 88.   5 Ibid., 104.   6 Ibid., 53-55.   7 Ibid.

of the existence of God is nuanced and subtle in form, shape, and pattern becoming a sensational vision that in philosophical terms is a pulsating cosmological argument for the existence of God. Hopkins and Mackay Brown express their arguments in language that dances metrically beyond the poetic conventions of their day to give a convincing prominence to what many know to be Catholic categories of thought. Unlike Mr. Frame the schoolmaster, Mackay Brown did not refrain from church attendance; the Greenfields Kirk gave him every reason to worship its Creator not only in the things He had made but in the eucharistic Christ who was as intelligible to him as He was to Hopkins.

Firstly, in Creation they found the Creator as the origin as First Mover, First Cause, Prime Mover in the classical Catholic Aristotelian categories from Thomas Aquinas. But Aquinas's analogical use of language, starting from origins and systematically moving towards ends compacted into the cosmological argument, set artificial constraints on the poetic perceptions and thoughtfulness of Hopkins and Mackay Brown. Their personal experience of the fragility of life had confronted them early on in a series of life events. They both emerged with a profound need to express the form, shapes, and patterns of what they understood to be an Illumination of the Divine. They were looking for what the Jesuit philosopher Frederick Copleston called in the 1948 BBC radio debate[8] with Bertrand Russell a "Principle of Sufficient Reason." Here they could find space for their poetic sensibilities to articulate new lines of artistic development. Their inner world needed innovative literary devices to bring forth what they were able to sense. Hopkins expanded the sprung rhythm of everyday diction and idiom with outriders, counterpoint, margaretting, quaining, the heart of which was inscape and instress. Where Hopkins expanded, Mackay Brown condensed, drawing from an Orkney poetics instilled by the rhythms of childhood, stored in the subconscious mind, emerging in kennings and litanies, to carving the runes. The sweet clear spirit of Hopkins driven by

---

8 The Copleston-Russell debate was an exchange concerning the existence of God between Frederick Copleston and Bertrand Russell in a 1948 BBC radio broadcast. There is a strong likelihood Mackay Brown listened in, as his knowledge of Copleston is well documented as is his passion for radio programs (see note 51). The debate centers on two points: the metaphysical and moral arguments for the existence of God.

a moral imperative led to a life-long artistic investigation into form, shape, and pattern that revealed an intellectual shift from causation to design suffused and illumined with moral purpose. This was their Principle of Sufficient Reason to pursue Duns Scotus's Theory of Univocity.[9] Both Hopkins and Mackay Brown thrived in their experience of the "particularities" of the natural world suffused as they saw it with God its Creator.

It is at this point while acknowledging the usefulness of the literary method of employing an analogical approach to language, this research study takes a univocal approach. Schmid gives an incisive reading of Mackay Brown that can "attest to his poetics of the visual imagination"[10] by giving evidence from the density of his poetic text within "a sacramental view of time."[11] Schmid gives voice to Mackay Brown's delight in the "making" of his poetry in all its patterns, dimensions, and technical aspects. Nevertheless, it is an analogical approach that on its own fails to open the renewed levels of language that Hopkins and Mackay Brown achieved through *univocity* that gave a challenging fullness and a radical departure from literary convention. Bicket also favors an analogical approach that aligns both Hopkins and Mackay Brown within a "sacramental understanding of the universe"[12] by citing David Tracey.[13] This study takes the view the analogical approach shrinks the poetic vision of Mackay Brown who unconsciously positioned himself in univocity in order to be true to his experience of the natural world and human nature, in keeping with the epistemic stream of Catholic thought that flowed through the Church Fathers into Newman, then through the Scotian and Jesuit Hopkins. These strands of thought are absorbed into the symphonic thought of Balthasar. An analogical approach moves in one direction as it seeks to draw out the complexity and hiddenness of poetic vision by all the literary techniques that compare and contrast, using human

---

9 Univocity of being is the idea that words describing the properties of God mean the same thing as when they apply to people or things. It is associated with the poetry of Gerard Manley Hopkins through the Scholastic theologian John Duns Scotus.
10 Schmid, *Keeping the Sources Pure: The Making of George Mackay Brown*, 194.
11 Ibid., 195.
12 Bicket, *The Scottish Catholic Imagination*, 39.
13 Tracey, *The Analogical Imagination: Christian Theology and the Culture of Pluralism*.

reasoning to elucidate difference by simplification to conceptualize what lies outside the limitations of human experience. Univocity was how Hopkins laid out new parameters to expand the use of language so that it was bi-directional and katalogical working linguistically to achieve a new level of articulation of the equivalence between reality and its expression. The universal and the particular became through Hopkins's innovations an expression of difference-in-unity and unity-in-difference as words were infused with personal experience and its empirical validity through faith and reason working seamlessly together. This is challenging for readers as they try to serially process the multiple dimensions that have considerable impact and force as well as rapture in the poetry of Hopkins and Mackay Brown.

Positioning and ranking Mackay Brown has always been a challenge that was in evidence as soon as he put pen to paper. The "rank"[14] of Mackay Brown before he came to Edinburgh in its various phases[15] over an eight-year span had been adjudicated on locally in 1950: "All I shall say here is it seems at least there is a chance—at the moment it would be foolish to say more—that Orkney has another poet whose best work will rank alongside Muir's."[16] Mackay Brown brought to his Edinburgh University postgraduate studies a substantial vision already at work through its formation within an Orkney poetics. He had already published two collections of poetry, *The Storm* (1954) and *Loaves and Fishes* (1959). His poetic vision was already conversant with "origins and ends" and Hopkins. Mackay Brown had already inscaped into his writings the patterns of the wild natural beauty of Orkney as it plunges headlong into the stuff of life: Church, Monastery and Hall, the brutish oppression of the peasantry, the fallen nature of man and woman, the crucible of marriage, the politics of the day, the remains of previous civilizations—all woven into the liturgy of sky, land and sea harbored within the Greenfields Kirk. Here was the seamless garment, the Orkney tapestry of the sacred and the profane. These are all Mackay

---

14 "Will George Brown Rank with Edwin Muir?"(unattributed) *Orkney Herald*, 10 January 1950, 5.
15 Newbattle Abbey College 1951-52, 1956. Edinburgh University BA 1956-60, Teacher Training (incomplete) 1960-61, Edinburgh University 1962-64.
16 "Will George Brown Rank with Edwin Muir?" *Orkney Herald*, 10 January 1950, 5.

Brown markers of his craft and his literary articulation of them takes us into a swarm of symbols that asks of its readers to be absorbed into a tapestry of life that gestures towards "the other place,"[17] to go through "the secret door"[18] via a "granary,"[19] to let go in a distinctive Orkney poetics where St. Magnus becomes the Christ-face of Orkney.

FABRIC AND FIRMAMENT OF AN ORKNEY TAPESTRY

Mackay Brown describes the decade 1941–1951 as having "very intense experiences that became part of the fabric of my life."[20] The published and unpublished writings from this decade are part of what Mackay Brown called "the fabric" because they are exactly that—a written record of these "intense experiences" that went with him throughout his life. I have chosen to accompany the Hopkins *Essays and Notes* with the earlier *Commonplace Book*[21] to specifically bring Mackay Brown's voice to the forefront of this study giving prominence to his inner world as it was before, during and after his time in Edinburgh. Hopkins and Mackay Brown do not present as kindly domesticated poets in their literary works. Their lives gave strong challenge and battle with those forces that try to keep us from being fully alive. They both felt the deepest emotions. God was at the heart of their personal darkness and confusion. This was a God never above their situation. It is God's nature to be in the crises at its deepest level. From beginning to end their inner turmoil was a spur to literary and spiritual enlightenment. The full range of Mackay Brown's published and unpublished writings show a continuously stable range of materials that piece together the complex poetic vision he so fiercely defended throughout his life. Mackay Brown wrote in "Summer Day 1947": "Vanity of vanities! By taper light / I read now, thrilled in Time, men walk

---

17 Muir, *An Autobiography*, 35.
18 Rendall, "The Riddle," in *Collected Poems*, 226.
19 Mackay Brown, *For the Islands I Sing*, 77.
20 Ibid., 79.
21 Cited in Murray, *Interrogation of Silence: The Writings of George Mackay Brown*. These notes were acquired by the NLS at the same time and from the same source as the Hopkins ms. The decision by the Literary Estate to release these materials at the same time gives an insight that these materials complement one another from the research point of view.

blind / The cloud-dappled alleys of God's eternal city."[22] Already the marks of Bunyan, Muir, Blake, and Hopkins are interwoven in the Mackay Brown fabric. Blindness is a biblical image for lack of spiritual sight, the inability to see things as they are. Mackay Brown was not blind to a metaphysics of creation that held the world as a participation in the creative energy of God. The blindness created by the vanity of the self-elevating ego and village mentality was overtaken within this decade by the tranced vision that the Greenfields Kirk of Orkney enraptured in him. He was led out-of-Orkney to the city of Edinburgh and then on (not back) to it, with the blessing (and suffering) that epiphanizes his audience. The seeds of the vision instilled within this decade swell their girth, exploding in the profusion and swarm of symbols, living in Stromness with an inner grace. It is this vision that effectively challenges the life with no eye for the spiritual.

According to biographical accounts, Mackay Brown showed certain instabilities in temperament and life skills[23] and the conventions of the times. But he was a poet, and he knew it. In Hopkins he found new lines of the old "firmament"[24] and its

---

22 Mackay Brown, "Summer Day 1947." See Gray: *George Mackay Brown: No Separation*, 43-44. (The context of this unpublished manuscript as one of the early drafts of the poem "Hamnavoe" held in the Orkney Archive is given in full.) This nine-versed "dream" poem bears witness to Mackay Brown's "classical" religious experience. The narrative of the poem is from the numinous sources of Orkney – its patterns of settlement, land, sky, sea, architecture and the place of man, woman, and child. Its echoing memories bear the marks of John Bunyan, the Book of Ecclesiastes, William Blake, and Edwin Muir. It is an absorbing point of reference that Mackay Brown's last words as recorded in Maggie Fergusson's *George Mackay Brown: The Life*: "I see hundreds and hundreds of ships sailing out of the harbor" resonate with those early 1947 lines in "Summer Day": "Fishing boats / Raised anchor. Offering red sails / To the west wind, drifting / In the tide-dark sound" giving emphasis to the "fabric of his life" from first to last. Fergusson made a similar reference in "The praise singers: poets George Mackay Brown and Gerard Manley Hopkins," *The Tablet*, 13 August 2020.
23 Fergusson, *George Mackay Brown: The Life*; Fergusson, *George Mackay Brown: The Wound and the Gift*.
24 The word "firmament" is first recorded in a Middle English narrative based on scripture dated 1250. It later appeared in the King James Bible. The word is anglicized from Latin *firmamentum*, used in the Vulgate (4th century). This in turn is derived from the Latin root *firmus*, a cognate with "firm." The word is a Latinization of the Greek *stereōma*, which appears in the Septuagint (c. AD 200). Like most ancient peoples, the Hebrews believed the sky was a solid dome with the Sun, Moon, planets and stars embedded in it. A detailed Christian view of the universe was based on various biblical texts and earlier

metaphysics of creation. As he writes in his customary understated self-appraisal of his intellectual nature, "It was essential to choose a writer of small output,"[25] as though he always took the effortless way out. His *Essays and Notes* defy this understatement. They record the poet as a man who had a distinctive grasp on the literary tradition and the "choruses"[26] or colonies of artists that converged around certain contemporary literary figures. The literary legends of the Rose Street set fashionable in Edinburgh in the 1960s[27] caught the attention of Mackay Brown for a time, but it is clear from the Hopkins manuscript collection there is an intellectual grasp on all things literary accompanied by an aspirational trajectory to make himself in the cast of Hopkins, as "one of the ancient smelters and smiths of poetry."[28]

Whatever was going on in his Edinburgh social life, Mackay Brown was coming to terms with Hopkins's new lines of an old firmament and he made a critical re-adjustment in his thinking. Hopkins's incarnational constellation with its keynotes of inscape and instress, haeccitas or thisness, the principle of individuation[29] became the infrastructure for Mackay Brown's Greenfields Kirk. While the old medieval firmament still held good

---

Greek and Egyptian christianized theories. The Catholic philosophers and theologians, St. Augustine and St. Thomas Aquinas emphasized the "solid nature" of the firmament. The Copernican Revolution of the 16th century led to reconsideration of these matters. In 1554, John Calvin proposed that "firmament" be interpreted as clouds. Calvin's doctrine of accommodation allowed Protestants to accept the findings of science without rejecting the authority of scripture. It is relevant to point out that when quoting scripture in his writings Mackay Brown draws from the King James Bible and Catholic translations (particularly in his novel *Magnus*).

25 Mackay Brown, *For the Islands I Sing*, 150.
26 Ibid., 144.
27 Fergusson, *George Mackay Brown: The Life*, 162.
28 Mackay Brown, *For the Islands I Sing*, 150.
29 Incarnation in Christian theology is the embodiment of God the Son in human flesh as Jesus Christ. According to Duns Scotus "the Incarnation of the Son of God, planned from all eternity by God the Father at the level of love is the fulfilment of creation and enables every creature, in Christ and through Christ, to be filled with grace and to praise and glorify God in eternity. Although Duns Scotus was aware that in fact, because of original sin, Christ redeemed us with his Passion, Death and Resurrection, he reaffirmed that the Incarnation is the greatest and most beautiful work of the entire history of salvation, that it is not conditioned by any contingent fact but is God's original idea of ultimately uniting with himself the whole of creation, in the Person and Flesh of the Son." *General Audience of July 7th, 2010*, where Pope Benedict XVI praised the *Doctor Subtilis*, Bl. John Duns Scotus.

because of the Incarnation, Hopkins's vision or way of seeing penetrated it in a manner that was empirically based, true to the forms in nature, true to innocence and experience, and true to the perceptions and intuitions of human nature. Hopkins's meticulous accumulations of the visual observation of the natural world flesh out his thinking and discoveries. He measured and quantified, named, and questioned the visual evidence as a means of coming to a realization of his empirical recordings. In addition, he went over and beyond the popular natural history quest that the Victorians were enthralled by. Whilst the Victorians were challenged by the evolutionary theories of Darwinism, Hopkins's *Journals* show his own absorption of the microscopic details or particularities of the natural world. Hopkins engaged in a process that tried to get at the world in a meaningful way to trace its journey from origins, through composition and its patterns, to "ends." Hopkins could not contain the excitement of his vivid sensed perceptions with the analogical use of language. The metaphysics of creation as understood by Hopkins substantiated his emerging epistemology: new lines for the old firmament were confirmed by his "data" collection and his keen interest in the science of the time. This is seen in the series of letters he wrote to the journal *Nature* in 1883.[30]

Hopkins built on the solidity of Augustine and Aquinas and he was able to see and understand the universe in its particularities. He discovered in Scotus how he could confirm his own thinking, centered as it was on the Incarnation. Mackay Brown found validation for his Greenfields Kirk within Hopkins's expression of the firmament in all its dynamic bi-directional oscillating vibrancy. He had personally travelled the incompleteness of the Reformation ethos with its accommodation of Calvinism[31] that to the Mackay Brown mind had a harsh and uncompromising stance towards the arts and spirituality. As Mackay Brown writes in his Edinburgh notes, "Many mystics closed their eyes the better to concentrate on the things of the spirit, but Hopkins opened them wide to find one ablaze in

---

30 Hopkins, *The Correspondence of Gerard Manley Hopkins and Richard Watson Dixon*, 161-66.
31 In 1554, John Calvin proposed that "firmament" be interpreted as clouds. Calvin's doctrine of accommodation allowed Protestants to accept the findings of science without rejecting the authority of scripture.

the many."³² And on Scotus: "the visible beauties of the world [are] a bridge between the finite and the infinite. Yet Hopkins's poetry must be judged for its artistic value, not for its religious value....The senses are not suppressed they are directed."³³

FINDING CONFIDENCE AND COURAGE IN ONESELF

One of the first impressions from the study of Mackay Brown's Hopkins *Essays and Notes* is a powerful sense of his own personal validation of "that taste of myself."³⁴ Hopkins's Jesuit formation aligned his own inner processes closely to the *Spiritual Exercises of St. Ignatius Loyola.*³⁵ There is no doubt that Mackay Brown read and thought widely and deeply during the postgraduate studies of Hopkins, but there was no evidence that he read the writings of St. Ignatius directly. Mackay Brown's notes are intuitive and heavily weighted towards his own inner processes. He aligned with the firmament of Catholic categories and the literary devices Hopkins confirmed as his own, but the Greenfields Kirk underwent change and development as he selectively filtered Hopkins's writings on St. Ignatius Loyola. Mackay Brown had written in 1947, in a defense of sorts for the Roman Catholic Church,³⁶ that he was attracted by the "The Communion of Saints."³⁷ Bearing in mind his life-long aversion to Calvinism, he wrote, "The bleak terror of the unshriven soul before God (which is the internal drama as pictured by the

---

32 Mackay Brown: *Notebook Three, NLS.*   33 Ibid.
34 Hopkins, "Comments on the Spiritual Exercises of Ignatius Loyola" in *Gerard Manley Hopkins: Poems and Prose,* 145.
35 *The Spiritual Exercises* (1548) of Ignatius of Loyola (founder of the Jesuit Order) are considered a classic work of spiritual literature. The main idea of Ignatian spirituality, is to help one "conquer oneself and to regulate one's life in such a way that no decision is made under the influence of any inordinate attachment." The Exercises are intended to give the person undertaking them a greater degree of freedom from his or her own likes and dislikes and focus on personal choice and discernment in accordance with God's will. Examination of oneself takes place within a 30-day (4 week) retreat in silence and solitude under a spiritual director. First week: Sin, and God's mercy. Second Week: episodes in the Life of Jesus. Third Week: The Passion of Jesus. Fourth Week: The Resurrection of Jesus and God's love. After the first week Ignatius recommends a form of contemplation *which he calls "application of the senses." For this you "place yourself in a scene from the Gospels. Ask yourself, 'What do I see? What do I hear? What do I feel, taste and smell?'"* Loyola Jesuit Centre.
36 Mackay Brown, *The Roman Catholic Church March 1947, NLS.*
37 Ibid.

Calvinists), is in the church for some made mellow and lovely by the intervention of the Saints on behalf of sinners on earth."[38] Mackay Brown finds great consolation in how the Catholic category of the interventions of the saints can be accompanied by the experience by which "each of us can bear a new infusion moving through time."[39]

As one reads the *Essays and Notes* there is a keen sense of Mackay Brown immersed in Hopkins and his ideas. Hopkins writes in the *Conclusion of the Principle or Foundation* certain key notions that Mackay Brown clearly absorbed to make his own, for example:

> Man was created to praise, reverence, and serve God our Lord, and thereby to save his soul...things on the face of the earth were created for man's sake, and to help him in the following out of the end for which he was created...BEGIN TO GIVE GOD GLORY...the moment we do this we reach the end of our being; we do what we are made for...this is a thing to live for...You cannot mean your praise if while your praise is on your lips there is no reverence in the mind; There can be no reverence in the mind if there is no obedience, no submission, no service...When a man is in God's grace and free from mortal sin, then everything he does, so long as there is no sin in it, gives God glory, and what does not give him glory has some, however little, sin in it...It is not only prayer that gives God glory but work. Smiting on the anvil, sawing a beam, whitewashing a wall, driving horses, sweeping, scouring, everything gives God some glory if being in his grace you do it as your duty.[40]

I have included these quotes from Hopkins to show the wave upon wave of Catholic categories that Mackay Brown absorbed that brought change and development. It is more an ever-absorbing love of God than points of doctrine and dogma that gave him confidence in his own sense of himself, his purpose and his duty. Clearly, Mackay Brown, raised as a Calvinist, knew at first hand "the bleak terror of the unshriven soul,"[41] found in Hopkins an ever-increasing Catholic frame of reference that

---

38 Ibid.   39 Ibid.
40 Hopkins, "The Principle or Foundation," in *Gerard Manley Hopkins: Poems and Prose*, 142-43.
41 Mackay Brown: *The Roman Catholic Church March 1947*, NLS.

resonated with his 1947 sense of the interventions of the saints as "mellow and lovely."[42] That "self-taste"[43] that haunted him is championed by Hopkins as an argument that convinced of a loving and compassionate God worthy of praise. The glory, the praise, the reverence, the forgiveness of sins, the grace of God, the life of prayer and work gave Hopkins and Mackay Brown a sense of their purpose, their dignity as human persons and as poets. Equally, life required a frame of obedience, submission, and service to go forward; and as Mackay Brown so distinctively wrote, "each of us can bear a new infusion moving through time."

Hopkins continued in his "Comments in the Spiritual Exercises of St. Ignatius Loyola"[44] to situate duty within the frame of the human person. Duty is to save one's soul by a life of service to the Glory of God, in things small and great, with a consciousness of the intention of the act. This is what he meant when he wrote of "following out of the end for which he was created."[45] Hopkins discovered his unique personal being in the patterns of his own experience of himself: "I find myself both as a man and as myself something most determined and distinctive, at pitch, more distinctive and higher pitched than anything else I see."[46] Within all the variegated richness of the personal patterns, "pleasures and pains, powers and experiences, deserts and guilt, shame and sense of beauty. Dangers, fears, all my fate," Hopkins saw the strongest argument for the nature of God. Only a God of this nature could bring the human person through a process of development and discipline for a unique purpose. Hopkins's argument for the existence of God was a blend of the design and moral arguments. The evidence was "my self-being, my consciousness and feeling of myself, that taste of myself, of I and me above and in all things, which is more distinctive than the taste of ale or alum, more distinctive than the smell of walnut leaf or camphor... searching nature I taste self at one tankard, that of my own being."[47] Reading the *Essays and Notes*, one has a strong sense of Mackay Brown's fascination with this line of Hopkins's thought.

---

42 Ibid.
43 Hopkins, "Comments on the Spiritual Exercises of Ignatius Loyola" in *Gerard Manley Hopkins: Poems and Prose*, 149.   44 Ibid., 145.
45 Hopkins, "The Principle or Foundation," in *Gerard Manley Hopkins Poems and Prose*, 142-43.   46 Ibid.   47 Ibid.

Hopkins amid the Victorians on his path into and out of the Oxford Movement was keenly aware of the developments in science and the newly minted variations on the Designer Argument for the Existence of God. From Paley, then to the depths of Augustine and Aquinas in his formation as an Aristotelian Catholic, Hopkins's observations and experience of the intelligent design in the natural world and his personal self are particular and universal, deeply shown in the nature of the human person. From inscape to instress, to individuation and *this-ness*, he ploughed the philosophical furrows following the sensational beauty that he perceived to come from the Creator God. Mackay Brown was no stranger to this path and like Hopkins recognized a dynamic appraisal of the natural world that included himself as a distinctive entity, duty-bound to go with his giftedness to the end.

Mackay Brown recorded Hopkins's key ideas and quotes and writes in *Notebook One*: "To seem the stranger lies 'my lot,' 'I wake and feel the fell of the dark' I am gall, heartburn.... Now we know what are his symptoms, though not perhaps the root of his sickness."[48] The healing power of poetry flowed from Hopkins to Mackay Brown. But from the *Notes* and then *Essays*, as much as the Hopkins influence is vital for Mackay Brown (and he is aware of the complete and utter Jesuit formation of Hopkins through the writings of St Ignatius), there is no evidence that he read the Jesuit saint's writings for himself. Mackay Brown commented on the *Spiritual Exercises of St. Ignatius* and the formation in Hopkins of that taste of myself, but there was no evidence he was going to put himself through the exacting rawness of the Jesuit formation. The *Notes* may document the influences on Hopkins, but they do not fire up Mackay Brown to seek them for himself. His quest for formation was through the infusion of the person, wordsmith, and poet, Hopkins. Hopkins found the taste of myself the most thrilling thing in existence and Mackay Brown wrote: "this distinctiveness informing all the objects and forms of nature too, (but meaningless unless his own lips drank from the tankard) can be the greatest curse, if emphasized in the wrong way. Then the amazing variety of life is ignored for the single existence."[49] Mackay Brown had

---

48 Mackay Brown, *Notebook One*, NLS.   49 Ibid.

a way of thinking that was distinctively his own, but found himself increasingly drawn into a Catholic flow of thought that stretched back to the Church Fathers, to Newman, to Hopkins and his Scotism and unintentionally he is positioning himself among his theological contemporaries such as Balthasar.

FINDING A VOICE IN A DARK FOREBODING WORLD

Having found confidence and courage in Hopkins, Mackay Brown consolidated his own distinctive "voice" during this Edinburgh period. In Orkney, "Finding a voice in the forties" (and 1950s)[50] had been "a complicated process," but one that rode the wave of "a renewed interest in language, local customs, dialect, folksong, co-operative ventures and—crucially—informed and passionate regional radio programs, and local magazines."[51] Mackay Brown was in at the start and was drawn into his first substantial chorus, a sort of "thronged bazaar" of mentors, artists, and drinkers.[52] In a ferment of "books, lectures, papers; of sitting and lingering and talking with a variety of people, many of them interesting, a few fascinating,"[53] he was sustained and nurtured first in Orkney, and then in Edinburgh for eight years as he journeyed through Newbattle Abbey and Edinburgh University. But the "hinterland" was always on his horizons as the only rightful place he could find himself as a poet who was a genuine and original wordsmith.

His conversion to Catholicism in 1961 has been scrutinized in various publications,[54] accompanied by a strong appreciation of Hopkins's influence: "Catholicism gave George Mackay Brown a loose structure of beliefs and a pattern of observances to which he could happily accommodate his native tendency as a poet to story-telling, myth and fable."[55] Most commentators leave it there, but his Catholicism is as much "a problem" in literary circles

---

50 MacInnes, "Finding a Voice in the Forties," *New Shetlander*, 30–33, 36.
51 Ibid., 30.
52 Mackay Brown, *For the Islands I Sing*, 144.
53 Ibid., 143–44.
54 Schmid, *Keeping the Sources Pure: The Making of George Mackay Brown*; Murray, *Interrogation of Silence: The Writings of George Mackay Brown*; Fergusson, *George Mackay Brown: The Life*; Ferguson, *George Mackay Brown: The Wound and the Gift*; Gray: *George Mackay Brown: No Separation*; Bicket, *George Mackay Brown and the Scottish Catholic Imagination*.
55 Gooding, *Sylvia Wishart: A Study*, 14.

and the fermenting choruses, as it is for scholars of Hopkins.[56] Mackay Brown was allowed his choice of religion, allowed his status as poet, but was he allowed an understanding of exactly how in the process of "doing as his neighbours"[57] he was deeply immersed in a formative relationship with a spirituality that kept him genuinely buoyant in the literary marketplace that was and is not overly receptive of the religious viewpoint? But as the critic Bold pointed out: "small criticisms do not alter my admiration for Brown's work...to disagree with him is one thing, to deny the awesome power of his work would be sheer folly."[58] The Mackay Brown form and content, the technicalities of his craft, were deeply interwoven to the point of "no separation." Gooding's chapter "Painter and Poet at Rackwick" in his Sylvia Wishart study gives a telling glimpse into the art of seamlessly gazing at the Orkney land, sea, and sky "scapes" and how it relates to Hopkins's articulation of the Scotian philosophical stance and attitude, for both Wishart the artist and Mackay Brown the poet. Equally, Sabine Schmid contributes a substantial chapter on Mackay Brown and Hopkins in her book, *Keeping the Sources Pure: The Making of George Mackay Brown*[59] as does my book *George Mackay Brown: No Separation.*[60]

But it is to the *23 pages of loose leaves* (cited as *Commonplace Book* in Murray's *Interrogation of Silence*) that are archived along with his *Essays and Notes* from his life and times in Edinburgh in the 1960s that attention now turns. Here it is important to take note of his thinking as it stood in the 1940s when he was "finding his voice." These tiny scraps of paper, aged and muted,[61] stand as evidence for Mackay Brown's "that taste of myself"[62] through a time that MacInnes describes as, "a burst of creative

---

56 Gardner, "The Religious Problem in G. M. Hopkins," *Scrutiny*, June 1937 in *Gerard Manley Hopkins: The Critical Heritage*, 373–83.
57 Newman, "English Catholic Literature" in *The Idea of a University*, 185.
58 Bold, *George Mackay Brown*, 113.
59 Schmid, *Keeping the Sources Pure: The Making of George Mackay Brown*. Chapter III, ("Sifted to Suit Our Sight: The Word as Sacrament in George Mackay Brown and Gerard Manley Hopkins"), 121–216.
60 Gray, *George Mackay Brown: No Separation.*
61 This collection is described as "torn from a notebook or notebooks" in the Lyon & Turnbull Catalogue Wednesday, 14th February 2018, 33 Broughton Place Edinburgh *Rare Books, Manuscripts, Maps & Photographs.*
62 Hopkins, "Comments on the Spiritual Exercises of Ignatius Loyola" in *Gerard Manley Hopkins: Poems and Prose*, 145.

activity and networking which had a very positive effect on local writers and artists alike."[63] But that "taste," that "individuation" of the poet during the 1940s, was a "grey" thing sparked with a series of life-giving moments. Included below are extracts that document the struggle of that "taste of myself" that serve to elevate the voice that will eventually find its way through the Edinburgh studies, and beyond. These notes position Mackay Brown in a place of depression as well as an intellectual struggle to rise against the dark foreboding world with a new strength of knowledge and intimate experience of God. He was caught up in a process of origins seeking ends wherever, since from the creation of the world God's invisible attributes of eternal power and divinity, His Presence, have been able to be understood and perceived in what he has created.

Mackay Brown writes in May 1947 through a character called Mazurin that, "He felt he was three parts dead already—a rather disgusting rag blown about on the winds of life."[64] He describes how a good angel came to speak to him, to reassure and point him towards his literary gifts.[65] As bleak as his life was, "the desert hills quaked with appalling menace."[66] Clearly, Mackay Brown found the courage to go on. These early notes are full of vulnerability and macabre images, but as one reads the aged leaves of notes one comes across a flash of inspiration, a moment of grace. Retrospectively he looks back to his childhood "...about the age of 7 or 8—I realized that man has made an orderly thing of time, that the hours and the months follow each other with the precision of marching soldiers (June 1946)." The intellectual development of the child led to a consistent recognition of the patterns of life, its form and shapes and an intense sense of Mackay Brown taking pleasure in that. Later as an adult he composed his own prayer: "A Prayer to cover much of life: Take me God. Use me. Pour through me as much life as I can bear. Increase not my knowledge of Good and Evil but my Innocence. Thy will be done (March 1947)."

Mackay Brown's early love of literature is well documented and, again, patterns of change and development trace the struggle

---

63 MacInnes, "Finding a Voice in the Forties," *New Shetlander*, 30–33, 36.
64 Mackay Brown, *Ms.: The Commonplace Book*. NLS.
65 Ibid.   66 Ibid.

he went through: "These wonderful lines from TS Eliot *The Family Reunion* 'In a world of fugitives the person taking the opposite direction will appear to run away...we are all running away from God, the whole world, like a stampeding herd. Those who turn back to seek the beauty and the terror 'will appear to run away'...which is just the accusation made in the world against mystics, monks, poets (March 1947)."[67] The pattern of struggle was intellectual, spiritual, moral, and emotional as he tried to keep moving forward in tune with a relentless calling towards what Muir had identified as the other place. True to form, Mackay Brown was "striving to create a current in the direction of Catholic truth"[68] that ran counter to the usual sociological strands that were expected of him: "Mazurin envied with a touch of bitterness the grace and energy of the swimmers, the lovers and the footballers because he was incapable of living in these strenuous physical ways. For he was ill, and the slightest exertion exhausted him. He felt that he was 3 parts dead already—a rather disgusting rag blown about on the winds of life. One evening the good angel spoke to him. Though he could not take part in the gay physical life he would enjoy watching it through his eyes. And the footballers that ran so swiftly and kicked so surely—what [were] Beethoven, Keats, Hilaire Belloc, and Lazarus but dull creatures in books to them? All their lives were long searches for sweet wells in immense deserts of boredom. As for Mazurin, well, he came on wells rather oftener than his fellows that were sweeter and cooler, even though for him the desert hills quaked with appalling menace. Mazurin loved books, but hated reading...the best thing was words that made images, that sang and drew fluent lines and gave birth to significant shapes. The best of all was poetry (May 1947)."[69]

This counter-current was frequented by macabre images that Mackay Brown navigated with care: "The kitten endured the first weeks of life in a dark forest piled with spider infested boxes and bric a brac. Sometimes it seems that we in this world may be living in such a confined and loathsome hole—'the sterile promontory' of Hamlet. But if we have patience, if we are supple

---

67 Ibid.
68 Newman, "English Catholic Literature" in *The Idea of a University*, 185.
69 Mackay Brown, George. *Ms.: The Commonplace Book*, NLS.

and yielding to what delightful meadows and perilous seas might we have access? (May 1947)."[70] The blend of dark and light was extremely familiar to him; but it proved, in spite of the threat to his physical and mental health, a place where the poetic vision in him was born: "The poet is able to enter into the visions of the dying and the unborn (June 1947)."[71] The direction of travel was to the artistic sense where "Art is not a frill nor a superior land of boredom...[it is] a vital necessity.... I want my poetry to be a pattern of the true images of this world—or rather of Orkney. The small part of it I know—so that, making it understood, we may bend it to our will, whether/wither for good or evil (December 1947)."[72]

The sense of triumph rises where "God overcomes the Devil." This in turn "means that God is harder and more perdurable than the Devil. Mercy, meekness, charity are harder than flint. Cruelty, meanness, self-indulgence are hard too, but not as hard as those (Jan 1948)."[73] How distinctively wise the Mackay Brown "voice" has become infused as it is with personal knowledge of the virtues as "hard." His use of this word for this purpose shows his distinctive word needle drawing the thread through the tapestry cloth at work. It is "hard" because he is drawing upon the words sense of resistance, an unbreakableness that cannot be easily bent or pierced, immoveable, a force and strength that is as bold as it is fatiguing and requiring a great deal of endurance and effort. The word is used univocally, not metaphorically but really, to speak to its spiritual sense in the same way as its material sense. "Mercy, meekness, charity are harder than flint"[74] and they are in his experience.

Mackay Brown's direction of travel returns to Eliot and "East Coker": "'Monsters, faery lights, enchantment' (EC)—the mysteries that haunt the minds of primitive people, are meant to be contrasted with the higher religious mysteries—faith, hope, love—into which they can be transmuted (April 1948)."[75] His own mind was haunted by the layers of his native tradition, but it was to the higher mysteries and its gifts that he turned to and saw the "Patterns: Life is untidy, a chaos, a meaningless flux, but if we stand remote from it, like a god or an artist,

---

70 Ibid.   71 Ibid.   72 Ibid.   73 Ibid.
74 Ibid.   75 Ibid.

the significant lines hold form, the pattern will leap into shape" (April 1948)."[76] Mackay Brown did as Hopkins had done and gave his "voice" to his craft because he had to "as long as I am the way I am."[77] Newman had set the tone in his *Apologia*. It enthralled Hopkins and Mackay Brown:

> I became excited at the view thus opened upon me...After a while I got calm. And at length the vivid impression upon my imagination faded away...I had to determine its logical value, and its bearing upon my duty...It was clear I had a good deal to learn...and that perhaps some new light was coming upon me. I determined to be guided, not by my imagination, but by my reason...that new conception of things should only so far influence me, as it had a logical claim to do so. If it came from above, it would come again, so I trusted—and with more definite outlines and greater cogency and consistency of proof.[78]

Emerging from the difficult post-war years that were formative for so many artists, it was lifesaving for Mackay Brown to embrace "definite outlines and greater cogency and consistency of proof."[79] All around him was "the cultural history—from the mid-1930s to the late 1950s—during a modernist revolution that, for all its dazzling excitement and stylistic freedoms, had in large part been fomented by apocalyptic fears...people were unable to shake off the memories of what they had just survived."[80] Mackay Brown highlighted one of these artists, Graham Sutherland,[81] writing, "I am thinking of his early painting"[82] that was of softly rounded landscapes, rather than "the far more raw vision that ensued post-war with their darkened colors and knotted lines stitching together broken forms. Sutherland brings the distortions of surrealism to bear on the deep familiarity of the biblical story."[83] Mackay Brown did not mention Stanley Spencer who was allied to Sutherland, nor did he mention David Jones, a Catholic

---

76 Ibid.
77 Mackay Brown, "Good Morning Scotland" (1 January 1974) BBC transcript, preparatory comment for recording, dated 24 December 1973, OLA.
78 Newman, *Apologia Pro Vita Sua*, 116 and 117-18.
79 Ibid.
80 Campbell-Johnston, "Turmoil and Trauma: Artists in an Age of Anxiety," January 17, 2020, *The Times*.
81 Mackay Brown, *Notebook Three*, NLS.
82 Ibid.
83 Campbell-Johnston, "Turmoil and Trauma: Artists in an Age of Anxiety."

artist and poet in a close alliance with other Catholic artists and intellectuals. The closest we get to this modernist movement was the one quote from the French Catholic philosopher, Jacques Maritain, who had a strong influence on the thinking in certain Catholic intellectual coteries and choruses: "the principle determining the peculiar perfection of everything which is, constituting and completing things in their essence and their qualities; the ontological secret, so to speak of their innermost being."[84] It is important to note that Maritain is never more than a mention in Mackay Brown's *Essays and Notes*. I would say, from the evidence of Mackay Brown's wide reading and cultural awareness, he didn't feel comfortable in any sort of alliance to these types of post-war groups. It is important to be aware of whom he writes notes about and of whom he doesn't. Whilst subjecting himself to the many credible influences of his contemporaries, it was Hopkins that held the center ground. And it is intriguing to me that, as engrossed as he was in Hopkins and the divine sequence of his new lines of the firmament, he cannot suppress the "very intense experiences that became part of the fabric of my life."[85] It was as though he "sees" as only the authentic artist can, and out gushed the swarm of symbols that he wove into the fabric and firmament of the Mackay Brown tapestry.

As Bold wrote in his study of Mackay Brown in 1978, "Modernism has become a library phenomenon with only a tenuous hold on the facts of life."[86] Balanced against the beige and unthreatening "*écriture*" of Derrida[87] and "documentary realism," Mackay Brown is not a good fit. The literary canon can't be honest about his place as he was "a law unto himself"[88] and "activated by a wide artistic vision."[89] The various literary camps and projects, try as they might, cannot hold the wealth and depth of vision of this deeply spiritual man. Despite obvious influences, the singularity of Mackay Brown's work made him difficult to classify. He was a man not forestalled by predecessors, nor to be classed with his contemporaries—and who indeed are his successors?

---

84 Mackay Brown, *Notebook Three*, NLS.
85 Mackay Brown, *For the Islands I Sing*, 79.
86 Bold, *George Mackay Brown*, 1.
87 See Introduction, note 72.
88 Bold, *George Mackay Brown*, 1.
89 Ibid.

But even those who dip in and out of Mackay Brown upon occasions are different for having absorbed him in his texts. As Bold acknowledged: "to deny the awesome power of his work would be sheer folly."[90]

The "unemployable, feckless boy who missed the war because of TB, who drinks, dreams and seems to have fallen by default into putting words together for a living"[91] has a strong "taste of himself." The extracts from the 1946–48 collection of diary-type notes were evidence of that "taste" of a "self" in the labyrinth. A dense and thick greyness of depression somehow could not entirely suppress the inner processes expressed in his writing as a way towards a deeply sensed beauty, the wild beauty of Orkney, his Greenfields Kirk. And there is no doubt education was key to the emergence from the labyrinth that was that distinctive self. Mackay Brown makes the classic Plato-out-of-the-cave journey. His studies at Newbattle Abbey, then Edinburgh University, both as under- and postgraduate, accompanied by the social and literary ferment of the choruses and illness, are transformative. As Mackay Brown wrote to his friend, Orkney artist, Ian MacInnes in 1960: "I'm no longer interested in letting half-baked stuff on to the counter, it'll be clean and crisp to the core, or I'll disown it."[92] The half-baked stuff was important, though, and Mackay Brown never concealed it from view. That "taste" of Mackay Brown, his self-awareness, that sense of the trajectory and formation of a poet, relied heavily in the first instance on his sources and some sort of negotiation with the concept of an audience.

Mackay Brown brought his own "gall" and "heartburn,"[93] "more distinctive than ale or walnut leaf"[94] in his combat to express himself and find an audience, encouraged by Hopkins who he knew was on the record with his "a poet is a public for himself"[95] and "Christ is the only true literary critic that he

---

90 Ibid., 113.
91 MacInnes, "Finding a Voice in the Forties," *New Shetlander*, 30-33, 36.
92 Ibid.
93 Mackay Brown, *Notebook One. Notes on the Dark Sonnets Sonnet 44 "I wake and feel the fell of dark, not day,"* NLS.
94 Mackay Brown, *Notebook Two. Notes on "Tom's Garland: Upon the Unemployed,"* NLS.
95 Hopkins, Letter to RB, January 19, 1879. *The Letters of Gerard Manley Hopkins to Robert Bridges*, 59.

cares about."⁹⁶ As he writes, "GMH found the most thrilling thing in existence (this distinctiveness informing all the objects and forms of nature too, but meaningless unless his own lips drank from the tankard) can be the greatest curse, if emphasized in the wrong way. Then the amazing variety of life is ignored for the single existence."⁹⁷ For Hopkins and Mackay Brown the kerygma, the Paschal Mystery, was inseparably at the heart of their life and literary projects. There was nothing generic about their spirituality. The new lines of the old firmament, according to Hopkins, that resonated so deeply and permanently with Mackay Brown pivoted on the Incarnation and Jesus crucified and risen. Their thought and poetry, their techniques, consistently and seamlessly echo the dangerous unnerving news concerning Jesus Christ risen from the dead. Their mutual insistence of the exacting nature of how Jesus died had a direct hold on their lives and poetry. Both poets show Newman's influence and did as their neighbors and as Mackay Brown specifies, it is the artistic sense not the religious sense, that will be the judge of their work. The relationship between the artistic and the religious sense set up a tension framed in the Salvation story and the struggle between the sacred and the profane. What John Pick writes of Hopkins's discovery of Scotus, "It was not that he found something he had not known,"⁹⁸ can be equally applied to Mackay Brown's discovery of Hopkins, then Scotus. Mackay Brown's Greenfields Kirk had formed in him a certain angle of vision that was distinctively his own; but for all his accumulated taste of myself he resonated with everything Hopkins believed in and lived for.

THE ANGLE OF THE MACKAY BROWN VISION

Half-baked stuff or not, what do we know about the angle of George Mackay Brown's vision? In September 1945 he wrote, "The Fiddler at the Fair (A Parable)":

> There is a great thronging fair that has gone on since the beginning of the world, and will continue, they say, to the end of it. From the hills and valleys at the uttermost

---

96 Hopkins, Letter to R.W. Dixon June 13, 1878. *The Correspondence of Gerard Manley Hopkins and Richard Watson Dixon*, 8–9.
97 Mackay Brown, *Notebook One. Notes on the Dark Sonnets*, NLS.
98 Pick, *Gerard Manley Hopkins: Priest and Poet*, 35 (note the edition Mackay Brown would have read would be the publication in 1942).

ends of the earth men come to visit this fair. They enter it through the gate called Birth and leave it through the gate called Death. Some men call the fair Vanity, some call it Probation; others call it, simply, the fair of Life. But whatever the name, in the end they are usually glad to leave it, and to live eternally in the light and silence of the hills surrounding.[99]

The Mackay Brown formed in the Calvinistic Stromness Kirk, knew the Bible first-hand, as did Edwin Muir before him. He was also deeply familiar with John Bunyan's *Pilgrim's Progress*. The simple imagery of "thronging fair" the "gates" of Birth and Death, the pilgrim "visits" of entrances and exits, probation or testing, the concept of a dream sequence, converged in his imagination. Here in his heart was a vivid childhood memory of "the blind fiddler who visited Stromness every autumn to play to the Lammas Market[100] crowds, and seemed to me so pathetic, ageless, strange, frightening."[101] We already know from Mackay Brown's autobiography that his childhood memories held strange fears and insecurities so much so that he worried "part of my mind was unhinged."[102] We also know about the influence and esteem of John Bunyan in the Brown household. His father "would say to us children, again and again: 'Whatever happens keep humble... Never get above yourselves.' Do I imagine it, that he recited Bunyan to us? 'He that is down need fear no fall, He that is low, no pride. He that is humble ever shall Have God to be his guide.' Whether he quoted us [children] this or not, it was his lifelong philosophy."[103] Mackay

---

99 Mackay Brown, unpublished TS "A Fiddler at the Fair (A Parable)." Sept. 1945. OLA, Ernest Walker Marwick Collection.
100 Lammas or Lughnasa is a harvest holiday which is celebrated on August 1st. The Anglo-Saxon Chronicle of 921 CE mentions Lughnasa as "the feast of first fruits." In Britain it is also called Lammas, from the Anglo-Saxon hlaefmass meaning "loaf-mass." A special Eucharistic thanksgiving for the first bread of the harvest was an extremely popular Christian practice during the Middle Ages. The "first bread" is brought forward with the offering, placed on the altar, blessed, and broken, and given to the people as the body of Christ, though the first bread blessing largely died out as a Christian ritual after the Reformation. After the Reformation it continued until the mid-twentieth century in Stromness in its mixture of the sacred and the profane. In essence, Stromness Shopping Week continues the "thronging" and "gaiety" to this day.
101 "The Fiddler at the Fair (A Parable)" Sept. 1945, OLA EWM Collection.
102 Mackay Brown, *For the Islands I Sing*, 46.
103 Ibid., 32-33.

Brown also wrote about Orkney house interiors: "In our parlor there was...John Bunyan dreaming of some episodes from the *Pilgrim's Progress.*"[104] Undoubtedly. John Bunyan was a companion for Mackay Brown from his earliest days.

The blind fiddler plays in the shadow of the temple for three travelers, each of whom have an attitude of life that evaluates their fitness for the afterlife. Music introduces another dimension with transformative results: prayer and light spring up. The fiddler addresses the weary travelers: "You have heard this music which God wrings from my soul in sharp sweet drops of agony. I ask no money in return. Instead you shall tell me of this mystery of light that is hidden from me. For sunrise and sunset glow and fade on the eyes of men: but I move eternally in darkness: the silent sources of light are hidden from me."[105] Called to respond, the first traveler makes the case for the simple rhythms of the natural world "in the slow lilting voice of his native islands."[106] He describes the movement of the sunlight in terms of its range of activity as it pivots through the day on his croft, across the hills and trout-loch, keenly sensitive to the pattern of sunlight from season to season and lives his life and feeds his family absorbing its life-giving power. This "simple good man"[107] is rewarded when his time for death comes for his plain-speaking with a burial and contentment in the ground, knowing he had provided for the family he left behind. On the other hand, the second traveler takes a strictly scientific view of things according to the laws of the universe and galaxies. When his death comes he has dug a six-foot hole and is devoured by worms. The fiddler is still none the wiser as he has expectations of a place called heaven. He ask the damned traveler about heaven who smiles "cynically."

It is the third traveler who can enlighten and convey a strong sense of the Light that he perceives Heaven to be: "Heaven? It is all around us, if only we would look with our real eyes instead of our vegetative eyes. You speak of the sun: what is it?" He can put aside the material phenomena and move on another dimension: "I see an innumerable company of Heavenly host crying,

---

104 Mackay Brown, "House Interiors 14/2/91" in *Rockpools and Daffodils*, 251.
105 Mackay Brown: Unpublished TS "A Fiddler at the Fair (A Parable)." Sept. 1945. OLA, EWM Collection.   106 Ibid.   107 Ibid.

'Holy, Holy, Holy is the Lord God Almighty.' His eyes shone with the ardor of his speaking."[108] "A man like this comes to the fair only once in many generations. He wears heaven about him like a cloak. Even in the cries of the ragged children, he heard the transcendent songs of the blest spirits, and he saw angels walking in the branches of mighty trees. Death to him was near and familiar, like passing from one room into another; and when he died, he had only to shed gracefully the heavy trappings of flesh and spring into the vault of heaven, a new-created angel clapping his hands for joy."[109] As the three men go on their way and are lost in the crowd at the fair the blind fiddler replete with what the third traveler told him of Heaven, falls asleep on the temple steps. When he woke it was the "morning" of his new life, "The warm sun was shining on his face. He put his fiddle to his shoulder and drew the bow across the strings. And as he played, it seemed to him that he translated the warmth on his face into the brightness which he could not see. And it seemed as he continued that he saw an innumerable company of the heavenly host crying, 'Holy, Holy, Holy is the Lord God Almighty.'"[110]

Mackay Brown seamlessly positions his angle of vision with an infusion of Blake when he writes: "See William Blake: 'A Vision of the Last Judgement.'"[111] Here we know for sure the elements of the Mackay Brown vision in his close reading and visualization given to what Blake had written and painted of the Last Judgment. As reviled as Blake was in the eighteenth century, there was a coterie of post-war artists[112] who were deeply inspired by Blake's artistic vision: Mackay Brown makes special note of Graeme Sutherland and his early work. Mackay Brown's Edinburgh postgraduate notes evidence the infusions: "I am thinking of the sculpture of Henry Moore, some of the music of Stravinsky, the early painting of Graham Sutherland, the prose of Joyce (parts of Ulysses for example)."[113] The categories of ideas that Mackay Brown adhered to were brought to Edinburgh in the 1960s and certain features of Blake's poetic

---

108 Ibid.   109 Ibid.   110 Ibid.
111 Blake, "The Last Judgement." *Life of William Blake (1880) Vol 2. Prose Writings.*
112 Campbell-Johnston, "Turmoil and Trauma: Artists in an age of anxiety," January 17, 2020, *The Times.*
113 Mackay Brown. George. *Notebook Three, NLS.*

thought, and literary language are well understood and continued. In fact, they were continued in his permanent structure of ideas to his death in 1996.

The early "finding a voice" period of the 1940s in Orkney underwent phases of refinement and development. Mackay Brown brought the post-Reformation firmament of Milton, Bunyan, and Blake to Hopkins's restoratively experimental innovations. And I would argue, even though the "literary revolution initiated by the 'men of 1914'—Joyce, Pound, Eliot, Wyndham Lewis—"[114] went with Mackay Brown and made their modernist or surrealistic marks on him, it was Hopkins's trajectory of the new firmament that enabled him to immerse his readers in his work. Critics such as Alan Bold are utterly convinced by the shape, images, and symbols, but less so by the ideas they carry with them. The literary critics of the 1970s could still recognize the depth of the Mackay Brown poetic vision as well as the enticement of its numinous surface.[115] Mackay Brown's angle of vision was particular and universal, all at once. It was bi-directional and katalogical as he moved with increasing deftness in the univocity of language.

Certain key features from Blake's text[116] are clearly infused into the angle of vision Mackay Brown pursued, for example, Blake defines, "The Last Judgement is not fable, or allegory, but vision" and then goes further: "Vision, or imagination, is a representation of what actually exists, really and interchangeably." Blake was "particular" about the relationship between "Fable or allegory" and its formation from "the Daughters of Memory." Biblically "The Hebrew Bible and the Gospel of Jesus are not allegory, but eternal vision" and "Pilgrim's Progress is full of it; the Greek poets the same." Mackay Brown's intense early experiences are just that—from the Orkney fable to the Orkney vision, always trying to go deep to get at the essence or soul of the experience within its echoes and memories. "The real vision of Time is an eternal youth"[117] or the blind fiddler, wherein "The world of the imagination is the world of eternity."[118]

---

114 Bold, *George Mackay Brown*. Oliver & Boyd: Edinburgh, 1978, 1.
115 Ibid., 113.
116 Blake, William. "The Last Judgement." *Life of William Blake (1880) Vol 2: Prose Writings*.   117 Ibid.   118 Ibid.

Mackay Brown had discovered a higher reality and that, "There exist in that eternal world the permanent realities of everything which we see reflected in this vegetable glass of nature."[119] In keeping with the christianization of the North Atlantic Mackay Brown committed early to "All things are comprehended in these eternal forms in the divine body of the Savior, the true vine of eternity."[120] The sense of the journey, the voyage, the pilgrimage, where "Man passes on, but states remain forever: he passed through them like a traveler, who may as well suppose these places he has passed through exist no more... everything is eternal."[121] His concept of Church goes beyond the Puritanism of Bunyan and the disillusion of Blake to a visualization, "I have seen, when at a distance, multitudes of men in harmony appear like a single infant, sometimes in the arms of a female. This represented the Church."[122] Unmistakably, Mackay Brown aligned with Blake's fixation on "Eternal vision," as his own experience was not allegorical or metaphorical but real.

His understanding of the sensational vision drew deeply within "Poetry, Painting, and Music, the three powers in man conversing with Paradise"[123] and in accord with Blake and Hopkins, "General knowledge is remote knowledge, it is in particulars that wisdom consist, and happiness too."[124] The Enlightenment that separated the arts from "Learning and Science" is interpreted as the act "that accompanies Adam out of Eden." To give glory to God was a liturgical act whether it be in the Greenfields Kirk or the biblical Temple, or the Eucharist, "Holy, holy, holy is the Lord God Almighty!"[125] The seamless gaze of faith embraced the profusion of the sacred and the profane, "I question not my corporeal eye, any more than I would question a window concerning a sight."[126] This window of vision was cognizant of the distinction between the method and the content, "I look through it, and not with it." Looking through the "window" Mackay Brown "sees" "The temple stands on the mount of God. From it flows on each side a river of life, on whose

---

119 Ibid.   120 Ibid.   121 Ibid.   122 Ibid.
123 Ibid.   124 Ibid.
125 Mackay Brown, Unpublished TS "A Fiddler at the Fair (A Parable)." Sept. 1945. OLA, EWM Collection.
126 Blake, "The Last Judgement." *Life of William Blake (1880) Vol 2. Prose Writings*.

banks grows the Tree of Life."[127] Through the eye of Blake, he too could stand within the canon of poets who "have put the Lord's Supper on the left hand of the throne, for it appears so at the Last Judgment for a protection."[128]

And so it was that Mackay Brown delivered not only on Blake but also on the Old Testament prophet Ezekiel and the reconsecration of the Temple,[129] wherein the configuration of the "thousand cubits" the "river wherever it flows, all living creatures teeming in it will live." This manifestation of blessings was a reaffirmation of the sanctity of life and deeply interconnected to the Book of Revelation that Mackay Brown was quite dogmatic about both in letters and conversation: "No Harm in studying the scriptures, so long as one knows what one is about. It is such a richly symbolic body of work, some people read into it (especially the Book of Revelation) all kinds of meaning."[130] Mackay Brown attributed the "all kinds of meaning" as a cause of the Reformation, "people were making private inferences" and I cannot overemphasize Mackay Brown's strict views on this historical point of contention. It mattered in his mind, and he strongly opposed the Reformation principle of private judgements. He asserted that the Church was "there to prevent such strayings." The Church says, "this is what scripture means" and is never tired of saying, "this and nothing else, unless the Holy Spirit unfolds some new meaning...it shouldn't be forgotten that the scripture we have is only a translation of translations—and meaning alters subtly with each translation."[131] He wrote this

---

[127] Mackay Brown, Unpublished TS "A Fiddler at the Fair (A Parable)." Sept. 1945. OLA, EWM Collection.
[128] Blake, "The Last Judgement." *Life of William Blake (1880) Vol 2: Prose Writings*. Although Blake was considered mad by contemporaries for his idiosyncratic views, he is held in high regard by later critics for his expressiveness and creativity, and for the philosophical and mystical undercurrents within his work. His paintings and poetry have been characterized as part of the Romantic movement and as "Pre-Romantic." A committed Christian who was hostile to the Church of England (indeed, to almost all forms of organized religion), Blake was influenced by the ideals and ambitions of the French and American Revolutions. Though later he rejected many of these political beliefs, he maintained an amiable relationship with the political activist Thomas Paine; he was also influenced by thinkers such as Emanuel Swedenborg. Despite these influences, the singularity of Blake's work makes him difficult to classify. [129] Book of Ezekiel 47:1-12.
[130] Mackay Brown, Letter to the author 15 November 1991. Included in Appendix in Gray, *George Mackay Brown: No Separation*, 203.
[131] Ibid.

in 1991. Yet in 1947 he was writing in a text that seems to be a "Defense" of the Catholic Church: "The Catholic on the other hand holds that the Bible is a dangerous book in the hands of ignorant men, because thought is indeed divinely inspired, it is full of subtleties and contradictions which no untrained human can hope to unravel and understand."[132] At the end of this text he concludes: "So the Catholic Church sees itself and knows itself as a living organism to which the divine truth is being gradually revealed through the Apostles" and then strikingly he conflates the dogmatic rhetoric with "as each of us can bear a new infusion moving through time we become ever more likely clothed in garments of spirit of Evil and Good, until in the end nothing of the divine is seen in us. But in Eternity we lay aside as outworn coverings, Evil and Good, and as naked souls breathe the pure Essence of Innocence."[133]

This is good evidence for his pre-Vatican II Catholic formation taking place alongside those very intense early experiences that were the fabric of his life, moving forward towards his reception into the Catholic Church in 1961 and remaining intact and undisturbed throughout the rest of his life. That is my impression. He had a strict doctrinal stance on matters Catholic that mellowed around the edges as time went on, but my personal experience is he would suddenly come out with a very spirited doctrinal view and an unflagging alignment with the Apostolic faith and papal authority. But he never left his allegiance to his formative experience of Bunyan and Blake and his "anti-hero" Calvin, as his Greenfields Kirk was assimilated into a post-Reformation eucharistic firmament through his own perceptions and thoughts finely tuned through Hopkins. The *Book of Revelation* documents: "the angel showed me the river of life, rising from the throne of God and the Lamb and flowing crystal clear... blessed are those who will have washed their robes clean, so that they will have the right to feed on the tree of life and can come through the gates into the city."[134] Mackay Brown carried his "new infusion moving through time,"[135] through "The Fiddler at the Fair

---

[132] Mackay Brown, *Unpublished MS The Roman Catholic Church. March 1947, NLS.* [133] Ibid. [134] Revelation 22:1-2, 14-15.
[135] Mackay Brown, *Unpublished MS The Roman Catholic Church, March 1947, NLS.*

(A Parable)"[136] in 1945, and by 1947 where he was able to align his writing within an increasingly ordered set of patterns and perceptions (or Catholic categories) where he could see how "we become ever more likely clothed in garments of spirit of Evil and Good, until in the end nothing of the divine is seen in us." Here are the marks of that very particular seamless garment he wove throughout his writing. It was his literary way of carrying that infusion. It is such a mix of the tangible and the intangible elements of life that he experienced in Orkney. Its moral intensity burned hot and cold for him, but he never stopped sensing that place "of pure Essence of Innocence" where the "outworn coverings" of "Evil and Good" would be laid aside to release the naked soul to breathe once again.[137]

Mackay Brown was held in high regard by his critics for his expressiveness and creativity in and out of Orkney, but below the surface many were (and still are) wary of what they interpreted as his idiosyncratic views out of keeping with a Protestant and secular Orkney and Scotland. This Chapter has traced the historical, literary, philosophical, and theological strands that evidence Mackay Brown's understanding of Hopkins's intelligent design. Certain philosophical and mystical undercurrents within his work push him towards being characterized as a Romantic but his poetic vision carried within it an intense Christianity from the outset as he scoped out for himself a place for his voice to be heard. Like Bunyan—then Blake and Hopkins—he came to understand the poet as an interpreter of a "crisis" that put him outside the many influences and constraints that marked his times. As a result, like Blake and then Hopkins, the singularity of his work makes him difficult to classify, especially so when he commits to Catholicism with its understanding of the co-inherence of the particular and the universal. The fabric, the firmament, the voice, the vision, was at an increasingly Catholic angle, especially so as Mackay Brown discovered the Eucharist as the ultimate set form in the leitourgia of the Greenfields Kirk that is Creation. Chapter Two continues with this ever-increasing Catholic angle of vision that was immersed in the Eucharist from which all Mackay Brown's genres radiate.

---

136 Mackay Brown, Unpublished TS "A Fiddler At the Fair (A Parable)." Sept. 1945. OLA, Ernest Walker Marwick Collection.
137 Mackay Brown, *Unpublished MS The Roman Catholic Church, March 1947,* NLS.

CHAPTER TWO

A Thousand Candles of Gorse

> "*The Mass is the most important action that anyone can participate in, the pure source of all goodness, truth, and beauty. Hopkins's total output [is] a kind of imitation of the Mass, a secondary spring where made of poetry, Catholic and non-Catholic might refresh themselves.*"[1]

THE MACKAY BROWN ANGLE OF VISION IN the 1945 "The Fiddler at the Fair (A Parable)"[2] is immersed in the Bible and the post-Reformation reconstruction of the firmament through Bunyan, Spenser, and Milton as it moved sequentially down to the eighteenth century of William Blake. Mackay Brown was very aware of the literary succession within the English language and beyond, and located himself within it with knowledge, conviction, and originality, as we have seen. Although his *Essays and Notes* are more a literary litany than systematic scholarship, he saw as the poet and lived as the poet, avowedly within the classical and biblical tradition that marked Western civilization. From this angle, Mackay Brown saw the literary canon as a secondary spring flowing from its source, feeding on the biblical Tree of Life and infused with healing and grace. As one ploughs through the "gorse" stripped of "outworn coverings" until all presence of the "divine" seems lost, it is then in our nakedness that according to Mackay Brown we can "breathe the pure Essence of Innocence"[3] and the "gorse" is illuminated into "a thousand candles."[4] The Greenfields Kirk was assimilated into the Temple wherein Mackay Brown found himself in the liturgy of April through the martyrdom of St. Magnus and the Passion of Christ. As such, his writing vies for its place in the literary canon alongside Hopkins to be judged

---

1 Mackay Brown, "*Gerard Manley Hopkins and the Mass,*" Notebook Three, NLS.
2 Mackay Brown, Unpublished TS "A Fiddler at the Fair (A Parable)." Sept. 1945. OLA, EWM Collection, D31/30/2.
3 Mackay Brown, *Unpublished MS The Roman Catholic Church. March 1947/NLS.*
4 Mackay Brown, "The Storm," in *The Collected Poems of George Mackay Brown*, 3.

not by the religious but by the artistic sense. This chapter examines the Eucharist as Mackay Brown's set form, within which he developed micro-set forms or genres to express the liturgical song for his people and their native tradition.

LITERARY LITANIES

Mackay Brown came to his principles early and they stayed with him all his life. As his mind was flooded with what he came to identify as a swarm of symbols, he gradually asserted a mastery over them as he seriously assumed the disciplined work of a writer. From the outset he used the "litany" as a way he could serialize and encapsulate an ever-flowing array of poetic materials. The litany as a set form is brief and formulaic covering a wide range of materials including the notion of time. Mackay Brown sharpened his use of the litany to generate dialogue using this biblical technique which functioned as a series of prayerful petitions rooted in the canticles and psalms. Writing as a journalist in 1989, he puts the tradition he chose to work within before his Orkney "public": first the Bible (Book of Ecclesiastes) and its confrontation of mortality and time "in the same way that great poets have always done."[5] His litany gathers in Shakespeare, Sophocles, Euripides, and Dante and the modern age with Yeats, Eliot, MacDiarmid, and Muir. But the "law of aesthetics" works with "many collaborative hands." Just as the Border Ballads were not written down by "one poet working alone; it might be said that a whole community shaped them orally in the course of generations."[6] Poets do not work in isolation: "it seems unlikely that Homer was one blind man with a harp. And what of the ancient literatures of Ireland and Scandinavia?"[7] The literary litany of great poets testifies to the "seamless garment"[8] that "confronts fearlessly whatever darkness, time and chance have in store for Everyman; and yet is able to break out in the same irresistible joy that Milton and Beethoven knew."[9] The poet, according to Mackay Brown, must do as in Ecclesiastes: "Let thy garments be always white. And let thy head lack no ointment."[10] Mackay

---

5 Mackay Brown, "Ecclesiastes 13/7/89," in *Rockpools and Daffodils*, 214.
6 Ibid.   7 Ibid.   8 John 19:23.
9 Mackay Brown, "Ecclesiastes 13/7/89," in *Rockpools and Daffodils*, 214.
10 Ibid.

Brown was clearly conscious of the biblical seamless garment at work as his leitourgia. The seamless undergarment that the soldiers who crucified Jesus gambled over, woven as one piece of cloth from neck to hem, was seen by the early Church and to this day as the blood-soaked passion garment or liturgical vestment of Christ the High Priest and His everlasting Kingdom. The symbolism of the garment is a powerful motif in Mackay Brown's thinking and surfaced repeatedly, especially so in his novel, *Magnus*.

The concept of the "audience," as it was for Hopkins, was always problematic for Mackay Brown. As poets they followed Newman's maxim, "Do as your neighbours"[11] and withstood the pressures of publishing. Hopkins knew his work was not "ready" to be received by the Victorians. He chose to work in the freedom of his own mind and heart with only a few close associates as readers. Mackay Brown adapted his writing accordingly for the Orkney audience through his journalism. He made complex materials and sources accessible in the company of other Orcadian literary figures and spun the threads and wove the textures keeping his pure individual poetic intensities at bay. It was the seamless garment that was a collaborative work, and his conversion to Catholicism made many unsure and uncertain of his message.

During his life, various Orcadian establishment interpretations found Mackay Brown problematic and some still do. Surely that is a healthy sign. He challenged their received notions about history, poetry, and spirituality because, as did Hopkins, he held a firm allegiance to origins and ends. To observe a certain "inhibition when it comes to capturing a different version of Orkney... After George... it is time for Orkney writers to step outside of the master's shadow and create their own versions."[12] The "post-modern *écriture*,"[13] which had a grasp of origins but not of ends and sees "existence, like our works, as an unfinished sentence,"[14] is for those who can live with an incompleteness in thought and belief. Mackay Brown and Hopkins were not intimidated by literary succession. The imaginative space of

---

11 Newman, "English Catholic Literature," in *The Idea of a University*, 188.
12 Ferguson, *George Mackay Brown: The Wound and the Gift*, 374.
13 Derrida, *Of Grammatology*. See Introduction, note 72.
14 Muir, "The Decline of the Novel," in *Essays on Literature and Society*, 144.

their predecessors did not intimidate or inhibit their creative processes.[15] The elevation of the ego and its *écriture* of "spotlights" revels in their "glittering surface."[16] This was the legacy of the private judgments that reformulated the pre-Reformation firmament and spawned the almost complete secularization of the borderless globalized literature that we see today.

The Reformation created new traditions and new firmaments. The tightly bound cluster of eucharistic symbols, treasured by Hopkins and Mackay Brown, disintegrated throughout the sixteenth and seventeenth centuries. Hopkins reinstated the pre-Reformation cluster of symbols in his verse, and Mackay Brown captured Hopkins's passion when he wrote, "The fervid time pattern of the Mass: for of course the Trinity is always there. It is the story of Man's Life on earth, the pure quintessence of all history both past and to come; the symbols are the key."[17] The impassioned use of symbols in the Eucharist burn and blaze as the priest transubstantiates them into "the Bread of Life."[18] In Mackay Brown's mind, Christ was festooned with thorns (gorse) that burst into candle flames. "It [the Mass] was the most important action that any man could participate in. It was the quintessence of all history, in particular it commemorated the life death and resurrection both recorded and to come. It was a channel for the release of man's finest energies—praise, gratitude, prayer."[19]

In terms of the literary succession, the language of poetry had negotiated various positions that rearranged and reinvented the firmament according to politicized theological developments and an evolving spirituality. The centerpiece within the power of symbols passed from the Eucharist to the Crown by the ascendancy of a metaphor that does not command a statement of belief. Truth and belief became private matters rather than the aesthetic experience that oscillates backwards and forwards through many layers of meaning and suggestion. The analogical philosophical temperament of the medieval period was understood in the community with its precision of belief and resonating symbols.

---

15 Bloom, *The Anxiety of Influence: A Theory of Poetry*, 5.
16 Bold, *George Mackay Brown*, 1.
17 Mackay Brown. *"Gerard Manley Hopkins and the Mass," Notebook Three. NLS.*
18 Ibid.   19 Ibid.

A sacramental Christianity was then able to penetrate the entire world of knowledge and the historical order. The realignment of the medieval world at the Reformation—and its subsequent cycles of suppression—became a linguistic mission for Hopkins, and then Mackay Brown, to repossess the "roots" of language at the point where it fully engaged with belief and enabled them to re-form and re-craft their world of poetry. They both moved from an analogical use of language to univocity. Instead of using words to compare God's properties to the world of phenomena, Hopkins, and then Mackay Brown, use words to describe the properties of God to mean the same thing unleashing a huge poetic energy and freedom that was empirically based, metrically irregular and spiritually illuminating.

The marked Protestant character of literature,[20] as observed by Newman, hastened Hopkins through the Oxford Movement to properly realize the integrity of what he interpreted as the "inscaped" thing.[21] This was Hopkins's lifework and legacy. Mackay Brown understood his own lifework as part of that succession. They founded their dancing metrics on the clear sweet spirit, the call of the curlew, where origins and ends control the narrative of the creation story with univocity rather than analogy. Both Schmid[22] and Bicket[23] interpret Mackay Brown's writing as committing to "the sacramental principle"[24] as an "affirmation of mystery in all reality"[25] and "permeated by a sacramental understanding of the universe."[26] Schmid and Bicket position Mackay Brown within a "tradition of sacramentalist poetics"[27] through the creativity of the powers of perception and the imagination. Their interpretation of Newman's *Grammar of Assent* falls short, especially so as they draw upon the more pluralist theological stance of McBrien,[28] Tracey,[29] and Greely[30] rather

---

20 Newman, "English Catholic Literature," in *The Idea of a University*, 188.
21 Ross, *Poetry and Dogma: The Transfiguration of Eucharistic Symbols in Seventeenth Century Poetry*, 242.
22 Schmid, *Keeping the Sources Pure: The Making of George Mackay Brown*, 154-55.
23 Bicket, *George Mackay Brown and the Scottish Catholic Imagination*.
24 Schmid, *Keeping the Sources Pure: The Making of George Mackay Brown*, 154-55.
25 Ibid.
26 Bicket, *George Mackay Brown and the Scottish Catholic Imagination*, 39.
27 Schmid, *Keeping the Sources Pure: The Making of George Mackay Brown*, 154-55.
28 McBrien, *Catholicism*. Cited by Schmid (154), Bicket (167).
29 Tracey, *The Analogical Imagination*. Cited by Bicket, 37.
30 Greely, *The Catholic Imagination*. Cited by Bicket, 37.

than the deeper Catholic intellectual and theological scholarship of Balthasar whose articulation of a theological aesthetics included the pre-theological understanding of the poets.

Schmid emphasizes that Hopkins saw "the role of the sacrament as a sign, rather than on the causality of the sacraments" and that "this suggests his interest in the renewal of a sacramental approach to both religion and poetry and is essentially a rediscovery and a celebration of the Thomistic perspective."[31] There is the idea in both Schmid and Bicket that a Thomistic analogical poetic language is evidenced in Hopkins and, by implication, Mackay Brown. This book takes the view that Hopkins and then Mackay Brown are pushing theological and poetical boundaries because of their absorption in the natural world and the human person as an expression of the Trinitarian doctrine that held God is a communion of persons (one nature three persons), where difference is experienced in perfect unity. Newman's articulation of his *Grammar of Assent* marks out his careful separation of the illative sense with its ability to reach a synthesis of polyvalent materials by multiple pathways in human consciousness and cognition. Newman did not assign the imagination a part in this process other than as an ability to serialize a range of images analogically at the point of perception.

By the time Hopkins discovered confirmation of his investigations in Scotus, he was able to express the power and rationale of difference in poetic language that went ahead to reintegrate difference within the unity of the Trinity. Balthasar drew upon the work of Newman[32] and Hopkins[33] to the point of elevating their specific contributions to Catholic thought as key contributions to his development of twentieth-century theology. Mackay Brown's own distinctive poetic work finds a place here in this stream of Christian thinking about truth and is part of the Western tradition. He too proves his grasp of the univocity of language in his Edinburgh *Essays and Notes* from the 1960s. Balthasar's katalogical, bi-directional theological project holds within itself poetical materials that can express difference-in-unity

---

31 Schmid, *Keeping the Sources Pure: The Making of George Mackay Brown*, 174, note 143.
32 Balthasar, *Theo-Logic I: Truth of the World*, 29.
33 Balthasar, *The Glory of the Lord: A Theological Aesthetics III: Studies in Theological Style: Lay Styles*, 353–99.

and unity-in-difference linguistically. An analogical perspective is one-directional where the emphasis is given to the human person's consciousness of God by comparing God in the first instance to something lesser and finite and then extrapolating towards his infinite being and presence in an upward (one-directional) movement. The convention of the literary method exemplified by Schmid and Bicket is the analogical approach that moves in this one-directional way with the idea that sacramental Christianity is that penetration of the entire world of knowledge and the historical order with the orderly succession of steps expressed through the sacramental principle and its seven sacraments. Hopkins, and then Mackay Brown, shift the perspective from analogy to univocity because their experience of the world and the human person needed a means that could express this experience, not metaphorically but really. The world and the human person radiate the actuality of Christ. Christ is sacrament and they see him everywhere descending and ascending bi-directionally. Their language becomes the paradox of being fuller, yet more condensed, more forceful, and yet more serene, all at once, as univocity allows their experience of Christ to open new frontiers of linguistic technicalities.

Hopkins re-drew the outlines of the older firmament, and Mackay Brown followed with his eucharistic litanies, already well on his way because of that "taste of myself" as a poet and in his perceptions of the inscaped phenomena of Orkney all around him. It is important to note that this "return to the sources" is in keeping with *la nouvelle theologie* (the new theology) that precipitated Vatican II, of which Balthasar was an integral part. The Oxford Movement opened the floodgates for Newman, Hopkins, and Mackay Brown, who enthusiastically embraced scripture and the multifaceted works of the Church Fathers. They could do no other. Catholic categories find time and place in the literary canon and, as Seamus Heaney[34] makes plain, the conscience *is that solitary place of realization that centers the bi-directional call of the curlew in the sensed-minds of Hopkins and Mackay Brown because they were alert to the* moral impetus that motivated their finely tuned and stabilized poetic vision and their seamless craft.

---

34 See Introduction, note 1.

REFORMATION LEGACY

The Reformation legacy was the spur for Hopkins and then Mackay Brown that made them push against literary conventions. For all their rejection of what they interpreted as the Reformation's linguistic suppression, their life and work found their purpose. They could do no other than linguistically move into their contemporary world and revitalize the medieval poetic and pre-theologic inclusivity that thrived prior to the Reformation. Layer by layer, they countered what they understood to be a great linguistic absence with the restorative unity of their poetic vision. The Protestant character of literature had reconfigured the firmament and institutionalized its legacy of what constituted a poet of stature; but both Hopkins and Mackay Brown pushed the contemporary literary boundaries to encompass the historicity of their respective centuries with language that was able to give difference its rightful expression as they caught hold of a unity powered by faith and reason keeping pace with development in society. They both infused into what had become a Protestant and then secular literary arena of supply and demand a reinvigorated richness that was as technically crafted as it was expressive of beauty. The openness of their approach took them over and beyond the Reformation legacy to express themselves in an organic univocity. An analogical view of the world seeded organic discrete growth from taking the simple experience and knowledge of the human person and pushing their understanding to things more complex through comparison. The learning curve was not only a powerful learning tool but a one-directional process from the particular to the universal by means of the trajectory of difference.

Bicket holds the view that there is such a thing as a "Catholic imagination" based on this one-directional approach, a sort of bottom-up cognition from what is known to what is unknown and that Catholic writers fall into this category. She understands Mackay Brown as "a particularly useful exemplar"[35] of this literary interpretation. Alternatively, the evidence suggests that this was exactly what limited such writers and poets throughout the Reformation period, and it was Hopkins who led the way for a bi-directional use of language by his mastery of univocity.

---

35 Bicket, *George Mackay Brown and the Scottish Catholic Imagination*, 11.

His passion, his piety, his priesthood, and his poetry were so radical as they converged in his linguistic expression that seeded such growth and development throughout the literary world. The disruptive seminality that Hopkins seeded was absorbed into the Balthasarian theological project that assigned Hopkins a chapter[36] in his multi-volume *Glory of the Lord*. A sacramental world view, an analogic world view that held within itself the power of symbols, was developed within a katalogical bi-directional Trinitarian articulation that brought such freedom and vibrancy to the language of Hopkins and then Mackay Brown.

The Mackay Brown *Essays and Notes* stands as an important testament to how he saw and positioned himself within the post-Reformation legacy. This was the reality Hopkins and Mackay Brown both contended with, and it was central to the development of their poetic craft. These manuscripts show Hopkins and Mackay Brown in agreement that their work was to be judged by the artistic sense rather than the religious sense because they understood the nature of the literary canon as the rightful place for the arts where religion does not cast a shadow over the ranking of poets. As Ross observes, "Milton is the last great Christian poet until Gerard Manley Hopkins. Between these two poets of stature are poets of stature who are Christian, but there are no Christian poets of stature.... It is not merely that Milton comes at the end of the great Christian tradition. In a real sense he ends that tradition."[37] To come to terms with the stature of Hopkins and Mackay Brown there is a need to consider that they saw themselves as re-starting that tradition within the remarkable inclusivity of the literary canon as it stood in their times and goes forward today.

The Reformation legacy brought about a purely literary appreciation of the Bible for some commentators, who saw it as the historical product of a visionary tradition that "records a continuous reshaping of the earlier and more primitive traditions, and as it goes on it becomes more explicitly prophetic, until the confused legends of an obscure people take the form of the

---

36 Balthasar, *The Glory of the Lord III: Studies in Theological Style: Lay Styles*, 353–99. Also see Gray, *George Mackay Brown: No Separation*. Chapter One, "Pre-theologics."

37 Ross, *Poetry and Dogma: The Transfiguration of Eucharistic Symbols in Seventeenth Century Poetry*, 183.

full cycle of fall, redemption and apocalypse."[38] The Bible was received by Blake, Hopkins and Mackay Brown as a code book or library of books. Blake took account of the visionary clarity of Hellenic literature and influence, but he rejected the abstract reflective thinking of Plato and Aristotle (as did the reformers at the Reformation in their quest to purify Christianity of Hellenic influence). Blake was the real heretic because ultimately his "firmament" could not quite relinquish the pre-Reformation literary roots that he admired in Chaucer and Langland. Blake was never an establishment artist or figure of any kind. The same can be said of Hopkins and Mackay Brown. Blake's vision was problematic for his contemporaries, but not for Mackay Brown. But Mackay Brown came to understand Hopkins's irritations with Blake. As Frye observes of Blake, "Every great vision is subject to the errors of its age and the Selfhood passions of its creator, but as culture matures and the Selfhood vision of life consolidates, the imaginative vision also may, if the refining smith is at work within it, become increasingly more accurate and complete."[39]

As Hopkins writes from Dublin to Canon Dixon, "You know what happened to crazy Blake, himself a most poetically electrical subject, both active and passive, at his first hearing: when the reader came to 'the pansy at my feet' he fell into a hysterical excitement. Now common sense forbid we should take on like these hysterical creatures: still it is proof of the power of the shock."[40] "Hopkins continues: "I have Blake's poems by me. Some of them remind me of yours. The best are of an exquisite freshness and lyrical inspiration, but there is mingled with the good work a great deal of rubbish, want of sense, and some touches of ribaldry and wickedness."[41] Furthermore, Abbott notes the influence of Blake on Hopkins as an artist: "the only imaginative drawing of his [Blake] that I have seen is the remarkable Blake-like heading to the manuscript of his early poem, 'A Vision of a Mermaid.'"[42]

The classicist Hopkins was immersed in Hellenic literature. The Jesuit Hopkins was keenly sharpened by Greek philosophical

---

[38] Frye, *Fearful Symmetry: A Study of William Blake*, 317.
[39] Ibid., 323.
[40] Hopkins's letter to Canon Dixon, Oct 23, 1886, in *The Correspondence of Gerard Manley Hopkins and Richard Watson Dixon*, 149.
[41] Ibid., 153.   [42] Ibid., 167.

tradition and its permeation of Catholic categories, as he confessed to Robert Bridges in 1879: "as we Aristotelian Catholics say, that the soul is the form of the body, yet the soul may have no other beauty, so to speak, than that which it expresses in the symmetry of the body."[43] It can safely be said that the post-graduate student Mackay Brown knew of Hopkins's irritations and delights. The Mackay Brown allegiance to Hopkins is shown here, "With idle[44] delight I turned the few pages of Hopkins *Collected Poems*, and also the astonished and not altogether approving notes of Robert Bridges at the end. I read his letters to Bridges, Coventry Patmore, and Canon Dixon."[45]

The 1945 Mackay Brown vision held the many seeds of the Reformation firmament. He was well read in classical literature, but his poetry did not rehash tradition; it was distinctly his own. Like Bunyan, Spenser, Milton, Blake, and Hopkins, his literary distinctiveness was notably divergent from those of his contemporaries and predecessors. The language of his poetry purposefully threw up a profusion of echoes from a pre-Reformation ethos in a blended Orkney poetics that wrapped itself around the literature of his contemporaries and flickered with a penetration into an unknown future. It was important to Hopkins and Mackay Brown that they would able to innovate within the literary canon alongside Spenser, but not be at war with Protestantism and its various phases since the Reformation. The Protestant view exemplified by Bunyan, Spenser, and Milton saw a Catholic Church full of corruption, and a determination that it was not only the wrong religion but the anti-religion. Hopkins and Mackay Brown found an ever-expanding workspace to work through this sentiment that had such an important influence on works such as *Pilgrim's Progress, The Faerie Queene*, or *Paradise Lost*.

The literary litany is scored with an orderly succession that Newman had seen to be the creators of a "Protestant literature." This observation was not a criticism. It was the reality, but Newman showed there was more to an English literature than the

---

43 Hopkins to Bridges 22 Oct 1879 in *The Letters of Gerard Manley Hopkins to Robert Bridges*, 95.
44 Using the word "idle" is characteristic understatement as that is one word I would never use about Mackay Brown. He was very disciplined and worked with great determination throughout his life.
45 Mackay Brown, *For the Islands I Sing*, 156.

parameters marked out by the much-admired Spenser. John Milton, William Blake, William Wordsworth, John Keats, Lord Byron, Alfred Tennyson and the many others who followed were well understood and studied by Hopkins and Mackay Brown. They both were distinctly aware of the literary esteem for John Milton and to a degree held it themselves. They also were aware their times were formed by a different crisis for which they became interpreters. Milton's confession in *Areopagitica*, "our sage and serious poet Spenser, whom I dare be known to think a better teacher than Scotus or Aquinas,"[46] was not a sentiment they would have shared. Hopkins and Mackay Brown[47] were in the flow of the seminal influence of the great poets and saw their faults without loving them any the less. Equally Hopkins and Mackay Brown were in a workspace that would find Spenser's sentiments towards the laws, customs, and religion of the Irish people as unacceptable and intolerant and not consistent with their quest to explore the very roots of language as a well-spring of inspiration. Although deeply affected by Irish faerie mythology, Spenser wished devoutly that the Irish language should be eradicated, writing that if children learn Irish before English, "Soe that the speach being Irish, the hart must needes be Irishe; for out of the aboundance of the hart, the tonge speaketh."[48]

Both Hopkins and Mackay Brown expanded and innovated within the English language with the infusion of what had been suppressed at the Reformation. Mackay Brown trawled the literary canon in its post-Reformation phases: "the verse of the eighteenth century seemed a huge desert—Dryden, Pope, Thomson. Again, it was only in my maturity that their marvelously polished couplets made sense."[49] He described himself as "an ardent revolutionary"[50] and then a "Shelleyan socialist"[51] against the backdrop of the Romantic movement. He processed the canon in a fluid manner as a cluster of problems and errors with a rising sense of his poetic distinctiveness that was more

---

46 Milton, *Areopagitica* (1644), 12–13.
47 Mackay Brown, *For the Islands I Sing*, 43. "I had a distaste for Milton, both the man and the poet...it was only years later, when I had matured, that the marvels of that elegy [Lycidas] revealed themselves, veil after veil."
48 Spenser, *A View of the Present State of Ireland*.
49 Mackay Brown, *For the Islands I Sing: An Autobiography*, 44.
50 Ibid., 43.   51 Ibid.

in accord (while being independent from) with Hopkins. He wrote to me in 1981 expressing the view in an exchange about Dryden: "at his best, is marvelous. But so much of his verse is contemporary satire, we of the 20th century miss the point. His craftsmanship is superb.... At the moment I am reading that pessimistic poet with the pity for poor suffering humanity and his hostility to God. Again, a marvelous craftsman in the art of verse; but, as G K Chesterton said, he likes to pose as the village atheist."[52] What the Catholic Dryden concealed in satire, Hopkins and Mackay Brown wanted to be free from, in order to express their heart-songs to the fullest. Mackay Brown resonated with the legacy of the "scorched earth policy" unleashed upon Ireland having been brought up within Orkney and its suppression of all things Catholic. It is interesting to note that on 13 July 1878 the *Orcadian* newspaper printed a lengthy discourse of a lecture given at the Free Church in Kirkwall by the Revd. Wylie of Edinburgh about the incoming re-establishment of the papal hierarchy in Scotland. Comparisons were made to the Irish "situation." The anti-Catholic rhetoric depicts a comparable situation appearing in Kirkwall where Catholics will be as likely to be incited to murder and violence by Canon Law "graven on the minds and consciences of the Popish populations of Ireland as with a pen of iron and received by them as truth from heaven."[53] Of course, tolerance did assuredly come, but not without the Spenserian "scorched earth" undercurrent so familiar to Mackay Brown formed in the Protestant ethos of Orkney.

Mackay Brown's literary odyssey fathomed the labyrinth and there was progression without jettisoning its delights and distastes. William Blake had considered Milton the major English poet and placed Edmund Spenser as Milton's precursor, seeing himself as Milton's poetical son. But there came a point where Mackay Brown moved convincingly to the Catholic philosophical categories marked out in a specific way by Hopkins. Mackay Brown would never cast off his Calvinist formation, but with certainty and conviction he was able to elevate his poetical

---

52 Mackay Brown in a letter to the author 18 August 1981, cited in Appendix *George Mackay Brown: No Separation*, 203.
53 Gray, *Circle of Light: The Catholic Church in Orkney Since the Reformation*, 79.

thought in a spiritual development that was wide and deep with a balance between faith and reason as it was for Newman and Hopkins while being true to an Orkney poetics.

Mackay Brown concludes his parable "The Blind Fiddler" with these words:

> One by one the sleepers of the fair awoke. The priest led the people to the temple for Matins. Some Pilgrims from the hills of eternal youth, attracted by the song, entered through the gate of Birth. Others passed out through the gate of Death and were glad to go. Among the quiet hills (which were the hills of home) the mystery of the song was made apparent to them.[54]

Bunyan and Blake are imprinted enduringly. But there was now a sense of the sacrament and the liturgy of the Orkney idyll, the Greenfields Kirk. Hopkins nurtured the Catholicism in Mackay Brown in a very particular way, all woven into the liturgy of sky, land, and sea as we see here when Mackay Brown writes: "The rich swarming never-exhausted beauty of the world: it was the garment of God. The Holy Spirit spreads bright wings over the hills at dawn Christ and all His hallows are there when the harvest stooks are brought in and participate in the rustic song and dance."[55]

A CATHOLIC HEART AND MIND

The Reformation legacy was not only the spur for Hopkins and Mackay Brown; it was also the forge for their literary experimentation and innovations. This spur and forge intensified their absorption into a Catholic heart and mind with its patterns of categories that appealed so much to them. For example, in January 1948 Mackay Brown jotted down *"A Prayer to cover much of life:* —Take me God. Use me. Pour through me as much life as I can bear. Increase not my knowledge of Good and Evil but my Innocence. Thy will be done."[56] His complex emotional turmoil drove his faith journey which manifested itself in the unforgettable images of life and power that sprang to life in his poetry. Mackay Brown and Hopkins took their respective journeys into their own

---

54 Mackay Brown, Unpublished TS "A Fiddler at the Fair (A Parable)." Sept. 1945. OLA, Ernest Walker Marwick Collection, D31/30/2.
55 Mackay Brown, *For the Islands I Sing*, 155.
56 Mackay Brown, *The Commonplace Book*, NLS.

inner hell, breaking through the ego with its narrow concerns, bringing space for a new healthy shift in their way of being and seeing. There is an awakening to the rich and unbroken grace in them and, as one can see in Mackay Brown's prayer, it was willed. The prayer itself reveals an Ignatian and Jesuit signature: it is generous and practical, investing in innocence whilst never under-rating knowledge as it gives a big space for obedience to God. "Pour through me as much life as I can bear" — and Mackay Brown did find life difficult. He is often presented as a caricature of his true self for his many social ineptitudes, but the reality of this literary man was the simplicity of his stance. It was serene, graceful, and intellectual and the Jesuit alignment continued through Hopkins and others. It is important to note that that the Society of Jesus is that one religious tradition of the Catholic Church (outside the more singular influence of the Oratorian St John Henry Newman) with which Mackay Brown aligned himself. The Jesuits played a decisive role in reinstating Catholicism in Scotland and Orkney during the post-Reformation period. The Jesuits also formally undertook care for the Orkney parish from 1958 to 2005. Mackay Brown's pastoral care was by the Jesuits, having been received into the Church when Father Frances Cairns, SJ, served as pastor, 1958–63. Mackay Brown used the Jesuit priests W. A. M Peters and Frederick Copleston to further his understanding of Hopkins's literary and philosophical ideas. And not to be dismissed is the Jesuit-educated James Joyce who features in Mackay Brown's *Essays and Notes*.

The passion of Mackay Brown's heart and mind was that of Christ and it moved forward in a liturgical frame. Mackay Brown's poetic forms and patterns progressively accumulated and clustered around what became his "Liturgy of April"[57] and "Stations of Cross"[58] sequences.. In 1983 he wrote of his poem "Rackwick Stations of the Cross: From Stone to Thorn"; "those fourteen couplets condense everything I wanted or want or will ever conceivably want to say."[59] Increasingly, what have been called "Catholic Categories" or a "Catholic structure of mind"[60] underpinned his poetic art wherein he expressed the Passion

---

57 Mackay Brown, "Elegy," in *The Collected Poems of George Mackay Brown*, 32.
58 Mackay Brown, A note held in EUL, Special Collections, George Mackay Brown, MS 2846.1.   59 Ibid.
60 Power, *James Joyce's Catholic Categories*, 16–17.

of Christ as it manifested itself to him in a many-layered pre-Reformation Orcadian Catholicism centered on the martyrdom of St. Magnus. As he did so, his poetic vision seamlessly embraced the sacred and the profane as one complete liturgical tapestry that held within itself a structure that brought a reinvigorated symmetry to the Reformation legacy of private relativistic judgment. Hopkins laid out the pioneering patterns of how to do this and Mackay Brown followed.

James Joyce clearly impacts Mackay Brown[61] within his *Essays and Notes* on Hopkins. Firstly, Mackay Brown makes a technical observation of Hopkins's poem "Inversnaid" when he writes, "curiously little of the kind of onomatopoeia that James Joyce and Hugh MacDiarmid delighted in when writing of streams and rivers."[62] Hopkins, by his estimation, did not use words to merely imitate the natural sounds of water. Hopkins did not try to mimic sound effects or merely describe just to be more expressive and interesting about water. According to Mackay Brown, he achieved a distinctiveness so much so that this is Inversnaid water that "nobody could think of it as being anywhere else."[63] The Hopkins innovation was to *inscape* the particular actuality of the water in its uniqueness giving specific authenticity to its location, "its pure landscape."[64] Mackay Brown captured the *inscape*: "'windpuff bonnet' is very good: those blown beads of froth that are the size and shape and color of the Scotsman's traditional cap; though comparatively light and airy in texture."[65] And again with: "'Broth of a pool'—the rush of water churns up the pool to the consistency and appearance of broth, that rich heavy dark soup that along with porridge and whiskey, is supposed to be Scotland's main nourishment."[66] Mackay Brown paid heed to Joyce's and MacDiarmid's technique and

---

61 Onomatopoeia: "Joyce's three different types of onomatopoeic language in the opening lines of the 'Sirens' chapter of *Ulysses* contain: conventional onomatopoeia with real words that sound like the things they refer to or describe eg Trilling, trilling...Peep!...tink...throbbing, non-onomatopoeic words used to create an onomatopoeic effect eg chips...chips...blew...blue, and onomatopoeia with made-up words eg steelyringing imperthnthn thnthnthn...peepofgold. In the latter type, Joyce fuses conventional onomatopoeic words ('ringing' and 'peep') with other words ('steely,' 'thnthnthn,' and 'ofgold') to create entirely new words with their own unique sonic effects."
62 Mackay Brown, *Two Landscape Poems*, a 10pp manuscript essay signed George M Brown 1964, each leaf 25.5 × 20cm.
63 Ibid.   64 Ibid.   65 Ibid.   66 Ibid.

their "structure of mind," but went alone towards Hopkins's Catholic "metaphysics of that ancient community of faith"[67] as one who has met the Orkney inscapes with his own senses. He discovered they had a reality outside the mind in a many-layered presence that aligns with Scotus's and Hopkins's formalitas[68] rather than the single inscape of the haecceitas.

Onomatopoeic theory explains the origin of the language as the natural human tendency to imitate the sounds of nature, but Mackay Brown saw Hopkins going over and beyond the natural tendency and technical mimicking of the sounds of nature in "water and streams" to align within Hopkins's sensational vision of the "multiplicity and intelligibility of multiple inscapes within a single thing."[69] Mackay Brown can stand alongside Joyce and MacDiarmid and their onomatopoeic "delight," but not their burgeoning internal conflict of mind swirling in its own stream of consciousness. He had his own internal conflict to contend with, and he had found a deep serenity in spite of, or because of, it that aligned him with a passionate love for the Creator and eclipsed the "half-baked stuff"[70] of his early interior monologues.

With Hopkins, he explored new artistic parameters, for example, in the "jets of excitement"[71] he experienced in Hopkins's poem, "The Sea and the Skylark." Here within a highly interactive and multi-disciplinary reading of the sensational Hopkins's vision he recorded his response: "I am thinking of the sculpture of Henry Moore, some of the music of Stravinsky, the early painting of Graham Sutherland, the prose of Joyce (parts of Ulysses for example)."[72] Finally, as the liturgical frame took precedence in Mackay Brown, he placed the anti-hero Joyce within the eucharistic chant: "Vere Dignum Est[73] [It is truly meet and just] (cf. James Joyce *Ulysses*)"[74] thus showing his affinity with

---

67 Ward, *World as Word: Philosophical Theology in Gerard Manley Hopkins*, 1.
68 Ward, "Philosophy and Inscape: Hopkins and the *Formalitas* of Duns Scotus."   69 Ibid.
70 MacInnes, "Finding a Voice in the Forties," *New Shetlander*, 30-33, 36.
71 Mackay Brown, *Notebook One. Notes on GMH poem "The Sea and the Skylark,"* NLS.   72 Ibid.
73 Joyce, *Ulysses*, "Wandering Rocks," 169. Father Conmee's pun on Paddy Dignam's surname is taken from the opening phrases of the various Prefaces that are intoned as part of the Eucharistic Prayer in the Catholic Tridentine Mass.
74 Mackay Brown, *Notebook Three. "Gerard Manley Hopkins and the Mass,"* NLS. This ambitious project is discussed in detail in Chapter Seven "Theological

Joyce's and Hopkins's Jesuit formation, both with a relentless focus on the Eucharist. Unlike Joyce, however, "Eucharistic Mutations and Permutations"[75] were not for him. Nor were MacDiarmid's political consciousness or any shades of modernism or the avant-garde.

Mackay Brown and Hopkins carried the instress within themselves and their poetry. That is the difference. The inscape is common to Hopkins, Mackay Brown, Joyce, and MacDiarmid, but Hopkins and Mackay Brown did not pursue the individuality or this-ness of their stream of consciousness. They instress the inscape, anchoring it to the Creator in a stem of infused grace. Joyce "streamed" his thoughts in the company of onomatopoeia: "Am I walking into eternity along Sandymount strand? Crush, crack, crick, crick."[76] Joyce can capture the *inscape*: "Under the upswelling tide he saw the writhing weeds lift languidly and sway reluctant arms, hissing up their petticoats, in whispering water swaying and upturning coy silver fronds."[77] With sight and sound Joyce inscaped water with "purling rill as it babbles on its way."[78] It all seems very familiar, but it could be any water at any location; whereas, as Mackay Brown specifies in "Inversnaid," the particular actuality of the water in its uniqueness gives specific authenticity to its location, "its pure landscape."[79] Equally, Mackay Brown moved over and beyond MacDiarmid's thought-stream: "So I have gathered unto myself / All the loose ends of Scotland, / And by naming them and accepting them, / Loving them and identifying myself with them, / Attempt to express the whole."[80]

Mackay Brown aligns with the Jesuit ethos that formed Joyce through his intensely experienced education. He was also abreast of Joyce's literary giftedness. Mackay Brown had his own bitter antipathies to contend with, but like Hopkins he was a convert who turned away from the Protestant tradition. It never left him, but he found his path and purpose and fulfillment in a many-layered pre-Reformation Orcadian Catholicism. Mackay Brown

---

Blades" where Mackay Brown tried to encompass Hopkins's poems within each liturgical phase of the Mass. Joyce is included above as a point of comparison within this incomplete project.
75 Power, *James Joyce's Catholic Categories*, 277–346.
76 Joyce, *Ulysses*, 37.   77 Ibid., 49.   78 Ibid., 123.
79 Mackay Brown, *Two Landscape Poems*, a *10pp manuscript essay signed George M Brown 1964, each leaf 25.5 × 20cm, NLS*.
80 MacDiarmid, "Scotland," *Complete Poems*.

steers clear of the institutional Church with its controversies[81] by keeping close to his sources quivering in their natural beauty. Following the Hopkins trajectory of new lines of re-engagement and development, he embraces the seamless difference between God and the things he had created held in the inscaped-instress. MacDiarmid meanwhile kept himself grounded in the natural world by "Loving them and identifying myself with them."[82]

Mackay Brown saw in Hopkins a certain dilemma that he resolved by quoting Jacques Maritain: "His is a loving contempt of all things other than the beloved. And the more he despises creatures in the degree to which they might be rivals of God, or objects of a possible choice to the exclusion of God and made by him as fair and worthy of our love... so we understand the paradox."[83] Squaring up to the paradox (to love the things of creation is to love its Creator) led Mackay Brown away from the Protestant tradition and secular wisdom to a spiritual enlightenment: "Whereby in the end the saint includes in a universal love of kinship and of piety—incomparably more free, but also more tender and more happy than any selfish love of the voluptuous or of the miser—all the weakness and the beauty of things, all he had left behind on his journey."[84] It is interesting to note Mackay Brown's insight into Joycean conflict and his notes on Maritain to find the way forward on Hopkins's journey that he made his own personal validation. It rings true with a letter he wrote to me in 1977, "Any sanctuary I had is all a heap of stones these days. I must gather the scattered blocks together and try, somehow to build anew."[85] This was a constant process for Hopkins and Mackay Brown and their poetry was evidence of their

---

[81] Mackay Brown. Letter to the author 18 August 1990. Cited in Appendix, *George Mackay Brown: No Separation*, 203: "I keep well clear of all kinds of Catholic controversy. I think the church seems full of energy nowadays (some misdirected, but that's the way it has always been)."
[82] MacDiarmid, "Scotland," *Complete Poems*.
[83] Maritain cited in *Notebook One, NLS*. I think it is fair to say that Mackay Brown was not as enthused as other Catholic artists and writers were about Maritain's philosophy. I would think this reflects his thinking that goes with Hopkins and Scotus rather than Aquinas. Again, it is the distinction between analogical language and *univocity* that leads Mackay Brown directly and completely to Hopkins to become a poetic practitioner rather than a commentator.
[84] Ibid.
[85] Mackay Brown. Letter (29 September 1977) to the author cited in Gray's *George Mackay Brown: No Separation*, 200.

marked resilience nurtured from Maritain's "all the weakness and beauty of things" that are scattered along the faith journey.

Hopkins redeveloped the new lines of the old firmament because of the insight and perception of things that became confirmed in him by his encounter with the philosopher Scotus. He did not deny his Catholic formation in Aristotle and Aquinas, but he was able to make good his knowledge of nature and the human person. This faith journey is well-documented in his *Notebooks* and *Journals* and *Letters*, as well as in his poetry. Mackay Brown read widely around Hopkins as a subject. Hopkins's explanations and articulations aligned themselves with his own experiences and perceptions. It was not his temperament to forensically dissect Hopkins's scholarly development. He read the literary criticism around Hopkins as it had accumulated by the 1960s. And he clearly read key books about Hopkins: John Pick and W. A. M. Peters are quoted in the Mackay Brown *Essays and Notes*, but it seems clear that it is Peters the Jesuit priest who captures Mackay Brown's attentiveness to Jesuit intellectual and literary insights.

Mackay Brown made brief notes on the Catholic spiritual tradition as in the writings of St. Ignatius Loyola, Jacques Maritain,[86] Marie Lataste,[87] St. John of the Cross, and St. Teresa of Avila, but there is no evidence for a strong affinity for these writers. Mackay Brown made a few jottings here and there, but it was Hopkins himself that was the supreme focus of his attention. Hopkins was the sounding-board for Mackay Brown's own preoccupation with the internal drama going on within him as it pulsated with echoing memories of Orkney and its manifestation to him as sensational vision. These jottings take on a serious tone that support Mackay Brown's understanding in specific areas of his intellectual development, but inevitably his interest was overtaken by Hopkins's Scotian theories and consequent development. The *Essays and Notes* give the sense that Mackay Brown was making brief forays into certain influences

---

[86] Jacques Maritain was a French Catholic philosopher. Raised Protestant, he was agnostic before converting to Catholicism in 1906. An author of more than sixty books, he helped to revive Thomas Aquinas in the twentieth century and had a strong influence on Catholic intellectuals and artists such as David Jones and his circle.
[87] Marie Lataste, 1822–1847, was a French Roman Catholic visionary, nun, and writer. Hopkins read her writings.

on Hopkins, but without any scrutiny other than to support his own personal ideas. They serve to elevate his convergence with Hopkins more than anything else.

Mackay Brown was conscious of the Catholic understanding and teaching of essences as evidenced by his jotting for Maritain: "the principle determining the peculiar perfection of everything which is, constituting and completing things in their essence and their qualities; the ontological secret, so to speak of their innermost being."[88] But, increasingly, he found resonance with Hopkins's theory of the individuating principle: inscape and instress, individuation or haecceitas or "this-ness" and the richness of formalitas. Aristotle and Aquinas held that the "first and proper object of our knowledge is the essence of things arrived at by abstraction, whereas Scotus holds that the first object of human knowledge is the individual as it is here and now presents itself to our senses." Gradually, a phased sensitive experience of the object is accompanied by an intuitive knowledge of the concrete individual and on this knowledge the mind works and reaches intellectual knowledge of the universal essence by the method of abstraction."[89] Mackay Brown knew from his own life and experience the high value of sense experience as material for the poetical mind to work upon. He had a series of powerful experiences growing up in Orkney and throughout the 1940s; certain of these experiences were key to his "taste of myself."[90] He knew his own individual essence and it was extraordinarily strong and distinctive, as it was in Hopkins. He was deeply aware of himself as selvèd. It cast a deep shadow over him all his life, but he made sense of himself as the poet in the cast of Hopkins and his ideas.

Mackay Brown's reading of Peters gave him access to the philosophical grasp of Hopkins's theory of the individuating principle. It is this principle that is Hopkins's proof for the existence of God:

> I find myself with my pleasures and pains, my powers and my experiences, my deserts and guilt, my shame and sense of beauty, my dangers, hopes, fears, and all

---

88 Mackay Brown, *Notebook Three*, NLS.
89 Peters, *Gerard Manley Hopkins: A Critical Essay Towards the Understanding of His Poetry*, 22.
90 Hopkins, "Comments on the Spiritual Exercises of St Ignatius Loyola," 145–50.

my fate, more important than anything else I see. And when I ask where does all this throng and stack of my being, so rich, so distinctive, so important, come from, nothing I see can answer me.[91]

Coming to terms with one's own nature is a crucial step to appreciating human nature in all its commonality and variety. Hopkins's ideas about being more "highly pitched" brought out the moral nature of human persons and their varying degrees of good and evil. Hopkins and Mackay Brown gravitated towards a consideration of themselves to the point of self-acceptance and that "consciousness and feeling" that Hopkins aligned with, "I and me above and in all things, which is more distinctive than the taste of alum, more distinctive than the smell of walnut leaf or camphor and is incommunicable by any means to another." Searching the natural world and finding one's purpose and place leads to that ability to "taste self but at one tankard, that of my own being."[92] Like Hopkins, Mackay Brown's poetry "originated from the deepest and most earnest realization of his own rich self."[93]

It has been argued that "Mackay Brown's Orkney isn't real—it's a heraldic, romantic vision;"[94] that leads at once to question "what is real," what is entailed in "Romantic" and "vision" and "imagination?" What do these words mean and how are they being used? Hopkins asked these questions in the nineteenth century. He was driven by these questions, as was Mackay Brown. A poem, a painting, a vision open the way to a higher reality. The classical tradition that Hopkins and Mackay Brown chose to work within could go high and deep and wide. It was coming from a full range of dimensions that were infinite and their language was used to express that. Both poets firmly rejected a catch-all use of certain generic terms in trying to place their work in the canon of literary succession. The Oxford Movement was no random trajectory that hastened a Protestant into a Catholic "movement." At its foundation was a search to release the suppressions of the past handed down by the politics

---

91 Hopkins, Notebook 309-10 cited in Peters, *Gerard Manley Hopkins: A Critical Essay Towards the Understanding of His Poetry*, 25.
92 Ibid., 28. 93 Ibid.
94 MacInnes, "Finding a Voice in the Forties," *New Shetlander*, 30-33, 36.

and theology of the times. Hopkins and Mackay Brown were impelled by the certainties they looked for as grounds for belief, and their art was refined and developed according to a fusion of antiquity and contemporary life in an intense engagement with the sources of both.

Romanticism peaked in the nineteenth century with its emphasis on emotion and individualism. It glorified the past and nature and championed the medieval age and ethos over the classical period. It was distinctively reactive towards the Industrial Revolution, the aristocratic social and political norms of the Age of Enlightenment, and the scientific rationalization of nature. There was a strong emphasis on intense emotion as an authentic source of aesthetic experience. There was also a strong belief and interest in the importance of nature and an elevation of folk art and ancient custom to something noble. The exaltation of reason on the one hand and emotion on the other—with a clear separation between them—released a lot of energy into literature and the arts. Hopkins and Mackay Brown were not immune to the Romanticism of those times or its legacy. But their story does not rest there. Newman had predicted that scientific humanism forged from the era of rationalist empiricism would reach its heights and then decline into an intellectual desolation "that might well last a very long time and require centuries to heal."[95] The Romanticism that drove the Oxford Movement elevated emotion to such an extent it was questioned by Newman from the position of the moral imperative of the conscience. To elevate the moral purpose of a literary text may once have been customary, well understood, and even admired, but now has lost its footing in the écriture. Hopkins and Mackay Brown were "philosophic in range and temper"[96] and moved within a tradition that had assimilated Greek philosophy, all things biblical and a litany of writers, artists, and musicians from the European cultural heritage. And, in the case of Mackay Brown, there was an expansion into Russian and American literature, but most decisively into the interplay of literary, historical, political, and religious energies in the world of the North Atlantic.

---

[95] Newman, *The Philosophical Notebook Vol I*, 30.
[96] Steiner, *Tolstoy or Dostoevsky: An Essay in the Old Criticism* (1959).

Hopkins, for his part, showed Mackay Brown how to find more in what many have considered the narrow path of Orkney. But Orkney, like Iceland, holds together a ferment of sources and a clearly defined poetics that could resonate universally as well as locally. Hopkins came through the ranks of Victorian times and artistry, through Ruskin and the Pre-Raphaelites. His classical mind, his intellectual stance, sought a spirituality that was soaked in a profound realism. Hopkins's own narrow journey was a voyage of discovery as he thought and sensed his way into Catholicism. He was absorbed in the natural world in a very empirical way. The empiricism of it generated a disciplined response as the evidence he could not stop gathering from the world of nature and the human person found expression in a bold and striking use of language.

Hopkins prepared to enter the Catholic Church through soul-searching in a world of sensation. He experienced the natural world and its patterns and form as being in perpetual motion. The phenomena of the natural world alerted his senses to an extremely high degree. His early impressive control of poetic form was insistent on God's presence in the world, not metaphorically but really. It was always his instinct to praise God. He saw mysteriousness and the design of Creation everywhere in its various stages of development and decay. Through successive stages of isolation and difference from family, and then from the wider community by conversion to Catholicism, Hopkins chose and formed himself in the Jesuit tradition. He had been influenced and shaped by the Oxford Movement and John Henry Newman. Newman studied, wrote, and acted upon the capacity to believe in all areas of life, including religion and its centrality to the human person. This was the Catholic philosophical temperament that came to the fore in Newman, Hopkins, and Mackay Brown. Newman was not the first advocate of an authentic capacity to believe, but he gave a lasting seminal and timely prominence to it. The whole person accumulated knowledge from being immersed in the world, not removed from it. Hopkins and Mackay Brown composed their poetry from the cumulative weight of their sensational vision with all the touchpoints that hovered between the natural and the supernatural. They were immersed in the world, and so was their verse. Equally they are immersed in that other place. Their poetic technique and content cannot but help "charge" the Greenfields Kirk with "the grandeur of God," because it actually and empirically was pulsating with a dynamic array of creative inscapes instressed with their Creator.

HOW TO INFUSE TEXT WITH THE "MAJESTY AND SWEETNESS" OF CHRIST

Mackay Brown's *Essays and Notes* evidence the prominence in his own Catholic heart and mind of Hopkins's thinking as well as writing and the convergence between the two. Mackay Brown took note how the radical Hopkins pivoted his place in the world on a God who spoke His revelation into the world by the Greek spirit and the Roman imperium. Through his immersion in Hopkins, he came to understand how the Church guarded this truth, giving frame and emphasis to the Greek speech of scriptures and the inherited doctrine that was received from Latin Rome. Hopkins was further integrated into this heritage and its classical and biblical authority through belonging to the Society of Jesus. The Patristic conception of the Christian mystery was further ignited by his participation in the Oxford Movement as it looked to re-engage with the Church Fathers in a post-Reformation secularization accelerating the detachment of literature from order, authority, and a coherent spirituality. This was the world that the critic Alan Bold refers to as the "old story,"[97] once remarkably familiar but now a strange version of existence that sits alongside the many chosen lifestyles recorded in the world of the *écriture*.

Hopkins, and then Mackay Brown, navigated the relativistic fragmentation as they embraced the firmament of sensation with its scales of light and sound. Hopkins commanded his own senses sharpened by the *Spiritual Exercises of St, Ignatius Loyola* and his empirical eye that puts natural phenomena under the microscope for adjudication within his frame of inscape and instress. Mackay Brown grew in confidence and certainty about his place in the authenticity of his own thinking and writing. Hopkins's new lines of departure from the "old, old story" achieve a challenging prominence in his poem, "God's Grandeur." His wordplay with the properties that belong to

---

97 Bold, *George Mackay Brown*, 44.

God's nature tumble over one another: The "grandeur," the "flame," the "shining," converge and coalesce, ever in a state of movement. As the "waves of generations" tread their way leaving a legacy of wreckage throughout Creation, Hopkins held humanity dear for all its fallen nature. But in spite of the worst humanity can do, the echoes of the casting out of Adam and Eve from the Garden of Eden and ensuing punishment for original sin (that marks us all) is not able to quell the joyous resilience, the deep-down freshness of the natural world of God's creation. This joyous resilience became a marked feature of Mackay Brown's own poetics as he too infused it with the majesty and sweetness of Christ.

As humanity hurtled into the darkness "off the black West," from the east assuredly came the Holy Spirit, with Hopkins's accustomed literal sighting of Christ. Oil oozes its tread, but is it an anointing under the compass of a brooding world gathered and transfigured in warmth and breast and bright wings? The Resurrection cannot be done away with: it is irrepressible in spite of everything to the contrary. The vision is vast but so simple, small, and particular. Hopkins develops and draws the new lines of the firmament as word by word, inscape by inscape, he turns to "God the Son, both Creator and Redeemer, as Light incarnate shining in stars, storms, sunsets of nature...This is the mystery of the incarnation in creation."[98] The divine energy was instressed into history through Christ and His sacraments. Hopkins believed, as did Scotus, in Christ's eucharistic presence working in nature. This was familiar territory to Mackay Brown, as his Greenfield Kirk, wherein the grandeur, the flame, and the shining spell out the firmament and forge as he honed his empirical eye to see the Creator God inscaped all around him, invested deeply in the divine energy of God through the Eucharist. Hopkins writes in his *Notebook* that all things "are charged with love, are charged with God and if we know how to touch them give off sparks and take fire, yield drops and flow, ring and tell of him."[99] This ability to charge or infuse text with God by the passion partners Hopkins and Mackay Brown

---

98 Heuser, *The Shaping Vision of Gerard Manley Hopkins*, 44.
99 Hopkins. N342, cited in Peters, *Gerard Manley Hopkins: A Critical Essay Towards the Understanding of His Poetry*, 7.

came from their repositioning in a newly understood firmament where they were completely fulfilled existentially within all its interwoven and seamless intellectual and spiritual strands. Their poetry radiated their unique vibrancy immersed in this world and the other with its pre theological materials.

Mackay Brown undertook a close reading of W. A. M. Peters, whose critique of Hopkins includes a study of his sensitive perception and how he understood that worked. Tracing Mackay Brown's reading and note-taking reveals his learning process concerning how to infuse text with the majesty and sweetness of Christ. Peters uses the term "personification" to mean "that figure of speech which cannot exist without a conscious act of the intellectual reasoning."[100] Peters argues that Hopkins's "angle of vision" is one of degree of difference rather than of kind in his observation and penetration of the natural world. His range of vision is an inclusive one that encompasses humanity, animate and inanimate things, as being possessed of the form of inscape. Humanity in man/woman is where God is most fully alive. Hopkins's consciousness of the presence of God in all things hinges on inscape as the precursor of the perception of God himself in the things he has made. God being present in this way charges them with his love and this love is personal. But Hopkins goes further to impersonate the objects he contemplates. "There lives the dearest freshness deep down things": here the inscape is caught by its dynamic energy (on the quiver). This was the Incarnation at work in the seamless interplay within the Trinitarian God in his Creation, in spite of the "reck" and "trod" of humanity. "The constant attribution of activity and life as a rule found its origin in Hopkins's impersonation of the object."[101]

Peters brings out the understanding of Hopkins's interplay between mythology and philosophy:

> Those things which like the common chattels of the house are in control of man entirely and offer no resistance except weight, become generalized, that is, cease to have individuality or personality, but all things which by their freedom from man's control, their irregular and unaccountable sequence, and their influence on man himself

---

100 Ibid., 8.   101 Ibid., 12.

most of all, look like persons and seem to have will of their own, these receive only personal names.[102]

This thought or "peculiar attitude" towards the things of nature is strongly developed in Hopkins and accounts for what Peters calls impersonation as the natural result of Hopkins having inscaped an object. Hopkins perceived the object as charged or instressed with God. This leads Hopkins to impersonate the object. This is the act of the poet in communication with the inscape, the presence of God in the "charged" object and discovering it to be what he called the instress. Hopkins and then Mackay Brown committed to what they perceived and understood to be an infusion of the majesty and sweetness of Christ. This was their discovery of the instress.

As wordsmiths, Hopkins and Mackay Bown unleashed in language the symbolization of those life-giving processes in the natural world. They locked into the Christian mystery inscaped with a swarm of symbols, and at the center of which is the Cross. Biblical narrative is elevated in "types"; its inscapes resonate in local folklore and cosmic realities. Hopkins the Jesuit brought intellectual and spiritual rigor to poetry turning the labyrinth of fragmentation from a place of disintegration to a trajectory where things were arranged in such a way "they become easy to survey and to judge."[103] This quality is attributed to the Jesuit fabric of James Joyce's literary works and drew upon the drive for some in literature to reclaim a coherency of order, authority, and spirituality against the tide of getting lost in the lesser personalities of different writers pursuing Muir's "unfinished sentences."[104] This quality can also be attributed to Mackay Brown. His *Commonplace Book (1940s)* and his Hopkins *Essays and Notes (1962–63)* reveal a movement from the grotesque and discordant that characterize surrealism to some inner place in Mackay Brown more serene where he could stand over and beyond himself to see the forms, patterns, and sequences of phenomena and human behavior within Catholic categories,

---

102 Ibid., 261. Peters cites Hopkins's undergraduate essay: "On the Connection between Mythology and Philosophy" (now published in Lesley Higgins, ed., *The Collected Works of Gerard Manley Hopkins, Volume 4: Essays and Notes.* D.V1, OUP, 2006).
103 Ellman, cited in Powers *James Joyce's Catholic*, 261.
104 Muir, "The Decline of the Novel," *in Essays on Literature and Society*, 144.

Catholic attitudes, and the Jesuit intellectual discipline. Here it becomes "easy to survey and judge."

Mackay Brown follows Hopkins's discovery of the *instress* further, extracting passivity from his own frame of poetic reference because to be passive or static in the dynamic interplay with creation does not fit what Hopkins or he himself saw as qualities of the natural world. Taking the Greek derivation of "stress" as "act," and absorbing the expressiveness of the Anglo-Saxon word to bring out the character of "stress" as a "force," demonstrates the processes that converged to keep things in existence and anticipates the tension of continued existence against opposing forces. As Hopkins writes in his notes on the *Spiritual Exercises of St. Ignatius*, the difference between stress and instress is that "passive power is not power proper and has no activity it cannot of itself come to stress, cannot instress itself (N310)."[105] Instress is that force that holds the inscape together. Inscape is perceived through the senses and bears description whereas instress is felt as it impresses upon the soul. Hopkins, through his formation from the *Spiritual Exercises*, trims everything down to an exactness that sharpened his poetic craft, making him exceptional in comparison with other poets of his day and beyond. His deep and acute awareness mark out a man who acknowledges the body and the soul in equal measure and how the sense perception and cognitive process operate to swim the tide of a Platonic realism and an Aristotelian structure punctuated by Scotus to bring out the new lines of the old firmament. The intensity of his experience integrated within his poetry gives it a hardness and precision that appears to many as a flatness and crudeness of diction. For example, he is very precise about bodily parts—his own and those of Christ Our Lord—these are Hopkins's signatures. My lips, my bones, my flesh and then the elevation to those of Christ—his foot, his shoulder, his finger. Mackay Brown follows this line of thought as the trajectory of "Christ moving in majesty and sweetness.[106]

In the collection of poems *Winterfold* published in 1976 Mackay Brown's pen distils a "Christian sequence" that the Scottish

---

105 Hopkins, *Gerard Manley Hopkins: Poems and Prose*, 146–47.
106 *Gerard Manley Hopkins: Two Landscape Poems*, a *10pp manuscript essay signed George M Brown 1964, each leaf 25.5 × 20cm. NLS.*

poet and literary critic Alan Bold has described as a "retelling of the Story (and implying the Fable) of Christ in our time."[107] Bold interprets Mackay Brown very sensitively, but sees him as battling against the sequence of clichés that are harbored within Christianity. "The biblical account is almost contemptibly familiar."[108] He argues that Mackay Brown imposes "a cunning structure on the old story so that something of the original brilliance shines through."[109] But is this true? Hopkins struck out against Victorian literary clichés with a confident expansion of language re-integrating the wild exuberance and moral seriousness of the Middle Ages via a temperament that does not deny the organic wholeness of the natural world and the human person in all their distinctive particularity. Symbols are then able to reengage with their sources once again, steered by Hopkins's inscape and instress to not only harness the medieval heritage but also to accommodate modern life and move forward into an uncertain future with an authentic literary craft. Mackay Brown would have been aware of Edwin Muir's observations: "the Scottish poets followed the tradition of Dunbar, who expressed the exuberance, wildness and eccentricity of the Middle Ages, not that of Henryson, who inherited the medieval completeness and harmony, and the power to see life whole, without taking refuge in the facetious and the grotesque."[110]

Ross has argued in *Poetry and Dogma* that the clichés that irked Hopkins were the result of "the capacity of the Eucharist symbol in poetry to function simultaneously at the levels of the natural, the historical, and the divine" but came under threat at the Reformation and were eventually lost in the course of the seventeenth century. In poetry, "'The Blood,' 'The Body,' 'The Sacrifice,' are reduced to metaphor, and finally to cliché. 'Fact' and 'value' disengage and draw apart."[111] The Reformation principle of private judgment with its permission to split and divide a wondrous unity brought to poetry the "utterly secular" and the various "-isms" across the spectrum of ideas to emerge as pseudo-sacred profanities that are pursued as norms. The radical Hopkins went into combat with the clichés and unleashed

---

[107] Bold, *George Mackay Brown*, 44.   [108] Ibid.   [109] Ibid.
[110] Muir, *Essays on Literature and Society*, 18–19.
[111] Ross, *Poetry and Dogma: The Transfiguration of Eucharistic Symbols in Seventeenth Century English Poetry*, viii.

an indisputable period of rupture with his intense engagement with spirituality and language that sought new lines of what for so many has become "the old story."[112]

So, is Mackay Brown the "cunning" poet who twists and turns his craft to take issue with the literary establishment? Or is he a disciple of Hopkins? Does he have a "firmament"[113] or a "pantheon"[114] that resonate throughout his literary craft? Hopkins and Mackay Brown both sought a reintegration of created reality, taking things within their times as they experienced them. Mackay Brown found his road and followed it from origins to ends. He wrote in 1986 on the subject of "The Scottish Predicament" that "if such a thing exists at all, [it] is connected with a whole history and ethos. Ought we write in Scots, or English, or Gaelic, or two or three tongues of Alba, or all, according to the demands of the subject? In the end this becomes a personal matter: he will soon find in what air his pen takes wing most eagerly."[115] He gave his full commitment to "his community, as a music that is not finished."[116] Mackay Brown, a writer of substance across many genres, saw his road, his duty, and vowed to "see that words are kept clear of all trashy accretions and are still clothed in their ancient power and beauty, while at the same time they are changed by new subtle shades of meaning."[117] Writers, he says, must "do what they can to keep the garden fresh and beautiful," to "toil his little patch" and to stay in tune with the "angels." Mackay Brown was very sensitized to the "audience": "In order to preserve words in their purity, increasingly in the past century poets have given up trying to communicate to the people they live among: they have withdrawn in to a smaller and smaller conclave—and they seem to write for each other and a few critics in obscure signs and symbols."[118] As a co-worker, rather than a disciple, Mackay Brown aligned himself within the literary succession, for better or worse, as a matter of duty: "Having found the road follow it to the end."[119]

---

112 Bold, *George Mackay Brown*, 44.
113 Ross, *Poetry and Dogma: The Transfiguration of Eucharistic Symbols in Seventeenth Century English Poetry*, ix.
114 Bold, *George Mackay Brown*, 44.
115 Mackay Brown, "Pen Mightier than the Predicament," 3.
116 Ibid.   117 Ibid.   118 Ibid.   119 Ibid.

In the poem "Creator" from *Winterfold* that is numbered "8" among a cruciform sequence, Mackay Brown speaks to and for a God who is Creator and in the manner of Hopkins in "God's Grandeur." Mackay Brown admired Hopkins, whilst all the time doing "otherwise" as we see in his "garden" where he toils in his "little patch," the Greenfields Kirk. The Creator is the Grain of Dust, the Raindrop, the Leaf, Forest, and Fall in the presence of his angels, not metaphorically but really. The seamless movement from the natural to the supernatural goes deep into the Bible: the Pitcher at the fountain, the Winter Tree, Flax, Wheel, Fold of linen. Impersonation at the fore like Hopkins the Creator God "fashioned the earth" on His "hands and knees." Suffering and chaos could not suppress the galaxies that grew from his "fingers." Creator is Street and the Daughters of Music "foregather." The form of the "worm" is inscaped by its atomic composition (but worm was code for the Mackay Brown depression). Creator is Adam "undone by the loom." Creator is Three Nails in a race to the bottom to be "least fruit of the Forge." Creator is Black Diamond at the center of time, burnt out "now." Creator is the Hollow in the Rock; He is the Seed locked in the House of Dust.

The new lines of the old firmament hold good. The resilience that was enshrined in the Seed is the great hope of Hopkins and Mackay Brown. Christian hope is fully integrated with their life-affirming vow to the movement of the faith journey. The inscaped natural world makes its presence felt as the instress of the Creator God. Faith brings security to an insecure world. Hopkins and Mackay Brown recognize the inscaping and instress of an adventurous God. They do not withhold their faith-response to such a God. This faith has a propositional form (the things that I believe) but it is the psychological or spiritual form and its luminous vision that the poetical language brought to the forefront of the reader's experience. The healing nature of poetry puts before the reader an attitude of trust in a God who is always holding out new possibilities. When Hopkins and Mackay Brown align their poetical sensibilities and language to such a God who is Creator, when Hopkins and Mackay Brown commit their wills to be directed according to His purposes, they become conduits of enormous poetical power.

In keeping with the new lines of the old firmament, Mackay Brown's litany of kennings (doing otherwise from Hopkins) inscape the "community" and its "music" in a visionary sensation that through loom and forge capture the potency and potentiality of the Creator. Mackay Brown wields his "theological blades,"[120] kenning by kenning, in the litany of inscape and instress, back and forth, back and forth. The music of the poetic symbolism hovers or quivers simultaneously at the levels of the natural, the historical, and the divine that had been "lost in the course of the seventeenth century"[121] and the relentless reductionism towards metaphor and then cliché. The form of "fact" and "value" are re-engaged and drawn together in a re-presentation of Hopkins's new lines of development of the old "firmament." This can be seen in the "music" of Mackay Brown's "blind fiddler." The poet first acknowledges the Creator, then the blindness of those who could not and will not see his works with the eyes of faith. The Fall had taken its toll and history traced out the presence of the Creator to us in his Son. The fountain of scripture, of human suffering, of the work and labor of human life in the community, the arts and the distress and tragedy of life, rise to a redemptive elevation against the dark at the center of time. The fabric of Hopkins's poem "God's Grandeur" wells up in Mackay Brown across his life and development never to leave him where he too was immersed in the belief that "And for all this, nature is never spent; / There lives the dearest freshness deep down things" that will defy the brooding world with the Creator's "warm breast" and "ah! bright wings."

The density of Hopkins's firmament with the assured movement between inscape and instress was a strong impetus to Mackay Brown's poetry. Mackay Brown knew his Greenfield Kirk, but doing otherwise forgoes density of expression. True to Hopkins's specification of body parts and the sense-gathering of netting things, Mackay Brown went fishing for beauty according to the inscapes of Orkney and he infuses the poem, "Rackwick,"[122] with the beauty of what he saw as Orkney's throne of Glory. Here

---

120 Mackay Brown, *Notebook Three*, NLS.
121 Ross, *Poetry and Dogma: The Transfiguration of Eucharistic Symbols in Seventeenth Century English Poetry*, viii.
122 Mackay Brown, "Rackwick," in *The Collected Poems of George Mackay Brown*, 5.

on the Island of Hoy "Let no tongue idly whisper here" gives a sense of the sacred, the instress of the Creator God found in the landscape where the chatter of the tongues is drawn into the silence that is the warp and weave of his life and work. The Greenfields Kirk had its own liturgy, its set form inscaped by the "strong red cliffs," "great mild sky," "hidden valley of light" "clouds pouring," "surging sea" and "fenceless fields." This is "Orkney's last enchantment." The "tongue" speaks up the person who was "between" and "under" and brought to a realization of "enchantment." Human endeavor conjures up the "fishermen with ploughs" and the "old heroes," all the while the liturgy of the Greenfields Kirk sweeps on in the strength of the cliffs, the greatness of the skies, mild they may be, moving into the hidden-ness of the valley.

The light and sweet and surging sea converges into songs that remind the reader no fences were needed for these fields. This is a place of song where sight and sound and memory reign supreme in the natural world that is lightly configured by the interlocking sustenance of the crofters who were also fishermen with their nets and boats and ploughs working with the land and sea. As memory throbs with the sense of the "old heroes," the liturgy awakens them from their sleeping to a Creator God whose nature is instressed by the hills that enfold with compassion. The instress is compassion. This is the nature of the God of the Greenfields Kirk, according to Mackay Brown and Hopkins in their poetic univocity.

The Hopkins's firmament inscapes up the form, the substance, the grasp of a dynamic interplay between the senses as the natural world hits the human eye, ear, mouth, tongue, skin, hair, breast, foot, hands, fingers. In his poem "Pied Beauty," the purposeful and organized array of the human body is a celebration of beauty first and foremost. The "pied" composition of beauty "dapples things" and draws praise to salute the Creator God who sees that what he has made was good. Hopkins gets particular as he conflates sky and cow in their coupled-color and brinded-ness. The particularity of movement in all its dimensions as chestnuts fall and finches" wings beat is always new and fresh. Each act of movement in its purposeful rhythm was a beat in the heart of time, unique to that moment, and it was the series of those acts that was in rhythm with their Creator God. The elements of human activity in the landscape are "plotted and pieced" in its "fold, fallow and plough" that hold a cave of echoes. The "trades" with their "gear" "tackle" and "trim" are conflated with "All things counter, original, spare, strange" bringing the "fickle" and "freckle" working their way across the landscape according to human notions of agricultural production for better or worse—who knows how?

As the loom weaves the light and the dark, it is the steady purposeful Creator that adjudicates upon human behavior and its stewardship of His Creation. His command is "swift" and "slow," "sweet" and "sour," "adazzle" and "dim." This sense of God's adjudication is the instress that impresses itself within the republic of the conscience. The inscaped form and its empirical patterns are held by the instress within the firmament. Hopkins had marked out his territory, his garden, his patch. This, Hopkins says, is a God whose nature is defined as infinite beauty, who as Creator was Father and sustains His Creation in a sequence and series of "fathering" acts, bringing "things" into being to fulfill their purpose in a God-given firmament. No clichés at work here. The "old, old story" is "freckled" with a "pied beauty" that is swift and slow, sweet and sour, adazzle and dim, in all its *inscapes;* and, as always, Hopkins starts with praise and ends with praise, having trod the movement from light into the dark to emerge, in spite of the worst that humanity can do to trash God's creation, in the effervescent resilience of Christian hope.

Hopkins and Mackay Brown never crossed the fine line between worship of the Creator and worship of the created thing as if it were God. Hopkins had a keen awareness and profound knowledge of the broad stream of Greek piety that was absorbed and transformed by Christianity's "pristine biblical simplicity."[123] Both poets well understood the tracing of the history of religion from the Greek myths into the mystical sacramental form of Christianity, and "having found the road follow it to the end."[124] The reciprocal influence between Christianity and the ancient mystery cults was a "very powerful and basic form of thinking that was common to antiquity as a whole."[125] At the heart of

---

123 Rahner, *Greek Myths and Christian Mystery*, 3.
124 Mackay Brown, "Pen Mightier than the Predicament," 3.
125 Rahner, *Greek Myths and Christian Mystery*, 3.

Christianity is the great drama of the world where the Christian sacraments and Christian redemption take their place in the final fulfillment in the mystery of Christ. As Mackay Brown writes, "what has become over delicate and subtle and civilized may draw strength from the savage roots that lie deep in the earth and the unconscious."[126] The wild proliferation of the different cult legends—Greek, Roman, Germanic, and Scandinavian—unfolded in oral and written traditions that were christianized in the various literatures as an "unceasing hymn to the cosmic mystery of the Cross."[127] Through Hopkins, Mackay Brown accepted the layers of the anthropomorphic paganism around him in Orkney, with their mirror images of vanity, arrogance, resentments and violence; but this pantheon did not put the human person under any moral pressure. Mackay Brown knew moral pressure at first hand. The republic of conscience could not and was not silenced in him. Through Hopkins, the realization came full circle as he could rise from "the savage roots" to be christianized in the Latin mysticism of praise that echoed "sharply defined formulations of ancient theology."[128] Mackay Brown's Orcadian vision absorbed the artistry of folklore and legend that was transformed through the medieval Christianity he found in St. Magnus, whose legacy existed and thrived within the Eucharist.

The understanding of the nature and purpose of symbols "was native to the culture in which Christianity developed."[129] Symbols draw their reality from the "savage salutary primitive power of nature that was always there, 'watching and waiting.'"[130] The piety of Hopkins and Mackay Brown resonates with this ancient Christian faith taking up the Gospel of Christ as a cruciform sequence of the realistic, brutal, shameful, and frightful historical events that document Christ's death. Hopkins, indeed, re-ignited the "fixedness of the essential pattern"[131] that imposed itself on the sacraments. This pattern was the Apostolic Tradition with its facts, ethical demands, and its mystery

---

126 *The Windhover* 11 MS pp on 6 leaves each 33 × 20.5cm signed George M Brown March 1964 in another ink. NLS.
127 Rahner, *Greek Myths and Christian Mystery*, 52.
128 Ibid., 40.   129 Ibid.
130 Mackay Brown, *Gerard Manley Hopkins: Two Landscape Poems*, a 10pp manuscript essay signed George M Brown 1964, each leaf 25.5 × 20cm. NLS.
131 Rahner, *Greek Myths and Christian Mystery*, 32.

of redemption from sin by Grace. There is one true God, the historic person of Jesus Christ. The faith placed in Christ was strictly monotheistic and had a sharply circumscribed form of dogmatic teaching that radiated out from the Eucharist.

Hopkins and Mackay Brown both use images familiar to their audience but their poetical configuration is intellectually demanding. They do not command the assent of audiences, but, at some point, their writing calls for a complete understanding of the natural world in terms of their observations and perceptions that are then taken on a journey of transcendent elevation to the realms of the supernatural. The "Pied Beauty" of the Greenfields Kirk is inscaped and instressed with runes, kennings, and symbols that all puzzle their way through a series of word games as much fun as they are luminous. No "glittering surfaces" or clichéd versions of "the old story" in these new lines are inscaped and instressed into poetical language. As Mackay Brown writes in the *Essays and Notes*:

> The fact is, I think, that Hopkins was really not so much different from Giotto and Fra Angelico and the painters of the age of faith. We know the Middle Ages had a great attraction for him. All his work, like theirs, sprang from a religious root, a vivid apprehension of Christ's presence in the universe. Unconsciously perhaps he answered Blake's question.[132]

Hopkins confirmed in him everything it meant for him to be a poet. He had already written in his first collection of published poems in "The Storm":

> I reeled past kirk and ale-house
> And the thousand candles
> Of gorse round my mother's yard[133]

Here from the outset is the mind of Mackay Brown and what exactly he sees as he swings past the Stromness kirk, a shrine to Calvin, then the ale-house, setting his sensations afire. By the time his speaker makes it through the storm to the safe haven of his mother's home and yard (at this point in the poem),

---

132 Mackay Brown, *GMH Two Landscape Poems*, a 10pp manuscript essay signed George M Brown 1964, each leaf 25.5 × 20cm. NLS.
133 Mackay Brown, "The Storm" in *The Collected Poems of George Mackay Brown*, 3.

the yellow radiance of the gorse flowers festoons what to his perception was the eucharistic altar with its "sharply defined formulations of ancient theology"[134] that resides and thrives within the liturgy to this day and beyond. Mackay Brown's literary litany becomes inscaped by the forge of the Reformation legacy. His Catholic mind and heart could not be quelled, as it was conscience-driven to infuse Christ in majesty and sweetness as radically as Hopkins had showed him how. Their partnership of passion is stationed in Christ and expressed itself in their writing bi-directionally, univocally rather than by a one-directional sacramental analogy. To inscape and *instress* according to Catholic categories created a challenging poetic craft bearing its infusions of the majesty and sweetness of the eucharistic Christ himself at every turn, not metaphorically but really. Chapter Three continues along this angle of vision where the radiant eucharistic narrative held within it the microcosmic inscapes that were fetched out in unison with the instress from what had become a post-Reformation world of absence.

---

134 Rahner, *Greek Myths and Christian Mystery*, 32.

CHAPTER THREE

Fetching Out Inscape and Instress

> "But to Chaucer, Spenser, Milton, Wordsworth, clouds were clouds, never 'cloud-puffballs, torn tufts, tossed pillows.' This is a new way of looking at things—here is a poet who wished to see the particular and not the general; such extravagance suggests a certain exhaustion of language."[1]

THIS CHAPTER SCOPES OUT THE FRAME of the angle of vision, "the new way of looking at things," that is specifically "particular" in the craft of "no separation" with its seamless sensations of pattern, form, and shape. The "new way of looking at things" is the artistry of fetching out inscape and instress that requires an eye for pattern, form, and shape. It has to be worked at with a disciplined constancy. Mackay Brown took his eucharistic narrative that holds within it the microcosmic inscapes as in the poem "Sunday in Selskay Isle."[2] He puts before his audience an image: "Selskay the island / Floats on a blue Sabbath silence." As the island is cradled in the blue sea, the inscapes that appear were elevated in Mackay Brown's mind as he assumed the craft of expressing univocity with the Sabbath silence. On one level he fetched out the anvil, the black creel, the open kirk door, accompanied by the sound of solemnity. The suppressive silence of the un-ringing anvil, the shuttered shop, the black-suited elders, the manse minister and wife, the laird, all of which were simultaneously at their stations as they moved out of the "death-ending darg[3] of a week to Sabbath and resurrection." At the same time, Mackay Brown layers in the world of absence, his world of the negative way with its echoes inscaped in a sort of via negativa that reinstates the loss and suppressions of the Reformation legacy.

---

1 Mackay Brown, *Notebook Two*, NLS.
2 Mackay Brown, *Northern Lights: A Poet's Sources*, 53–55. Also in *The Collected Poems of George Mackay Brown*, 413.
3 Merriam-Webster. Chiefly Scottish. First attested in late Middle English; a syncopic form of daywork, developed through the series of forms: daywork → daywerk → daywark → dawark → *da"ark → dark → darg. "Darg."

Solemnity in the seven cries of the bell summoned island folk to the small stone steeple, yet all the time the big narrative prevails holding within the little story, the particular version of the Reformation legacy. The historicity cannot quell the compelling story rising in the natural world as the horse gallops in the Glebe field. "Mr Frame" the schoolmaster on the Isle of Selskay, not an atheist, worshiped in the Greenfields Kirk that was the Orkney world of sensation. According to the schoolmaster, the divine is everywhere, a place where the senses are sharpened by art, maths, optics, and music. The artistic frame stimulated in Mackay Brown during the Edinburgh study of Hopkins, the ever-developing craft of mastering the poetic flux with pulsating yet controlled image sequences.

The inner psyches of Hopkins and Mackay Brown pushed them to exercise their keen eyes, listening ears, to get to grip with their own inner consciousness, immersed as they were in the natural world. Their response was a creative one. They both pursued form and composition and anchored themselves within a deep stable harmony that they discovered to be Christ himself, where all inscapes are sourced. They feasted on the phenomena of lightened sound, the radiance of sunlight and birdsong. Their senses were in perpetual motion with sun-risings and sun-settings with their changing spectrums of color, their music soaring and sinking in wind and bird. The flux threw up a profound experience of beauty, but it also pulled them back into an emotional life that was as desolate as it was inspired. The crimson-white radiance of the sky and the blue dye of the sea shake in the wind as the sun descends and fluctuates in color-scale, intensity, and depth projection into a maze of interchanging hues. The throbbing of the clouds, the deep sources of light, soaked deep into the reflections on the water. An intensely patterned visionary sensation was inscaped giving form and composition with an authenticity evidenced by the strong harmony secured in their poetry. The forceful intensity of the godhead through the songs of nature in all its textures and sounds in a giddying blinding daze was counterpointed with their own personal dread of the labyrinth.

Mackay Brown fetches out his sensational vision in a series of inscapes throughout his literary writings. As he wrote in 1951,

> I like to watch the behavior of clouds. They interest me more than birds or flowers. Soon a great solid-seeming wedge of cloud split off from the main mass, and sped away northwards, driven by the trumpeting wind. Against the cliffs and fields of Sandwick a deluge would burst in fifteen minutes. Meanwhile the large cloud over Hoy reached up and swallowed the sun. I was looking at the wet Coolags when the shadow fell over Stromness town and parish. The effect was dramatic and frightening.—Yet over towards Orphir the hills lay in full sunshine, and the waters of Hoy Sound were of an indescribably beautiful blue.[4]

In December 1954 in his column "Island Diary", he wrote with great confidence as he seamlessly crafted the natural with the supernatural, the Greenfields Kirk with its intense pattern of the instressed inscapes in a drama of the sacred and the profane.

> We in Orkney, despite all the pleasant vagaries of our weather, have become used to fairly definite patterns. There is the good year when snow falls plentifully in January and February and blots out the islands with dazzling whiteness. The snow comes in a succession of dark storms—little hard pellets thundering for a whole day on the frozen earth; then, a few mysterious days, when the air is a three-dimensional curtain of undulating snowflakes; then about three weeks of flawless weather under a blue breathless sky, the earth brighter than in summer, sea, and loch a harsh purple. In such winters, the people are transformed. And with their bright glittering eyes and fine complexions seem to be taking part in some delightful but slightly unreal pantomime. These winters of pure deep snow are usually followed by equally marvelous summers. The year 1947 was a classic in this respect. And I cannot forget the lovely swarming colors of the world after the long snow of the year had melted. The earth was like a butterfly of rare stained-glass breed breaking from its chrysalis. I had never seen the grass so green, or the daisies so pink, or the slates on the road had a fine brave tint, after the whiteness so virginal and delicate to begin with, so shroud-like towards the end—had melted away.[5]

---

4 Mackay Brown, "A Sky-Scape in March" (1951), in *Northern Lights: A Poet's Sources*, 97.
5 Mackay Brown, "The End of a Sinister Year" in "Island Diary," *The Orkney Herald*. December 28th, 1954, 5.

Yet there was another Orkney climate classic when the more sinister labyrinth pattern of greyness took hold. All the seasons melted into one "common wash of greyness" with alternating days of dark, wet, and dry. "The spirit wilts and grows sick with the sheer monotony of it." Mackay Brown's mirror-image of the natural world ebbed and flowed in cycles or inscapes of weather and in 1954, "The post Hogmanay winter was a skinflint, and doled out snowflakes as if they were sixpenny pieces. The spring was a poor, spineless half-awake thing. The summer was melancholic to the point of insanity. Autumn was still-born. And the winter came in again early, with a malignancy the like of which I never remember."[6] Mackay Brown's moods ebbed and flowed, but, like Hopkins, he could not live with aimless drift. They both exerted control in word form, shape, and pattern as the consistency of design led them towards enlightenment. Their literary composition is the teleological argument[7] in the trajectory of the arrow that aims and hits its target. Hopkins gave it shape and form in the innovative inscape able to penetrate intelligent design in all a thing's particularity by word and metric. This was the re-launch of the old firmament that can re-engage the post Reformation world in all its historical and cultural phases.

"A VIVID APPREHENSION OF CHRIST'S PRESENCE IN THE UNIVERSE."[8]

The new way of looking at things through processing the full range of sensations experienced at first-hand led to the ciphered world of the Greenfields Kirk through the inscape of Christ. This was not a symbol or figure of Christ. It was Christ in the

---

6 Ibid.
7 The teleological argument for the existence of God, commonly known as the "argument from design" originated from the Fifth Way of St. Thomas Aquinas, and was developed through history. "The fifth way is taken from the governance of the world. We see that things which lack knowledge, such as natural bodies, act for an end, and this is evident from their acting always, or nearly always, in the same way, to obtain the best result. Hence it is plain that they achieve their end, not fortuitously, but designedly. Now whatever lacks knowledge cannot move towards an end, unless it be directed by some being endowed with knowledge and intelligence as the arrow is directed by the archer. Therefore, some intelligent being exists by whom all natural things are directed to their end; and this being we call God." *St Thomas Aquinas, Summa Theologica: Article 3, Question 2.*
8 Mackay Brown, *Two Landscape Poems, a 10pp manuscript essay signed George M Brown 1964, each leaf 25.5 × 20cm. NLS.*

mind of Hopkins and Mackay Brown. Dappled through Mackay Brown's writing, the "vivid apprehension of Christ" is inscaped in strategic linguistic placements, for example, with "a thousand candles of gorse"[9] seamlessly interchanging between stars and altar candles. "Over the carnival hill the stars trooped out"[10] as time turns towards the ploughman turning the pages of the "liturgy of spring,"[11] furrow by furrow. In the new organic way of looking at things, Mackay Brown gave thoughtful witness to Hopkins's poem, "That Nature is a Heraclitean Fire and the Comfort of the Resurrection," with clouds performing as "Heaven-roisterers etc—they are a crowd of carnival folk; they are soldiers with shining weapons, going on in order."[12] Mackay Brown exerted order, but in a way that is never an artificial constriction to the reality that "clouds are down, soft, and fleecy, some with the appearance of rough hearts some smooth as whitewash. Against this immaculate changing skyscape the elms perform their lovely ritual."[13] True to Hopkins's ciphered empiricism, Mackay Brown writes,

> But neither is the elm as elm—it is the gristle and iris and lashes of an eye forever opening and thinking regularity. The inrushing torrents of light. So far, we have the impression of a windy summer day. The poet perhaps is lying on his back looking up at the sky through the disturbed branches of an elm. The lines that follow confirm this idea. There has been a storm that has thrown the world into confusion, a storm with plenty of rain in it that has filled the ruts with pools.[14]

Mackay Brown knew Hopkins's inscape of the ritualistic fire, where the elm tree becomes the body part of the resurrected Christ. The elm's "gristle" leaves are Christ's eyelashes shielding his iris as it controls pupil size and the amount of light getting into the eye.

Later in the poem "The Abbot"[15] he is just as precise: "This is a day of sheaves at Innertun / And five crisp circles." The number

---

9 Mackay Brown, "The Storm" in *The Collected Poems of George Mackay Brown*, 3.
10 Mackay Brown, "The Night in Troy," 16.   11 Ibid.
12 Mackay Brown, *Notebook Two notes on Hopkins's "That Nature Is a Heraclitean Fire and the Comfort of the Resurrection,"* NLS.
13 Ibid.   14 Ibid.
15 Mackay Brown, "The Abbot," in *The Collected Poems of George Mackay Brown*, 42-44.

"five" immediately freights with the inscape of the five wounds of Christ. Then, in a steady building of light and sound, "A yellow wind walks on the hill. / The small boats in the sound / Pluck this brightness and that from the nets" is squared with the Crucifixion and the Easter liturgy, "Our cow watched a black field in March." / "And deepening greens, all summer,"... / "Today she cries over a sudden radiance, / The clean death of corn." And there is "Christ, crofter, lay kindly on this white beard / Thy sickle, flail, millstone, fires.... / they shout across the broken gold. / The boy has found a lark's nest in the oats." For Mackay Brown, the Greenfields Kirk holds in its heart the Lord Christ configured in his Passion and Resurrection in the natural configuration of the seasons. The swarm of symbols seamlessly inscaped bear the Christ instress as Mackay Brown harks back to pre-Reformation Orkney when the lark was called Our Lady's Hen.[16] "Popish dregs"[17] rose again in Orkney in the inscape of the "lark's nest in the oats." Christ is nested in the Greenfields Kirk through Our Lady, the Virgin Mary. Hopkins's Heraclitean fire was the natural world of the Greenfields Kirk in all its glory, and it is the reality for these poets that the Resurrection is everywhere to be found if one has an eye for it.

This was the Mackay Brown journey in its quest to sharpen and reinvigorate linguistics with word-codes and idea-images deeply connected or instressed with their origins: recording types and patterns in nature, looking for striking, distinctive words that actually univocally are the ringing sounds of that natural world, as immediate to the senses as to the mind. Mackay Brown has been quoted as having "not the faintest idea what the word [inscape] meant"[18] and that "the Yanks have done all the scholarly and pedantic stuff... No room for another spade... it's best to leave the great dead where they are with the eternal light on their brows; not soil them with our vain breath from below."[19] Mackay Brown cultivated a social persona according to the precepts of his father and John Bunyan: "Whatever happens keep humble... Never get above yourselves."[20] Mackay Brown's self-deprecation hid the truth of his knowledge and

---

16 Brand, *Brand's Description of Orkney*, 760–64. 17 Ibid.
18 Fergusson, *George Mackay Brown: The Life*, 174.
19 Ibid. 20 Ibid., 32–33.

understanding of inscape. He lived and breathed inscape and had read deeply and widely around the subject focusing on key texts. Although his postgraduate *Essays and Notes* are marked more by his journalistic style than the analytical "spade," his distinctive poet's mind was intently at work showing his favorite ideas and developing them throughout his own poetry in accordance with the writings of Hopkins. The *Essays and Notes* are important because they evidence the convergence between the poets as passion partners, whose distinctive piety held a consistent vision of their difference-in-unity and unity-in-difference, centered on Christ as the primary form, the primary inscape wherein all else flowed and was sustained.

Hopkins was shaped by a consistent vision described by Alan Heuser[21] in terms of scales of light and sound as the senses processed the flooding flux of the natural world. Hopkins had "a vision of creation, from its beginnings in Pre-Raphaelite sensationalism and Greek philosophy, through its modifications and applications, psychological, poetic, moral, theological, to its final stage of discovery."[22] Hopkins's artistic sense was brought to maturity through his Ignatian and Scotist formation. So, what did this vision look like to Mackay Brown? How did he understand Hopkins? What evidence was there of his influence? How did inscape and instress manifest themselves in Hopkins and Mackay Brown poems? To what degree did they give form and shape to spiritual realities in spiritual or secular terms that did not overwhelm or undermine their artistry? Mackay Brown, already transfigured[23] by his personal struggles through the 1940s, was fully aware of the intertwining of the sacred and the profane, allowing it to flush his writing with an illumination that he came to identify as grace.

So far we have seen a range of examples in the poetry of Hopkins and Mackay Brown that demonstrate an outflow of influence in the liberation of their wordplay in poetical language. Hopkins articulates and justifies the deeply rooted connection by stretching experimentally, going deep into the past whilst he carries marks of development from the Victorian age. Hopkins

---

21 Heuser, *The Shaping Vision of Gerard Manley Hopkins*, 6.
22 Ibid.
23 See the unpublished poem "Summer Day" in *George Mackay Brown: No Separation*, 43–44.

opened the floodgates towards the narrow path of sight that thrive in the particularity of things without separation from the instress of their Creator God. Hopkins and Mackay Brown aspire to collaborate with the artists who belong to an "age of faith" where work "sprang from a religious root, a vivid apprehension of Christ's presence in the universe."[24] Hopkins showed and proved to Mackay Brown that, although this age of faith went against the times they were living through, they could express themselves in a renewed age of faith by the exertion of a seminal linguistic influence that carries that faith within it through the ciphered world of the inscape and the instress.

Mackay Brown's definitions of inscape are well documented and cited throughout his *Essays and Notes* on Hopkins. For example, when he writes that Hopkins "sensed the uniqueness of Oxford, its inscape, how it differed from all other cities everywhere"[25] he demonstrates that he saw location as uniquely one and whole, holding within this uniqueness the difference-in-unity and the unity-in-difference. This is the katalogical perspective made manifest as he pushed the boundaries of poetic conventions beyond the analogical serialization to write as truthfully of the natural world as he could using empiricism as Hopkins had done. Univocally, he expressed his grasp and experience of language as, "this rhythm, this dance, is part of the inscape of the man, that is, it is a part of the living landscape within, his soul's scenery."[26] Mackay Brown endorses univocity at every turn in these *Essays and Notes*. "Hopkins saw everywhere distinctiveness, inscape, separateness, a splendor of individual forms and essences and souls, and this vision comes out of his loneliness."[27] He understood Hopkins's vision because he had one of his own that also made demands upon him to truthfully actualize his own vivid apprehensions. There is a remarkable convergence between Mackay Brown and Hopkins because they both "wanted at one and the same time to inscape the actual

---

24 Mackay Brown, *Two Landscape Poems*, a 10pp manuscript essay signed George M Brown 1964, each leaf 25.5 × 20cm. NLS.
25 Ibid.
26 Mackay Brown, *Hopkins and His Metric* a 12pp manuscript essay signed George M Brown 1964, each leaf 25.5 × 20.5cm. NLS.
27 Mackay Brown, *Gerard Manley Hopkins and His Public*, 12 manuscript pp on 4 leaves each 33 × 20.5cm signed George M Brown November 1963. NLS.

Fetching Out Inscape and Instress

vivid flight of the bird."[28] To infuse their poetic craft with their own vivid apprehensions meant more than describing, comparing, or visually reproducing images. They both wanted to achieve the integrity and reality of the inscape, the intelligent design instressed by their Creator.

Mackay Brown shows his grasp of the inscape when he writes:

> John Pick on this poem speaks of the inscapes of the sky, but this seems to me to show a lack of knowledge of what inscape is. Inscape is, in part, a thing is the way it is and cannot possibly be other—why a reed, say, is green and skinny and thickish and tough and ridged and sword-shaped and stands stiffly among other reeds and grows near water—'that unified complex of characteristics which constitute the outer reflection of the inner nature of a thing' (W. A. M. Peters, SJ), and not only so, but why every individual reed is unique and different from all other reeds though it belongs to the same species. Also, it can be observed from first growth to decay, and so it presents a sequence of inscapes, all equally interesting and beautiful. As the poet says in his notebook 'if the behavior [of a plant] could be gathered up and so stalled it would have a beauty of all the higher degree.'[29]

Mackay Brown balanced in his own mind and experience the intelligent design of the inscape and its serial sequence, but, by underlining Hopkins's own words "so stalled," he demonstrates his appreciation of the dynamic flow of life and growth that could be controlled within his own perceptions and apprehended to be expressed in poetic text that reached a higher degree of beauty. This is the artistry of infusing text with the majesty and sweetness of Christ, once perceived and apprehended, and using words to re-present Christ univocally. This is the craft of Hopkins and Mackay Brown.

Again, and again, Mackay Brown whilst irritated by Pick's interpretation, pushes the literary conventions in his own mind to go beyond analogical language where things that are known are used through comparison to explain or give an insight into what is not known:

---

28 Mackay Brown, *The Windhover* 11 MS pp on 6 leaves each 33 × 20.5cm signed George M Brown March 1964 in another ink. NLS.
29 Mackay Brown, *Two Night Poems and manuscript pp* on 4 leaves each 33 × 20.5 in blue and black ink, signed George M Brown 1963. NLS.

> The series of joyous exclamations in the octet of "The Starlight Night" are not inscapes at all. They are old-fashioned similes with all the 'likes' and 'as's' swept away in a rush of joy; and some of the similes, if you think about them for a moment, are not too convincing... And who has ever heard of fire-folk, diamond delves (mines)? But it is not as Pick claims, an inscape; it is a simile (and here I can't judge, for I have never seen white beam or abeles) the farmyard line is the only striking simile in the octet. Why it is specially important will appear later.[30]

As was Hopkins, Mackay Brown was pushed towards univocity to express the realism of how things actually are. They both were in awe of the beauty they experienced in the natural world, but equally they were in awe of their inner world: "Inscape—the landscape within, soul's scenery—'O the mind, mind has mountains, cliffs of fall sheer, no man-fathomed.'"[31] The depression that they both knew intensely drew them into the Passion of Christ wherein the "Inscape is the inner form...the ontological secret behind a thing."[32] Their depression, their experience of the dark forces, is also inscaped in their "soul scenery." They understood the electrifying radiance of Christ-birds that were inscaped into their selves and the world of nature. Mackay Brown called "As Kingfishers Catch Fire" "The great inscape poem"[33] wherein being "created in the image of God" is personal and particular with its patterns and shapes apprehended by the poets as they too become channels of Christ's Passion in the radiance of their verse. Mackay Brown understands the uniqueness, the difference-in-unity, the unity-in-difference, in nature and the human person, when he writes: "As Father Hopkins, the poet must have met in church and home thousands of labourer's and navvies like Tom, but each with his own quirk, mole, flourish, inscape, flavor 'more distinctive than ale or walnut leaf.'"[34]

Mackay Brown records in his autobiography[35] what he called his "dalliance" with Hopkins:

> Inscape? It is somehow related to 'landscape.' It is the 'scape' inside a man. The sweep and range and mind

---

30 Ibid.
31 Mackay Brown, *Notebook One notes on Dark Sonnet 42*, NLS.
32 Ibid.   33 Ibid.   34 Ibid., notes on "Tom's Garland."
35 Mackay Brown, *For the Islands I Sing*, 157.

and spirit, the diversity and abundance and flow and fall and aspiring that, seemingly so various, are yet a unity. But the inner scape does not exist by and for itself; it is balanced, held in a sweet tension and harmony by the lovely world outside, the 'scape' that is always changing as the man moves here and there in space and time, himself a center of infinite horizons, always questing, never satisfied.[36]

He described his sketches for the postgraduate essays in the following terms: "I was much happier fixing on some idea or image and writing cursive sentences and paragraphs and rounding it out to some kind of conclusion."[37] Here again and as always, Mackay Brown plays down his intellectual grasp of ideas. He understood and knew exactly what Hopkins had elucidated in the new lines of the old firmament, but it was not his quest to express himself in precisely articulated conceptualizations to prove it.

Mackay Brown wrote about the senses because he had a sensational vision. He was aware that "The senses are not suppressed they are directed."[38] Furthermore, he experienced the "Senses tongued like angels proclaiming the glory of God."[39] Like Hopkins, Mackay Brown understood the threefold nature of the senses: as the sensed object that sends out a sensation that is received by a sense organ. An Orkney poetics had already instilled in him the probing aesthetics drawn from the wild beauty of those islands where air, water, and land assumed scales of light and sound able to be refracted prismatically in the following way "the man moves here and there in space and time, himself a center of infinite horizons, always questing, never satisfied."[40] Mackay Brown was aware that beauty is a series of relations that take an absolute form in an ideal type. Its reflection takes up an appearance in a concrete world. These reflections are the many particulars of the One universal being. Hopkins restates his Platonic[41] theory of the naturalistic ideal disentangling himself from materialism. Mackay Brown follows the same path in his own pursuit of beauty.

---

36 Ibid. 37 Ibid. 38 Mackay Brown, *Notebook One, NLS*.
39 Ibid. 40 Mackay Brown, *For the Islands I Sing*, 157.
41 Mackay Brown had a copy in his personal library of Plato, *The Symposium*, trans. W. A. Hamilton. Harmondsworth: Penguin, 1951. Paperback. GMB signature. See Peterson, GMB Personal Library.

Through the artistic sense, Hopkins established a series of fixed points in his discovery of inscape and instress with his strong focus on the world of nature and the human person. Mackay Brown had forged for himself a similar pattern through his "half-baked stuff"[42] of the 1940s and then moving through his own stages of development. First the experiences of personal vulnerability were refined within family, kirk, and schooling. Then came the blossoming of his love for literature, which, accompanied by a consciousness of "fate" as a gifted storyteller, took on an Orcadian trajectory. The journey through two world wars and the various cultural developments that thrived in post-war Britain and Europe had quickly disseminated throughout the traditional way of life in the islands to point him in a specific direction that ran counter to conventional expectations. As Mackay Brown had written in 1947, "These wonderful lines from TS Eliot 'The Family Reunion.' In a world of fugitives, the person taking the opposite direction will appear to run away...we are all running away from God, the whole world, like a stampeding herd. Those who turn back to seek the beauty and the terror 'will appear to run away,'...which is just the accusation made in the world against mystics, monks, poets."[43]

What started as an organic Greenfields Kirk was quickly inscaped with what appeared at first surrealistic perceptions and distortions of human life. Mackay Brown's series of inscapes were stressed by the forces winding through creation with their evidence of life and the impulses behind them. These stresses intensified a certain set of emotions and experiences of will, which then became instressed. While the one-shape of the inscape took stem-form, it was the instress that shaped the force and stemmed feeling. What Hopkins crafted as a "string of being" in the interplay of the inscape and instress, Mackay Brown crafts as tapestry where knowing and feeling integrate in their illuminated text: from coined words to an aesthetic vision and on to a metaphysics that will hold. This was the Hopkins journey of sprung rhythm to its super-naturalization in new lines for a poetical language that to Mackay Brown, "suggests a certain exhaustion of language"[44] in the then prevailing linguistic usage.

---

42 MacInnes, "Finding a Voice in the Forties," *New Shetlander*, 30–33, 36.
43 Mackay Brown, *March 1947 Commonplace Book*, NLS.
44 Mackay Brown, Notebook Two "*That Nature Is a Heraclitean Fire and the Comfort of the Resurrection*," NLS.

He also knew his place and the problems of accommodating his vision to an audience. "For Mackay Brown's non-Catholic readers, the willing suspension of disbelief is becoming increasingly difficult, however high one's admiration of his humanity and his technical skill."[45] Mackay Brown knew about the problems the audience had with his writing, and he held the tension in balance as a honing feature of his craft. I would go as far as to say that even his Catholic readers can be rightfully challenged as they overlay their own perceptions and practices of Catholicism on his writing, seeing some sort of endorsement and triumph that is a source of validation for them. The intellectual and spiritual richness of both Hopkins and Mackay Brown also generously bowed to the empirical gathering of evidence. It never forced assent. It was not their intention to do so. As Mackay Brown confesses, "Yet GMH's poetry must be judged for its artistic value, not for its religious value."[46] Mackay Brown equally claimed artistic value as the measure of his own work.

For Mackay Brown, to reach beyond the Parnassian heights in poetry was a spur to a technical mastery super-naturalized by a simultaneous emergence of vision. The patterns of this vision were already in evidence in his work, as we have seen, before Edinburgh. Hopkins had written in his diary in April 1864

> Poetry at Oxford. It is a happy thing there is no royal road to poetry. The world should know by this time that one cannot reach Parnassus except by flying thither. Yet from time to time more men go up and either perish in its gullies fluttering excelsior flags or else come down again with full folios and blank countenances. Yet the old fallacy keeps its ground. Every age has its false alarms.[47]

Mackay Brown was ambitious and competitive in the manner of Hopkins before him, and he certainly would have appreciated Hopkins's humor. Mackay Brown's ability to fix on some idea or image made him happy. It worked for him to walk his narrow path along the lines Hopkins had marked out, giving the seamless patterns of what he would identify as a work of tapestry.

---

45 Scott, "Scottish Poetry in the Seventies," 109.
46 Mackay Brown, *Notebook One, NLS*.
47 Mackay Brown, *Gerard Manley Hopkins and His Public, cited in 12 manuscript pp on 4 leaves each 33 × 20.5cm signed George M Brown November 1963. NLS*.

An Orkney poetics is the gathering of lines and curves as visible unitive signs giving witness to the wild beauty of Orkney. The halo of the Northern Lights manifests themselves in the vitality of creation with their rays and beams and arcs of rainbows. Shafts and stems of wood and stone weave in the patterns of plants, trees, and pillared rock formations. The waves and ribs of air and water are captured in the swirling ferment of currents and tides that play host to the islands. The clouds throng the skies. These curves radiate from a single root. Hopkins the artist crafted the particular lines and curves as organic wholes in a linguistic shaping he learnt from drawing and sketching the unitive life of objects in all their dimensions, relations, position of parts in a whole and perspective. Mackay Brown was able to identify this power of sight in his own perceptions, and it was his gift to draw and sketch with words that cannot be blocked or suppressed or separated from their source and origins. He opened the shutters and out flowed an Orkney poetics that adhered closely to the Hopkinsesque craft suffused in the natural world whilst seamlessly giving sight to a higher reality. For an audience seeking a rich visual and aural experience, it was immensely satisfying. To go further—to embrace the intellectual and spiritual formulations that underpin the wordplay—took the artistic sense from the religious root to new heights of literary adventure.

As an Orkney poetics bore the evidence of its many-varied inscapes, the force and pressure strained into life informing the shapes of its creatures. Its distinctive curvature winds through creation with the very impulse of life behind it. A flash of intuition works through the threefold action of the senses. Sequentially, the whole shape of creation in little or one type of it, in a detail, in a creature, emerged into consciousness (knowing and feeling) fixed in a string of being. The stem-shape point of energy gathered inwardly infusing a particular object with a particular subject in a simple moment of emotion (fervor) or will (choice). Both inscape and instress were fore-drawn to a point of unity of being in a prior idea and both have a common root. The cognition of the inscape was seamlessly and simultaneously unified with the instress or felt pressure. It was here that Hopkins discovered that a natural sensation was ready to receive supernatural understanding and an intellectual formulation. As Mackay Brown had quoted from

Maritain, inscape is the "the principle determining the peculiar perfection of everything which is, constituting and completing things in their essence and their qualities; the ontological secret, so to speak of their innermost being."[48] And again, the inscape is the "inner form... ontological secret behind a thing."[49]

The few key quotes Mackay Brown chose to record of Maritain demonstrate the processes in Mackay Brown's mind searching for the unity behind existence, while at the same time realizing how difference is part and parcel of that unity. But it was Hopkins, and not Maritain, that Mackay Brown was absorbed in. It was Hopkins's mind that he converged with finding within it an experience of Catholic spirituality that was univocal rather than analogical. Other Catholic literary elites may have found validation in Maritain, but that was not for Mackay Brown. His poetic and pre-theologic intuitions, like Hopkins, pushed him onto a literary path that shaped a craft absorbed in empirical realities rather than the abstract unity of the ontological secret as the existential answer to everything. The practical day-to-day realities of being a wordsmith required of him to take his faith journey in the direction of the Jesuit poet and priest Hopkins whose radical experience of Christ as the source of all inscapes was for Mackay Brown "a vivid apprehension of Christ's presence in the universe."[50] This was something Mackay Brown could rejoice in, and the *Essays and Notes* are convincing in this validation.

EPISTEMOLOGY: A THEORY OF KNOWLEDGE HOLDING FAST TO THE ROOTS OF LANGUAGE

It is important to follow Mackay Brown's poetic craft in terms of Hopkins's theological and philosophical ideas and how they flow into Balthasar's theological project in the twentieth century with its understanding of the pre-theological status of literature. Balthasar took the view that after Aquinas theology had become commentary rather than an expression of the glory of revelation.[51] The convergence between Mackay Brown and Hopkins is

---

48 Mackay Brown, *Notebook Three*, NLS, quoting the neo-Thomist philosophy of Jacques Maritain, *Art and Scholasticism with Other Essays*, 20.
49 Ibid.
50 Mackay Brown, *Two Landscape Poems*, a *10pp manuscript essay signed George M Brown 1964, each leaf 25.5 × 20cm. NLS.*
51 Gray, *George Mackay Brown: No Separation*. See Chapter One, "Pre-Theologics."

Catholic and epistemic. The emergence of inscape and instress from Hopkins's deeply contextualized philosophy was not re-articulated by Mackay Brown; he had already made it work for him prior to coming to the Edinburgh studies. Mackay Brown held a natural allegiance to Hopkins's re-invigorated firmament and the twentieth century ethos of the Balthasarian project to reconnect with God as Primary Form. Mackay Brown the poet worked directly within his sources. He had been challenged to do so by his experience and perceptions of Orkney.

What may to some appear to be a light touch approach in his *Essays and Notes* to academic study and literary analysis was, in fact, his "method" of going to the essence of "things." His *Essays and Notes* defies the art of commentary and literary analysis. The essays have a pattern of their own that blends into his published and unpublished writings. This Mackay Brown pattern exhibited itself very distinctively because he had a central vision and experience of God that animated his thought and language to the degree that he was constantly in "back to the sources" mode, first within Orkney, then with the ethos of the Oxford Movement through Newman, and then with the specific craft of the word-smith Hopkins. So, word derivation was the place to start. It mattered to Mackay Brown that the classical scholar Hopkins elevated the Latin scapus and Greek skapos drawing towards the *scape* as bridge and stem of stress. Scape was the shaft of a column of a balance/flower stalk, stem. Then came the inclusivity of the Old English derivation sceap/shape/scape giving a universality in that inscape can cover forms anywhere and everywhere.[52] The Old English shape throws up the meaning of creation, creature/make, structure/decree, destiny. Mackay Brown made this pursuit of word derivation his own, and his poetic craft thrived as it followed the Hopkins trajectory. The words used and how and where he used them become strategic as he pushes the boundaries for him to be as exact as one could to match the integrity of the inscapes.

Heuser was clear that "it is not unlikely that Hopkins's double word meant 'created form held fast by evidence of creative power. The concrete emblem of a fixed type in the scale of nature, bearing within it a sign of the Creator (a string of creation; later, in

---

52 Heuser, *The Shaping Vision of Gerard Manley Hopkins*, 25.

the 1880s, a thread of destiny).'"⁵³ And it is likely that Mackay Brown, too, was at one with Heuser's compact definition knowing his fascination with word games and derivations is very much part of his "back to sources" modus operandi. This compact approach that keyed in the Greek to Latin to Old English is the impetus of Hopkins's Platonic realism, a new reinvigorated realism ready to encompass a powerful expression of the empirical gatherings from the natural world to give metaphysical and supernatural insights into the Creator God. As Hopkins held to the roots of language, so did Mackay Brown.

According to Hopkins, instress "feels deep," the inscape that holds fast in a fixed position and shape. Instress is the force or pressure that bridges the gap downward towards unity of being in feeling and as immersed as the senses are in the particularities the instress holistically presses towards the direct experience of the universal, in unity and oneness. It is here the term "bridge," "stem of stress," "the prepossession of feeling" come into play in the articulation of the presence of the Creator God. Hopkins made good the "leading lines of form" and the "flush in composition." These are the new lines of the old firmament re-integrating the breach created at the Reformation. Mackay Brown made sense of his own "feels deep" that is the instress; and through this emotionally charged energy he could see the process of weaving the seamless tapestry that is the seamless garment of his writing in its entirety.

Through the labyrinthine flux, Hopkins identified a series of relations never static, always vibrant with energy. The literature rightly gives much attention to Hopkins's use of classical sources and the Victorians Pater, Ruskin, and Pre-Raphaelites but it is also significant to be aware of Newman's *Essay in Aid of a Grammar of Assent* (Hopkins wanted to write a commentary, but the offer was declined by Newman). Whatever sources Hopkins and Mackay Brown were shaped by in their voyage of discovery, at its core was the thinking spirituality that circulated within the Oxford Movement. Reconnecting with a pre-Reformation ethos was alongside the developments in science and emerging psychological perspectives on the personal nature of the human person and their interactions with the environment.

---

53 Ibid.

It is important to trace all the lucid threads between Hopkins and Mackay Brown to keep pulling together some sort of epistemic edifice out of what may appear to be a confusing mix of fragmentary aspects. The evidence for a co-inherency between them stands in the rawness of their pre-theologic materials where both poets found a new field of play as they pushed the boundaries of their metaphysical range to give expression of their knowledge of the created world. As Hopkins writes, "that is Christ playing at me and me playing at Christ only that it is no play but truth; that is Christ being me and me being Christ."[54] The "play" of the poet was in Christ as Truth, Beauty, and Grace with its seraphic form of the Cross. The complementarity between man and woman is that between Christ and the Virgin Mary. Hopkins's language was unashamedly a theological phenomenon and Mackay Brown followed with his own distinctive poetic vision that he wove as a miniature of life itself. This is the power of their poetry.

It is also important to note the influence of the thinking of Newman on both poets. His study of the processes of the ratio, the rational self, documents his observations of the flow of sense materials through reason and emotions in unison. He separated "real apprehension" from "notional apprehension," even though he recognized the prior role of perception as "the informations of sense and sensation are the initial basis of both of them."[55] Newman's project in the *Grammar* is to investigate the potentiality or capacity of the human person to possess or be possessed by the image of God. He discusses language, reflects on a theistic concept of God, provides evidence to support theistic belief, explores whether traditional theistic belief could be reconciled and supported by scientific investigation of nature, explores the distinctiveness of the Christian style of life that springs from doctrine, and operates with a forward-looking perspective that actively searches for new directions and insights. The blend of curious philosophical minds from Newman to Hopkins to Mackay Brown is also expressed in literature and specifically poetical language and composition.

---

54 Hopkins, *The Sermons and Devotional Writings of Gerard Manley Hopkins*, 154.
55 Newman, *An Essay in Aid of a Grammar of Assent*, 29.

Newman's systematic method is enormously appealing to the poets not only in intellectual terms but also for its emotional richness. Epistemically, it puts faith and reason on a renewed footing with an understanding of the emotional life in all its moods, hues, and shades.

Hopkins brought the distinctive Jesuit Ignatian spiritual discipline to his understanding of Newman's thinking that accentuated in him the inscape as intelligible form or "notional apprehension" and the intensely felt instress as the "real apprehension." The great pathos of the Passion of Christ penetrated the souls of Hopkins and Mackay Brown as they navigated their own personal moods, their consolations, and desolations. Training the senses and directing them into their craft made both these poets very conscious of their own inner workings. Hopkins found concrete form in inscape, the notional apprehension of sense information. But why stop there when he had a ready theory for those inner workings of the mind closely quartered to the emotional life represented in the Greek concept of the psyche? Those inner feelings of undergoing sudden force and tension give instress. Suspension and relaxation give slack or collapse. Hopkins, through the Ignatian discipline of *The Spiritual Exercises*, filters through to the experience of Mackay Brown in his own personal life drama.

Reason accompanies the processes of coming to and the deepening of faith as it explores the borderline between the conscious and unconscious. The experience of an uncontrolled emotional release or the voluntary choices formed a stemmed trajectory of pressure, of strong cumulative impressions on the senses to the point where Hopkins identified mysterious feeling or unconscious cerebration that could call up a different sense, for example, humming a tune. This humming is something I (and others) witness with Mackay Brown. In many a conversation in his company at Mayburn Court, he would be given to humming, and it was immediately apparent to me that it came from a deep place as one explored various poetic themes and notions. The humming was thrown up and one was aware of psychic pressure of some sort. It soothed him. Mackay Brown had a well-established vision that worked according to his experiences of memory and dreams that flow between stress and slack, and feeling was clustered along those fibers. Hopkins had a vision as well, but he also speculated wherein Mackay Brown did not. Hopkins filtered the speculative character of his theories through to him. That was more in line with the directions of his energies already firmly instressed and inscaped in accordance with his rich perceptions of islands of Orkney.

Hopkins discovered in his reading of Scotus the confirmation of his own experience; and, in turn, this came as a revelation to Mackay Brown. For both, sensation is a spiritual sense linked to innate memory rising out of and falling back to unity of feeling in a quivering dialogue between the conscious and the unconscious of the deep realities of stored being—in the person and their community. Mackay Brown uses his writing to explore himself. This can be seen in the comparison of his "half-baked stuff" of the 1940s with the Edinburgh post graduate work. A particular fine-tuning and refinement takes place through the influence from Hopkins. Mackay Brown explored his inner life with its deep Orkney lore and memories. Both Hopkins and Mackay Brown put a strong trust in primitive levels of feeling, sensation, innate memory, and unconscious knowing. In fact, they committed their lives to these as "fibers of being." Through Hopkins's vision and speculation, Mackay Brown moved from a vague awareness of nature's created being to great confidence in the visionary sensation of his own perceptions, dreams, and memories as they manifested themselves in him. He was able to experience a validation of his own dramatic personal life in all its moods and hues and falling shorts. Increasingly, his experience of a common nature within the human person filtered through the thinking and feeling craft of Hopkins and brought him to a realization of the created nature of Christ. Mackay Brown did not live in a world of abstractions. He was deeply connected to a fixed type between natural form and essential idea (to use the language of Scotus). The one-shape he committed to was Christ in the inscape of St. Magnus. All the stemmed pressure of feeling he had accumulated over the years refined itself and gained momentum through his knowledge and experience of the Orcadian Earl Magnus.

Hopkins's vision of Christ was "particular" in that it took the form of the sequence of patterns he saw in the natural world. "The eyelid in the clouds, eyelash in ashsprays, lip in flowers, shoulder in mountains, limb and foot in glaciers, beard in waterfalls, taperlift face in snowdrifts."[56] Here was the manhood of Christ according to Hopkins. In his *Journal* Hopkins explicitly gives an exacting witness to Christ in all his created beauty and which drew from him praise and glory: "As we drove home the stars came out thick: I leant back to look at them and my heart opening more than usual praised our Lord to and in whom all that beauty comes home."[57] Epistemically, the lucid linguistic threads between Hopkins and Mackay Brown converge in their sources to become raw poetic materials extracted and absorbed from the substance and concrete form all around them in Creation. Their epistemic unity is seamlessly universal and particular, holding within itself linguistic unity-in-difference and difference-in-unity.

THE ONE-NESS OF GOD IN HIS BLUEBELLS, DAFFODILS, AND STARLIGHTS

The more that Hopkins's inscapes mixed the strength and sweetness of his poetic materials, the more he was drawn intuitionally to evidence of the Incarnation. It was this doctrine that radiated through the old firmament and Hopkins knew well its new lines of direction that re-integrated the fragmented reality of the post-Reformation legacy. He documented the mystery of the bluebell in its consummate particularities, tracking the inscape and giving way to the baffling of the senses in its rays of unusual light. The light from the bluebells "to float their deeper instress in upon the mind"[58] brings him to the Presence of Christ. The deeper the instress, the more evidence of God's incarnation. Hopkins articulated this evidence as an example of what he perceived as an accumulative stem of pressure. This is spiritual experience. This in turn leads the human person to the personal acknowledgment of Christ as an unforced act of will. Assent, then, is at the discretion of the beholder. Hopkins draws his readers or beholders into the inscaped bluebell that, as Heuser points out, is a "sort of altar light standing for the Real Presence": "I do not think I have ever seen anything more beautiful than the bluebell I have been looking at. I know the

---

56 Heuser, *The Shaping Vision of Gerard Manley Hopkins*, 38.
57 Hopkins. Journal (IV.205), cited in Heuser, *The Shaping Vision of Gerard Manley Hopkins*, 38.   58 Ibid. (IV.174), 39.

beauty of our Lord by it. Its [inscape] is mixed of strength and grace, like an ash tree. The head is strongly drawn over backwards and arched down like a cutwater drawing itself back from the line of the keel."[59]

Meanwhile, Mackay Brown in his collection *Loaves and Fishes* (1959) had documented the daffodil[60] as one and many. He examines it as a particular and as a universal, possessed of inscape and instress, truly fetched out. Like Hopkins, his sensational vision hones into the form, to the inscape, flushed with feeling. The special radiance of Orkney in its liturgy of Spring is those darling daffodil: "Heads skewered with grief," interchanging with "Three Marys at the cross" seamlessly on the quiver stemmed down to the bracketed "(Christ was wire and wax / Festooned on a dead tree)." The inscapes from "Head" to "Guardians of the rock," are instressed with "emerald tapers" that "touch" "The pale wick of the sun." It is all very tactile as Mackay Brown goes deep into the impending Passion of Christ, "the rose" that "Bleeds on the solstice stone" "the cornstalk" that "unloads" "Peace from hills of thorn." The Orkney tapestry is true to its nature and for Mackay Brown, like Hopkins, what at first is a radiant glimpse of Christ Himself becomes a traveling trajectory continuing its stem and expansion into "Spindrifting blossoms" and the long curling sea wave of the grey March "comber" that thunders on to the world shores then splashing "our rooms coldly...with First grace of light," stemming through time to the pulsating "throb" of the "corn-tides." The "fields" will "Drown in honey and fleeces" "Shawled in radiance" in their "Tissue of sun and snow." A trinity (the inscape of the tri-unity) of "Three bowl-bound daffodils.... In the Euclidian season.... When darkness equals light" are the Pythagorean theological mathematics at work to rein in the form of "the world's circle shudders.... Down to one bleeding point" at the foot of the Cross at Calvary where "Mary Mary Mary," daffodil by daffodil by daffodil, is a "Triangle of grief."

This lyrical poem is a seamless tapestry woven from the fibers of creation. These are the patterns of the instressed inscapes threaded with force and pressure straining into life. They inform

---

59 Ibid.
60 Mackay Brown, "Daffodils," in *The Collected Poems of George Mackay Brown*, 35–36.

the shapes of its creatures with the great pathos of the Passion of Christ in all its moods, hues, and shades. Inner feelings undergo sudden force and tension that gives instress. Then the suspension and relaxation slacken or collapse to rise again in the throbbing tides of creation. Innate memory rises out of and falls back to unity of feeling in a quivering dialogue between the conscious and the unconscious of the deep realities of stored being—in the person and their community. Mackay Brown was absorbed by evidence of creative power through the instress that sustained the created form or inscape of the daffodil. The concrete emblem of a fixed type, the daffodils in the scale of nature, bears within it a sign of the Creator (a string of creation, a thread of destiny) all held by the instress that "feels deep" the inscape that held fast in a fixed position and shape.

Mackay Brown enshrined the wild natural beauty of Orkney in a flow of interchanging imagery: from daffodil heads to the Marys at the foot of the Cross, from Calvary to the stringed and chained flowers, the Mary heads garlanded with the wire (bone) and wax (torn flesh) of the crucified body of Christ on the tree of His death. The force, the pressure, the beauty of imagery, sweeps in the particularities of the interchanging instressed-inscapes with emotional tension, a mix of grief and unmovable strength (women the guardians). Their grief rose towards the Light to fall in the passion of the violent death, the blood falling onto the altar. Mackay Brown gives an example here of an Orkney poetical form able to conflate the archaeological layers of the solstice stone of Maeshowe or the temple complex with their hint of violent death and sacrificial rites, with the later era of Christianity. The crucified Christ rises again as the golden cornstalk unloads the Resurrection in his poetic mind at work. Swathes of peace from the violence of thornèd scourges are harbored in the hills. From Orkney to Jerusalem, from Jerusalem to Orkney, the biblical trajectory inscapes and instresses the peaceful flow of the Orkney Islands with its corn-tide throb and fields, is woven in the waters of thundering grey combers and the drowning in honey and fleeces. The sights and sounds, the tactile presence of the Lord in his creation, is palpable and articulated in a consummate mastery. The sweep of the ages is a conflation of the Neolithic to the early christianization period and medieval pieties, through the Reformation period to the new lines of the old firmament, under the artistry and spirituality of Hopkins and Mackay Brown. Both poets partnered together in a passionate re-weaving and re-crafting of word play. Their religious experience manifested as a distinctive artistic vision within a secularist world that had grown intentionally deaf to the voice of the Spirit. This mastery of an epistemology was in place before the Hopkins studies in their various stages of the Edinburgh period.

Hopkins writes in his *Journal* Aug 17, 1874 that "As we drove home the stars came out thick: I leant back to look at them and my heart opening more than usual praised Our Lord to and in whom all that beauty comes home." Mackay Brown exercises a degree of adjudication in his Edinburgh essay, "The fruit of that opening of the heart is this sonnet 'The Starlight Night.' It seems to me that there is more beauty in the sound of the poem than in anything precise or clear-cut or original in the way of observation. It is difficult to describe starlight better than to say, as the journal does, 'the stars came out thick.'"[61] Mackay Brown was always highly independent and was not going to give way to Hopkins's craft lightly, but it is clear he had grasped the core of Hopkins from his own study of sense phenomena. He dallied with literary criticism:

> John Pick on this poem speaks of the inscapes of the sky, but this seems to me to show a lack of knowledge of what inscape is. Inscape is, in part, a thing is the way it is and cannot possibly be other—why a reed, say, is green and skinny and thickish and tough and ridged and sword-shaped and stands stiffly among other reeds and grows near water—'that unified complex of characteristics which constitute the outer reflection of the inner nature of a thing' (W. A. M. Peters, SJ), and not only so, but why every individual reed is unique and different from all other reeds though it belongs to the same species.[62]

But his focus does not stay with Pick or Peters. He was more interested in the sense phenomena itself and then what Hopkins himself recorded in his journals and crafted into his

---

61 Mackay Brown, *Two Night Poems and manuscript pp on 4 leaves each 33 × 20.5 in blue and black ink, signed George M Brown 1963.* NLS.
62 Ibid.

poems. Mackay Brown had already proved his poetic credentials (and he knew it) in his collections of published and unpublished writings prior to Edinburgh giving evidence of his expertise in inscape and instress. What was most influential was his discovery that he was not alone in his inner life and sensibilities. Learning to be strong in his own convictions against the various tides of misunderstandings and misinterpretations that he had contended with in Orkney needed strengthening and this was finalized in the Edinburgh phases of development that were personal as well as educational. He goes on to write, "Also it can be observed from first growth to decay, and so it presents a sequence of inscapes, all equally interesting and beautiful." As the poet says in his notebook "if the behavior [of a plant] could be gathered up and so stalled it would have a beauty of all the higher degree...."[63] He validates the concepts of inscape and instress and their dynamic nature with sequential flooding that flushes out the ever-emerging vision. Mackay Brown puts on show how to "stall" with its sense of slowing and stabilizing long enough to see the patterns to bring their proliferation to his Orkney tapestry. Hopkins steered him to give them life and substance as they tracked the new lines of the old firmament into verse and other genres.

Why did he quibble then with, "The series of joyous exclamations in the octet of *The Starlight Night* are not inscapes at all. They are old-fashioned similes with all the 'likes' and 'as's' swept away in a rush of joy; and some of the similes, if you think about them for a moment, are not too convincing."[64] "And who has ever heard of fire-folk, diamond delves (mines)?" "But it is not as Pick claims, an inscape; it is a simile...(and here I can't judge, for I have never seen white beam or abeles)...the farmyard line is the only striking simile in the octet...why it is specially important will appear later...."[65] Any ambiguities between what is a simile and what is an inscape in Mackay Brown's mind seems to have been based on his experience of the sense phenomena. If he had not experienced it directly, he reserved the right to question the existence of "fire-folk" or "diamond delves." Yet for all his misgivings about this poem, his own heart opened to the resolution in the last closing lines:

---

63 Ibid.   64 Ibid.   65 Ibid.

"these are indeed the barn; withindoors house." Here is a configuration of the interplay between inscape and instress that he had direct experience of in his interchanging perceptions of the Orkney farm buildings and his "withindoors" inner life. The alignment of barn/church is inscaped as primal form "stalled" from history, recognized, and identified, yet "on the quiver," in the stem of the instress that does not permit any static institutionalization. The purposeful barn is the "Christ home" invested with Christ, his "mother" (Mary) and "all his hallows" (the saints). This extract from the *Essays and Notes* is important, as it shows Mackay Brown moving from the literary conventions of analogical language and pushing his own boundaries into the univocity of the inscape.

In 1947, Mackay Brown crafted the unpublished poem "Summer Day" (that later re-emerged as "Hamnavoe") "One lyrical star Prologued night's pageantry."[66] Mackay Brown in the 1954 poetry collection *The Storm* "stalls the inscapes of stars" and their swing and sway: "In the Road Home":[67]

> A sower, all in tatters,
> Strode, scattering the seed, immense
> Against the sunset bars,
> And through his fingers, with the night,
> Streamed the silver stars.
> ...
> The northern lights
> Were streaming broad and high.
> The tinkers lit their glimmering fires...[68]

Here is the mastery of the seamless interchange between points of light in the dark as the poet uses his needle to draw its thread through the tapestry cloth. The Mackay Brown fabric and firmament swing and sway in their eucharistic liturgical song, not metaphorically but really. The sensational poetic vision continued into the poem "The Storm" with "And the thousand candles of gorse around my mother's yard."[69] The saturation of light in "The Fisherman" trembles and quivers in "a quiet scattering of stars."[70] In the 1959 collection, *Loaves and Fishes*, Mackay Brown continued the upswell of song in the poem "Childsong": "Stars

---

66 Cited in Gray, *George Mackay Brown: No Separation*, 43.
67 *The Collected Poems of George Mackay Brown*, 2.
68 Ibid., 2.   69 Ibid., 3.   70 Ibid., 10.

reap the blue / Swept corn of night. / Westward they surge, / their sickles bright."[71] The pulsating throb of the inscapes of light was and is a seamless interchange of their reality. The immediacy that Mackay Brown scopes out word by word, inscape by inscape is flushed together by the instress. The leitourgia rises and falls according to the sprung rhythm of the actuality passing through the mind and heart of Mackay Brown. The dialect[72] poem "Stars" from the same collection glows with its soundings of honeyed tones, "And light on an uncan star, / A tinker in space!... / when Venus shook her hair / Owre the Soond."[73] And of course the gospel star is never far away from the conflation from land to sky to sea "a herald o God!" In "The Lodging" "The Stones of the desert town / Flush; and, a star filled wave, / Night steeples down,"[74] where the warp and weave of the narrative is inseparable from its sights and sounds so immediately present to the poet and his audience. In the poem, "The Shining Ones," the vision is all-consuming: "But the night / was a funnel of darkness, roaring with stars"[75] as we are outfoxed by the mystery of the Creator God so present to his Creation. This sampling of poems derives from before the 1960s Edinburgh studies. The Mackay Brown poetic vision and its craft is so distinctive in its strength and vigor. Elementally, it can be traced across his writings from first to last, from origins to ends, as is the influence of Hopkins on his formation.

There is a distinctive poetic sensibility that surrounded both Mackay Brown and Hopkins, a common ground that became holy as it assimilated the phenomena of the natural world in all its variegated and particular forms, transfiguring it with a spiritual atmosphere. The great drama of Redemption was native to the culture within which Mackay Brown developed. He could not but be fashioned by its mass of ideas and images that streamed throughout Orkney across time and space. Early in his life this world was intelligible to him in a very specific

---

71 Ibid., 23.
72 Hopkins and Mackay Brown chose to write in an inclusive but not dialect form of language. Both Hopkins and Mackay Brown studied the poetry of William Barnes, a copy of which is in Mackay Brown's personal library. See Barnes, *One Hundred Poems*. Inscribed to GMB. See Peterson, GMB Personal Library.
73 *The Collected Poems of George Mackay Brown*, 25.
74 Ibid., 28.   75 Ibid., 33.

way through his surrender to the instressed Christendom of St. Magnus the Martyr. Like Hopkins, all his inscapes are Christ, formed as they were in the natural world we inhabit and in the human person. And also like Hopkins, he crafts linguistically the many that are One and the One that is the many, seamlessly instressed, showing difference-in-unity and unity-in-difference.

CHRISTBIRDS: SYMBOLIC SENSE OR THE REAL PRESENCE?

We have seen how the one inscape Hopkins and Mackay Brown were working with was not an abstraction. That inscape was Christ, the primary form, whose spiritual power filtered through the perceptions and intellect of Hopkins and Mackay Brown. They would go as far as to accommodate their craft to Christ precisely in the dense particularity of his Mystical Body across space and time. They were compelled to go beyond literary conventions of their respective times because of their knowledge of Christ through their perceptions and intellect. They took Christ straightforwardly over and above poetic metaphor and the range of analogical language. This is the Catholic tradition and its insistence that Christ should be taken straightforwardly. Hopkins's Christ poem, "The Windhover" is given a special attentiveness by Mackay Brown in his essay[76] where he writes, "He wanted at one and the same time to inscape the actual vivid flight of the bird, so that we should all recognize it as a windhover and not any other bird and also to make it a religious poem ad majorem Dei Gloria." Mackay Brown is not putting before us a tour de force in academic and literary criticism. He is however, taking care not to forget the things that his own eyes had seen in Orkney, and it was his method to "rely on one's own memories rather than an ornithologist."[77] His attentiveness to memory in the same essay shows his lifelong call to "teach them [memories] to your children and to your children's children."[78]

Mackay Brown argues that Hopkins "worked" the Christ bird, "in 2 stages, first by comparing the hawk on the wind to a horseman on a horse, understanding it, controlling it, dominating

---

[76] Mackay Brown, *The Windhover* 11 MS pp on 6 leaves each 33 × 20.5cm signed *George M Brown March 1964 in another ink.* NLS.
[77] Ibid.
[78] Mackay Brown brings to mind the scripture Dt 4:1, 5–9 and its call to parental duty.

it; and not just any horseman, but a princely medieval horseman, and it seems, a French one at that. Of course the French have always had the reputation of being great horsemen; several passages in Shakespeare speak of their skill in the art; and Hopkins wanted [the] overtone of superlative skill in his poem."[79] Hopkins's inscapes were a biological mimicry that was the closest external resemblance of an animal or plant (or part of one) to another animal, plant, or inanimate object. Mackay Brown had the realization that Hopkins's artistry was pushing towards linguistically being able to express the perfection of nature. The new level of realism in Hopkins's use of language stretched the linguistic boundaries to the point that Christ was the windhover and the windhover Christ, not figuratively but actually.

Mackay Brown followed Hopkins's reinvigorated trajectory that made "appeal to the medieval" that was "fashionable at the time Hopkins was writing...the time of Tennyson, Morris, Rossetti, and it enabled him to bring ideas of grace and chivalry and royalty...which prepare the mind for the final comparison with Christ as hero, the royal conqueror riding through the world in his armor, yet humble as the poorest peasant acclaiming him, as happened in Piers Plowman."[80] In love and humility, the bird Christ, the windhover, is Jesus, risen from the dead, present and alive in the Church, still seeking us out, coming into our line of vision, not waiting for us to crawl to him, but seeking us out in love and humility. To this effect, Mackay Brown dallied in some word-study: "'Dapple-drawn-falcon' dapple is H's favorite word." Mackay Brown identified the favorite words of other writers by way of comparison making the point that these favorite words were some sort of psychological signature: "Keats cloy," "Arnold moon-blanched," "DH Lawrence dark," "TS Eliot broken."[81]

As much as Mackay Brown admired the *"The Horseman... medieval horseman knight-at-arms"* as an "imaginary sketch, piece for a stained glass window" he saw "that the movements of the hawk and rider have indeed a remarkable similarity." But Mackay Brown relied on his own Orcadian experience and memories: "And while these horses and horsemen weave their

---

79 Mackay Brown, *The Windhover* 11 MS *pp on 6 leaves each 33 × 20.5cm signed George M Brown March 1964 in another ink.* NLS.
80 Ibid.   81 Ibid.

courtly ritual, humbler men are driving slow clumsy plough-horses over the fields in an action which looks like ritual, but which is primarily concerned, like the windhover, with getting food."[82] Mackay Brown was attentive to his close reading of Hopkins's "Sermon" with his "martial heir of heaven,"[83] but as he was always insistent to me personally in letters and conversation, he "always firmly denied he was a mystic and declared on the contrary that he was very earthbound." Nevertheless, he writes things that are pure mysticism, as in that letter of 2 September 1983, "one must be passive often, to let the swarming delights of the world in, and things beyond,"[84] Mackay Brown was never comfortable with having his inner being exposed in conversation. He reserved his inner being for his writing. His starting point was the real-life phenomena, but his curious mind, like that of Hopkins, followed through with integrity a line of vision that inevitably could not help being saturated seamlessly with things beyond. Mackay Brown, like Hopkins, perceived

> Christ was no mere historical figure, the redeemer of the world who was once on earth for a short time and is now in heaven until his final coming at the end of all things. To think of Christ in this way is to make him in a way even more remote than the piece of medieval heraldry we have just been considering. To appreciate the poem fully one must give at least some kind of imaginative consent to the doctrine of the Real Presence: Christ is actually and really present in the world every day, on the altar and in the tabernacle and in the bodies of communicants as they leave the church for their homes and fields and workshops. So that H writes 'I caught-minion' he means it literally.... Christ actually present in the physical sense as he was present at the stable in Bethlehem and at the wedding in Cana, on the Lake of Galilee in the storm and in Gethsemane and Golgotha.[85]

Mackay Brown returned to his Orcadian sources with the ploughman and his Liturgy of Spring, turning the pages furrow

---

82 Ibid.
83 Hopkins, "Christ Our Lord the Eternal Hero." Sermon Bedford Leigh Nov 23 1879, in Devlin, ed., *The Sermons and Devotional Writings of Gerard Manley Hopkins*.
84 Gray, *Circle of Light: The Catholic Church in Orkney Since 1560*, 98.
85 Mackay Brown, *The Windhover* 11 MS pp on 6 leaves each 33 × 20.5cm signed George M Brown March 1964 in another ink. NLS.

by furrow: "For most of us, any kind of perfection—physical, courtly, spiritual—is an ideal that can never be achieved. The hard clumsy toil of the ploughman is a symbol of all our strivings,... 'a sheer plod' far removed from the beauty of the bird's flight, the ritual of the joust, or the Incarnation. We turn dark seemingly profitless furrows; no fire of beauty or holiness breaks immediately from those broken 'blue-black-embers; yet out of the earth wounds rise in due course ripe.'"[86] The biblical "Fields of corn" were deep in Mackay Brown's formation as a person and as a poet:

> (We know that Christ used many parables and images and similitudes from agriculture—the sower, the fields white into harvest, the corn and the tares etc). Without that bread that is won by toil and sweat, beauty and valor would not exist; and a small part of that same bread will, on our altar, become Christ himself, the Bread of Heaven, the highest beauty, and the rarest chivalry. So Christ unites himself with our toil forever. So the work of humble people, far from being ugly or useless, is gathered into God's plan for the redemption of the world; and all trades give him glory.[87]

As Hopkins had written himself:

> It is not only prayer that gives God glory but work. Smiting on an anvil, sawing a beam, whitewashing a wall, driving horses, sweeping, scouring, everything gives God some glory if being in his grace you do it as your duty. To go to communion worthily gives God great glory, but to take food in thankfulness and temperance gives him glory too. To lift up the hands in prayer gives God glory, but a man with a dungfork in his hand, a woman with a slip pail, give him glory too. He is so great that all things give him glory if you mean they should. So then, my brethren, live.[88]

The oneness of Hopkins and St. Ignatius Loyola is also at one with Mackay Brown and the Muir fable,[89] with its firm founda-

---

86 Ibid. 87 Ibid.
88 Hopkins, "The Principal of Foundation. An address based on the opening of *The Spiritual Exercises* of St Ignatius Loyola," *Gerard Manley Hopkins: Poems and Prose*, 143–44.
89 Mackay Brown, "The Story of Scotland: Edwin Muir," 21 November, 1988. OLA, GMB Collection, 2. *Edwin Muir: An Autobiography*, 35.

tion from Muir's upbringing on the Orkney island of Wyre. As has been written more recently, Muir's childhood on Wyre is, "one of the richest descriptions of Orkney anywhere in literature."[90] Mackay Brown, standing in the literary canon alongside "Dante or Blake,"[91] with his particular development and progression through Muir and Hopkins truly gives testament to an Orkney poetics.

It is clear Mackay Brown's supervisor Winifred Maynard was not in tune with her student when she makes the comment "illuminating vs manufactured." Mackay Brown is enchanted by Hopkins and the swarm of symbols which effected in him a state of trance. Maynard interprets this as an artificial illumination. This experience of being tranced is the swarm of the inscape and instress in their stemming and stalling rhythms of life on the quiver. The illumination is the Mackay Brown signature, whereas the "manufactured" hints at a paucity of skill in the art of literary criticism. But Mackay Brown sensed and knew the "work" of the soul, that still point at the heart of every person, that deepest center, that point of encounter with the transcendent yet incarnate mystery of God. Hopkins and Mackay Brown both had a living relationship with God. For all the personal messiness of their lives, they recognized the flow of spiritual energy and their part in it. Their craft consisted in teaching people how to see, how to hear, how to walk their path, how to be free of themselves to discover God. Their writing confirms this as they plough the furrows giving meaning at the deepest center of the human person. Mackay Brown alerts his readers and critics across the time span of his literary project to the meaning of his craft. For example:

> I try often to suggest the swift dangerous rhythms of the sea, and (even more important) the slow dark fruitful rhythm of the earth from seedtime to harvest. (One of my books of verse is called *Loaves and Fishes* and a later one *Fishermen with Ploughs*.) The bread that is the result of the crofter's hard labour on the earth is a recurring symbol: meaning the simple nourishment of the body, and the mysterious sign of the godhead. The poem 'Stations of the Cross'—which has been set to music recently by Peter Maxwell Davies—is a key poem.[92]

90 Hall, *The History of Orkney Literature*, 71.   91 Ibid.
92 Mackay Brown, *The Orcadian Poet George Mackay Brown Reads His Poems and a Story*.

Fetching Out Inscape and Instress

In August 1951 Mackay Brown had written,

> And we saw a kestrel in the gathering darkness, cutting a superb graph of flight against hill and sky—the long downward glide on level wings, the sudden fluttering rise, the incredible hover, pivoted motionless in space—and then that downward glide again, till we lost him in the hollows. We had one more fine sight as were coming down by another route. Suddenly a yellow segment swam up, until the harvest moon appeared over the Orphir hills, and stood precariously balanced, like a large improbable orange, on the sheer crest. We turned the binoculars on it, and saw the peculiar map on its surface. Now it was clear, and the sky had a new splendor in addition to the few stars, the red west, the hovering kestrel.[93]

Intriguingly, Mackay Brown did not leave it there. He went on to affirm the church in a very distinctive shift of faith from the Greenfields Kirk towards the Eucharist: "We climbed down into the silent town, all four of us, and thought that, from the point of view of worship, it was almost as good as being in church."[94] Mackay Brown was consistent within an Orkney poetics and his various stages of development. The streaming underground sensibilities of Mackay Brown were now ready to appear fully in the light of a steady stream of publications.

Later in the 1971 poetry collection *Fishermen with Ploughs*, in contrast to Hopkins's "The Windhover," the illumined Mackay Brown inscribed with inscape and instress how to see the Kingdom of God, how to hear the voice of the Holy Spirit, how to keep walking the way of spiritual energy to be free of the self in the discovery of God, in his small poem "The Big Wind."[95] Hopkins in his poem "The Windhover" had instilled the force and majesty, the rise and fall, the hovering, in a dynamic quiver of verse, "the hurl and gliding / Rebuffed the big wind." By way of contrast, Mackay Brown captures the momentum of the big wind more domestically in his native tradition with "trundles our pail" a "clanging bell" sounding its way "through the four crofts." The big wind gives sight of the broken circles of waves and gulls as its force pushes and pulls in its sway. The big wind

---

[93] Mackay Brown, "Under Brinkies Brae," *Island Epiphanies* in *Northern Lights: A Poet's Sources*, 104. [94] Ibid.
[95] Mackay Brown, "The Big Wind," in The *Collected Poems*, 128.

"laid," "beat," and drove" and "whirled" and "set." The drifts of high hay, the stones of the dead, the grounding of boats, the petulant immodesty of petticoats and then the smooth unbroken all-embracing word-strokes of sound and sight blending the hen-house seamed with raging cockerels blown out on the crested sound. All the while, the scanning-hawk-eye of an all-powerful and all-seeing God: "The kestrel stood unmoving over the hill." The Orkney wind, the Orkney pail and clang, the Orkney crofts, the Orkney waves and gulls, the Orkney hay drifts, the Orkney stones of the dead, the Orkney boats, the Orkney petticoats, the Orkney hen-houses and cockerels, are a patch-worked tapestry over which the Christ-bird presides.

The question must be asked of Hopkins and Mackay Brown: what first got the attention of their audience? It was not what they said, but the way they said it. What did the audience notice? People were astonished at Hopkins's poetry; for he wrote it as one having literary, philosophical, and spiritual authority. "But the difficulty remains," for Mackay Brown,

> I for one, while admiring the achieve[ment] and mastery, do not experience that final peace and resolution which came out of the greatest poetry. There is a violence, a deliberate feeling of uncouthness and barbarity about 'The Windhover' that is, I think, meant to disturb cultured readers brought up on smooth combed meters of English verse. The poet himself was a bit scared; he speaks of 'his heart in hiding,' half appalled by what he has written—as a man at first light must be at once frightened and fascinated by the slow glide and savage plummet of the kestrel; as a priest must be awed every morning by the fact that Christ is in the circle of bread on the altar and that he is holding the creator of the universe in his hands.[96]

One senses here in "The Windhover" essay that Mackay Brown's experience of the natural world was one of an awed serenity rather than Hopkins's forceful savagery. Here Mackay Brown shows his native tradition with its distinctive Orkney poetics. His Orcadian friend and fellow poet Robert Rendall wrote of the shore as a margin or sacred space that left a "profound influence

---

96 Mackay Brown, *The Windhover 11 MS pp on 6 leaves each 33 × 20.5cm signed George M Brown March 1964 in another ink*. NLS.

on the subconscious habits of Orkney people." Here between land and sea at the shore, "There is healing in the sea for mind and body."[97] The savagery of Christ's Passion is tempered by Mackay Brown's desire "for final peace and resolution"[98] that he found so convincingly in his native tradition. This was especially so for him in his devotion to the life and death of St. Magnus that brought him great personal serenity.

Mackay Brown had also been held to account by his audience. He continued to disturb cultured readers, and this was as healthy a sign as it was for Hopkins. The all-embracing texture of their writing absorbed the dynamic flow of the patterns and perceptions of the sacred as well as the profane. This continues to challenge the literary, philosophical, and spiritual ethos of our times. Mackay Brown observed the extraordinary in Hopkins as a distinct positive in terms of technique:

> It was an extraordinary way to treat the sonnet form, which had with neatness and economy contained so much of the courtliness and economy of Spenser, the anguish of Donne, the sensuous delight of Keats. It looks like a deliberate attempt to smash something that has grown too smooth and effete—one remembers the tastelessness of the Rossettis' and Tennyson's sonnets—and to remake the mould in harsher stronger lines.[99]

The passion of Hopkins was a turning point for many poets, and especially for Mackay Brown. Remaking the literary "mold" to take account of a wider and deeper vision did the literary world a service. Hopkins's new lines of development reinvigorated the old firmament in accord with his close engagement with sources of language and the human psyche. What emerged was a freer but more tightly disciplined seamless integration between form and content. Bloom's "clear imaginative space"[100] was given a firm epistemological basis that was able to engage with the post Reformation world and beyond. The nature of their spiritual "orthodoxy" was a radical force that opened new horizons which had been suppressed for centuries and could once again engage with their contemporary times in a radiant act of praise.

---

97 Rendall, *Orkney Shore*, 150.
98 Mackay Brown, *The Windhover* 11 MS pp on 6 leaves each 33 × 20.5cm signed *George M Brown March 1964 in another ink*. NLS.   99 Ibid.
100 Bloom, *The Anxiety of Influence: A Theory of Poetry*, 5.

Mackay Brown concluded with a certain ambivalence that,

> H himself never attempted anything so extreme in the sonnet form again, except perhaps 'Sybil's Leaves' and 'Heraclitean Fire,' and these seem to me much less successful than 'The Windhover.' Henceforth the mountains he scaled, though some of them were higher and lonelier, had not the savage grandeur of 'The Windhover.' Nor did the poem open any new directions for the sonnet form to take; it was impossible in any case for a poet ever to attempt to write like that again, in that bizarre wayward highly sèlved kind of way.[101]

Mackay Brown tried to fathom the trends unleashed by Hopkins from his 1960s perspective in Edinburgh. "Perhaps it remains an early symptom of a new 20th century kind of art," he writes, "—a simultaneous development in painting, music, sculpture, literature, the dance—which attempts to unite the sophisticated and the primitive, so that what has become over delicate and subtle and civilized may draw strength from the savage roots that lie deep in the earth and the unconscious."[102] He himself gained strength from Hopkins's "sweet clear spirit,"[103] and with conviction and confidence became an increasing presence in the literary world for his authority, technical competence, and his wholehearted faith (not immediately transparent to many because like Hopkins he kept "his heart in hiding").[104] Mackay Brown expanded into a range of forms from traditional stanza forms, sonnets, ballads, free verse, prose poems, runes, choruses, haiku, kennings, and litanies having served his literary apprenticeship of which "Edinburgh" was an integral part for its complex mix of higher education as well as for the relationships he welded. And, as Newman had prescribed in "English Catholic Literature," Mackay Brown's literary style "henceforth becomes a property of the language itself that hitherto did not exist."[105]

---

101 Mackay Brown, *The Windhover* 11 MS pp on 6 leaves each 33 × 20.5cm signed George M Brown March 1964 in another ink. NLS.
102 Ibid.
103 Mackay Brown, Letter to Jeanette Marwick, 12 October 1962. OLA, EWM Collection.
104 Mackay Brown, *The Windhover* 11 MS pp on 6 leaves each 33 × 20.5cm signed George M Brown March 1964 in another ink. NLS.
105 Newman, "English Catholic Literature," in *The Idea of a University*, 188.

This chapter has fetched out inscape and instress as the craft of a thoughtful and always thinking engagement with the world we live in. Hopkins and Mackay Brown grounded their writing and their readers in Christ to whom all truth and beauty belonged, in their minds at least. Their piety was flushed with Grace that instressed the natural world with its seraphic inscape of the Cross. They crafted their vivid apprehensions into a language that was anchored in the epistemic roots of language. Once again, the dynamic energy of the Trinitarian God was restoratively secured in language with the Real Presence in a seamless interweaving of unity and difference. This was Newman's critical point: did these poets bring into the English language in their poetry new properties? Hopkins and Mackay Brown moved their field and range of poetic play from the analogic nature of literary convention to univocity. This meant moving from likening bluebells, daffodils, starlights and birds to God, to radically asserting the presence of God in their difference rather than the likeness. It was the Scotian difference that defined unity and its particularity. Oneness and thisness found the new expression of energy that radically gave majestic force and radiant tenderness to the seamless language of Hopkins and Mackay Brown. Chapter Four will further explore how Hopkins and Mackay Brown expressed this critical difference in their craft by "stalling" and "stemming" with their incisive infusions of the elements of verse, number, meter, and music.

CHAPTER FOUR

Stalling and Stemming with Stars and Stations

ELEMENTS OF VERSE

*"But you shall walk the golden street
And you unhouse and house the Lord."*[1]

NUMBER, METER, AND MUSIC WERE SO important to Hopkins and Mackay Brown because they translated their experience of the poetic from their selves to their audience, inscape by inscape, in the patterns they forged as heraldic shields and stations. Hopkins invigorated the old firmament to set right a disjointed universe and Mackay Brown followed in the new lines of its development. This chapter focuses further on that restorative process in these soulèd and selvèd poets who worked their craft beyond abstractions to give what they interpreted to be the redemptive voice of poetry within the salvation religion of Christianity. They wrestled with dark existential forces from their first-hand experience of the powers that lurk in the human person. Clearly in their frame of reference they never lost sight of negative forces, the inscape of which was "sin," for to do so would be to lose sight of Christianity. Like the "Hound of Heaven"[2] in Francis Thompson's poem, the windhover-Christ comes relentlessly searching after us.

There is a strong moral character to their craft. Their poetry is based on an understanding that a salvation religion made no sense if all types of behaviors were equable in terms of good and evil and the various shades between these two points. The human person from their understanding and experience needs an in-depth explanation. They go deep with inscape as it "stalls"

---

1 Hopkins, "The Habit of Perfection," *Poems and Prose*, 5.
2 Mackay Brown, *For the Islands I Sing*, 50.

with its sense of controlling the demiurge-driven chaos of the flux. The "stem" of the instress feeds the inscape its divine-life-giving sparks, quivering and pulsing towards the highest good. The act of stalling and stemming was crafted in unison with intelligent design and purpose by an infrastructure of number, meter, and music. The question must be asked: is this exertion of order a manifestation of their own personal disorderly experience of the world expressed as another flight of poetic fancy, or is it an actual documentation not only of the power and range of human cognition but of God Himself as a radiant and rational reality?

Mackay Brown explains the workings of inscape in plants in his notes on the poem, "The Starlight Night": "every individual reed is unique and different from all other reeds though it belongs to the same species. Also, it can be observed from first growth to decay, and so it presents a sequence of inscapes, all equally interesting and beautiful. As the poet says in his notebook 'if the behavior [of a plant] could be gathered up and so stalled it would have a beauty of all the higher degree.'"[3] To stall is that act that could serialize the behaviors of plants and persons as a sequence of inscapes that are observed and experienced within that sequence. The poets invite a cognitive judgment towards evaluating how each contributed to their purpose by their design. The greater the alignment between inscaped behavior and its particular nature and its universal purpose, the greater the good. The poet's craft is to align the particular elements of verse with the instressed stem of the Creator.

The act of stalling is this alignment, and its ordering is achieved by Hopkins's use of number, meter, and music. He articulates these elements of verse to such an exactness Mackay Brown was able to recognize that he was already in possession of these natural organic elements in himself and his composition. Yet Mackay Brown knew for certain he was no crude imitator of Hopkins. He was also working within an Orkney poetics that had its own particular raison d'etre. But his distinctiveness did share the process, the frame of reference, the stall of the inscape and the stem of the Creator. In Mackay Brown's study of Hopkins's landscape poems "Inversnaid" and "Duns Scotus

---

3 Mackay Brown, *Two Night Poems and manuscript pp on 4 leaves each 33 × 20.5 in blue and black ink, signed George M Brown 1963. NLS.*

Oxford" his light academic touch concealed how influenced he was by the visual arts. In his "seeing" you can also hear the songs of nature and the sense of the divine action of the Creator. Seamlessly, he was fore-gathered in by a sequence of great artists with "vivid apprehensions of Christ" and the stem of the "religious root."

> GMH is famous for the fresh and vivid beauty of his landscapes. They seem to me like the paintings of Van Gogh, who was working about the same time—the same bright rush of wind, the secret rising of the sap into the branches. Certainly, many humanists have thought H did wrong to drag the deity in at the end of so many of his poems, like a bar at ten o'clock as if H was only doing this to please his religious superiors. But the fact is, I think, that H was really not so much different from Giotto and Fra Angelico and the painters of the age of faith. We know the middle ages had a great attraction for him. All his work, like theirs, sprang from a religious root, a vivid apprehension of Christ's presence in the universe. Unconsciously perhaps he answered Blake's question.[4]

Mackay Brown continued, giving precedence to Hopkins over Blake, "With a ringing affirmative; and not only in ancient time but this very morning and forever. Through sonnet after sonnet moves the Creator—Christ in majesty and sweetness."[5] Hopkins developed new lines for the old firmament that had passed through the heart and mind and soul of Blake to emerge with what appeared to Mackay Brown as "answers."

To align Hopkins first with van Gogh, then Giotto and Fra Angelico speak to their formation in the Passion of Christ so forceful in their art, yet equally conscious of the particularities of their craft and how they form harmonic composition. As van Gogh wrote to his brother Theo from London in 1874, "Always continue walking a lot and loving nature, for that's the real way to learn and understand art better and better. Painters

---

4 Mackay Brown, *Two Landscape Poems, a 10pp manuscript essay signed George M Brown 1964, each leaf 25.5 × 20cm. NLS.* [Blake, William. Jerusalem. "And did those feet in ancient time Walk upon England's mountains green: And was the holy Lamb of God, On England's pleasant pastures seen! And did the Countenance Divine, Shine forth upon our clouded hills? And was Jerusalem builded here, Among these dark Satanic Mills?"].
5 Ibid.

understand nature and love it and teach us to see."⁶ Mackay Brown's artistic appreciation moved from Hopkins's contemporaries and his own, then irresistibly he found himself aligning with the medieval period, the age of faith, before the world as he understood it became disjointed and rent of the sweetness of the old religion. But still Mackay Brown carried with him the imprint of the radical firmament of William Blake and the stem or religious root to his questioning poetic mind and vision. The influence of the visual arts showed Mackay Brown's mind and heart to be ringing with sensations that sought the fullest range of expression that he and many others found in Hopkins.

THE SPRUNG RHYTHM OF CHRISTIAN ILLUMINATION

The *Essays and Notes* elevate the evidence for Mackay Brown's own distinctive development in how to give the fullest range of poetic expression whilst retaining one's own literary integrity. Mackay Brown recognized Hopkins's poem "Inversnaid" as the single instance "where he tried anything approaching pure landscape... Inversnaid is a Scottish landscape; nobody could think of it as being anywhere else."⁷ Mackay Brown registered his literary judgment on a "scale" where, he observed, "there is curiously little of the kind of onomatopoeia that James Joyce and MacDiarmid delighted in when writing of streams and rivers."⁸ These observations were interpreted by his tutor as "illuminated or manufactured"⁹ token attempts to measure Hopkins against his own literary "choruses."¹⁰ These were the colonies of artists that converged around certain literary figures within the contemporary culture, but Mackay Brown very quickly moved to the realm of his own thoughts and insights into Hopkins as "one of the ancient smelters and smiths of poetry."¹¹ Mackay Brown admired in Hopkins, "An astonishing thing is how he uses Scottish words to such effect. Shakespeare has been praised

---

6 Cited at the Tate Britain Exhibition *Van Gogh and Britain*, Mar–Aug 2019. It was interesting to see this quotation above Van Gogh's painting *Shoes* 1886 in the guidebook. Mackay Brown was intrigued by Hopkins's focus on "shoes" throughout his poetry.
7 Mackay Brown, *Two Landscape Poems*, a 10pp manuscript essay signed George M Brown 1964, each leaf 25.5 × 20cm. NLS.
8 Ibid. See also Chapter Two "A Catholic Mind and Heart."
9 Ibid. Comment by Winifred Maynard.
10 Mackay Brown, *For the Islands I Sing*, 144.   11 Ibid., 150.

for the vivid Celtic atmosphere of Macbeth; 'Inversnaid' in its smaller scape is just as good."[12] He went on to record Hopkins's inclusive and particular lexicon, "barn" "bonnet" "broth" "braes" "bonny." He continues along this line of thought: "A malicious critic might suggest that H has hurriedly [taken up] some dictionary of the Scottish tongue to give authenticity to the landscape, and got no further than 'b,' but in fact the words are imaginatively deployed. A random selection of Scottish words made a picture like a cheap Scottish calendar."[13]

In fact, Mackay Brown put the whimsical aside to show his enthrallment with word study: "Darksome (coining of the poet) vs Sct. word lightsome (check OED)." He recognized the unique ability in the English Hopkins to go deep into the Scottish landscape and compose a genuine word painting of its "pure landscape" untarnished or embellished by the presence of persons. Inscape and instress, the stall and stem of his technique are not a romantic reverie but a linguistic display of realism, "taking things as they are"[14] within the interlacing of all their natural and cultural connections beyond the stereotypes. This is seen in the following examples where Mackay Brown digs deep into the roots of language. The sounds, touches, sights, sensationally interweave and interlace with identity in place and person to the point of unmistakable nationhood: "'windpuff bonnet' is very good: those blown beads of froth that are the size and shape and color of the Scotsman's traditional cap; though comparatively light and airy in texture." Then with another optimization of the senses: "Broth of a pool—the rush of water churns up the pool to the consistency and appearance of broth, that rich heavy dark soup that along with porridge and whiskey, is supposed to be Scotland's main nourishment." Again and again, Mackay Brown took note: "Heathpacks—often heather is not evenly spread out over the hillside, but in clumps and cushions, the word 'flitches' emphasizes this picture." Sounds and sight wrapped the vision, or was it the vision wrapping the sounds and sights? The pure art of it is real, not metaphoric: "the beadbonny ash that sits over the burn—this is the rowan,

---

12 Mackay Brown, George *Two Landscape Poems*, a *10pp manuscript essay signed George M Brown 1964, each leaf 25.5 × 20cm. NLS.*
13 Ibid.
14 Newman, *An Essay in Aid of a Grammar of Assent*, 197.

the mountain ash, a squat solitary beautiful tree crammed in summer with scarlet berries."[15]

With echoes of Edwin Muir, Mackay Brown went on to recognize that "The Scottish poets followed the tradition of Dunbar, who expressed the exuberance, wildness and eccentricity of the Middle Ages"[16] when he wrote: *"Inversnaid* is most Scottish of all, perhaps, in a kind of dark infernal gaiety that is reminiscent of Dunbar and Burns; the wild imagined rout of horses, death in the spate (the floating 'windpuff bonnet') like Tam o' Shanter with a more sinister end to it. Somewhere near here, one would imagine, the witches waited for Macbeth."[17] Then again echoing Muir's words on Robert Henryson as an exponent of "the medieval completeness and harmony, and the power to see life whole, without taking refuge in the facetious and the grotesque"[18] he observed in Hopkins: But the poem is not to end on this stark note. The beadbonny ash brings in, tentatively, the idea of prayer. This wild apparently Godforsaken beauty (it is one of the few H poems which doesn't mention God or Christ the HG[19]) is necessary in the world, to remind men of the savage salutary primitive power of nature that is always there, "watching and waiting."[20] He observed in Hopkins that the "telling" story of "Inversnaid" does not rest in the "savage salutary primitive power." Mackay Brown himself knew the eddying enclosure of the "pitchblack." He was sensing spiritual light in the "beadbonny ash" that conflated in his mind with the seamless water-scarlet-blood-berry-prayer beads rising in an upward surge towards healing and wholeness out of the "rounds and rounds / Despair to drowning."[21] Hopkins's "groins of the braes" did not bear comment. Hopkins's propensity to see Christ's body parts as he trawled through his particularities in the landscape was not a focus, but "wiry heathpacks" (muscles) and "flitches (fleshy

---

15 Mackay Brown, *Two Landscape Poems*, a 10pp manuscript essay signed George M Brown 1964, each leaf 25.5 × 20cm. NLS.
16 Muir, *Essays on Literature and Society*, 18.
17 Mackay Brown, *Two Landscape Poems*, a 10pp manuscript essay signed George M Brown 1964, each leaf 25.5 × 20cm. NLS.
18 Muir, *Essays on Literature and Society*, 18–19.
19 Holy Ghost.
20 Mackay Brown, *Two Landscape Poems*, a 10pp manuscript essay signed George M Brown 1964, each leaf 25.5 × 20cm. NLS.
21 Hopkins, "Inversnaid," *Poems and Prose*, 50.

sides)²² of fern" was alongside the blood-scarlet rowan berries. Hopkins and Mackay Brown have Christ in their sight, as they did throughout their poetry, one way or another.

It is also significant to take note at this point of Mackay Brown's reading and pencil markings in his own copy of Kurt Wittig's *The Scottish Tradition in Literature*[23] where he was drawn to key paragraphs. For example, he noted: "Scots Makars...carried on the various strands of native tradition...vernacular...aureate Chaucerian"[24] and "There is no other poet [Dunbar] of the Middle English period whose works contain such a wealth of dazzling colors and other pulsating sense images."[25] With reference to Burns's poem "Tam o' Shanter," Mackay Brown annotated a Note[26] "Or like the snow falls in the river" with a comparison to Hopkins with "How about GM Hopkins's 'O hero savest O Hero savest.'" The comparison was between Burns's "Tam o' Shanter" and Hopkins's "Loss of Eurydice" to make the point of the Scottish poet's "constant interweaving of diverse traditions" to generate great poetic "fertility and vitality" drawn from the real world of Scottish land and life.[27] It might be fair to say that the journalist in Mackay Brown got the better of him as he goes from the sublime to "Nowadays" observing that Hopkins "implies (as often in his poems), there is too much sophistication, too great a concern for security and safety first,"[28] but inevitably he came back to one of his great themes, "we need the wildness and the wet of "Inversnaid" to remind us of our sources."[29] The energy of language in its dancing power was critical to Mackay Brown's visualization, "It is conceivable that, given "Inversnaid" to work on, a painter could put the scene down on canvas with fair accuracy." As the poet-stream of Dunbar, Burns, and Hopkins work in and out of English and Scots they aureated their use of language drawing upon English for concreteness and Scots for color and music, doing so in masterstrokes of linguistic unity.

---

22 From Middle English *flicche*, from Old English *flićće* ("side of an animal, flitch"), from Proto-Germanic **flikkiją* ("side, flitch"), from Proto-Indo-European **pleh₁k-* ("to tear, peel off"). Cognate with Low German *flikke*, French *flèche*, Icelandic *flikki* ("flitch"), Middle Low German *vlicke*.
23 Wittig, *The Scottish Tradition in Literature*, GMB signature. OL/S (Stromness Academy). See Peterson.
24 Ibid., 58. 25 Ibid., 67. 26 Ibid., 201. 27 Ibid., 150.
28 Mackay Brown, *Two Landscape Poems*, a 10pp manuscript essay signed George M Brown 1964, each leaf 25.5 × 20cm. NLS. 29 Ibid.

Stalling and Stemming with Stars and Stations

In Mackay Brown's examination of Hopkins's "Duns Scotus's Oxford," he saw that landscape "in a very different style, half symbolical and abstract, like a man who by a cold act of memory omits all but the important things," paring down to the "dapple-eared lily...an important symbol"[30] that lay beneath Hopkins's Oxford, concealing the "innocence and purity" of the Virgin Mary that once was openly honored in the countryside and town of Oxford. Mackay Brown writes that he was able to understand Hopkins's forceful perceptions. Mackay Brown could now "look at the city with a new eye; and of course, 'towery' [city] and 'branchy' [between towers] give a quiver of life to the line." He then cross-references to the last line of Hopkins's poem, "Repeat that, repeat"[31]—"the whole landscape flushes on a sudden at the sound." The scales of light and sound, the visionary sensation, flush and pivot on the inscape of the Incarnation as Mackay Brown recognized—and was at one with—the instressed "quiver of life." Oxford, "Thou has a base and brackish skirt there," was according to Mackay Brown "an earthy town, with rooks as well as larks in it." He glided over the poem without academic penetration, but intuitively was at one with Hopkins, "The poem is a celebration of DS [Duns Scotus] and the uniqueness he saw in everything. He more than any other man could have sensed the uniqueness of Oxford, its inscape, how it differed from all other cities everywhere."

The Oxford of the old firmament was a pre-Reformation Oxford [Catholic in Mackay Brown's and Hopkins's minds] "Oxford, from its medieval freshness and gaiety, had a base and brackish skirt now" and Mackay Brown pursued the feminine, "like a woman gone sour and slatterly a little, though still retaining more than a remnant of her former beauty." The Virgin Mary was now "unhonoured," and "how can modern Oxford help but fall prey to sourness and gracelessness? This I think is the crux of the poem. Drive out religion with its images of goodness, truth, purity, beauty and useless ferments and spawns everywhere." But all was not lost: "Yet the place was haunted by wise good ghost, DS, though he had been dead

---

30 Ibid.
31 Hopkins, "Repeat that Repeat" (Unfinished poems and fragments), in *Poems and Prose*, 80.

for centuries, Oxford is still his city." Hopkins's new lines trace the particularities of Scotus in an articulation of inscape and instress, fetching out the old firmament as a beacon of light for Mackay Brown: "His continual presence was a kind of reassurance for H that the old beauty and grace would never be completely trodden down into uniform grayness [greyness] of modern industrialism." And as Mackay Brown wrote to me at Easter 1993, "Duns Scotus: Gerard Manley Hopkins held the Blessed D. S. in most high regard: D. S. 'most swayed my spirit peace'... They were dunces[32] themselves who put that label [dunce] on him."[33]

All the "particularities," inscaped and instressed, mutually indwell in an illumined manuscript of tapestry. Poetry is the inscape of language, the sprung rhythm of Christian illumination as it dwells within the natural world. Hopkins's new lines of the old firmament are interwoven designs turning in and around on each other, in a pulsating dance of play. The old firmament was lovingly conceived, expressed, and lived, not as a romantic idyll, but as a life as close as one could be to an awesome and wondrous interweaving and interlacing of the particular in the universal as one in the other. All particular facets and phenomena of life are utterly implicated in each other, and Hopkins and Mackay Brown understood that and crafted that sensational poetic vision into their language. These word-games are an illuminated array of inscapes stemmed by instress. Hopkins and Mackay Brown were like the twelfth century Icelandic Pingèyrar monks and their associates for whom "the application of Christian learning,

---

32 The word is derived from the name of the Scottish Scholastic theologian and philosopher John Duns Scotus. Along with Thomas Aquinas and William of Ockham, he was one of the leading Scholastic philosopher-theologians of the High Middle Ages. Duns Scotus wrote treatises on theology, grammar, logic, and metaphysics, which were widely influential throughout Western Europe, earning Duns the papal accolade *Doctor Subtilis* (Subtle Teacher). Duns Scotus remains highly esteemed in the Roman Catholic Church, and was beatified by Pope John Paul II in 1993. The followers of Duns Scotus were called the Dunses, Dunsmen, or Scotists. When in the sixteenth century the Scotists argued against Renaissance humanism, the term *duns* or *dunce* became, in the mouths of the Protestants, a term of abuse and a synonym for one incapable of scholarship. This was the etymology given by Richard Stanyhurst. Samuel Johnson, on the other hand, maintained that the source of the word was unknown, https://en.wikipedia.org/wiki/Dunce.
33 Mackay Brown, Letter to the author, Easter 1993. Cited in Appendix *George Mackay Brown No Separation*, 198.

especially biblical typology and symbolic thought, was not an intellectual game."[34] Both Hopkins and Mackay Brown placed themselves within that underlying thought that originated in Patristic literature wherein salvation is articulated against the backdrop of the "fickle fortunes of the temporal world"[35] whilst seamlessly asserting "the native tradition."[36] Christian illumination was able to absorb Hopkins's nineteenth century and Mackay Brown's twentieth century "like melted wax"[37] with a new sensitivity to "the mystery found in the scriptures" as "a many-sided and involved thing; and it takes first one form, then another."[38] Stalling and stemming was a natural and organic poetic process that gave both Hopkins and then Mackay Brown the power to hammer and forge blazing elements of verse that is a Christian illumination of sprung rhythm, seamlessly interlaced with their heart-song.

THE CURVATURE OF SOUND

Tracings of the interlaced heart-song can be seen in Mackay Brown's essay, *"Hopkins and His Metric."*[39] Mackay Brown's poetic craft was consciously reflective as he glided through the various literary giants to arrive at some obvious truths as well as his own metrical dance with "some of the old original sources of poetic rhythm." He recognized "that poetry of his [Hopkins's] age has gone stale and flat in its movement" and there had been a loss of "vitality."[40] Whatever the inner processes within a poet, Mackay Brown thought each must find his/her rhythm that fits one's talent. No matter how much the poet may study the theory, it is not useful unless there was the very individual gift, "this rhythm, this dance, is part of the 'inscape' of the man, that is, it is a part of the living landscape within, his soul's scenery."[41] His writing in this essay and across the years gives considerable appraisal of how poetry is composed:

---

34 Antonsson, "Salvation and Early Saga Writing in Iceland: Aspects of the Work of the Pingèyrar Monks and Their Associates," 130.
35 Ibid., 118.   36 Ibid., 130.
37 Joachim of Fiore, *Liber figurarum* (Reeves 1950), 67; cited in Antonsson, "Salvation and Early Saga Writing in Iceland: Aspects of the Work of the Pingèyrar Monks and Their Associates," 71.   38 Ibid.
39 Mackay Brown, *Hopkins and His Metric a 12pp manuscript essay signed George M Brown 1964, each leaf 25.5 × 20.5cm. NLS.*
40 Ibid.   41 Ibid.

> The important thing, I think is: poetry must have a structure. It is not to be confined, it is to be forced to seek resources in language, to mine deep for the right word and phrase that yet chime in felicitously with the rest. Nowadays—alas—verse looks too easy. I think any new poet should spend a year at least learning the traditional forms of English prosody. After that, he should see his way clear.[42]

The art of interlacing is a Christian illumination flushed with the curvature of sound, and it was recognized and endorsed in part by the critics.

Mackay Brown never took the easy road. He saw his way clear before his early immersion in Hopkins, during the intensive study in Edinburgh and after the Edinburgh phase. His composition was co-inherent with Hopkins's, but he held his own distinctiveness as he covered a range of forms from traditional stanzas, sonnets, ballads, *free verse*, prose poems, runes, choruses, haikus, kennings, and litanies. There is also a convincing evidence base for considerable emotional range, both "from poem to poem but also within a single creation, moving from religious ecstasy to wry realization of human weakness."[43] Mackay Brown illuminated and sang his song as he composed. He was appraised by his critics as often achieving, "a singing directness not unworthy of Yeats, a legendary richness not inferior to Muir, and a verbal resonance not less remarkable than Thomas." The literary criticism does not stint when it comes to appraise Mackay Brown's forms and sources. His language is "bare and poised,"[44] illumined with "visionary poetic energy," "intense," all of which "suggests that Brown's imagination is most at home when he attempts to disguise the fact."[45] Mackay Brown's emotional range is full of tenderness "...his whole feeling...his quiet meditative rhythm...its beauty and delicacy...suggests that this poet, this man fixed in the task of the 'interrogation of silence' as he calls the poet's work, is not

---

42 Cambridge, "'A Thread Too Bright for the Eye': An Appreciation of George Mackay Brown." *Chapman*, no. 84 (1996): 36-40, cited from personal correspondence from Mackay Brown to Gerry Cambridge.
43 Scott, "George Mackay Brown." In Murphy, ed. *Contemporary Poets of the English Language*, 144-45.
44 Cairns, *The History of Scottish Literature. Vol. 4: Twentieth Century*, 320.
45 Corcoran, in Vinson, James, and D. L. Kirkpatrick, eds. *Contemporary Poets*, 97-98.

altogether a fully contemporary poet."[46] Mackay Brown's style is "at its best, is superbly simple, combining conciseness with clarity in phrases which are functional and fine."[47]

But is this the whole story? This essay on Hopkins's metrics draws from Mackay Brown not only the closest measure of the world they both inhabited, but also their chosen metrical co-inherence. Mackay Brown chose to "chime" in with Hopkins "when he attempts to disguise the fact."[48] As he writes: "No other English poet has been so concerned about meter as GMH. For the most part poets have accepted the traditional meters and rhythms without question, making where necessary their own personal variations... so slight most readers would never know;[49] gliding through the literary greats a "sensitive reader... could tell vintage Dryden from Pope, a (Sydney, Spenser, Burns, Ferguson, Eliot, Pound) by the movement of the verse alone."[50] Mackay Brown highlighted Tennyson as having "an exquisite ear," even if "his lapses in taste are nearly always visual: (In Memoriam) 'The filthy bylane rings to the yell of the trampled wife.'"[51] Although Mackay Brown allowed Tennyson an "exquisite ear," he can't resist a spiked comment towards, "That was enough to make him the laureate of the reporters and hack writers."[52] Mackay Brown conceded his liking for "the rhythm is rather impressive, with its abandon and irregular thud of boots."[53] He preferred Browning's rhythms as "more interesting and dynamic than Tennyson," as in the poem "Bishop Blougram's Apology," "No more wine?" and in "Home-Thoughts, from Abroad"... "all the swallows."[54]

Mackay Brown comes to the point: "H was much more concerned, I think, to give us the essence of himself, to probe for a pure wellspring through the increasing tedium and boredom and sordidness of life, 'there dwells the dearest freshness deep down things.'" Mackay Brown kept close to his sources, and he loved to quote Hopkins's call to "go deep." He recognized that "rhythm was part of his freshness, a pure welling up from

---

46 Ibid.
47 Scott, "George Mackay Brown," In Murphy, ed. *Contemporary Poets of the English Language*, 144-45.
48 Corcoran, in Vinson, James, D. L. Kirkpatrick, eds. *Contemporary Poets*, 97-98.
49 Mackay Brown, Hopkins and His Metric *a 12pp manuscript essay signed George M Brown 1964, each leaf 25.5 × 20.5cm. NLS.*
50 Ibid.   51 Ibid.   52 Ibid.   53 Ibid.   54 Ibid.

secret sources." Equally he put aside the shallow deployment of language by "the mass media of communication, so terrifying in our own times." Hopkins keenly felt this, "even then by means of newspapers and fifth rate novels in cheap editions, was beginning to make itself felt, threatening the language he loved with sterility and drought."[55]

The problematic, erudite, complex, pious, Roman Catholic Hopkins knew the tastes of his times. Mackay Brown recognized the excitement in Hopkins on his journey to develop the new lines of the old firmament through his English temperament: "New sources of vitality had to be discovered; and the drilling went on in that important part of himself that had thought long and eagerly about language, its origins and behavior and possibilities." He sensed Hopkins's poetic art was called to judgment by means of a set of contradictions: "Paradoxically he sought to 'purify the dialect of the tribe,'"[56] borrowing the line from T. S. Eliot's poem "Little Gidding." Mackay Brown understood the relationship between belief and words and brought a strong focus on Hopkins's linguistic craft that rose to a majestic visionary illumination. This was Hopkins's artistry. He saw the world as shattered and shallow. Through the Oxford Movement, he became illumined in that "new springtime" that re-called a pre-Reformation culture many sensed they had lost. The new springtime of spiritual rebirth, gave new lines of development by means of a poetic language that shone brightly in the face of the tired and the trite where the mind had no command of the "aftersight and foresight" driven as T. S. Eliot exposed by "the cold friction of expiring sense without enchantment... as body and soul begin to fall asunder."[57]

Mackay Brown had engaged with Eliot early on in his development and the evidence here in this essay shows his own interest

---

55 Ibid.
56 Eliot, "Little Gidding" from *Four Quartets* II.IV, first published in 1942. Eliot had an incisive influence on Mackay Brown in his early development. This can be seen in Mackay Brown's use of quotes in the Commonplace Book and in his unpublished letter poem to Ernest Marwick reproduced in Gray *George Mackay Brown: No Separation*, 31–36. See also Fergusson, *The Life George Mackay Brown*, 130–31 for a discussion of Mackay Brown's reaction to Eliot, who had "become in his mind, a suspect figure." The divergence between them clearly represents Mackay Brown shaking off vestiges of being categorized within modernism or its offshoots.   57 Ibid.

in language and its patterns inscaped in dialect and tribe or "the native tradition."⁵⁸ But as Eliot represented a much more diverse movement of the poetical tradition than the category of Modernism had dictated, Mackay Brown, through Hopkins's influence, distinctively marked out his territory to decisively pursue the vernacular language strongly identified with the Orkney Islands through an artistry pivoted on the seamless unity of words and belief. Hopkins's firmament gave Mackay Brown a communal poetic space within which to write—with conviction and great beauty where thought was seamlessly interwoven in his controlled crafted language. What Hopkins had seen and heard on English and Welsh paths, lanes, and streets, what Mackay Brown had seen and heard on Orkney walks and Stromness streets, are the inscaped patterns of spoken words, the sprung rhythm "that approximates to the slackness of ordinary speech" and its "running rhythm." Mackay Brown illustrated this with the convention, "common in English verse use measured in feet of 2 or 3 syllables. V, v-, -vv, vv-, v-v: To be or not to be, that is the question, The Assyrian came down like a wolf on the fold."⁵⁹

As words eddy and fall, the reader of the poets can accompany their minds at work in the lines of the running rhythm as it subdivides in counter-point and non-counter-point. The poetic style uses opposition keeping the reader guessing and surprised about what comes next. They brought to the vernacular and dialect the sprung rhythm from their knowledge and store of Greek and Latin lyrics and such older English verse as "Piers Plowman." The poet's mind could seamlessly meld and weave a mixture of "running" and "sprung rhythm," but Mackay Brown wrote, "H argues these rhythms endlessly repeated become 'same and tame' and so poets introduce variations with 'reversed feet.'" As Mackay Brown later wrote in an autobiographical essay in 1987:

> Writing is a gift one is born with: that is a platitude, but true. It can never be taught. The born writer waits for the rhythms and patterns that have always been there since words began, the loom of language; then his work can begin; though a lifetime of strict discipline is necessary

---

58 Antonsson, "Salvation and Early Saga Writing in Iceland: Aspects of the Work of the Pingèyrar Monks and Their Associates," 130.
59 Mackay Brown, *Hopkins and His Metric a 12pp manuscript essay signed George M Brown 1964, each leaf 25.5 × 20.5cm.* NLS.

too. Unconsciously I had absorbed rhythm and pattern in the classroom, at an early age, when the teacher read to us the great biblical stories—Noah, Abraham, and Isaac, Joseph and his brothers, Samson and Saul and David. The Border ballads provided rich nourishment, and the classical stories like Ulysses and the siege of Troy. Rhythm and pattern: these are the graces that a writer needs. Professors of literature, however brilliant or trenchant and penetrating their understanding of texts, don't have the key to 'the workshop of looms.' It may be given to any passing scoundrel or vagrant.[60]

Later he wrote of his time studying Hopkins's "theories of prosody": "In the end, I think it is not all that important that people should understand them; that marvelous anvil-ringing poetry is what matters."[61] But Mackay Brown did understand the theories of prosody. Taking up the mantle of the "scoundrel or vagrant" more readily than evidencing academic brilliance, he came to Hopkins already poetically formed in so many ways. He assumed as his mantle the rhythms and patterns of the Earldom of the Orkney Islands. He had immersed himself in *The Orkneyinga Saga* and absorbed the "bareness of the narrative, interspersed with elaborate poetical 'kennings.'" This was his world, and he was confessional about it: "I have exploited it to the full."[62]

Working within this poetic stream of crafting verse according to fixed patterns of the inscape his composition became flowing rhythms of sound fully engaging with the life of thought in a dancing drama of movement. Mackay Brown recognized there was fixed shape but also a sound curvature that was irregular when he wrote: "The slight irregularity is not a flaw; in poetry it is the stir and breath of life."[63] The distinctiveness of sound also applies to persons: "It is like those slight departures from the normally accepted code of behavior that make our friends unique and interesting and dear."[64] As irregularities express their distinctiveness as they rise, rock, or fall, their rhythm finds sound curvature as it employs alliteration, assonance, inner rhyme to give sound-color and echo, woven syllable by syllable by vowel by

---

[60] Mackay Brown, "George Mackay Brown," in Sarkissian, ed., *Contemporary Authors: Autobiographical Series*, 61–75.
[61] Ibid. [62] Ibid.
[63] Mackay Brown, *Hopkins and His Metric* a 12pp manuscript essay signed George M Brown 1964, each leaf 25.5 × 20.5cm. NLS. [64] Ibid.

stress-beat by chiming "in the workshop of looms."[65] Hopkins's legendary devices illumined his verse, mostly in sonnet and ode form, with color music. It is personal, provincial, and loud-soft as it explores language and life through the inscaped-instress utilizing to the full the process of stalling and stemming.

Again, Mackay Brown recognized the fixed core: "People delight to recognize fixed artistic forms—sonnet, madrigal, the changeless ikon of the Madonna—because it gives feeling of stability, it is a rock under their feet, a bond of union between all people who share the same culture."[66] He also recognized there was at the same time: "equally the delight in variation, a slight assertion of independence; for this is a mark of freedom and of that subtle secret life which obeys other laws than those crude laws hammered out to contain all creative energy."[67] In addition, he writes, "In poetry this reversal of feet, [is] an alternative gratification and teasing of the ear."[68] His study of words was sharpened and illumined by his mastery of Old English, prior to the intensive Hopkins study: "to trace everyday words back to their source was a constant delight: to understand, for example, that 'lord' means 'keeper of the bread' and 'lady' means 'baker of the bread.'"[69] But Mackay Brown, like Hopkins, did not stop with the etymology and derivation. They both exercised and exploited to the full the unity between word and belief. Mackay Brown writes: "This is to dignify the humblest toil; this is to 'scatter the proud in the imagination of their hearts.' There were profound spiritual undertones; but all rooted in the four elements and the five senses."[70]

In his new lines of development, Hopkins explored and exploited the seamless overtones and undertones at work in language. Whether the audience are selective and go no further than the overtones of their poetic language and just revel in the rhythms, the color-music, or the patterns of the word dance, this does not deny the existence of the profound under-toning of their

---

65 Mackay Brown, "George Mackay Brown," in Sarkissian, ed. *Contemporary Authors: Autobiographical Series*, 61–75.
66 Mackay Brown, *Hopkins and His Metric* a 12pp manuscript essay signed George M Brown 1964, each leaf 25.5 × 20.5cm. NLS.
67 Ibid. 68 Ibid.
69 Mackay Brown, "George Mackay Brown," in Sarkissian, ed. *Contemporary Authors: Autobiographical Series*, 61–75. 70 Ibid.

work as it veers into the depths of existence. And as Mackay Brown wrote of his pursuit of the narrative: "I never strayed far from my first love, poetry... Poetry has strayed, perhaps dangerously, into my stories... My imagination nourishes itself chiefly on narrative—on events in time—and, according as a true rhythm is found and maintained, these narratives may be compacted into poems; and a poem may be so handled that it bears with ease and grace the very different balances and tensions of a story."[71] Mackay Brown used the narrative to spark the allegorical and pursues levels of correspondence between the natural and moral, pagan, and Christian—as Hopkins modeled so exquisitely.

Using univocity as Hopkins did constantly, Mackay Brown was able to mirror the levels of sensation as they resonated with each other in a serene seamless exchange of sound and echo, under-thought and over-thought, under-tone and over-tone, inside-time, and outside-time. It raises the possibility in my mind that Mackay Brown was himself the Blind Fiddler whose musical ear honed in Orcadian rhythms of land, sea, sky, and dialect liturgically dancing forth in an Orkney Poetics. Although Mackay Brown never explicitly talked or wrote about Hopkins's chime, that "brilliancy, starrieness, quain, margaretting" which feeds off a fixed inner oneness, he shared with Hopkins an intense absorption in echo and memory and its expression in music. This level of intensity gives their verse a powerful assimilation of sense and intellect within which the curvature of sound is then stalled and stemmed in interwoven infrastructure of number.

PYTHAGOREAN NUMBER THEORY

Hopkins and Mackay Brown employed numbers as words. Numbers were interesting to them. This was the strong anvil-like structure upon which their work, although different in obvious ways, was founded. While Mackay Brown was the master of understatement regarding himself and his place in the literary tradition: "There is no easy way of getting to the place of poetry. Even if one gets to the gates and knocks, there are severe and grave questions to be answered. Only the princes of verse know the mysterious password." He saw himself doing "honest work" in the "weavers shed outside" the palace. "I will not get to the

---

71 Ibid.

inner sanctum where the crown jewels are; but the journey to the place has been good."[72] If Hopkins was obscure once, he is not now. If Mackay Brown is considered obscure, that will change. For, in fact, he recognized that obscurity is "often the last refuge of the poetaster."[73] But obscurity in verse was another matter. Mackay Brown, as did Hopkins, was "reaching deep under the normal currents of meaning—a kind of verse that moves us in a way we don't understand. But only the greatest poets can use it: those who breathe the pure serene of the realms of gold."[74]

Mackay Brown walked deep in the poetical firmament of Hopkins and had a keen eye for structure. He stuck by some current of a mathematical basis to his art in his "good"[75] journey. Hopkins wrote and practiced the theory of mathematical proportion and ratio in metrics and music. Mackay Brown also shared this interest. While Mackay Brown used many forms of composition, Hopkins favored sonnet and ode. Both poets lived in the energy of the Incarnation and soaked up musical and metrical time according to their surroundings. Through Hopkins's pursuit of St. Augustine's christianized Pythagorean theory with his intense scholastic vigor, Mackay Brown was able to work within that frame of reference bringing precision to his own composition. The focus for Mackay Brown was the interworking of numbers in Pythagorean theory that rose so prominently in Plato and the Christian allegorist St. Augustine. He talked and wrote about number theory with his characteristic understated simplicity evidenced in his *Essays and Notes* on Hopkins's storm poem "The Wreck of the Deutschland."[76] He observed,

> The number 5 is given a mystical meaning in the poem, 'Five! The finding and sake / And cipher of suffering Christ'...5 seems to the modern mind a quite arbitrary number;...yet the number was God-devised, it had a mystical meaning beyond its merely utilitarian function in mathematics...(7 = creation-time/number of cardinal virtues and deadly sins, the spectrum span, number of loaves and fishes (5 + 2) with which Christ fed the multitude—a significant number)...5 × 40 souls on the Deutschland (40 probably favorite number in holy writ)...5 × 10 drowned

---

72 Ibid.   73 Ibid.   74 Ibid.   75 Ibid.
76 Mackay Brown, Notes on *"The Wreck of the Deutschland," 17 manuscript pages on 20 leaves each 33 × 20.5, signed GM Brown Feb 1963. NLS.*

or rather...5 × 5 × 2...2 is another important number in the poem, redeeming the unit from solitariness, necessary for balancing, contrast, 'dappling', that is the art and soul of nature...5 words in the title...5 letters in the Holy Name...At mass priest utters 5 words so that bread may become the body of Christ Hoc est enim corpus meum (this is my body).

Mackay Brown boldly gave total support to Hopkins, "Better to see too much in it than nothing at all. GMH announced the number 5 with such a trumpet call and then proceeds to scatter it and there are multiples of it throughout the poem." Mackay Brown's intense allegiance to number theory is based on what Hopkins saw as a deep resounding truth in number combinations. Hopkins saw these number combinations in nature as he is working from an understanding in Pythagorean "doctrine."[77] The numeral system was treated as a scale of fixed points and intervals and number was a source of rhythm (meter) and harmonia (music). Fixed points equated with finite nature and the spaces between them equate with the infinity of the supernatural. Geometrical dimensions are fixed in certain shapes and the infinite (instress) was breathed into the finite (inscape).

Plato had further developed the doctrine with the conceptualization that numbers were between the sensed object and their idea. Hopkins followed St. Augustine's and Plato's lines of development to an understanding that numbers were derived from sense-objects as symbols of ideas. Hopkins's study of mathematics and music put his composition in verse in a downward trajectory—from the supernatural or metaphysical melody of ideas down to the wordplay in verse. This feature of Hopkins's thought and craft is important because it convincingly moves

---

[77] "The Pythagorean doctrine of numbers took as the beginning of all figures and qualities the right-angled triangle, consisting of the numbers 3, 4, 5, in the equation $3_2 + 4_2 + 5_2$. Three stood for the heavenly triangle, four for the earth square. The sum of the first three numbers, the triad, was the number of the whole, a unity in multiplicity, cause of all things; the sum of the first four numbers, the tetractys or quadrate, was the root of eternally flowing nature. For St Augustine...number 1 is God, Jehovah; in the Triad is the Holy Trinity: the diad is the dual nature of Christ in Trinity; 5 stands for the 5 wounds; from the triune principle of God and the quadruple principle of man are produced the universal symbols 7 and 12...It should be noted that Scotus took over through Avicenna the Platonic theory of number." Heuser, *The Shaping Vision of Gerard Manley Hopkins*, 83, 115 note 3.

from the one-directional upward use of analogical language to the katalogical bi-directional perspective (descent and ascent) to expand into the realism of univocity. That is the "why and how" Hopkins was able to bring such force and penetration to his poetic language. Both poets conceived their poems at source within the energy of the Incarnation. The Christ-bird of the "Windhover" descends and ascends in unison, not metaphorically but really, and does so mathematically. Mackay Brown had spent years "at least learning the traditional forms of English prosody."[78] He gave his time to the study of Hopkins's "theories of prosody" and concluded, "In the end, I think it is not all that important that people should understand them; that marvelous anvil-ringing poetry is what matters."[79] He had found the way clear[80] for himself long since, but Hopkins mentored him as no other in his Platonized Pythagorean number theory that had flowed into Christianity through St. Augustine.

Mackay Brown's own "clear way" hovers around the number seven: "It is a mysterious and beautiful number in itself, and it occurs often in nature and in ceremony: the colors of the spectrum, the continents, the days of the week (the seven-syllabled Word of Creation), the deadly sins, the cardinal virtues, the ages of man, the family ('seventh child of a seventh child')...the five loaves and two fishes of the miracle; the sorrows of the Blessed Virgin."[81] He specified the heptahedron[82] as his particular pattern, "the number seven has an extraordinary power." This was his epistemic way for his "art" to hold a fixed pattern at its center while the tensions and contradictions contended with each other in "the endless flux." "I have relied often on the seven-faceted poem or story." A character is stalled and stemmed in the fixed pattern of the inscape, "it is caught and held in the mystery of

---

78 Mackay Brown, Notes on *"The Wreck of the Deutschland,"* 17 manuscript pages on 20 leaves each 33 × 20.5, signed GM Brown Feb 1963. NLS.
79 Ibid.
80 Cambridge, "'A Thread Too Bright for the Eye': An Appreciation of George Mackay Brown," *Chapman*, 36-40. Cited from personal correspondence from Mackay Brown to Gerry Cambridge.
81 Mackay Brown, *For the Islands I Sing: An Autobiography*, 168-69.
82 A heptahedron (plural: heptahedra) is a polyhedron having seven sides, or faces. A heptahedron can take a surprising number of different basic forms, or topologies. Probably most familiar are the hexagonal pyramid and the pentagonal prism. Also notable is the tetrahemihexahedron, whose seven faces form a rudimentary projective plane. No heptahedra are regular.

number seven, and there it is imprisoned till the song, or the fable is finished and free to go, like Ariel."⁸³ The dominance of "the seven" and its "charmed circle" in Mackay Brown's mind is not a random superstition or an eccentricity. It "dictates the whole tone and structure"⁸⁴ of his art. Mackay Brown makes composition look easy, but in fact he had drilled down into the sources of language and philosophy so much so that a distinctive vitality surfaced with an artistic uniqueness suggesting that he was "most at home when he attempts to disguise the fact."⁸⁵ He had discovered the katalogical perspective although he never used that theological classification from Balthasar. Yet his own line of thought, validated by Newman and then Hopkins, led him to share that perspective because that was his poetic vision. His postgraduate study on Hopkins gave him a consciousness of the underlying epistemology that had been at work within his own writing for a good long while.

Hopkins wrote to R.W. Dixon 23 October 1886, "there have been in history a few, a very few men, whom common repute, even where it did not trust them, has treated as having had something happen to them that does not happen to other men, as having seen something, whatever that really was."⁸⁶ Hopkins as an artist had "seen something"; so too Mackay Brown: "human nature in these men saw something, got a shock; wavers in opinion, looking back, whether there was anything in it or no; but is in a tremble ever since."⁸⁷ Hopkins wrote with references to Plato, Wordsworth, and Blake who in the expression of their philosophy or art evidence the "proof of the shock."⁸⁸ Mackay Brown very individually immersed himself and his art in this "seen something" and, like Hopkins, placed himself and his art within the idealist Platonic tradition that found its most immediate expression in the writings of John Henry Newman.

---

83   Ibid. Note: Ariel is the fairy-servant of Prospero in Shakespeare's play *The Tempest*. He was imprisoned by the witch Sycorax when she ruled the island, but Prospero saved him. Now he obeys his master's every command, with the expectation of his eventual freedom. Ariel has integrity and loyalty and is eventually freed by Prospero.
84   Mackay Brown, *For the Islands I Sing: An Autobiography*, 168-69.
85   Neil Corcoran, in *Contemporary Poets*, 97-98.
86   Hopkins, letter to R.W. Dixon 23 October 1886 in *The Correspondence of Gerard Manley Hopkins and Richard Watson Dixon*, 147.
87   Ibid., 148.   88   Ibid.

Newman's exploration of the Church Fathers underpinned the Oxford Movement and lent a compelling form of mysticism to the Tractarians. After the long centuries of the suppression of the sacramental principles and divine indwelling, Newman connected deeply to the early Alexandrian (Platonist) theology of the Fathers, Clement, and Origen in his Tractarian phase. For him, nature is a parable and scripture an allegory. Deep truths lay under the appearance of words that were packed with meaning in undertones as well as overtones and would be revealed in their time and season. Clement and Origen opened this energy source to Newman and then Hopkins and later Mackay Brown. The energy of the Incarnation led them to "see something" not immediately obvious. This was an intuitive apprehension through the intellect and functioned as a sustaining principle of faith.

Newman and then Hopkins were surrounded by the Romantic attitudes that had released the Tractarians into this ancient form of Christian contemplation. The swarm of symbols that carried Hopkins and then Mackay Brown away from a dry rational utilitarianism that suppressed the sacramental principle prompted their conversions to Catholicism that indwelled in their art. Yet it was an artistic sense by which they both wanted to be judged. Their poetry conceals an inner narrative that, if penetrated according to its echoes, memories, and metrics, reveals a glimpse of the God they sought in the mysterious recesses of their minds. Neither Hopkins nor Mackay Brown self-identified as a mystic. But their Patristic roots were immersed in the divine energy of the Incarnation and surfaced in their metrics and number theory that brought a distinctive illumination to their compositions. Mackay Brown's pursuit of the heptahedron worked from this tradition, and he used it to significant effect coming up with a surprising number of different basic forms. The Mackay Brown collection of heptahedra are irregular, and this is a feature of their form. He said himself, "often the demands of story or play or poem force me into a ten-sectioned or twelve-sectioned work" as he found himself straying from "the charmed circle of the seven."[89] His familiarity with structured seven-faced forms allowed for an expansion into the ten or the twelve planed platforms that were held within the illumination of the seven.

---

89 Mackay Brown, *For the Islands I Sing*, 168-69.

Hopkins's and then Mackay Brown's illuminative verse kept in step with the difference-in-unity and unity-in-difference using sound and number as its elements, stalled, and stemmed with points of reference (inscape) flushed with energy (instress). They needed a form of expression that could re-create their experience of the world they lived in as authentically as they could. This led them to break with convention and find majesty and beauty in a dark fore-boding world with its ever-increasing relativity and existential deconstruction, first in themselves and then in their verse. Hopkins blazed the trail and Mackay Brown followed to give expression to a new form of symmetry.

IRREGULARITY AS A FORM OF SYMMETRY

Hopkins is the master of irregularity as a form of symmetry. The sprung rhythm leapt and bounded, oozing with vitality as he reinvigorated the epistemological development of the "old" firmament. What may have first appeared as idiosyncratic sprung rhythm tracking the natural and organic trajectories of thought is welded seamlessly into language to become totally rational. Mackay Brown followed with his idiosyncrasy that served him well as he wrote: "(Incidentally, why 'feet'?) I suppose because the human foot is a unit with different parts, it is meant for movement—walking or running (in prose) dancing (in verse). To move at all the feet must beat on the ground with a characteristic rhythm—the rhythms of a drunken fair, a secret rendezvous, a pilgrimage; each has its own pace and style."[90] Always in thrall to the "Blind Fiddler" in pursuit of "green corn," Mackay Brown's mind was at work in his inner synthesis of the inscapes of an Orkney poetics within the universality of a rich classical counterpoint. He conflated stitch-by-stitch the inscape of the "Everyman" who "has his own particular mode of going" stalled and stemmed, within the incarnational energy of the instress. Conflation or the seamless interchange of all the component parts tracks the dynamic oscillation between the universal and the particular in the manner of Hopkins, held or stalled on the quiver, is expressed "in speech as in movement" where Everyman "must put one foot in front of the other many

---

90 Mackay Brown, *Hopkins and His Metric, a 12pp manuscript essay signed George M Brown 1964, each leaf 25.5 × 20.5cm. NLS.*

times to get to the place he is going to, or to finish his dance."⁹¹

While the essay on Hopkins's metric called for an academic critique, Mackay Brown was absorbed in his own thoughts and literary processes and how his own artistic mastery could "see" the technique of Hopkins, but still be thoroughly individual and independent. Mackay Brown could appear to be whimsical too when he alluded to Hopkins's view of "what he said about the poetry of inspiration and Parnassian poetry."⁹² Hopkins distinguished between the range of poetic diction that crossed the spectrum from high inspiration in mood and moment to the more consistent competency of the mediocre "spoken from the poet's mind"⁹³ to the true greatness where there was the gift of genius that "sings." Parnassian poetry, for Hopkin, did not "sing." As Mackay Brown wrote, "It is strange that nowhere in view of that, H did not invent for the movements of verse, instead of the rather ugly 'feet', some words like 'wings.'"⁹⁴ Furthermore, "H knew well enough how few lines in all the verse that was ever written is winged; though indeed there are a few dancers who sometimes dance so well that their feet seem hardly to touch the ground."⁹⁵

The energy Mackay Brown observed in Hopkins held a liturgical rhythm brimming with the energy of the Incarnation. The concrete nature of Hopkins's linguistic formation with its Scotist haeccitas or thisness of things was not lost on Mackay Brown. He did not offer up a forensic analysis and discussion of the syntax that drew consistently from Greek, Latin, and Anglo-Saxon structured by syntactic inversion. Hopkins deliberately deployed his skill in compression and energy from an Anglo-Saxon vocabulary resonating with the echoing overtones and undertones in his inversion of word order according to the structures of inflected languages. Hopkins never abandoned meaning for the sake of an empty vacuous rhetoric. By using asyndeton, a device that omits connecting words such as "and" and "but," with crosscurrents of alliteration, assonance, and rhyme, his sprung rhythm reclaimed the center ground for "the

91 Ibid.   92 Ibid.
93 Hopkins, letter to A.W. M. Baillie Sept. 10, 1864, in *Gerard Manley Hopkins Poem and Prose*, 155–56.
94 Mackay Brown, *Hopkins and His Metric, a 12pp manuscript essay signed George M Brown 1964, each leaf 25.5 × 20.5cm. NLS.*   95 Ibid.

current language heightened."[96] Mackay Brown had taken note and Hopkins equipped him with "finer tools"[97] to not only compose, but to refine his own poetic diction.

With an Orkney poetics that had already set out his credentials before he drafted these *Essays and Notes*, Mackay Brown could now re-read Milton and Shakespeare afresh. Of Milton's "Samson Agonistes" Mackay Brown writes: "But the groundswell is still there; the reader can find his way through the cross currents, and the slight peril heightens the enjoyment...it is called counterpoint. But Milton only does this occasionally."[98] He goes on to comment: "H argues the principle can be extended to cover the entire poem. The original common rhythm that the ear expects is then, he claims, destroyed; what is left is an entirely new rhythm, which he called 'sprung rhythm'...The ear does not know what is coming...all is unexpected and strange."[99] Mackay Brown offers up some examples of the "extraordinary effect," such as "Wrenching from the norm e.g., Shakespeare 'age, ache, penury and imprisonment,'"[100] Donne "all whom warre, dearth, age, agues, tyrannies/Despair, law, chance."[101]

Mackay Brown examined Hopkins's sprung rhythm in "Each stanza as a unit in itself."[102] But according to Mackay Brown there lay, "The ugliness of much of its rhyming."[103] It could be justified, "if we agree with H that the stanza rather than the single line is to be the unit." Another main innovation "hangers" or "outrides"...seem to hang below the line or ride forward or backward from it in another dimension than the line itself."[104] Mackay Brown was not entirely convinced or clear about Hopkins's theory of art, "But I for one would welcome a little explanation of Hopkins's SR [sprung rhythm] as the most natural of things" and "rhythm of common speech and of written prose,

---

96 Hopkins, letter to Robert Bridges 14 August 1879 in *The Letters of Gerard Manley Hopkins to Robert Bridges*, 89.
97 BBC Scotland. George Mackay Brown 70th Birthday, *One Star in the West*, Broadcast April 1996.
98 Mackay Brown, *Hopkins and His Metric*, a 12pp manuscript essay signed George M Brown 1964, each leaf 25.5 × 20.5cm. NLS.
99 Ibid.
100 Claudio's word to Isabella in Shakespeare's *Measure for Measure*, III.1.
101 Donne, "Holy Sonnets" no. 4. (1609).
102 Mackay Brown, *Hopkins and His Metric*, a 12pp manuscript essay signed George M Brown 1964, each leaf 25.5 × 20.5cm. NLS.
103 Ibid.   104 Ibid.

when rhythm is perceived in them."[105] Clearly, Hopkins challenged Mackay Brown and the society around him: "This seems to me one of the most extraordinary statements ever made by a poet. Common speech had its rhythms, of course, broken and blunt and disjointed though they normally are (just eavesdrop for a few minutes on a casual conversation between strangers in a queue) and prose has an enormous variety of rhythms from the jargon of the *Daily Express* to the complex rhythms of poetry, and this is only natural (except in announcements and laws and proclamations)."[106]

However, there was no doubt in Mackay Brown's mind that ultimately: "It is the individual tone and emphasis that comes through, and this varies with every writer; whereas it is likely that poetry comes from an altogether deeper level of experience where the individual personality is almost submerged and the poet is speaking for the whole tribe, the whole community."[107] Mackay Brown had taken T. S. Eliot's maxim to heart and given his allegiance long since. And Mackay Brown knew his Orcadian community having heard its call to poetics from his earliest days, even if this community struggled to know him, and still do. Mackay Brown could see Hopkins as the literary outsider, on the margins because of his sensational visionary art immersed in Catholicism: "It seems to me H was the complete heretic when he tried to approximate the rigid severe vatic rhythms of poetry to the slack anarchical rhythms of common speech and the more purposeful utilitarian rhythms of prose, he was asserting a kind of literary Protestantism which, however, far from bringing down anathemas on his head, has made him one of the most acclaimed poets in an age athirst for novelty and the cult of the individual."[108] Hopkins's nevertheless had taken his rightful place in the classical literary trajectory, not for his religion, but for his art. That laurel cannot be denied him. He witnessed to Mackay Brown how his art, too, could rise above the Parnassian and "sing" above the parapet of the popular.

But Mackay Brown proceeds to question who Hopkins's successors might be. "It remains a curious thing, however, that no poet of importance has thought it necessary or possible to adapt any of H's theories to his own work. There is no evidence that

---

[105] Ibid.   [106] Ibid.   [107] Ibid.   [108] Ibid.

the machinery of poetry was worn out on 'H's day, and still, two generations later, the best poets are writing in traditional meters. Trochee and dactyl are still the healthy heartbeat—beats of the language; they have been for a long time and perhaps they will be for a long time to come. They have been, at least up to the present, a sign of poetry's well-being and vitality."[109] Was Mackay Brown ambivalent about Hopkins's legacy? Or was he at some all-absorbing level finding a way through from his own natural serenity:

> To return for a moment to the image of the dancing foot: In spite of the many fine things in Hopkins poetry, there is something a little hectic, a little hysterical, about the tone in which he celebrates the beauty and glory of creation. It was as if he were saying, 'In this time of decay and degeneration of language, look at the extraordinary lengths I must go to preserve the old joy inviolate.'[110]

The "old joy" was critical to understanding Hopkins and Mackay Brown. This is what makes their verse "sing" along with the great poets of the tradition:

> The former poets, Shakespeare and Keats and Chaucer, could do it with simple natural easy movements of their feet, but today it can only be done with the greatest difficulty and contortion. And if we compare H's line about the Skylark[111] with one of Chaucer—'Tak any brid and put it in a cage'[112]—it can be seen how quick and nervous H's is compared to the largeness and tranquility of the old poet.[113]

"Tranquility" was of the utmost importance to Mackay Brown. At his core he had found a space he could be most truly who he was, and it was a workspace where he could "carve the runes and keep silent."[114] During this study and very emotional period in his life he also was socializing within the bustling choruses in Edinburgh having to weigh up his place. As Mackay Brown struggled to formulate his elements of verse in the process of

---

109 Ibid.   110 Ibid.
111 Hopkins, "As a dare-gale skylark scanted in a dull cage," "The Caged Skylark," in *Poems and Prose*, 31.
112 Chaucer, "The Maunciple's Tale," in *The Canterbury Tales*.
113 Mackay Brown, *Hopkins and His Metric, a 12pp manuscript essay signed George M Brown 1964, each leaf 25.5 × 20.5cm*. NLS.
114 Mackay Brown, "A Work for Poets," in *The Collected Works*, xvii.

stalling and stemming, he could see among his contemporaries that "It may well be that the rhythms of poetry are slowly changing and evolving, and that they must inevitably change with the changing environment of language... some recent poets recognized need for change."[115] In addition, as he pithily observes:

> Free verse is a kind of melting down of the old metric until something more suitable to the age we live in is discovered. The broken lines of The Waste Land, the delicate subtle flow of Lawrence's animal poems, Pound's attempt to weld image and rhythm more firmly together, are all signs of poet's dissatisfaction with the traditional English meters. And yet the attempt to create a new mould is proving far from easy. Hardy, Yeats, Muir, Auden, Dylan Thomas, Stevens, Lowell, in spite of those innovators, are still moving their feet in the same way as Chaucer and Donne and Wordsworth did.[116]

Finally, he concludes: "The dance is recognizably the same to depend less and less on sprung rhythm in favor of the old traditional meters. It is possible that, in the future, the example of H will modify the rhythms of English poetry in subtle and unexpected ways, but it seems that trochee and dactyl will survive his assault for some time to come."[117] Disciples and acolytes of literary greats do not become a Hopkins or a Shakespeare or a Chaucer. The poets that "sing" to hearts and minds as they accept their part in the development of language in their times are "vatic," far-seeing and prophetic for a purpose. To forge their craft in the combat of history brings meaning through poetry to the human person. Hopkins may have been "hectic" and "hysterical" with his "dare-gale skylark scanted in a dull cage"[118] contrasting with Chaucer's "bird in a cage,"[119] but they were both old firmament poets, to whom Mackay Brown aligned himself in "subtle and unexpected ways." He sensed, felt, and knew this within himself, then in Edinburgh and more assuredly as time went on into his poetic future. The dissonance of the English Hopkins was for Mackay Brown a source of "measure" against which he could configure his Orcadian poetics. The co-inherence of their

---

115 Mackay Brown, *Hopkins and His Metric*, a 12pp manuscript essay signed George M Brown 1964, each leaf 25.5 × 20.5cm. NLS.
116 Ibid. 117 Ibid.
118 Hopkins, "The Caged Skylark," *Poems and Prose*, 31.
119 Chaucer, "The Maunciple's Tale," in *The Canterbury Tales*.

distinctive patterns and shapes of words and rhythms, sights and sounds that rise, fall, turn, repeat, suspend, resolve, in a swarm of symbols were distilled by Mackay Brown into traditional stanza forms, sonnets, ballads, *free verse*, prose poems, runes, choruses, haiku, kennings, plainchant and litanies, in their many projections from the central core of the heptahedron. Entranced by the dancing metrics of the curlew, the "sweet clear spirit"[120] of Hopkins, confirmed in him a passion for the "finer tools"[121] at his disposal. The *Essays and Notes* confirm along with his writings prior to, and after this Edinburgh study period, his thinking craft where these finer tools address elements of verse in an illumination of sound and number as they dove-tail in the instressed inscapes. This is the reinvigorated new firmament where irregularity is assimilated into a new pre-theologic symmetry. Irregularity finds its place not in analogical language but in *univocity* with its difference-in-unity and unity-in-difference.

ASSERTING "THE NATIVE TRADITION"[122] IN A DARK FOREBODING WORLD

Somewhere in the private deeps of the "Anchorite of God," Mackay Brown is the private oracle revealed in the unpublished poem "Summer Day."[123] As he had "raised his eyes / One golden summer morning" he walked "The cloud-dappled-alleys of God's eternal city."[124] In the tradition of the twelfth century Pingèyrar monks and their associates, Hopkins, and Mackay Brown "bring from his [God's] storeroom both the new and the old"[125] and reassert the native tradition. For many of Mackay Brown's contemporaries, T. S. Eliot's *The Waste Land* marked out a version of a post-war landscape. The disassembling of what had passed as a civilized culture, harbored an ethos of anger and resentment and a profound sense of loss. Mackay Brown dissolved anger and resentment, public and private, into the native tradition of his deeply-rooted Orcadian powers of perception.

---

120 Mackay Brown letter to Jeanette Marwick, 12 October 1962. Orkney Archive. Ernest Walker Marwick collection, D31/30/4.
121 BBC Scotland. George Mackay Brown 70th Birthday, *One Star in the West*, Broadcast April 1996.
122 Antonsson, "Salvation and Early Saga Writing in Iceland: Aspects of the Work of the Pingèyrar Monks and Their Associates," 130.
123 Unpublished MS reproduced in Gray, *George Mackay Brown: No Separation*, 43–44.   124 Ibid.   125 Mt 13:47–52.

Through "current language heightened,"[126] he decisively displaced private and public anger and resentment with a sensational vision of Redemption. As he wrote in a long unpublished letter-poem to Ernest Marwick in 1954: "On this blind road I take and bless / The night's star-piercing bitterness."[127] He was decisive about his call to the "native tradition" and did not see himself within the Eliot coterie: "In a London office Eliot sits, / Prince of intellectual wits, / Writing a few lines every year / Between a wry grin and tear, /.... and after him a whole host swarms / Of purblind ineffectual worms, / Weaving not from hearts but tails / A labyrinth of silvery trails."[128] It brought once again "enchantment" to "St Magnus' healing bones" / in the midst of "...the storm, I am content / It is my chosen element."[129] In 1981, Neil Ascherson observed Mackay Brown "to be the least tormented, the most spiritually secure"[130] in the study of his Scottish contemporaries. His "half-baked stuff" was penetrating and illuminating about where he had come from and where he was going. He went high and deep and surfaced with an Orkney poetics that captured history within a private oracle. This experience pushed him towards a new poetic freedom to be tenderly received by many in some shape or form of illumination in a dark foreboding world.

Like Hopkins, he aspired to avoid "the suspicion of 'Parnassian' by deliberate use of counterpoint and sprung rhythm"[131] whilst firmly aligned within the orthodoxy of the literary tradition. As Mackay Brown observed of Hopkins: "Later he chafed at the restriction of 14 lines of iambic pentameter (even his own violent kind of iambic) [and] tried to vary [the] scope of [the] sonnet, compressing eg 'Pied Beauty' and 'Peace' (6 lines followed by 4 with brief coda) 'Peace' having an extra stress each line expanding in 'Felix Randall,' 'Henry Purcell,' 'The Soldier,' with a six stress

---

126 Hopkins, letter to Robert Bridges 14 August 1879, in *The Letters of Gerard Manley Hopkins to Robert Bridges*, 89.
127 Unpublished MS, reproduced in Gray, *George Mackay Brown No Separation*, 32-36.   128 Ibid.   129 Ibid.
130 Ascherson, *Seven Poets: Hugh MacDiarmid, Norman MacCaig, Iain Crichton Smith, George Mackay Brown, Robert Garioch, Sorley Maclean, Edwin Morgan*, 23.
131 Mackay Brown, *A Note on the Sonnet Form as used by Hopkins in Hopkins and His Metric* a 12pp manuscript essay signed George M Brown 1964, each leaf 25.5 × 20.5cm. NLS.

line though otherwise they keep orthodox shape."[132] The more he tried to be critical of Hopkins, the more the "sweet clear spirit"[133] impressed upon him that "imagery is strange too, almost surrealistic. The great stormfowl of the sestet incongruous; I remember the bird jarred on me for a long time, until I saw that, in fact, he makes no sudden appearance in line 10, but has been there from the beginning."[134] Being "disturbed" or challenged by Hopkins, he turned his mind to the "rich" and the "strange" running together seamlessly where belief and words are one, with no separation. It was an intense experience of beauty.

So, what was the evidence that Mackay Brown aspired to avoid "the suspicion of 'Parnassian' by deliberate use of counterpoint and sprung rhythm"?[135] The problem of a private vision taking aim at a large undefined audience is the certain death of many a poet. But to work from an already received public vision of Christian redemption, as Hopkins and Mackay Brown did, gave scope for the long term where the audience could grow and thrive long after the death of the poet and stretched back to the twelfth century and further as partners or associates in the Passion of Christ. Mackay Brown did not show any form of triumphalism in religious matters and never plunged headlong into Hopkins's endeavors to articulate "a cosmological scheme of salvation"[136] through his understanding of Scotus. But Mackay Brown was aligned with Hopkins's key ideas of nature, self, will, and pitch. Providence, free will and the spiritual response to grace[137] were central to the poetry of both poets. Mackay Brown emerged from the half-baked stuff phase to have the serenity that marked all his writing as well as his "person." His self being or oneness was integral to him. His pitch, that individual degree in the tonal scale of being, or in Scotus's terms the thisness or haecceitas[138] emerged early and late on the Mackay Brown poetic journey.

---

132 Mackay Brown, *The Henry Purcell Sonnet of Gerard Manley Hopkins*, 10 manuscript pages each 20.5 × 25 cm, signed George M Brown. NLS.
133 Mackay Brown letter to Jeanette Marwick, 12 October 1962. OLA, EWM Collection.
134 Mackay Brown, *The Henry Purcell Sonnet of Gerard Manley Hopkins*, 10 manuscript pages each 20.5 × 25 cm, signed George M Brown. NLS.
135 Mackay Brown, *A Note on the Sonnet Form as used by Hopkins in Hopkins and His Metric* a 12pp manuscript essay signed George M Brown 1964, each leaf 25.5 × 20.5cm. NLS.
136 Heuser, *The Shaping Vision of Gerard Manley Hopkins*, 64.
137 Ibid. 138 Ibid., 65.

Stalling and Stemming with Stars and Stations

He had his pitch, his self-determination in the native tradition; and he did not deviate.

Hopkins's sonnet "Henry Purcell" and Mackay Brown's view of it[139] reveal their difference in unity and unity in difference. Mackay Brown's sonnet, "Chapel Between Cornfield and Shore,"[140] is included here for its sharp contrast between the two poets to reinforce difference and unity. Firstly, in Hopkins's sprung rhythm where the current language is heightened, the force and flow of "Henry Purcell" is the place where "the forged feature finds me," and there was the "scatter a colossal smile / Off him" raised by the word-stream of music in "so arch-especial a spirit as heaves." Hopkins's use of asyndeton within crosscurrents of alliteration, assonance, and rhyme, keeps the shape orthodox but true to the instressed-inscapes, stemmed and stalled, the old firmament fetching-out seamlessly each fitting word, phrase and line as thought flowed towards balance and much more. Hopkins introduces this poem of praise for the musician and his music that goes beyond the "moods of man's mind" to "the very make and species of man as created both in him and all men generally."[141] Through Hopkins's spirited inscapes — the angelic voice or bird, with its intensity of love, threaded with spiritual combat and the mystery of the self — lies a word-painting rooted in an underworld. Here the preconscious and the primitive are musically interwoven with ideal types and mirror images among pagan myths and Pythagorean numbers.

Hopkins mastery of the "pitch" is also witnessed in Mackay Brown's "Chapel Between Cornfield and Shore." Clearly Mackay Brown could use the orthodox shape of the sonnet form with its symphonic ebb of the ocean dance as it rose from within. The grey stone chapel, not "arch-especial," but inscaped with its arch, chancel, and sanctuary, flushed and infused with a timeless liturgical force, kept its continuity within the Reformation storm. Mackay Brown was perpetually sparing in his diction, but nevertheless the word-stress-rhythm was in tune with the natural world he knew so well. His poetic instinct was for the narrative in all he did as the poet and storyteller

---

[139] Mackay Brown, *The Henry Purcell Sonnet of Gerard Manley Hopkins*, 10 manuscript pages each 20.5 × 25 cm, signed George M Brown. NLS.
[140] *Collected Poems of George Mackay Brown*, 35.
[141] Hopkins, "Henry Purcell," in *Poems and Prose*, 41.

in keeping with his native tradition. His inversion, "the wave turns round," is as pointed as Hopkins's "reversal / Of the outward sentence low lays him, listed to a heresy." The contrast is sharp as the Hopkins and Mackay Brown pitch was one of asyndeton versus non-asyndeton. Mackay Brown found Hopkins's language disorientating, yet so successful at instilling the "image" in spite of resistance. Mackay Brown was more covert and with an ease that disguised its composition, he used the word "thrawn"—the twisted and wrenched Scottish acre that was the space for the new ceremonies (not rituals) as the locus for the re-crucifixion of Christ, the green corn, as it riseth from the seed. The symphonic ocean dance in all its "sounds from her lucent strings" bears the bird-angel's counterpoint with "bell nod and cry above," their inscapes bearing down into the elements with "Ploughshare" and "creel" pressing their furrows into the hard-heart-earth to be caught and clustered as they are "sieged with hungry sins." The "fisher priest offers our spindrift[142] bread," its spray gale-force-blown from its cresting waves. The eucharistic bread-spray "drifts" in the direction of the gale with speed and force to find "the hooked hands" to receive "the harrowed heart of Love."

In his poem, "The Poet,"[143] Mackay Brown is never far from the "blind lyrical tramp" who caught the call of the curlew in true Orkney style. This was Mackay Brown, the poet, leaving the "pool of silence" donned in the persona of "mask and cloak" moving in strings of rhythm "among the folk," gifting an "invading" infusion of "gaiety" to the sobriety that suppresses the human vitality of the "Fair." With hints of Bunyan's *Pilgrim's Progress* and the extinguishing of light in the retreat of dancers and masks, it is the poet, Mackay Brown, who was receives into the familiar force and flow of "cold" penetration, the "interrogation of silence." Like Hopkins in his poem "The Habit of Perfection," Mackay Brown finds in "Silence" a place that could "sing to me,"[144] but silence is also a hard taskmaster. In the

---

142 Spindrift (more rarely spoondrift) usually refers to spray, particularly to the spray blown from cresting waves during a gale. This spray, which "drifts" in the direction of the gale, is one of the characteristics of a wind speed of 8 Beaufort and higher at sea.
143 *Collected Poems of George Mackay Brown*. "The Poet," 45–46.
144 Manley Hopkins, "The Habit of Perfection," *Poems and Prose*, 5.

"double dark" is found "the uncreated light." Shut in and curfewed "all surrenders come" "Which only makes you eloquent." The dance of eloquence pitches its rhythms of "ruck and reel," its "Coils" and "keeps" that "teases simple sight." This place of contemplation is "the golden street" where Mackay Brown along with Hopkins's "unhouse and house the Lord,"[145] together. The contrast between the two poets couldn't be stronger as the priest-poet takes on the song of silence and its "ruck and reel"[146] while Mackay Brown with the interrogation of "ploughshare and creel"[147] disrupted the conventional appearances of things for the sake of stripping everything down from the "Fair"[148] to "double-dark"[149] to find the "uncreated light" and the force and flow of dancing "eloquence."[150] This is the process of the poet "to unhouse"[151] and build again to restore "the maimed rockpool"[152] thereby "surrendered into the "simple sight"[153] that sees the divine indwelling that "houses"[154] the Lord.

The "housing" of the Lord took Mackay Brown by surprise in "Henry Purcell": "The great stormfowl of the sestet incongruous; I remember the bird jarred on me for a long time, until I saw that, in fact, he makes no sudden appearance in line 10, but has been there from the beginning."[155] Mackay Brown was noted for his own "visionary poetic energy," that "is intense" and "suggests that Brown's imagination is most at home when he attempts to disguise the fact."[156] As he said himself: "The ear does not know what is coming"[157] "The imagery is strange too, almost surrealistic,"[158] but yet there was a complete "surrender" as all the senses are seamlessly engaged in a process of inscape stalled and stemmed by instress to "house the Lord." Mackay Brown takes a slow pace

---

145 Ibid.   146 Ibid.
147 "Chapel Between Cornfield and Shore," *Collected Poems of George Mackay Brown*, 35.
148 Ibid.   149 Manley Hopkins, "The Habit of Perfection," 5.
150 Ibid.   151 Ibid.
152 "Chapel Between Cornfield and Shore," *Collected Poems of George Mackay Brown*, 35.
153 Hopkins, "The Habit of Perfection," *Poems and Prose*, 5.
154 Ibid.
155 Mackay Brown, *The Henry Purcell Sonnet of Gerard Manley Hopkins*, 10 manuscript pages each 20.5 × 25 cm, signed George M Brown. NLS.
156 Corcoran, *Contemporary Poets*, 97–98.
157 Mackay Brown, *Hopkins and His Metric*, a 12pp manuscript essay signed George M Brown 1964, each leaf 25.5 × 20.5cm. NLS.   158 Ibid.

and a steady rhythm and when he does catch the audience by surprise, like Hopkins, it is completely as it should be.

In his poem "Horseman and Seals Birsay,"[159] he writes, "On the green holm they built their church." "There were three arches." Nothing "arch-especial" about this "house" yet the tide of ritual ebbs in slow feet as it carried the tread of a litany well said, intoned with what at first gaze and hearing was grey and dull and quaintly retrospective. But was it? The village, the house, the milk, the farmer, the peats, the fishermen are seamlessly stitched with their "basket of mouthing silver" and "gifts from heaven." The narrative turns round-by-round in the prayèred voices of the monastery where the counterpoint of the "bell" and the "seven sounds of the sea," the "eight times chant of the murmuring psalms in that deep pasture." Hopkins, and then Mackay Brown, worked within the "clear influence the Greek models had in the development of the Latin Chant and found in the system of modes. These were worked out by the ancient Greeks and expounded by Pythagoras. They differ from the system of major and minor scales, and of the various keys, on which post-Renaissance Western music is based. There are eight different standard modes. The modes variously prescribe the arrangement of tone and semi-tone intervals within the scale. Any piece set in that mode must conform to this arrangement."[160] The Pythagorean modal system coalesces with the numerical observations of nature as Mackay Brown sequences his inscapes: "The sea lay round the isle, a bright girdle...from shore to shore pierced cries of gull and petrel."

Mackay Brown was not one for asyndeton. His lyrical litanies held to a strict form of composition by his use of numbers—seven for heaven, eight for the conflation of the eight tides (divided up into two high tides becoming four and two low tides becoming four) and the monastic Liturgy of Hours (Vigils, Lauds, Prime, Terce, Sext, Nones, Vespers, Compline) for which each hour is accompanied by the bell calling to prayer. Mackay Brown used a 3/3 stressed, halved and paused Old English line to open: "On the green holm/they built their church," 3/2 "they walked to the village/across the ebb," 3/2 "Fishermen left a basket / of mouthing

---

159 *Collected Poems of George Mackay Brown*, 41.
160 Hardy, *An Introduction to Gregorian Chant*.

silver," 3/4 "And missed their bell / with the seven sounds of the sea," 3/2 "They murmured their psalms / in that deep pasture" counterpointing and reversing iambic feet to slow and quicken, slow and quicken in the positioning of the "stress and slack." As Mackay Brown said himself: "The ear does not know what is coming,"[161] "The imagery is strange too, almost surrealistic."[162]

Mackay Brown's heptahedron, his particular pattern, in which "the number seven has an extraordinary power," was never far from view. This was his epistemic way for his "art" to hold a fixed pattern at its center while the tensions and contradictions contended with each other in "the endless flux" where he "relied often on the seven-faceted poem or story."[163] A character was stalled and stemmed in the fixed pattern of the inscape, "it is caught and held in the mystery of number seven, and there it is imprisoned till the song or the fable is finished and free to go, like Ariel."[164] The dominance of "the seven" and its "charmed circle" in Mackay Brown's mind was not a random superstition or an eccentricity. It "dictates the whole tone and structure."[165]

Like Hopkins, Mackay Brown's re-cast speech as sound in a stalled sequence of inscapes gives a rhythm that "rocks" with lyrical ups and downs, falling and rising with foot and metered word. Therein time, beat, and count interweave in an intensive repetitive syllable-by-syllable design. Hopkins modeled how to keep close to the sources, his devices only serving to be as true to a sound-color that befitted the natural world and its persons. He was the master of the "echo" as it reverberated between beginning, middle and end-sounds of syllables. Mackay Brown followed suit with a special prominence given to the intonation or chiming of a series of well-placed vowels. Heuser cited Hopkins's Roehampton lecture notes[166] for his exploration of "vowelling on" (echolalia or Platonic shadow) and "vowelling off" (an alphabetical scale of vowels). Chiming on vowels gave "brilliancy, starriness, quain, margaretting."[167]

---

[161] Mackay Brown, Hopkins and His Metric *a 12pp manuscript essay signed George M Brown 1964, each leaf 25.5 × 20.5cm. NLS.*
[162] Ibid.   [163] Mackay Brown, *For the Islands I Sing*, 168-69.
[164] Ibid.   [165] Ibid.
[166] Heuser, *The Shaping Vision of Gerard Manley Hopkins*, 40. Lecture notes given when Hopkins taught as Professor of Rhetoric (1873-74), "Rhythm and Verse, Poetry and Verse."   [167] Ibid.

It is important to note here that Mackay Brown's patterns of sprung rhythm, for all their textbook English, are illuminated not only by the rooted source of Old English but also the Orkney cadence. Mackay Brown did not confuse the properties of language with the properties of the world for verbal convenience. In the Platonic, and then the Hopkins, technique, he understood that the universe was perfect, but its observed imperfections come from the limitations of human cognition and perception. Yet poets such as Hopkins and Mackay Brown bear witness to how to meaningfully connect with that perfect universe through their verse. Readers and listeners have a need to explore his verse through its Orcadian spoken accented diction, for example, as recorded in *For the Islands I Sing: A Collection of Poems and Short Stories by George Mackay Brown*.[168] The listener can hear the Orkney "vowelling" whether it be on or off, soft and weathered, independent of the Scottish brogue and echoing certain features of Old Norse and more specifically the Orkney version of Norn.[169]

Mackay Brown heard and held the "gentle silken-voiced"[170] Orcadian farmer and "ancient harp" of the sea in "a heraldic stillness and a hoarded symbolism"[171] as he flushed sight and sound in "the sheer sensuous relish of utterance."[172] He made a strong statement for his "firmament" in alignment with Hopkins, never to use words as "functional ciphers"[173] for "Poetry is a fine interpretation of ghost and kernel."[174] Like Hopkins, he saw that the "decay of language was always the symptom of a more serious sickness."[175] Hopkins considered Wales and its language "always to me a mother of Muses."[176] Mackay Brown "heard" and "flushed" his poetical language with the inscapes of the Orcadian dialect specific to its Norn retention[177] of the rising and falling of the gliding vowels of "diphthongs."[178] Hence the

---

168 *For the Islands I Sing: A Collection of Poems and Short Stories* by George Mackay Brown. CD.
169 Davis, *The Early English Settlement of Orkney and Shetland*, 65.
170 Mackay Brown, *An Orkney Tapestry*, 15.
171 Ibid., 19.   172 Ibid., 22.   173 Ibid., 21.   174 Ibid.   175 Ibid., 23.
176 Hopkins, (I.227) Cited from his unpublished papers in Peters, S. J. *Gerard Manley Hopkins: A Critical Essay Towards the Understanding of His Poetry*, 41.
177 Davis, *The Early English Settlement of Orkney and Shetland*, 82-86. The process called *i-mutation* between AD 450 to 500. It happened everywhere in the Germanic world in every language except for Orkney and Shetland Norn.
178 Orkney Dictionary, for example: English oa becomes Orcadian o as in "sound" becomes *soond*, English ou, ow becomes Orcadian oo as in "boat" becomes *bot*, English au, aw becomes Orcadian aa as in "haul" becomes *haal*.

Stalling and Stemming with Stars and Stations

striking difference of tone between the two poets, yet they were sourcing an authentic shared firmament into their composition that asserted the native tradition reinvigorating English language and literature.

The "starriness" of Mackay Brown's "mouthing silver" is shades of Hopkins's color-music-words for primroses as "the strong swell given by the deeper yellow middle."[179] Mackay Brown counterpoints "Fishermen left a basket" with "of mouthing silver." Tone and semitone and consonant chime were set against or intermingled with a vowelling that "swells" in the echoes of his color-music-words. The inscaped herrings flail and flash in the "margaretting" device weaving the vowels "into a daisy-chain of notes"[180] and are "quained" by the "brilliant star-angled consonants used to square-in the shining vowels."[181] For example, the daisy-chain of vowels are squared in by the surround of consonants:

> "A horseman stood at the shore, his feet in seaweed"...
> And mixed their bell with the seven sounds of the sea...
> Then the ebb subtracted one sound...
> From the seven-fold harmony of ocean.
> The tide lay slack, between ebb and flowing, a slipped girdle.
> Till the flood set in from the west, with a sound like harps....

It may seem a stating of the obvious, but to see Mackay Brown at work at his desk humming and deep in thought,[182] his play of consonant and vowel was set to a pitch that held the daisy-chains and colour-music-words together within the Orcadian "ring or tang or grain"[183] in its "loudness and softness, accent of meaning, logical, rhetorical and ethical emphasis and intonation."[184] Like Hopkins, Mackay Brown demonstrates a complex and irregular use of the ratio of consonant and vowel, "stress and slack parts, the periodic and flowing, hovering between random and metrical speech."[185] Like Hopkins, Mackay Brown also uses "chromatic colour-music" ("mouthing silver")

---

179 Heuser, *The Shaping Vision of Gerard Manley Hopkins*, 41.
180 Ibid. 181 Ibid.
182 Seen in BBC Scotland's George Mackay Brown 70th Birthday, *One Star in the West*, Broadcast April 1996.
183 Heuser, *The Shaping Vision of Gerard Manley Hopkins*, 41-42.
184 Ibid. 185 Ibid., 42.

and "diatonic type-shape"[186] (his preference for the heptahedron as a centerpiece could absorb irregularity into symmetry).

And then the enigmatic "horseman." Was this the Earl Magnus, "in need of God"? The heavy repetitive alliterative chiming intonation of the "h" with "horsemen," "he," "his," "him" is coupled and softened with the sea-skirl-of the skerry. The "bright girdle" of the sea anchored in the vastness of a cosmic awesome silence "pierced" with "cries of gull and petrel" while "seaweed" commands the "patience" of a man on a journey to his martyrdom. Timing is everything, as the Trinity is aureated in "the cold triangular pools" and the "Dominus Pascit Mei" (The Lord is My Shepherd of Psalm 23), gathers and pulsates as surely as Paul's gathered-whelks-in the basket. Seals are conflated seamlessly with the "gentle old men's faces" of the monastics who turned their faces in unison towards the "seven-fold harmony of ocean." Tides ebbing and flowing hold them in their water-embrace and as the high tide floods in "with a sound like harps" the seal-prayered-men are elevated in grace, "one-by-one" to the "new water" of Eternal Life. The surging back and forth of litany and liturgy, the curvature of sound, the deeply rooted language, illuminate in sprung rhythm the sequence of inscapes that asserts "the native tradition"[187] in a dark fore-boding world. Mackay Brown had not seen Hopkins's "stormfowl" coming, but its "unhousing" released in him how to "house" the Lord in the love of his life, St. Magnus. This was no poetic flight of fancy. Here was the exertion of order working from the real world through Mackay Brown in an actual documentation, not only of the power and range of human cognition but of God Himself as a radiant and rational reality. The stall and stem with its elements of verse take the artistic sense to new heights and depths of achievement as we shall see in Chapter Five where the "unhousing" of the human person as poetic subject thrived in the sprung rhythm of Christian illumination.

---

[186] These terms may mean different things in different contexts. Very often, *diatonic* refers to musical elements derived from the modes and transpositions of the "white note scale" C-D-E-F-G-A-B. In some usages it includes all forms of heptatonic scale that are in common use in Western music (the major, and all forms of the minor).

[187] Antonsson, "Salvation and Early Saga Writing in Iceland: Aspects of the Work of the Pingèyrar Monks and Their Associates," 130.

CHAPTER FIVE

Hurrahing in the Harvests

*"But hold dear the martyr in you
And the martyr, the sufferer, in all men,
And the martyr in Magnus,
And Christ, the eternal martyr."*[1]

THE EMERGENCE OF ST. MAGNUS IN THE work of Mackay Brown is pivotal in understanding everything he wrote. Herein lay the inscape of the "Everyman," the human person as poetic subject, fetched out in the mind of Mackay Brown as he asserted the native tradition in its christianized form. The trajectory from his "half-baked stuff" of the 1940s followed a set pattern from the outset where the uniqueness of the human person made for a stunning view of man, woman, and child as poetic subjects. In an unpublished poem, "Everyman,"[2] Mackay Brown fetched out the set pattern, the inscape, the "Fallen, angelic seed,"[3] created from "the calm wheel of God's man-dealing hand."[4] Mackay Brown's Boethian[5] conceptualization of "the wheel of life" is within the western literary canon and in spite of its almost clichéd status (both in the medieval period and now), it clearly evidences Mackay Brown and Orkney's Platonist and Christian heritage. But Mackay Brown set out the reproductive processes in poetic language—"the phallic gale that consummates the ceremony of the rose."[6] Even the cellular nature "Everyman" must pass through time and seasons that "forged his delicate armour of blood and bone / In the womb's glare, and at his trembling stations,"[7] but it was

---

1 Mackay Brown, "Saint Magnus Cathedral," Easter 1944. Unpublished MS OLA, EWM Collection.
2 Mackay Brown, "Everyman" (probably 1944). Unpublished MS OLS, EWM Collection.
3 Ibid.   4 Ibid.
5 Boethius, Platonist, and Christian philosopher, explored the question in *The Consolation of Philosophy* — is this world ruled by chance or is it governed by the rational principle, God?
6 Mackay Brown, "Everyman." Unpublished MS OLA, EWM Collection.
7 Ibid.

not long before "Everyman" was portrayed as Christ through his Passion that according to Mackay Brown defined us. The serious elegiac tone of all Mackay Brown's work shines through the "half-baked stuff" as Everyman contains man and woman who complement each other "where tall women under the red tree lament."[8] The man Christ on the Cross of the "red tree" held around his death "tall women" who stand out historically and spiritually in their "lament" or heartsong of passionate grief.

Mackay Brown, in the manner of Hopkins, created within a shared cypher or poetic algorithm, with the swarm of symbols that followed the set pattern of the instressed-inscape in a series of well-defined steps. Asserting the native tradition was never left to an aimless fluidity or a disorderly flux of energy. As with the twelfth century Icelandic Pingèyrar monks and their associates, the salvation story is the one narrative to which everything simultaneously returns and sets forward. Their illumination takes in the Creation account, the Incarnation and Nativity, the Passion, and Resurrection. Hopkins's metrical illumination reinvigorated the firmament, but Mackay Brown did not feel inclined to adopt what he felt was a more confrontational "tone" by Hopkins: "There is a violence, a deliberate feeling of uncouthness and barbarity about 'The Windhover' that is, I think, meant to disturb cultured readers brought up on smooth combed meters of English verse."[9] Mackay Brown was a disruptor, but differed from Hopkins in degree, if not in kind. He observed in Hopkins, "The poet himself was a bit scared; he speaks of 'his heart in hiding,' half appalled by what he has written—as a man at first light must be at once frightened and fascinated by the slow glide and savage plummet of the kestrel."[10]

How frightened was Mackay Brown when he compared the Christ-bird to, "a priest [who] must be awed every morning by the fact that Christ is in the circle of bread on the altar and that he is holding the creator of the universe in his hands."[11] This was the core of their Catholicism. Whether it was a problem or not for the audience, this seamless transition from the particular to the universal is not a contrived literary device. It works because it is

---

8 Ibid.
9 Mackay Brown, *The Windhover* 11 MS pp on 6 leaves each 33 × 20.5cm signed George M Brown March 1964 in another ink. NLS.
10 Ibid.   11 Ibid.

able to demonstrate the certainty, the conviction, the experience of eucharistic belief as the act and power of their vision, their understanding of the world; but, to be clear, it is optional for the audience and never imposed. This is disruptive and disturbing to the cultured literary audience who want more of the same of the "smooth combed verse,"[12] in an array of vibrant images that come in and out of culture with no sense of permanence. They are finite and meant to be so. But the illumined consciousness of these two poets was driven by the moral imperative to substantiate the seamless drift between particularities and the universal, between the *inscape* and the *instress*, the physical and the metaphysical, the natural and the supernatural.

WE ARE ALL HALLOWS[13]

Mackay Brown wrote in his study of Hopkins's "The Starlight Night" that "The starlight is God's; by merely existing it praises God, though it doesn't know that it does so."[14] The human person receives sense impressions and makes judgments upon them, but Mackay Brown made an important distinction between the radiating light of a star that by its mere existence praised its Creator God because of its completeness and purposefulness regardless of the evidence of intelligent design experienced as *inscape* to the poet's mind. As he continues, "but man can mean to give praises to God."[15] The human person has intellect and will to choose to believe and act to praise God, but why would the human person choose to do so? Mackay Brown answers: "If God doesn't exist, the beauty of the night sky is a cold empty thing, all our wonder would be lost like corn growing wild."[16] The poet's mind and emotions, interwoven as they were in the search for meaning, for origins and ends, undertook the discipline of the inscape, the fetching out of design and its life force. It was not rational to accept a position of random arrays of contingent and accidental phenomena (like corn growing wild) purely by force of its experience as sensual beauty. Stars factually exist, whether we see them or not. They exist for a reason and a purpose, and their inscape captures that seamless

---

12 Ibid.   13 Ibid.
14 Mackay Brown, *Two Night Poems and manuscript pp on 4 leaves each 33 × 20.5 in blue and black ink, signed George M Brown 1963*. NLS.
15 Ibid.   16 Ibid.

instressed understanding. Their existence does not depend on whether there are human persons or poets to see them.

Mackay Brown was clear, as was Hopkins: "But as things are... Stars issue from the hand of God, are there for a divine purpose, and we cannot possess or win any true knowledge of beauty unless our lives are somehow touched with grace."[17] To these poets there is an experience of freedom to willingly praise God in his stars as an act of joyous participation in the co-inherent dynamics of God's being and to convey that to their audience, unashamedly being disruptive in doing so. The experience of God is expressed by Hopkins as the "stem." This infusion of grace is achieved by the poetic technique of the "stall" of the dynamic vibrancy always on the move in experience. To insert the "stem" into the "stall" of grace that our experience of God is, evidenced the presence of a discerning spiritual detachment from the conventions of their times—Victorian and beyond. Here are new lines of development of what to many was the cliché of the old firmament. Hopkins wrote the stemmed instress was, "the issue from the hand of God," the cognition of which he said, "Ah well! it is all a purchase, all a prize. / Buy then! bid then!" the price being "—What!?—Prayer, patience, alms, vows."[18] But Mackay Brown knew, as did Hopkins: "This is not to say that an atheist cannot appreciate any kind of beauty, a starlight night for example, or a sonnet. But his enjoyment can never be wholly satisfactory; it lacks an essential element, being an end in itself and not (as it should be) a means to a richer delight and beauty."[19] These are poets who cannot rest in the *inscape*; they are always pressing for something more. This processing of sources stands as a documented witness and surrender to the Divine in the instress.

Mackay Brown saw the vocation of the poet within this divine indwelling and incorporated it seamlessly into his poetics: "The image of the barn" in the midst of a world that is a "May-mess" of the sprung rhythm of new seed-bearing growth that sent disruptive "shocks" into the literary status quo. The seasons

---

17 Ibid.
18 Hopkins, "The Starlight Night" in *Gerard Manley Hopkins: Poems and Prose*, 27.
19 Mackay Brown, *Two Night Poems and manuscript pp on 4 leaves each 33 × 20.5 in blue and black ink, signed George M Brown 1963*. NLS.

turned according to their rhythms and Mackay Brown observed, "as at the end reminds us of the labourer—too few—sent out into the harvest; but here it surely includes poets as well as religious. The harvest is beauty as well as holiness."[20] The world of work, wherever it may be, is a place where, according to Mackay Brown, "We are meant to remember such parables as The Sower, The Tares and The Corn, and that great pronouncement of Christ, 'I am the Bread of Life.'"[21] Eucharistic "barns" contended in the "May-mess" of the "withindoors house" of the inner human person.

Mackay Brown could be quite dismissive of Hopkins, and there are certain aspects to this poem and its inscaped alignment that irked him ("diamond delves" and so on).[22] Yet, as dismissive as he tried to be, he fell into line when it came to Hopkins's grasp of the infinite and its dancing metrics that held its own workings within. Mackay Brown wrote, "In this poem H, who is both priest and poet, has cut swathe after swathe of loveliness with the bright scythe of his verse."[23] So, it was the priest-poet who labored for the gospel-harvest to be stored in the barn-church; yet there was no extraction from the messy workings of the world. Mackay Brown goes back to the text, the ciphered code stitched seamlessly holding its own workings within itself and again, with certainty, he wore his heart and mind on his sleeve for all to see:

> These are indeed the barn. All beauty of this night is like a granary. Inside are the true riches—what a—granary is really for—the harvested grain, all the loveliness and goodness that men have imagined and wrought on earth; and there is too the great harvester himself and all his heroic and gentle labourers—'Christ and his mother and all his hallows.'[24]

The sensational vision of baby barns, particular barns, was swept metaphysically into the universality: "But the Barn is the whole church where you will see the statues of Virgin and Saint in the riches, and hidden in the tabernacle Christ himself, the Bread of Life, source of all nourishment and insight and true delight, the power and the glory."[25] Mackay Brown, for all

---

20 Ibid.   21 Ibid.   22 Ibid.   23 Ibid.
24 Ibid.   25 Ibid.

his doubts about Hopkins and this poem, nevertheless sweeps his audience into his own visionary reckoning. "Granary" is a Mackay Brown (not Hopkins) inscape that rises repeatedly to swarm in his own distinctive tranced Orkney poetics.

The Hopkins infusion continued, circling, according to the call of the Orkney curlew of Christ-bird-song. The moral imperative took aim at the human person as poetic subject and took on the more complex nature of personhood, of the selvèd thisness of the human person. It is here that both Hopkins and Mackay Brown stand or fall in their understanding of the seamless integration of the universal and the particular. Or was there a struggle on the part of Mackay Brown to align himself with Hopkins and Duns Scotus's Theory of univocity? The univocity of being implies there is no real distinction between essence and existence. They are seamlessly one. Aquinas (and his subsequent theory of analogy) made a distinction between the two, Scotus did not, and neither did Hopkins or Mackay Brown (or did he?). Hopkins's poetry evidences an understanding that there is no distinction between the thing that exists and what it is. How completely did Mackay Brown adhere to that principle? From his considerable poetic study, he often talked about essences especially regarding the human person.

The sense and form of the human person for both poets arose through experience first and then aligned and developed further within the Scotian innovative and incisive understanding of the Incarnation. Hopkins used the language of the inscape to express the experience of humanity and validate its physicality contextualised with the meta-physicality of the instress. Mackay Brown often explored the human person with language of the "constants in human nature"[26] that led him to speak and compose according to the "Everyman."[27] As Mackay Brown's poetic technique develops and grows in confidence, a slow infusion is seen at every level: "Slowly theology is beginning to insert its blade into the poem."[28] Mackay Brown's understanding of humanity moved from the individual physicality of the "Everyman" to the universal essence. Hopkins spoke of "manmarks"[29] as that trace

---

26 Mackay Brown, *Magnus*, 129.
27 Ibid., 130.
28 Mackay Brown, *Notebook Two "That Nature is a Heraclitean Fire and the Comfort of the Resurrection," NLS*.
29 Ibid.

of the human person that abide in work and play within the realm of Creation (Mackay Brown's Greenfields Kirk). Mackay Brown reflected on the human person in Hopkins's scheme of things, the reinvigorated firmament in his poems "Harry Ploughman" and "Tom's Garland." Ploughman and workman were particular to the everyday individual but given a hallowed or sainted extrapolation with the universality of the platonized type. Linguistic extrapolation fitted the dovetailed poetic technique of both poets. They took known experience and projected, extended, and expanded it into areas not known or previously experienced. This was their field of poetic play to epistemically arrive at a knowledge of the unknown by using curvature of sound and Pythagorean number theory as points of reference within an illumined infrastructure that pivoted on the tension of light and dark as we have seen in Chapter Four. This was their mastery of the dynamic art of compression and expansion that brought new properties to the English language, and it gives a fullness to the expression of the human person as poetic subject.

Mackay Brown's characteristic resistance to Hopkins's disruptive, disordered word-play, leads him to the portrayal of Harry as "snarled up in his own devices, not a complete figure, [with a] broken vividness about him, [a] foretaste of one of those Cubist portraits where the subject is all fragmented" and then there was the "GMH obsession with footwear" to consider alongside the manner in which "all his arguments with God end in his own willing defeat."[30] Mackay Brown held of both sonnets, "Tom's Garland," and "Harry Ploughman," a "hesitation in calling them sonnets"; and he didn't think they looked "like them on the page." Mackay Brown always looked for an alignment more serene. He thought Hopkins a poet who "moves through the sextet in violent ritual action" without a "wave like surge and fall." In the octet Mackay Brown writes that Hopkins "went further to "stall" all motion caught up and movement" and that this act of stalling "does preserve traditional feeling."[31] Mackay Brown recognized that Hopkins worked "the traditional feeling" of poetic form to absorb the irregularities or the differences within human nature into a timeless symmetry as the human person moves

---

30 Mackay Brown, *Notebook One, NLS*.   31 Ibid.

through historical time. As Hopkins successfully linguistically assimilated difference and unity into his poetic language of sprung rhythm, its symmetry brought a new realism to literature. Hopkins's existential crisis and the reinvigorated firmament that emerged disrupted the "traditional feeling"[32] of his times and gave line and lead to Mackay Brown's own existential crisis. As Newman had defined, the classics of a National Literature are those literary works that are outstanding examples of a particular style and have lasting worth with a timeless quality. The creators of these "classics" are in a line of succession, "a type of a generation or the interpreter of a crisis." They are each in their turn made for their day and their day made for them.[33] Their "peculiar talent" arose in the circumstances of their times. They were able to give their language flexibility in expression of a variety of thoughts and feelings accompanied by a penetrating discernment, a clarity of vision or intellect that provided a deep understanding and insight. The new symmetry could expand and compress, disrupt and challenge in its relentless push to keep poetic vision fresh and real and it was not afraid of the dark forces within the human person.

Mackay Brown in his *Essays and Notes* on "The Windhover" has a strong consciousness of the action of the ploughman: "driving slow clumsy plough-horses over the fields in an action which looks like ritual but which is primarily concerned, like the windhover, with getting food."[34] Mackay Brown is understated when expanding his vision from the particular worker to the universal food gatherer underpinning the survival of the community. This insight holds within it acts of "courtly ritual" as the Christ-windhover-bird takes liturgical form and shape overseeing "humbler men ... driving slow clumsy plough-horses over the fields" pressing the vision to see Christ the food-gatherer in his eucharistic body-bread.[35] Mackay Brown and Hopkins work in unison in their treatment of the world of work. This unity is demonstrated in Mackay Brown's poem "Masque of Bread."[36]

---

32 Ibid.
33 Newman, "English Catholic Literature," in *The Idea of a University*, 187.
34 Mackay Brown, *The Windhover* 11MS pp on 6 leaves each 33 × 20.5cm signed George M Brown March 1964 in another ink. NLS.　　　35 Ibid.
36 Mackay Brown, "The Masque of Bread," *Collected Poems of George Mackay Brown*, 19.

Mackay Brown seamlessly fetches out the difference and the unity in the ritual getting of food from seed to corn, harvested and ground to the making of bread and all quivering in the action of the human person. Holding the "martyr, the sufferer, in all men"[37] close to his heart as he descends into the dark foreboding world of the "seventy hungry streets, / Each poorer than the last" until at rest at "the Inquisitor's door."[38] The persona of the Inquisitor goes either way, first towards a harsh and severe official searching out the roots of heresy contrary to the doctrine or teachings of the Catholic faith. But secondly the public persona gave way to the seeker on the narrow path that is "like a nightmare round his winter feet."[39] The masked persona[40] happens upon "a white bakehouse with a little arch"[41] aureated with curvature of sight, sound, and smell, "a creaking sign" and "fragrant doorpost" sensationally drawn into where the "Inquisitor" poet clings "like drifted snow," interrogating silence and shutter by shutter the baker's "oven" opens out "on hills of harvest sun and corn." The eucharistic "loaf," laid out on the altar, "the long shelf"/ "was bearded, thewed,[42] goldcrusted like a god." Just as Hopkins's "Harry Ploughman" is inscaped with "his thew," the curvature of sight and sound open out the "masque": "Each drew a mask over his gentle eyes / —Masks of the world, the boar, the hawk, the reaper—" and the ritual on the altar plays out "the mock passion" as they "clawed the bread."[43] Mackay Brown in Edinburgh had within him already

---

[37] Mackay Brown, "Saint Magnus Cathedral," Easter 1944. Unpublished MS Orkney Archives: EWM Collection.
[38] Mackay Brown, "The Masque of Bread," *Collected Poems of George Mackay Brown*, 18-19.   [39] Ibid.
[40] Persona is a derivative from the Latin to mean mask.
[41] Mackay Brown, "The Masque of Bread," *Collected Poems of George Mackay Brown*, 19.
[42] Old English thēaw "usage, custom," (plural) "manner of behaving," of unknown origin. The sense "good bodily proportions, muscular development" arose in Middle English. Synonyms give vivid echoes of the swarm of meaning, for example, robustness · healthiness · hardiness · strength · stamina · sturdiness · fitness · good shape · power · bloom · radiance · sap · energy · activity · liveliness · life · spryness · sprightliness · vitality · vivacity · vivaciousness · verve · animation · spiritedness · spirit · enthusiasm · fire · fieriness · fervour · ardour · zeal · passion · might · forcefulness · determination · intensity · dynamism · sparkle · effervescence · zest · dash · snap · spark · gusto · pep · bounce · exuberance · drive · push · elan · zip · zing.
[43] Mackay Brown, "The Masque of Bread," *Collected Poems of George Mackay Brown*, 19.

the art form of how to sustain his incarnational stance punctuating or aureating the natural world with the supernatural as symbols swarm and are brought into the embrace of the eucharistic harvest. His rhyme and reason allow his audience to rest in the natural images of Orkney fauna, flora, and work, much of which was historical to the Orcadian audience rather than a symphonic vision of God's creation. He was not romantically yearning for a world long gone. His rhyme and reason were intended to stitch the tapestry and illumine his visionary sensation by means of an incarnational stance.

Furthermore, there is the conflation of the "Everyman" "the martyr, the sufferer, in all men,"[44] as he stands between "the cold Plough and the embers in the door of death"[45] with Christ and all his hallows. The language of the "constants" stall and stem the *inscapes* with "door" and "stations" that hold the inscape to its instress as the symbols swarm. Death on Calvary interchanged with all acts of death, for and with Christ, in "that simple act Of terror or love." The Tree of Life's "Angel with a sword" holds ground against the Grim Reaper's "Grinning Rags" and an enigmatic figure appears, "He knelt in the doorway."[46] This is St. Magnus and the native tradition. Mackay Brown writes in his novel *Magnus*, first published in 1973, that the hallowed "Everyman"[47] gestated "astride the kindled seed?"[48] and

> the whole web of history trembled...He saw himself in the mask of the beast being dragged to a primitive stone. A more desolate image followed, from some far reach of time: he saw a man walking the length of a bare white ringing corridor to a small cube-shaped interior full of hard light; in that hideous clarity the man would die. The recurrence of pattern-within-flux touched him, momentarily with wonder.[49]

The Mackay Brown dream vision of "Fragmented light and song" eucharistically emerges when "the bread lay broken" and "the first steeple / Shook out petals of morning, long bright robes / Circled in order round the man that died."[50]

And, sure enough, Mackay Brown while at his post graduate studies in Edinburgh, was busy sketching out a frame for "A

---

44 Ibid.   45 Ibid.   46 Ibid.   47 Ibid., *Magnus*, 131.
48 Ibid., "The Masque of Bread," 19.
49 Ibid., *Magnus*, 131.   50 Ibid., "The Masque of Bread," 19.

Magnus piece 7 parts? It is the year of Our Lord 1075 1085 1098 1115 1116 Easter 1116 Orkneyinga Saga."[51] These *Essays and Notes* on Hopkins confirm the Mackay Brown technique as it then stood in the 1960s but opened out other lines of development, some Parnassian, some not:

> The hard clumsy toil of the ploughman is a symbol of all our strivings, 'a sheer plod' far removed from the beauty of the bird's flight, the ritual of the joust, or the Incarnation. We turn dark seemingly profitless furrows; no fire of beauty or holiness breaks immediately from those broken 'blue-black-embers'; yet out of the earth wounds rise in due course ripe fields of corn.[52]

The hallowed human person exemplified by St. Magnus faces his own light and dark forces as did Hopkins and Mackay Brown. Is this a literary symmetry alone that has no basis in real life? Or can literature once again give authentic linguistic expression of the nature of the human person? Being "hallowed" for Hopkins and Mackay Brown is where divinity and humanity come together, in Christ. These passion poets found themselves in many a dark place and roll of emotions, but they saw something of the divine power breaking through in the form of Christ, a man of sorrow and suffering, who they believed gave them their place and purpose.

THE GRIME OF POLITICAL MANMARKS AND FOOTPRINTS

Both Hopkins and Mackay Brown pass through the political realm in their literary quest. They put out into the depths, for them a place of transformation for the human person in existential combat. As Mackay Brown, in his notes in "Gerard Manley Hopkins and Politics," writes, "I am not much interested in politics myself."[53] But he did have a high degree of political literacy and was intellectually sensitive to the injustices endured by the agricultural underclasses when he wrote of the "impression of horse hooves and ploughmen's boots and all the wandering feet (arcumambient[54]) of the country folk.

---

51 Mackay Brown, *Notebook Three. NLS.*
52 Mackay Brown, *The Windhover* 11 MS pp on 6 leaves each 33 × 20.5cm signed George M Brown March 1964 in another ink. NLS.
53 Mackay Brown, *Notebook Two*, "Gerard Manley Hopkins and Politics," NLS.
54 The etymology of *arcus* is the same; the root arc not only means to hurl, but to sing or resound.

Their treadmill toil suggests meaningless, futility. The 'footprints' are marks hiding man's one true direction."[55] The rhythms of his childhood flourish image by image in his close study of Orkney, and he was often quoted to this end: "I realize now how lucky I was to be brought up in Orkney. Not only are the islands beautiful in themselves and layered with history and prehistory but here live the food providers, the farmers, and fishermen whose work keeps the breath in us all. I don't need to go in search of themes. Rhythms and images and legends are everywhere."[56] And here we have a prime example of such a quotation fetching out the "existence versus essence." So, the biblical echoes, the "breath" ("In him we live and move and have our being as even some of your poets have said"[57]), favor the Scotian and Hopkins alignment with "existence." In other words, the instressed inscape holds within itself a profound grasp of the old firmament made new by Hopkins, and is able to transcend, simultaneously ascending and descending on the quiver of the instress as the inscapes held to the doctrine of Incarnation. Some of his critics see this as a defect or weakness, descending into "archaism is a problem"[58] which "deteriorates into mannerism"[59] or Georgianism[60] "worked in a very strange and personal way almost obsessive."[61]

Mackay Brown considered the human person as central in Hopkins's "Tom's Garland": "Tom and Dick and (later) Harry Ploughman emerge in H's representative figures of the English workman—strong, stupid, beautiful, uncomplicated (well-digestioned)."[62] This was a poem that Mackay Brown did not think successful, and he clearly was not at one with Hopkins's Conservative Tory politics: "Tom's Garland is a false poem, then,

---

55 Mackay Brown, *Notebook Two. Notes on "That Nature is a Heraclitean Fire and the Comfort of the Resurrection," NLS.*
56 Campbell, "Carried along by the Rhythms of Childhood," in *The Scotsman*, Saturday 13 October 1990, 13.   57 Acts 17:15, 22–18:1.
58 Scammell, "Hard as Granite, Sweet as Grass," *The Scotsman Weekend: Books & Poetry*, 1991.
59 Nye, "Turning Fables into Life," *The Scotsman Weekend*, 15 June 1991, 7.
60 Ibid. The aesthetic principles of Georgianism included a respect for formalism as well as bucolic and romantic subject matter. The devastation of World War I, along with the rise of modernism, signaled the retreat of Georgianism as an influential school of poetry.
61 Cloud, "Splendid Isolation." *Spectrum Review*, 32.
62 Mackay Brown, *Notebook One. Sketches for Essays, NLS.*

from the foundation up. I am not much interested in politics myself and I have no partisan prejudge[ment] against H's attitude in this poem. It just seems, in the light of history, to give a false picture. This sickness erupts in the poem itself—it is certainly one of his worst performances, harsh, clumsy, unharmonious."[63] This essay sketch does flush out the strength of Mackay Brown's political orientation and his clear disdain for Conservatism, certain forms of socialism; even further, he saw politics as a skewed version of the true purpose of the nature of the human person. It was the genius of Mackay Brown that journalistically he did at times give the appearance of running with the hare and hunting with the hounds but inevitably the irresistible force of his literary work, his "Masque," was founded on a sensational vision that carries worldly or political concerns within a firmament possessing a divine reach and purpose. In the minds of these passion poets, divine life and power break through at every opportunity. The business of politics is "grime". Surface dirt ingrained but never given the elevation or last word in any way that could suppress the dignity of the human person and the world of work. Christ was not a politician, He was Redeemer, Savior, and Sacramental Healer. Hopkins and then Mackay Brown never stopped being enthralled by His Presence in this world and beyond.

Nobody reads Hopkins or Blake or Mackay Brown for their politics, even if their political context was undoubtedly of considerable importance in an examination of their participation in society.[64] Mackay Brown never once talked to me about Catholic social teaching, and I am not aware he used the phrase "the common good,"[65] but then I never discussed that with him in conversation or letter. We did talk about John Paul II and, although he was a great admirer, he did not think the pope's poetry was convincing. He did, though, soften his spiky stance by saying that one would have to take into consideration what

---

63 Mackay Brown, *Notebook Two*. "Tom's Garland: Upon the Unemployed," NLS.
64 MacBeath, "Under Equality's Sun: George Mackay Brown and Socialism from the Margins of Society."
65 The notion of "the common good" may be the most familiar concept of Catholic social teaching. The Compendium of the Social Doctrine of the Church cites it as the first principle of CST, and as something "to which every aspect of social life must be related" (164), and as the "primary goal" of society (165).

was lost in the translation into English. He framed his politics as he wrote to me on 30 October 1994: "Has the great socialist dream vanished in the gray light of day? I hope not: because we must always keep that ideal alive."[66] He did expend his energies on a politicized version of Christ in the days of his "half-baked stuff" when much of his imagery reflected his inner struggles with the macabre, for example, in the unpublished "Christ Poem" from July 1944. He tried to cast the trial of Christ before his accusers in the modern stance of the radical carpenter challenging the warped class structure at every turn ending with the death penalty (death by hanging): "Meantime the membership of the underground Communist Party increases by leaps and bounds."[67] Later, in the unpublished story "Magnificat,"[68] he never truly manages to centralize the Virgin Mary, Mother of Christ the carpenter, with "The widow... all alone. Her man died years ago. Her son was hanged." He tried to draw on the ancient prayer of the Magnificat,[69] but it does not come off and the manuscript is scored with crossing outs and big segments "canceled" (not that this was unusual for Mackay Brown's textual method). Mackay Brown tried to put the ancient prayer on the lips of Mary the widow and sorrowed mother in this prose narrative, but it comes across as awkward and unreal. Nevertheless, it does position Mackay Brown as a poet who had a political consciousness that was part of his view of the world of Orkney and beyond.

Mackay Brown gives the political context and its purpose some weight in the study of Hopkins's sonnet "Tom's Garland (upon the Unemployed.)" In *Notebook One* he sketches out his first impressions of Tom the worker who appears as the "least successful of characters, symbol abstract figure, in fact as things

---

66 Mackay Brown, letter to the author 30/10/94. In the author's personal correspondence.
67 Mackay Brown, "Christ Poem." July 1944. Unpublished MS in OLA, EWM Collection.
68 Mackay Brown, "Magnificat" unpublished short story, June/July 1994, manuscript. D124/18/2/6.
69 The Magnificat (Latin for "[My soul] magnifies [the Lord]") is a canticle, also known as the Song of Mary, the Canticle of Mary and, in the Byzantine tradition, the Ode of the Theotokos (Greek: Ἡ Ὠδὴ τῆς Θεοτόκου). Mackay Brown was totally familiar with OT ideas given prominence here by Mary the Daughter of Zion: God comes not to help the rich and the powerful but the poor and the simple. Ever since Abraham received the promises Gn. 15: 1a. 17: 1a Israel has been God's favored one. Luke 1: 46–55 Note 1z. *The New Jerusalem Bible*.

have turned out...Tom-heart-at-ease has a television set now goes to Butlins every year for his holiday with the wife and kids, misses mass every other Sunday and votes Labour & Tory alternatively. [A] faded outworn image, Tom must take his place beside Peter Pan in a never-never land."[70] Mackay Brown writes with the sparks and spikes of a social, political, and religious critique that could not hold his interest other than to generate colorful and idiosyncratic images of the political tensions and pressures that swayed in Hopkins as he wrote this experimental curtal sonnet. Tensions and pressures on the poet drove the experimentation, the new lines of development of the old firmament making it longer (caudal) or shorter (curtal). The Petrarchan form was pressed into service with new expansion and compression, not purely for effect, but to accommodate the poet's thinking and feeling meshed in a ferment that sought accurate expression. Mackay Brown does not comment on this, but here was his license to experiment that increasingly was optimized by him after this study period. The complex inner worlds of these poets needed a form that could hold and stabilize and be true to their moral consciences. Driven by the imperative, the call of curlew and its curvature of sound, the Christ-bird always gains the upper hand, over and above the political zeitgeist of their times.

Mackay Brown comments that Hopkins was at once the "Englishman, patriot, chauvinist" who was less than sympathetic to Irish politics. It puzzled him that the intelligent Hopkins could not see a "false and strident jingoism" all about him in "his age." "Surely an intelligence like H's could see that the same establishment he lauds in 'Tom's Garland' wielded the knife that tore out Edmund Campion's[71] entrails and sent the Catholic Church into the wilderness 300 years ago."[72] Mackay Brown struggled with his own vehement tone as he recognized the late nineteenth century that may have given a certain appearance of

---

70 Mackay Brown, *Notebook One*, NLS.
71 Edmund Campion, S. J. (24 January 1540–1 December 1581) was an English Catholic Jesuit priest and martyr. While conducting an underground ministry in officially Anglican England, Campion was arrested by priest hunters. Convicted of high treason, he was hanged, drawn, and quartered at Tyburn. Campion was beatified by Pope Leo XIII in 1886 and canonized in 1970 by Pope Paul VI as one of the Forty Martyrs of England and Wales.
72 Mackay Brown, *Notebook Two*, "*GMH and Politics*," NLS.

harmony at a time when civilization was breaking down. He tried giving a rationale for the emergence of the shapeshifters, Hangdog and Manwolf (socialists, levelers from the industrial slums of England). Mackay Brown is reading Hopkins's letters and poems concurrently and forms his rationale greatly influenced by Hopkins's point of view.[73] Hopkins examined the "necessity of socialism" including "Engle's description" and Edith Sitwell's view of Queen Victoria. Mackay Brown takes the Russian Revolution into account as he writes that Hopkins's portrayals of "Tom," "Dick" and later "Harry" are "strong, stupid, beautiful, uncomplicated" even "well-digestioned." As Mackay Brown writes. "Tom has manwolf in him too, Tom has a touch of hangdog. There was great danger in that squat and surly steel. It was only the leaven of liberalism in English politics that kept Tom and Dick and Harry out of the red drama of revolution and preserved them as respectable (usually Labour) voters."[74]

Mackay Brown swiftly extricated himself from the political to the realm wherein he was more "at home" and able to express what he really believed and wanted to say: "It is the traditionally Xt [Christian] (especially Catholics) view I think of the poor as being especially blessed of God. And here is a poor man, Tom. Here is a Catholic showing him to us. Yet Tom is not really poor, in the Xt's [Christian] sense, at all, when the poem is examined. He is well shod, well fed, well bedded, sound in heart and body, not troubled, like Houseman's lads, with 'the thoughts that hurt.'" And then he goes to scripture and speaks his mind: "But the real poor of this world are those so vividly and terribly depicted in scripture—the halt,[75] the blind, the maim, the lepers, the devil-possessed—and this has nothing much to do with economics—those who share the wounds of Christ, and, accepting them in love as part of the inevitable human lot—will likewise share in the great feast of the Bridegroom when "the tears will be wiped from all eyes."[76] Mackay Brown's heart was with outcasts, those on the margins of society. He did not place

---

73 Hopkins, *The Letters of Gerard Manley Hopkins to Robert Bridges*, 264–66.
74 Mackay Brown, *Notebook Two*, "*GMH and Politics*," NLS.
75 Mackay Brown is using the King James Bible here by using "halt" in Luke 14:21, John 5:3, an archaism for those with a physical disability (Old English *healtian* (verb), halt, healt (adjective), of Germanic origin).
76 Mackay Brown, *Notebook Two*, "*GMH and Politics*," NLS.

the core of his faith in institutions. His faith was in Christ ministering to "The gospel poor" who "are not only the labourers in the vineyard and the sower who goes out to sow, they are the centurion whose servant is sick and Pilate with his terrible doubts and the rich young man who clung to his poverty-making wealth and went away sorrowfully out of God's presence. The poor we have with us always."[77] And then he writes with his signatory spark and spike of grace, "If Rockefeller and the rat-catcher if they are without grace; gnaw the same unhallowed crust."[78] Mackay Brown, like Hopkins, sees the dignity of the human person as the central form that keeps breaking out in the coming together of the divine and human in spite of their unhallowed grime, manmarks and footprints. This "Everyman" instressed-inscape gave tremendous hope to all their writing.

Mackay Brown gives the impression of annoyance at times. Specifically he notes down that Hopkins is "looking at Tom politically and as I suggested, falsely." The poem fails in his view because "As the priest, H [is] the nourisher of immortal souls." And again, he denies the credibility of the political, "It would have been written to the order of the Conservative Central Office of the time."[79] Then Mackay Brown "peers a little way" to see how Tom would have fared in "recent social history" with National Health Insurance and family labor to bring in money to offset the effects of poverty and sickness. He reverts again to the circumstances where "Hangdog and Manwolf might seem to him like the good hounds in a fable who (who know where the grouse has fallen into the heather and where the rabbit have their burrows)."[80] His heart and mind were ever Orkney and "the chant of the agricultural poor" was something he was in tune with and with which he had community experience. The Mackay Brown verdict on socialism, then, goes like this: "In other words, socialism of some kind, as H well knew, was a necessity at this period of Western Europe's social history; if it did not come peacefully, it would come violently (as in Nazi Germany) And that was what the poet was afraid of. The 'Socialists, radicals, levelers,' something to be a new group in history, without roots or responsibilities underneath the chant of England's agricultural poor." And his resolution was a gospel

---

77 Ibid.   78 Ibid.   79 Ibid.   80 Ibid.

one: "But only Xts [Christianity] was able to feed the total multitude. The politicians of the 19th century were certainly not able to do so—one remembers the ghastly story of Ireland between 1849 and 1858."[81]

Mackay Brown argues that "Tom is one of H's least successful characters partly because a little of the grime of politics adheres to him (H was not a political simpleton as this sonnet suggests)." He had read the *Letters (Hopkins to Bridges)*[82] where Hopkins is quite politically opinionated and conflicted by the economic and political controversies surrounding him as he taught classics at University College Dublin. The political pressure of his university appointment combined with the instability of the British Empire in the face of economic and political threats sought some sort of psychic resolution in the symbolism of the Queen. The Protestant legacy of the Reformation increasingly endowed the Church of the reformers with a level of divine authority from its Kings and Queens as it appropriated the rites and rituals of Catholicism. The Oxford Movement put Newman and then Hopkins in the religious dimension of Catholicism that extracted them from national allegiances that had to accommodate all the anti-Catholic sentiment in English society and anti-English sentiment in Irish society. Amidst all the tensions Hopkins and Mackay Brown had to live with, they were not abandoning reformed Christianity in its various forms; rather, they were expanding, developing, and restoring the old firmament anew from their position within society. They were not limited and bound by the Protestant ethos of those times and struck out on their own against popular literary tides of convention.

Mackay Brown equally found himself in such a position with the added anti-Catholic sentiment within Orcadian and Scottish

---

81 Ibid.
82 *The Letters of Gerard Manley Hopkins to Robert Bridges*, 26-27. "But it is a dreadful thing for the greatest and most necessary part of a very rich nation to live a hard life without dignity, knowledge, comforts, delight, or hopes in the midst of plenty—which plenty they make. They profess that they do not care what they wreck and burn, the old civilization and order must be destroyed. This is a dreadful lookout but what has the old civilization done for them? As it at present stands in England it is itself in great measure founded on wrecking. But they got none of the spoils, they came in for nothing but harm from it then and thereafter. England has grown hugely wealthy, but this wealth has not reached the working classes; I expect it has made their condition worse."

society and the overlap between the two. As he wrote in 1984, "To Orcadians Scotland had always been a problem. We belong and we do not belong."[83] The "Scotification" of "one of the great medieval earldoms" began with a temporary arrangement in 1469, "but it was for keeps as things turned out." Mackay Brown described the Reformation politics of those times as an "unpleasant business" when "Scotsmen flooded in and sat in the high places of Orkney." The subsequent history of those times was brutal, forcefully imposed and a contradiction of the legacy recorded in the medieval Orkneyinga Saga. "It vanished like a rich dream once the Scottish carpet-baggers came. In a generation or so Orkney, the powerful medieval earldom, had shrunk to the status of a minor Scottish county. The ancient frames of the earldom with their graces and ceremonies were torn down, almost overnight. And soon the beauty of the old religion was taken from Orkneymen, and Calvinism established."[84] This was what Mackay Brown thought, believed, and wrote throughout his life; and any attempt to mute this lacks integrity. His voice still stands, whether it is agreed with, reinterpreted, or compromised by subsequent generations. Like all the genuinely great poets, Mackay Brown left politics to the politicians and put his heart and soul into "the ancient harp-strokes," the sprung rhythms of the community with his own strong consciousness, not only of the flow and workings of history, but of words. The mesh of racial composition in Orkney and the speech that "goes down and up, like waves or little hills. If the people speak a kind of Scots-English, the music of their tongue is unique. Those who know about such things compare the rhythms and intonations to certain valleys in Norway."[85] Distinctively, Mackay Brown resonated with the "ancient frame," the old firmament made new, not trying to "beat the bell back" but to quarry words, harness the swarm of symbols, carve the runes, in order to keep in step with the "Orkneys" and their own culture, traditions, and history slightly removed from the ethos of others, "in the far reaches of the ocean...the islands...new-washed from the foam of perilous seas."[86]

---

83 Mackay Brown, My Scotland: "Orkney and Scotland," in *The Scottish Review: Arts and Environment*, 15.
84 Ibid.   85 Ibid.   86 Ibid.

Mackay Brown thought "Tom's Garland" fell short with its political view of the human person, but his own political consciousness was an important part of his life and work. When I went back to re-read my correspondence, Mackay Brown, like all of us, observed the doings of the world. Yet his difference was seen in his allegiances that are on the record publicly as a journalist and privately as a letter-writer. For example: "A lot of unemployment here too...the hideous patchwork that's best, it seems, that politicians of whatever creed can manage (25 Sept 1981). "Neither State socialism nor freebooting Capitalism seems to be the answer to the world's material ills (18/8/90)," "The election caused a small stir here, but I suppose it doesn't matter all that much who gets in, the government has such a narrow room for maneuver (25 April 1992)," "Everyone here speaks of recession (8 Oct 1992)," "I thought New Zealand was the original welfare state until I saw a TV program recently: wealth to the rich, the gutter for the poor...things are rapidly going that way here, too. Has the great socialist dream vanished in the gray light of day? I hope not: because we must always keep that ideal alive (30/10/94)."[87] But it was the ancient frame of Christianity, the sweetness of the old religion that held his mind and heart. As for Hopkins, the Incarnation was the pulsing stem of Mackay Brown's hurrahing in the poetic harvest, "Christmas gives me more fruitful images than anything else (28 Sept 1982)."[88] He needed breadth and depth and in his distinctive grasp of Orkney and Catholicism he interweaves between the two with politics stitched in its rightful place.

THE HUMAN PERSON AS POETIC SUBJECT

Mackay Brown, like Hopkins, had his poetic "feet" astride two worlds—this world and the other. Their sense of place was geographically peripheral "far from the sites of Christian world history"[89] as it was to the Catholic literary elite of the Middle Ages. The christianization of the North Atlantic, closer as it

---

[87] Mackay Brown, Correspondence in possession of the author are included (except for 30/10/94) in the Appendix "Excerpts from the letters of Mackay Brown to Gray, 1977-1993," in *George Mackay Brown No Separation*, 191-205.
[88] Ibid.
[89] Jakobsson, "Centre and Periphery in Icelandic Medieval Discourse," in *Preprint Papers: The 14th International Saga Conference*.

was to a palpable proto-Christian experience, once again given literary prominence when the Oxford Movement unleashed in Hopkins his passion for Christ in accordance with his interpretation of his times in "crisis." As we have seen, Mackay Brown was not entirely happy with the portrayal of Hopkins's "Tom" and "Dick"[90] as well as "Harry."[91] Nevertheless, Hopkins's disruptive approach is an assimilation of sorts that indeed captured Mackay Brown's attention and alerted him to the discordant ethos of Hopkins's and his own times. Mackay Brown observed Hopkins's "Tom" as "made to stand in the glare of a false romanticism."[92] Giving Hopkins his due, he understood that Hopkins wrote of "people he knew, and especially of people he met in the course of his priestly duties, it could be very good."[93] However, Mackay Brown saw Tom as a "symbol, and abstract figure," the "Everyman" that "Father Hopkins, the poet must have met in church and home thousands of labourers and navvies like Tom, but each with his own quirk, mole, flourish, inscape, flavor 'more distinctive than ale or walnut leaf'; no-one, it's safe to say, exactly like this dumb contented ox who is made to stand for the British working class."[94] The characterization of particular persons "more distinctive than ale or walnut leaf" anchors "Tom," "this dumb contented ox" as well as "Harry" a "fragmented Cubist portrait" as seamlessly interwoven within the universal. Already adept at mastering a dynamic flow of particularities in the swarm of symbols, Mackay Brown had another, more Orkney, version in mind.

The human person as poetic subject takes on a piercing tactile sense based on scholarship as well as feeling and intuition. Mackay Brown made his own discoveries and developed them along the Hopkinesque lines of the renewal of the old firmament trying to restore and heal what he saw as the "wreck" that the Reformation forcefully imposed upon Orkney.[95] Poems,

---

90 Mackay Brown, *Notebook Two*, "GMH & Politics," NLS.
91 Mackay Brown, *Notebook One*. "*snarled up in his own devices, not a complete figure, broken vividness about him, foretaste of one of those Cubist portraits where the subject is all fragmented,*" NLS.
92 Mackay Brown, *Notebook Two*, "GMH & Politics," NLS.
93 Ibid. 94 Ibid.
95 Gray, *Circle of Light: The Catholic Church in Orkney Since 1560*, 15. "There was a dismantling of medieval culture, and its onset was sudden...The Reformation Parliament of 1560 forbade the Mass; tradition has it that the

whether Hopkins's or Mackay Brown's, may at first reading appear strange and adrift from the conventions of their times. The religious stance of their audiences, not to mention their literary critics, inevitably affects how they are read. Hopkins turned from external nature to the spiritual and moral condition of the human person. The human person has a universality where fallen nature implies a sense of judgment and a sense of redemption. The humanity of Christ is seen at work by Mackay Brown in St. Magnus as an Orkney prototype, inscaped and instressed by a life of dedication, obedience, and service in the sacrifice of the Passion of Our Lord. Individual lives of devoted service through physical discipline and moral duty are then analogues of religious obedience. Christ inscaped into the human person, made in the image of God, exemplifies the particular shape and pattern of the unique person. The essence of the human person is held in the tension of the form of the servant. Keywords and sounds proliferate in repeated figures such as birds of flight, the windhover and stormfowl, angels and archangels, horse and rider, laborer and ploughman. Heroic conduct is therefore the tough struggle of mastery. The presentation within the dramatic narrative hovers between under- and overstatement, falling and rising across the life drama all the time anchored in the *instress* fastened in concrete type. The ordered array of phrase, of feeling in the raw spontaneity of fixed types/essences reveals nature, pitch and will, thisness, that taste of myself, the self of being. Here in the selvèd person is the basic fiber of being, pitched or tuned in the instress, the grace of God. The will is exercised in choice. A life of moral discipline carries the imagery of battle.

Hopkins expressly denied the Romantic atomism of personality in art calling it "damned subjective rot."[96] Hopkins's "long ramble on literary matters"[97] enclosed the "keepings"[98] of a succession

---

last Mass was officiated at Rapness on Westray. The break-up of Catholic Orkney was led by Bishop Bothwell, who quickly reorganized land ownership, personnel, and family power." For a fuller account of the impact of the Reformation on Orkney see Chapter Seven "Reading Orkney" in *George Mackay Brown: No Separation*.

96 Hopkins, letter to Robert Bridges, June 22, 1879, *The Letters of Gerard Manley Hopkins to Robert Bridges*, 84.
97 Hopkins, letter to Canon Dixon, 1 December 1881. *The Correspondence of Gerard Manley Hopkins to Richard Watson Dixon*, 98–99.
98 Ibid.

of English poets and painters as they moved through various phases of artistic and language development. "Keepings" or those properties that were retained or kept from each historical phase had to pass through the literary canon and its prime traditions like going through the "eye of the needle." This art of refinement set up an objective essence or intrinsic nature in the cluster of the properties of the English language. Its orthodoxy could withstand enrichment by its heresies. Although he concurs that "the Lake poets and all that school represent, as it seems to me, the mean or standard of English style and diction...which culminated in Milton"[99] their "keepings" are "their weak point, a sort of colorless keepings."[100] "They were faithful but not rich observers of nature."[101] Hopkins was always pressing towards a strong and realistic eye away from the mere subjective, the sentimental, the colorless classicism, the archaic, even the biblical, to arrive at the inscape as the objective essence fastened in concrete type.

Hopkins and then Mackay Brown understood the work of the poet to elicit a piercing sight into things and persons. The expression of their art was disruptive and stunning in its use of word-color-sound-play that was sharper and clearer than normally perceived by the common eye. Both poets created sharp visual impressions and remote comparisons with finer tools of technique to fetch out the inscape and instress. This technique ran in parallel to the experience of life. The intellectual deployment of Platonic realism and Pythagorean imagery with geometrical and musical figures form the basis for Hopkins's theory of inscape and instress. It was developed at Oxford from a fusion of philosophy of beauty, a metaphysics and science of being. Later Duns Scotus and a close reading and living of Ignatian experience released in Hopkins an immense fire of passion. Mackay Brown found in Hopkins a spiritual and intellectual credibility he could live with, after much pondering. But he had already turned and tuned his mind and craft towards "workers in field and mill and mine"[102] as well as tinker, saint, crofter, tramp, lifeboatman, fisherman, doctor, librarian, tailor. Mackay Brown portrays the inscaped pageant of Orkney folk in their fibred goodness in spite of their dark struggles in the

---

99 Ibid.   100 Ibid.   101 Ibid.
102 Mackay Brown, "Prologue," *Collected Poems of George Mackay Brown*, 1.

"eerie carnival, and frightened folk / Fluttered on the cliff edge."[103] Again and again, the human person errs on the side of the good, like the clever Doctor Guthrie[104] with his "dark smirk" but for all his contempt for the Orcadian "way-of-life" and their genetic mix as a "curious hotch-potch," his sense of conscientious duty never failed as he went out on his calls "well after midnight." Through his eyes, the poet explores the historical fusion that assimilates all comers into the "pageant" of life and death in the face of "sea's cold fermentation."[105] The human person, for all his moral endeavor, "flutters" precariously "on the cliff edge" as they each and all are constrained to face the truth of the natural world. The miracle of life takes precedent over its dark challenges. Inevitably and surely, Mackay Brown rises to his best with the "dark plinth"[106] giving way to his "liturgy of April,"[107] having experienced first-hand the "undersong of terrible holy joy."[108] The human person emerges with an undone goodness for all his or her failings. Mackay Brown, like Hopkins, releases his passion into the "fire of images." He tells the story of a people, each and all, particular and universal. He accepts the dark chaos of the encounter between this world and the other, having learned without realizing it how to *inscape* with shape and rhythm conceived in simplicity and silence.

It is pertinent to take note of Edwin Muir's profound influence on Mackay Brown as he spread his literary wings to get a clear view of the human person as poetic subject. Muir was in from the beginning of Mackay Brown's literary formation in many ways. Mackay Brown soaked in the subtlety of Muir's literary arguments and educational ethos as he advanced in his own development. Muir steered him towards a wide appreciation of literary ability regardless of the religious or political views that a literary person may or may not hold. In an essay "The Political View of Literature" (1949), Muir thoughtfully gives voice to the view that subsequent generations of readers and critics of a work are "not entitled to transform it into something else and then assess it as something else."[109] About reli-

---

103 Ibid., "Lifeboatman," 9.
104 Ibid., "Doctor," 12.
105 Ibid., "Lifeboatman," 9.
106 Ibid., "The Night in Troy," 17.
107 Ibid.
108 Ibid., "The Old Women," 16.
109 Muir, "The Political View of Literature," in *Essays on Literature and Society*, 139.

gion, he asserts: "Anyone who cannot enter into it is not in a position to understand it; all that he can do therefore is to interpret it in his own terms, which are foreign to the experience itself."[110] Whether James Joyce or T. S. Eliot (or Mackay Brown) were being critiqued in Muir's view, a literary critic is duty-bound to understand their work before settling on any errors the literary work may or may not contain. To understand, the critic has to know "the essential thing...what is it that determines the pattern and scale of emphasis, what is the real work, and what are the by-products of it."[111] Mackay Brown and Hopkins were very sensitized to potential audiences. They fully realized the dilemma of how to be tune with an audience who lacked their epistemic formation. Using real people and genuine experience from a knowledge of life in a very particular way ensured that the audience was able to step back and recognize characterization regardless of the age in which they were living. Hopkins and Mackay Brown do this by a piercing study of the particularities of moral character of the human person. Whether one agrees with their characterization or not, there is no doubt by doing so they both consciously locate themselves in the classical literary canon. They passionately and conscientiously worked within the artistic sense but never deconstructed the Catholic moral ethos. Their Catholicism mattered. Their work has endured to this day and goes into the future because of the authenticity and the moral gravitas of their composition. As Alan Bold writes, "criticisms do not alter my admiration for Brown's work: to disagree with him is one thing, to deny the awesome power of his work would be sheer folly."[112] And it is also important to consider that Mackay Brown left a vast paper trail (published and unpublished) that ensured his voice would be heard throughout his development. He did not conceal the "half-baked stuff" or his psychic turmoil from view. They are there for the serious researcher alongside the more selective autobiography[113] that some believe leaves more questions than answers.[114]

---

[110] Ibid.   [111] Ibid., 140.   [112] Bold, *George Mackay Brown*, 113.
[113] Mackay Brown, *For the Islands I Sing*.
[114] MacBeath, *Under Equality's Sun: George Mackay Brown and Socialism from the Margins of Society*.

Mackay Brown turned with positivity towards Hopkins's poem "Felix Randal."[115] This poem, in his view, was Hopkins's "greatest portrait"[116] of the human person with "no sentimentality"[117] in spite of the "disorder that unraveled all his strength."[118] Mackay Brown values Hopkins the parish priest and his pastoral care of his people in London, Liverpool, Bedford Leigh, Oxford, and Glasgow. As Hopkins shared with Canon Dixon: "My Liverpool and Glasgow experience laid upon my mind a conviction, a truly crushing conviction, of the misery of town life to the poor and more than to the poor, of the misery of the poor in general, of the degradation of our race, of the hollowness of this century's civilization: it made even life a burden to me to have daily thrust upon me in the things I saw."[119] Hopkins was a deeply diligent and committed parish priest who may have been wearied by his tasks, but his priesthood was always at the forefront of his mind and heart. The poet Hopkins was all tenderness towards the farrier Felix as he administered the sacraments: "this seeing the sick endears them to us, us too it endears." The words of the sacrament, "My tongue had taught thee comfort." The touch of the Sacrament "had quenched my tears." The tears "touched my heart." As Mackay Brown rightly observes, there is "no sentimentality" in spite of the "disorder that unraveled all his strength." Felix Randal, the farrier or blacksmith receiving the Last Rites or Sacrament of the Anointing of the Sick, had now "a heavenlier heart" prepared and shriven to make the final journey: "Being anointed and all." Hopkins the poet felt the pressure of his priestly experience and his articulation of the human person was re-shaped and expanded in accordance with his "feelings." The Petrarchan sonnet was reconfigured to accommodate what Mackay Brown identifies as the "chafing at the restriction of 14 lines of iambic pentameter (even his own violent kind of iambic)"[120] and tried to bring variation to the scope of sonnet with "an extra stress each line expanding in 'Felix Randal,'... with a six stress line though otherwise they keep orthodox shape."[121]

---

115 Mackay Brown, *Notebook One*, NLS.
116 Ibid. 117 Ibid. 118 Ibid.
119 Hopkins, letter to Canon Dixon, 1 December 1881, *The Correspondence of Gerard Manley Hopkins to Richard Watson Dixon*, 97.
120 Mackay Brown, "A note on the sonnet form as used by Hopkins," *7 manuscript pp on 4 leaves each 33 × 20.5 signed GMB March-April 1964 in pencil*. NLS.
121 Ibid.

Hopkins began in the first line, "Felix Randal, the farrier, O is he dead then?" This sprung rhythm also holds true for Mackay Brown's sonnet "Farm Labourer"[122] where it resonates in the first line "God, am I not dead yet? Said Ward, his ear meeting another dawn." No sign of the priestly anointing other than in the last line, "a lark flashed its needle down the west"[123] after a long life of arduous work struggling with and against the elements as the food-gatherer. Mackay Brown was not an expander. Hopkins's mix of intricate metrical forms and complexity of poetic language expanded in accordance with his psychic processes as he re-ordered and reinvigorated the old firmament elicited from a time when the medieval worldview from the twelfth to the fifteenth century held within itself the predominance of Catholic clerical elites. As written culture had gained ground in Iceland in the twelfth century "literary neophytes,"[124] such as the Pingèyrar monks and their associates, worked to infuse this worldview into their own native tradition. Hopkins and Mackay Brown retrieved that worldview within their own much changed time period.

The holy centers of the Mediterranean were tangible poetic materials. The passion poets carried the Holy Land as their epistemic center as they moved into a world infused with the matrices of many worldviews to emphasize their native tradition. Mackay Brown moved deftly into regional difference and the distinctive characteristics of the Orkney Islands in all its interactional layering. The Nordic narrative and skaldic tradition kept his Christian faith still and strong through St. Magnus. The poise of St. Magnus as a Christian within the matrix of intruding worlds exudes a seamless spectrum across the various phases of the North Atlantic christianization. The christianized firmament absorbed the matrix in all its paganism and was Mackay Brown's ultimate poetical and spiritual adventure. He did not feel the pressure of his emotions to expand the iambic pentameter like Hopkins. As he emphasized the Orkney native tradition, he did so with an accompanying decrease in metrical linguistic complexity as he powered his writing with

[122] Mackay Brown, "Farm Labourer," *Collected Poems of George Mackay Brown*, 46.   [123] Ibid.
[124] Jakobsson, "Centre and Periphery in Icelandic Medieval Discourse," in *Preprint Papers: The 14th International Saga Conference*.

an ordering of words and phrases, runes, kennings, and specialized vocabulary set within a liturgical frame that intoned his sprung rhythm through his litany of devices. Whatever psychic processes he was going through as the poet it bore fruit as his art of compression honed down towards silence. In "Farm Labourer,"[125] Ward's ear is taken up by the music of creation, the throb of the blackbird, the stretched barbarous throats of the gulls, the musical visualization of the creels, the haddock lines, the boats, all anointed by the lyrical web of his days in spite of his bodily pain.[126] The world of work was sanctifying. A seminal Orcadian poetics surfaced within the classical literary canon and the Hopkins "world-wielding shoulder Majestic—as a stallion-stalwart, very-violet-sweet"[127] was transposed to become Mackay Brown's conduit of Christ, St. Magnus. This was the Mackay Brown signature inscaped across all his work in a "matrix of intrusion of worlds."[128]

Hopkins and Mackay Brown intersect in the movement of the spirit as it undertakes descent and ascent in unison, its release as in Hopkins's poem "Caged Skylark" where "man's spirit in the prison of the body... operating close to the borders of (on the one hand) music, and in the other of impressionistic painting."[129] Sound and visual imagery mesh seamlessly as a sensational vision: "There never was in English a more sensuous poet, not even Keats."[130] Mackay Brown then makes a declaration: "Intellectually the poetry of GMH is commonplace. He says nothing surprising or original; it is all lilt, pattern—the roll, the rise, the carol, the creation."[131] This is surprising. What does Mackay Brown mean? The intellectual stance of Hopkins was stable and scholarly, and it was Catholic. The theory of knowledge they both adhered to was the anchor where the "Senses tongued like angels"[132] were able to proclaim "the glory of God."[133] This is the purpose of their verse and the purpose of the human person, to live their lives within that proclamation. This was not

---

[125] Mackay Brown, "Farm Labourer," *Collected Poems of George Mackay Brown*, 46. [126] Ibid.
[127] Hopkins, "Hurrahing in the Harvest," *Gerard Manley Hopkins. Poems and Prose*, 31.
[128] Jakobsson, "Centre and Periphery in Icelandic Medieval Discourse," in *Preprint Papers: The 14th International Saga Conference.*
[129] Mackay Brown, *Notebook One, NLS.*
[130] Ibid.   [131] Ibid.   [132] Ibid.   [133] Ibid.

surprising to Hopkins and Mackay Brown, but very surprising and disruptive to the literary classes of their times and now.

Of all Hopkins's verse it was "St Alphonsus Rodriguez"[134] that Mackay Brown declared the "best." "This is one of the simplest of H's poems and I feel one of his best; for the balance is held in almost perfect delicacy not so in some of the earlier sonnets where the balance between the natural and the religious element is deliberately weighted in favor of religion."[135] Mackay Brown was very alert to overweighting his own composition in the same direction. His early mentor Ernest Marwick had written to Mackay Brown in 1947 advising him to "substitute 'Christ' for 'Our Lord,' as it is very possible that the audience will not be a devout one and might regard the latter as a piece of unsupportable presumption. I will risk letting them think the whole thing is a religious tract."[136] Hopkins gave Mackay Brown clear lines of development to seek literary "balance" in a seamless all-encompassing serenity of spirit. More intriguingly, Mackay Brown favored this sonnet and portrayal of Alphonsus, Jesuit and lay brother, in a manner I think hit home to him personally. Mackay Brown himself was characterized with a good measure of passivity and he guarded the quiet life increasingly: "What particular kind of saintliness was in such a quiet life? What H is doing in this poem is making a contrast between active and passive virtue—Holiness dwells in everything great and small."[137] The life of action was totally invested in his disciplined work as poet and its fruitfulness as journalist, novelist, and dramatist. His daily work routines at his kitchen table were testimony to "The active stress and the passive stress are exquisitely balanced

---

134 Hopkins wrote a sonnet about his fellow Jesuit in which he praised St. Alphonsus for his heroic sanctity in daily service. Born in Segovia, Spain, in 1532, he is the patron saint of the lay brothers of the Company of Jesus (the Jesuits). Jesuit lay brothers are men who are called to the religious life as Jesuits but who are not called to priestly ministry. Although they are not ordained, they share the mission of the Jesuits, carrying out various responsibilities. "I'm on my way, Lord," is the phrase he repeated every time the doorbell rang at the Montesión College in the Spanish city of Palma, on the island of Majorca, where he lived for more than 40 years. He exercised the role of porter (or doorkeeper) with a prayerful passion. St. Alphonsus's sensitivity towards others and to God's will, which inspired him to conduct his task as porter with great joy, led many people to seek him as a spiritual guide.
135 Mackay Brown, *Notebook Two, NLS*.
136 Marwick to Mackay Brown 15 Feb. 1947. Cited in Gray, *George Mackay Brown: No Separation*, 26.   137 Mackay Brown, *Notebook Two, NLS*.

and equally potent."[138] Alphonsus, the "Holy Doorkeeper,"[139] lay brother and Jesuit, was extolled by Hopkins: "God...with trickling increment, / Veins violets and tall trees makes more and more."[140] This brings more meaning for Mackay Brown: "The beauty of the mountain and violet is the same, is born of the same stress, though in different form."[141] To my mind, his passive nature found worth and dignity in his active work as a poet. Here was his consciousness that "Holiness dwells in everything great and small."[142] The moral imperative, the call of the curlew, energized him with purpose and authenticity. He was not seeking a devout audience in the conventional sense. Devoutness lies elsewhere—in the Mackay Brown "Greenfields Kirk" creation set as a baseline with which many readers find themselves in tune. His barn-church, his Bethlehems, and Nazareths, rose up from the Greenfields Kirk with their peoples inscaped and instressed as human persons who are "all hallows" in the Communion of Saints.

With such an attitude (passive virtue), Mackay Brown pays tribute (active virtue) to the human person as poetic subject. So, who were his protagonists? Working as the poet, whether it was with his craft of "melted wax"[143] or "the palimpsest"[144] or the painstaking reconstitution of texts and their layers through the centuries, Mackay Brown increasingly gave a strong still center of unity to his literary work. The impetus from Hopkins found clear lines of development into the history and culture of the christianized North Atlantic and its intersecting matrix of worlds. As he became one of the timeless literary elite, whether it was acknowledged or not, he had found his reason and purpose deeply affirmed in the very personal quest into St. Magnus.

---

[138] Ibid.
[139] Having read of Mackay Brown's declaration for this poem as his favorite makes me wonder if he saw himself as a "Holy Doorkeeper" in the tradition of St Alphonsus. He had many knocks on his door at Mayburn Court from those near and who had come far. He was very accessible to his callers. Did he too say to himself, "I'm on my way, Lord"?
[140] Hopkins, "In honour of St Alphonsus Rodriguez Laybrother of the Society of Jesus," *Gerard Manley Hopkins. Poems and Prose*, 67.
[141] Mackay Brown, *Notebook Two, NLS*.   [142] Ibid.
[143] Joachim of Fiore, *Liber figurum*: cited in Antonsson, 71.
[144] Fengler, "Aspects of Catholic Spirituality in the Poetry of George Mackay Brown," in Zirra, Ioana, Potter, eds., *The Literary Avatars of Christian Sacramentality: Theology and Practical Life in Recent Modernity*.

Mackay Brown was well able to draw upon a wide range of sources and edge his work with a critical historical attitude, smoothing the edges but retaining the tensions of political relations between peoples and nations in a very particular literary and spiritual journey. He inflected his writing with the ethos of his times as a collector of tradition in his moral drama that dipped in and out of many worlds, natural and supernatural. The Scandinavian heritage fused within his Catholic epistemic attitude and his protagonists—fisherman and farmer, men, and women in their rites of passage from conception to their journey across birth and death to Tir-nan-Nog are smoothed and melted in grace oscillating between center and periphery. They emerged as a plethora of inscapes moving on the horizons with instressed stealth as literary figures, the harvest of symbols, making their presence felt in their particularities as a universal cosmic pageant. This was a cosmic pageant that Mackay Brown, in asserting the native tradition, dovetailed into the "narrative of Christian and Greco-Roman world history, Old Norse ancient history became a corollary of this greater metanarrative—a parallel history that shadowed the greater events occurring at the world's center."[145]

The poetic text and its metrics took its shape and form and energy from the saga tradition and its playfulness between this world and the other. Whether it was "Thorfinn" or "Country Girl" or Earl Magnus they were experienced through Mackay Brown's mind turning off the road of convention and taking a less traveled path, entering a wilder landscape where fewer people venture into "the transitory landscape of the Other World."[146] The footpaths were broad in this world because lots of people traveled on them: humanity intruded on the landscape to make it more accessible to them, the more people who go down a footpath, the wider it gets.[147] Just like the saga writers, before their audience knew it, they had arrived through the subtle changes from the poet's pen in the Other World—the world of the supernatural had materialized. Narrative patterns were inflected deeply into Mackay Brown's work, more so than that of Hopkins. This

---

[145] Jakobsson, "Centre and Periphery in Icelandic Medieval Discourse" in *Preprint Papers The 14th International Saga Conference*.
[146] Leslie, "Border Crossings Landscape and the Other world in the Fornaldarsǫgur" in *Preprint Papers: The 14th International Saga Conference*.
[147] Ibid.

narrative influence was from the saga tradition emphasizing the native tradition in a natural fusion of Orcadian history, culture and folklore and its seamless layers of Icelandic and Celtic analogues. This was a majestically inscaped Orkney poetics that was more Fornaldarsǫgur[148] than an institutionalized Christian hagiography or some sort of literary stereotypic Catholic imagination. An Orkney poetics held no distinction between what was real and unreal. It operated on a platformed narrative that absorbed and assimilated all phases of historical development and the matrices of worlds and worlds within worlds. Mackay Brown did this organically from his Orcadian forge, infusing his work within the reinvigorated firmament released so abruptly by Hopkins onto an unsuspecting literary world.

CAGED SKYLARKS IN THE REDEEMING WAVES

The human person as poetic subject was released into the redemptive ferment and swarm of these intersecting worlds. Thorfinn[149] is Mackay Brown's protagonist, his version of Hopkins's caged skylark. This was the epistemic unity-in-difference and difference-in-unity of Hopkins and Mackay Brown interwoven in their poetic craft as death intersects life or is it life intersecting death? Haunted, in the song of his drowning, Thorfinn, in the type of the "Everyman," rowed to his death, "his little boat behind the holm / To take the purple samurai of the flood." He "Turned a salt key in his last door of light." In the extrapolation from the "heart sick" Thorfinn to the inscape of the Everyman ascending from this world of "weeded rock and plangent pool," God took him with "his beautiful claws" in the swarm and shoals of "Sweet algae and tiny glimmering fish / The dropping surfeits of the rich Atlantic / Ravelling its rivers through the corn-patched Orkneys." God with his "beautiful claws" is the "Owner of these lobsters." The univocal seamless interchange between God and the lobster, both possessing "beautiful claws," not metaphorically but really. It is God's nature to absorb by means of Love, "abroad in a seeking wave," able to lift Thorfinn "from the creaking rowlocks of time" as his

---

148 (Old Norse: "sagas of antiquity") class of Icelandic sagas dealing with the ancient myths and hero legends of Germania, with the adventures of Vikings, or with other exotic adventures in foreign lands.
149 Mackay Brown, "Thorfinn," *Collected Poems of George Mackay Brown*, 20.

little-soul-boat fires into the flood to be "flung a glad ghost on a wingless shore." All the while those he left behind are none-the-wiser when the "empty boat is found stuttering on the rocks" as the "dawn-cold cocks" biblically cheer an infused light "along the links" of the matrices of intersecting and intruding worlds. Thorfinn is Hopkins's "Caged Skylark," where "man's spirit in the prison of the body was "operating close to the borders of (on the one hand) music, and in the other of impressionistic painting."[150]

Mackay Brown worked within his native tradition with the upswing from Thorfinn, the particular Orcadian, to Everyman in the aspirational form of Earl Magnus from the *Orkneyinga Saga*.[151] The sainted Magnus was and is the crown and center that unified all his literary work. From his "center" he made many literary expeditions in terms of genre. The Mackay Brown poetic protagonists, in a vast compilation from his own self as skald and scholar, were crafted by this poet of passion through the sanctity of St. Magnus. With power, passion, and potency he explored the violent death of Magnus, the hallowed Orcadian, reinvigorating his veneration within the Hopkins firmament with its theological blades and ethical component. Questions of theodicy and divine providence, free will and the problem of evil, sexual identity and behavior, flow seamlessly through his work that encompasses the native tradition in all its phases. A new paradigm of sanctity assimilated the legend, the prayerèd religion of a christianized North Atlantic pivoted on the gospels and the holy sites of the Mediterranean without a forsaking of the crystalline Nordic metanarrative. As the St. Magnus component of *The Orkneyinga Saga* was its mainstay (30 pages of text), so too was the literary work of Mackay Brown anchored in poem, story, novel, and drama. The coalescing sources from saga passed through his immediate and direct experience of St. Magnus for the people of Orkney to ruminate over with their Reformation cast of minds mired in a firm secularization of the "never-ending-sentences"—exactly what Muir cautioned against.

Through each collection of poems, published one by one, the "shining life" of the "blessèd and brave Saint Magnus Who bowed

---

150 Mackay Brown, *Notebook One, NLS*.
151 *Orkneyinga Saga: The History of the Earls of Orkney*.

his head and died"[152] is inscaped into the world of "Grinning Rags" standing "between the cold Plough and the embers in the door of death";[153] his sèlved-seeking answers were as Christ had sought in Gethsemane, "and still he knew no answer";[154] whose body would lie broken, circled with "fragmented light and song" in this world and the other in its "riot of masks."[155] Then the redemptive rhythms of "a bird / Winged with fivers... smothered him in flowers."[156] Mackay Brown hurrahed in the harvest of his symbols with each word, and each phrase could stand within a text and alone. Alone and together his language was highly charged with ideas and thoughts as they wrapped around regular and irregular instressed-inscapes with the definitive beauty of an Orkney poetics. This was the infrastructure of his sensational vision where, "the red ploughs cleave their snow and curve forever / Across the April hill," and the "liturgy of April"[157] swept with "The Magnustide long swords of rain."[158] The native tradition, the Orcadian Fornaldarsǫgur of the St. Magnus Way,[159] unfolds liturgically: "In Birsay they move in their furrows, bread is broken / Half way to the sacrament. / Here Magnus was born, here they laid his bones."[160] Mackay Brown's absorption of the narrative expanded his literary prowess as he moved from sonnet and lyric and ode and ballad to accept the great themes that drew him on, absorbing into his tapestry all the new irregularities as Hopkins had done. From his center he used the heptahedron and liturgical and litany forms drawing from his novel *Magnus* a consolidated shift of emphasis that was as contemporary as it was timeless. Here was "the new paradigm of sanctity," the self-sacrifice of the martyr intimated by "the strange wave that washed over" Magnus according to the

---

[152] Mackay Brown, "The Road Home," *Collected Poems of George Mackay Brown*, 2.
[153] Ibid., "The Masque of Bread," 18–19.
[154] Ibid.
[155] Ibid., "December Day, Hoy Sound," 19.
[156] Ibid., "The Death Bird," 26.
[157] Ibid., "Elegy," 32.
[158] Ibid.
[159] Pilgrim route in Orkney recently reinstated that traces the locations and storyways of the trans-positioning of St Magnus's body from Egilsay to Kirkwall and its cult of veneration: see further Sarah Jane Gibbon and James Moore, "Storyways: Visualising Saintly Impact in a North Atlantic Maritime Landscape" in *Open Archaeology*, 235–62.
[160] Mackay Brown, "Places to Visit," *Collected Poems of George Mackay Brown*, 60.

Orkneyinga Saga[161]—this same wave that washed over Mackay Brown, anointing him with grace that trembled at the many stations throughout his work.

Magnus of the "Way," Magnus the "Keeper of red stone," Magnus wearer of "white coat" and "red martyr coat" Magnus, the "friend" was the human person as poetic subject for us all. Mackay Brown gave poetic intercession to reinvigorate the Christ-face of Orkney once again, not metaphorically but really. "The stories, legends, poems / Will be woven to make your sail. / You may hear the beautiful tale of Magnus / Who took salt on his lip. / Your good angel / Will be with you on that shore."[162] Mackay Brown did not impose Magnus on his people. He invoked Magnus as intercessor to sanctify, heal, and make the spiritual journey whole again, making much space for all-comers as they dipped in and out of texts accompanied by Christ-birds and shoals of fish in the swing and sway of the "big wind" with its scoops of grace and shards of light in the dark. It was a compilation as was the *Orkneyinga Saga*. It was a reconstitution in "the redeeming wave." It was a palimpsest; it was a seamless intersection and intrusion of worlds that coalesced wave by wave, tide by tide, through the eons of time to make it through to the heavenly shores.

Here were his portrayals, those characterizations that were seamlessly particular and universal in the manner of Hopkins, but yet his dancing metrics were independent in their composition. The ancient harps of the old firmament, "the old, old story" accepted the new lines of development within a classical literary canon that harbored no ambiguity as did the one-dimensional world of the "never-ending sentence."[163] This was new wine in fresh skins. The human person as poetic subject was hallowed, in spite of everything, as they were Hurrahed in the Harvest of redemptive waves of grace surging in to transform the grime of sin. Chapter Six is more specific about the dark mire Hopkins and Mackay Brown found themselves in and explores how it brings development and expansion of the artistic sense so critical for their writing and sense of achievement.

---

161 *Orkneyinga Saga: The History of the Earls of Orkney*, 93.
162 Mackay Brown, "A New Child: ECL 11 June 1993," *Collected Poems of George Mackay Brown*, 328-29.
163 Muir, "The Decline of the Novel" *in Essays on Literature and Society*, 144.

CHAPTER SIX

Immortalizing Storms and Shipwrecks

*"Drop my harp through a green wave, off Yesnaby,
Next time you row to the lobsters."*[1]

THE HALLOWED HUMAN PERSON AS POETIC subject, grimed and vulnerable, mired in the dark, discovers personal illumination through the experience of the absence of light. The poetic infrastructure had to be as full as it could be to authentically write the truth of the human person. Poetic form had to match reality and Hopkins and Mackay Brown went deep into the workings of their experience of the dark night of the soul. The Mackay Brown algorithm was the heptahedron, that penetrating and all-encompassing shape and pattern inscaped into his writings with precise positioning and poise. This algorithmic "harp" innovatively accomplished the task of absorbing what appeared discordant and awkward into a timeless symmetry through the imposition of order on phases of disorder and disruption within nature with its storms and shipwrecks.

Hopkins fashioned his literary art with great creativity and precision to have seminal capacity that aligned and absorbed regular and irregular literary conventions. His reinvigorated firmament, the new wine in fresh literary skins, forged a close examination of the human person in the fight of their lives, in their "dark night" of spiritual combat. Both Hopkins and Mackay knew extremely well the vicissitudes of their "annunciations of terror"[2] and immortalized them in storm and shipwreck giving potency and weight to the moral character of the firmament to which they aligned themselves. This moral character had a particular pattern and shape subject as it was to mood shifts and

---

1 Mackay Brown, "The Five Voyages of Arnor," *Collected Poems of George Mackay Brown*, 63–64.
2 Mackay Brown, Notes on *"The Wreck of the Deutschland,"* 17 manuscript pages on 20 leaves each 33 × 20.5, signed GM Brown Feb 1963, NLS.

the sway of the emotions. Its rational ballast was able to hold or "stall" the irrational in a fibred scale of tension laid bare in a living and breathing understanding and articulation of God's nature. This was the voyage of their discovery that played to their individual uniqueness, their thisness, within the universal cosmological reality. The intellectual and spiritual energy displayed in their writing was at first disruptive of the conventions of their times and then slowly became more intelligible, one way or another, to their diverse audiences and critics.

The Scotian theory of univocity gave them epistemic freedom to apply the principle that there is no real distinction between essence and existence. They are seamlessly one. Whereas Aquinas had made a distinction between the two, Scotus did not—and neither did Hopkins or Mackay Brown. Their poetry evidences an understanding that there is no distinction between the thing that existed and what it was. Their writing is built upon an assumption that we can never know whether something exists unless we have a concept of the thing itself. The strong emphasis on cognition and the senses working in unison validates this for both poets. They did not attribute to the human person a bland common nature because of their experience of the unique thisness of the individual held seamlessly within the instress of the Creator. What seemed most abstract was actually in reality earthed by individuation. Mackay Brown had pithily observed how the "healthy heartbeat of the trochee and the dactyl"[3] continued to march to this end counterpointed in the expansion by Hopkins and his own powers of compression. They instill a potent thisness into their ciphered language of number, meter, and music within the literary canon. They were not the types of poet to elegantly wander "lonely as a cloud" and be content to work within the steady stream of images from "the inward eye." They were more likely to get biblical as in "Let the clouds rain down the Just One,"[4] for they saw the Christ-inscape of the rainclouds bringing justice in the harvests for the food-gatherers in their communities. Their passion for poetry gave rise to a bigger project more majestic and confrontational as they tried

---

3 Mackay Brown, *Hopkins and His Metric*, a 12pp manuscript essay signed George M Brown 1964, each leaf 25.5 × 20.5cm, NLS.
4 Isaiah 45:8.

to heal the breach of the Reformation with a poetic reformation of their own that took full account of the whole person and their navigation of the universe in this world and the next. Wave upon wave, the Scotian theory of univocity enters into the Christ story through the inscapes, the form and pattern of Passion, Resurrection and Redemption immortalized in storms and shipwrecks. These poets took up their ancient harps with a distinctive compatibility within the erupting discordancy of their times. As Mackay Brown writes: "Christ Our Lord...To any Catholic, to a Jesuit priest especially perhaps, Christ is, in his human form, the best and rarest and bravest and most beautiful of all creatures."[5] Christ gave form and pattern and pitch to Alphonsus, Felix, Harry, and Tom, Magnus, Thorfinn, Arnor and many more as Hopkins and Mackay Brown presented humanity through the instressed-inscape of their particularities. This was the eye of their literary needle and, stitch by stitch, wave by wave, they laid out their thoughts, perceptions, and beliefs.

WRAPPING ANNUNCIATIONS OF TERROR IN A LITURGICAL FRAME

Hopkins emerged from his Jesuit priestly formation and the intensity of its Ignatian Spiritual Exercises to re-present the fate of the wreck of the Deutschland[6] in a composition of what Mackay Brown experienced as "Stanzas like waves," according to his *Essays and Notes*.[7] The vocation of the poet was problematic for Hopkins. Jesuits by their nature break with convention and historically they have had a very distinctive path. This was not lost on Mackay Brown, and although he dallied here and there with the call to priesthood, it was the empathy he had towards Hopkins as Jesuit, priest as well as poet, that enabled him to stand in the conflict of his own shoes and arrive at some measure of his own vocation as the literary anchorite, bard, skald, and

---

5 Mackay Brown, *Notebook Three*, NLS.
6 In a snowstorm on 6 December 1875 the emigrant ship, outward-bound from Bremen, in Germany via Southampton for New York, struck the infamous Kentish Knock offshore sandbank at the entrance to the Thames Estuary. She broke her back on the sands and foundered with the loss of about 57 passengers, including five Franciscan nuns exiled by the Falck Laws (enacted in the German Kingdom of Prussia during the Kulturkampf conflict with the Catholic Church).
7 Mackay Brown, *Notes on "The Wreck of the Deutschland," 17 manuscript pages on 20 leaves each 33 × 20.5, signed GM Brown Feb 1963*, NLS.

Makar, all in one. The Jesuits had played their part in the post-Reformation development in Scotland and in Orkney. Mackay Brown's development as a Catholic held this dear, but in the privacy of his interior castle, his within-doors barn. And as he read Newman, as the Jesuit Hopkins had done before him, he found symmetry and a marked serenity in "those passages, all exquisite and soaring as violin music, that rise clear above his own dilemmas and difficulties."[8] The "dilemmas and difficulties" of the human person could be expressed in their rise and fall, in the frame of the regular and the irregular, the difference-in-unity and unity-in-difference especially so as Hopkins exemplified how to do so in his poem, "The Wreck of the Deutschland."

And so it was that Mackay Brown found how to give shape and form to "annunciations of terror" "with something of waves" of "irregular broken rhythms." He made the judgment that the "whole poem [was] a 'bright battering sea.'"[9] He had by this time composed his own poem "Storm" for the collection of the same name published in 1954. As he wrote in his autobiography "there is no doubt that writers whom one enjoys so much are taken into the creative imagination and influence one's writing; but one should never be so foolish as to imitate them."[10] "Storm" carries the assimilation and absorption of Hopkins's own storm poem, yet Mackay Brown was markedly independent with his difference-in-unity. Storms and shipwrecks were of critical importance to these poets. Mackay Brown was no stranger to "the bright battering sea" as he inscaped his native Orkney's Scapa Flow as a timeless "anchorage, a quiet stretch of water"[11] where a succession of seagoing vessels from the Viking longships to the British navy ships of World War I and II "took up their silent stations."[12] The Battle of *Jutland* (1916), the wreck of the *Hampshire* at Marwick Head (1916), the scuttling of the German High fleet (1919), and the sinking of the *Royal Oak* (1939) give a strong profile to the strategic importance of the Orkney Islands poised in the North Atlantic. The war historians gave warp and weave to fact and fiction, but the poet Mackay Brown, by his

---

8 Mackay Brown, *For the Islands I Sing*, 51.
9 Mackay Brown, *Notes on "The Wreck of the Deutschland*,*"* *17 manuscript pages on 20 leaves each 33 × 20.5, signed GM Brown Feb 1963, NLS.*
10 Mackay Brown, *For the Islands I Sing*, 65–66.
11 Mackay Brown, *An Orkney Tapestry*, 9.   12 Ibid., 9.

own curious nature, went over and beyond the truncated data of the meaningless "prosaic."[13]

Significantly, he quoted the Orcadian poet Ann Scott-Moncrieff in *An Orkney Tapestry:* "Wide Waith[14] that wreaths[15] the salt tide wi" the fresh, Whaur swan and eider sweem,[16] Whaur[17] weed meets ware."[18] Here was an emphasis of the native tradition in its "eye" in to that night when the *Royal Oak* went down and Mackay Brown described it as a "Wagnerian drama" that he watched from his back door in Stromness.[19] Here was the historical event and a celebration of sorts in the local dialect with its Old Norse infusions. Scott-Moncrieff's lyrical empiricism gave sound and sight to that night with a keen sense of the waters, salt and fresh, that turn and twist in an angry ferment to become a wistfully plangent garland of weed flowers laid down for the war-dead on the weir. This was pure inscape for Mackay Brown and while Scott-Moncrieff lacked the potency of the instress, the native tradition that was exerted by Mackay Brown across his development, gave high prominence to Orcadians, who to this day bear the form and pattern of that place[20] with its echoes and

---

13 Ibid., 19.
14 Waithe: The name comes from the Old Norse "vað" meaning "wading place" or "ford."
15 Wreath: Old English *wriða* «fillet, bandage, band» (literally "that which is wound around"), from Proto-Germanic *writh-* (source also of Old Norse *riða*, Danish vride, Old High German *ridan* "to turn, twist," Old Saxon, Old Frisian *wreth* "angry," Dutch *wreed* "rough, harsh, cruel," Old High German *reid* "twisted," Old Norse *reiða* "angry"), from PIE *wreit-* "to turn, bend" (source also of Old English *wriða* "band," *wriðan* "to twist, torture," *wrap* "angry"), from root *wer-* (2) "to turn, bend." Meaning "ring or garland of flowers or vines" is first recorded 1560s.
16 O. Sc. *sweme*, to swim, a.1400. The form corresponds to Mid.Eng. *sweme, swime*, to swim, with lengthening of the vowel in an open syllable, and not therefore directly descended from O. E. *swimman*, but rather from O. N. *svima*, to swim.
17 Old English *hwǣr, hwār(a)*; related to Old Frisian *hwēr*, Old Saxon, Old High German *hwār*, Old Norse, Gothic *hvar* [Old-lore Miscellany of Orkney, Shetland, etc. 1907-20 (Sh.)].
18 [O. Sc. *were*, to defend, 1375, *werwall*, 1450, to guard an entry, 1475, to ward off, c.1480, O. E. *werian*, to defend. The *n.* is partly direct from the verb, partly from O. E. *wer*, Eng. *wear*, dial. ware, a river barrier, from the same stem, *wer-*.] See Mackay Brown, An Orkney Tapestry, 9.
19 Mackay Brown, "Bombs at the Brig-o-Waithe," in *Northern Lights: A Poet's Sources*, 22-23.
20 The Brig o' Waithe is a small arched bridge that crosses the mouth of the Stenness Loch, a large sea loch in Orkney's West Mainland, as it outflows into the Bay of Ireland and Scapa Flow beyond.

memories of war. He took his artistry further into the literary canon where the native tradition was a vehicle of honor in the far reaches of the christianization of the North Atlantic. The Brig o' Waithe, as Mackay Brown understands Scott-Moncrieff's poem, is "the actual Brig o'Dread which, according to medieval religious folk tradition, all souls had to cross after death."[21] The christianization of Orcadian inscapes is a well-documented fusion throughout the writings of Mackay Brown and his elevation of the liturgical frame.[22]

Mackay Brown relished word study and derivation, word sound, shape, and pattern and their correlation, if not equivalence, with the natural world. His visionary sensations were flushed with the very purpose of language. Rowena Murray makes the point in her study of the influence of Norse literature on Mackay Brown that "He never studied Anglo-Saxon or Old Norse when he was a student at the University of Edinburgh, nor has he done so since"[23] and "He has therefore, had to rely on translations for his knowledge of the saga style."[24] My impression is that he had a strong working knowledge of Old (and Middle) English and a life-long delight in searching out etymology and derivation for the natural in-depth grasp he had of the native tradition both oral and textual. This was reinforced by his own personal library, specifically as evidenced in the MacInnes Collection.[25] Further evidence of more formal study can be seen in his *Essays and Notes* with its references to the Oxford English Dictionary. It accompanied him in his exploration of Hopkins's lexicon. Murray tracked Mackay Brown's development from "paraphrase" to "compactness, matter-of-fact tone, and irony" to its art of compression that concealed the complex in a "style that is deceptively simple."[26]

---

[21] Mackay Brown, "Orkney Common Reader," *Orkney Herald*, 12 November 1953, 5.
[22] For example, the short story "Brig-o-Dread" in *The Sun's Net*, with its direct link to the *Lyke-Wake Dirge*. The assimilation of the pre-Christian eras and their Nordic and Germanic heritage was well studied by Mackay Brown and his peers.
[23] Murray, "The Influence of Norse Literature on the Twentieth Century Writer George Mackay Brown," in Strauss, Dietrich, Drescher, eds., *Scottish Language and Literature: Medieval and Renaissance.*
[24] Ibid.   [25] Peterson, Mackay Brown Personal Library.
[26] Murray, "The Influence of Norse Literature on the Twentieth Century Writer George Mackay Brown," in Strauss, Dietrich, and H. W. Drescher, eds., *Scottish Language and Literature: Medieval and Renaissance,* 547–57.

Murray took note of Mackay Brown's utilization of the saga tradition and technique elicited from translation into English and called it a "reconstruction."[27] Later Murray makes the telling insight: "Brown perfects a style which effortlessly charts the movements of the mind itself to be punctuated with 'echoes of silence'"[28] characterized by "the rich aura that has grown about them from the start and grows infinitesimally richer every time they are spoken."[29] Mackay Brown lays out his intentions in *An Orkney Tapestry:*[30] "I have had to wrench skaldic verse into a shape acceptable to modern readers." Murray notes the genius of Mackay Brown was very alert to the modern mind and in the way he sought to render his writing and language within its ethos. Mackay Brown's reading and markings in his well-thumbed Wittig[31] volume give emphasis to his understanding of "aureation" and Murray confirms his willingness to exercise this specific art as had Chaucer and Dunbar.[32] Mackay Brown accepted the native tradition from his people, their islands and their "annunciations of terror," and placed them within a literary canon that was as classical as it was fiercely independent.

Throughout the Hopkins *Essays and Notes* there is a powerful sense of Mackay Brown working through Hopkins's poem with an intellectual energy that to date has not been a marked in-depth feature of the study of his work. The *Essays and Notes* conveyed Mackay Brown giving the evidence as he analyzed it. And his analysis was understated. His readers are drawn by the vivid imagery and its keen sense of the natural world that did not lie to readers who knew the Orkney heritage and its native tradition. The Orkney layers of sight and sound, touch, taste, smell, emerge on a frame, a design, a pattern, and shape, as his studious poetic eye contextualized ocean and water and weather moving at pace within the natural pulse of creation. Here was the act of composition infused and flushed with visionary sensations according to musical and metrical time. The dance in twos and fours, the symmetry or quadrature frame, elicit the sprung rhythm of a naturalistic meter. But somewhere along the

---

27 Ibid.   28 Ibid.   29 Ibid.
30 Mackay Brown, *An Orkney Tapestry*.
31 Wittig, *The Scottish Tradition in Literature*.
32 Ibid., 58, 62–63.

line, Mackay Brown started to place things in a liturgical frame to really make his mark.

Hopkins drives his sea poem with a frame of fours to *inscape* the intensity of natural phenomena, stressed with a beat of three giving a metric ratio of 4:3. The proportional use of language flushed with sight and sound according to number theory is never so tightly controlled by the softer and more free-flowing Mackay Brown. Though he took a Hopkins feature here and there to express a profound truth in his number combinations, compression was his signature (rather than expansion) as he fetched out the inscaped Nordic corridor instressed with the liturgical frame of litany and chant. More than any other of Hopkins's poems, "The Wreck of the Deutschland" gave Mackay Brown the freedom to draw upon his experience of the Mass wherein the worshiper is free to roam, to weave in and out of its set liturgical phases. And, of course, for so many of us the Latin language gives that extra sense of spiritual intimacy where the mind and emotions and the senses wrap around each other in a unique way.

Mackay Brown first looked to the "shape of the stanza on the page" and saw "resemblance to spread wings, after the fashion of George Herbert."[33] But the great sea poems of literature took second place to Mackay Brown's formation within the natural Orcadian rhythms of weather and water and its biblical frame: "Through the storm and the poem a dove is flying, sometimes fiery and terrible, but in the end it has the palm in its beak... or one might see a resemblance to a ship in full sail."[34] Mackay Brown had first-hand experience: "Sometimes God, in order to stir us out of our lethargy and faithlessness, darkens our lives with annunciations of terror; sometimes he steals through us secretly and sweetly, like sap in a tree."[35] The first method Mackay Brown applied to those on the *Deutschland*; the second to Hopkins himself. The ship *Deutschland* "is modern Europe, all rationalism, free thinking and materialism."[36] Hopkins dra-

---

33 Mackay Brown refers to Herbert's poem "Easter Wings." The layout of this poem is the first thing that strikes the reader: when it was first published in 1633 it was formatted sideways on adjacent pages, with the lines arranged to form the shape of a bird's wings. See Mackay Brown, *Notes on "The Wreck of the Deutschland,"* 17 manuscript pages on 20 leaves each 33 × 20.5, signed GM Brown Feb 1963, NLS.

34 Ibid.   35 Ibid.   36 Ibid.

matized the newspaper reports current at the time giving the snowstorm the power and potency of God that called for a human response inscaped as it was in the Franciscan nuns kneeling in prayer on the deck.

Mackay Brown had a palpable sense of the terror inscaped with the instress of a merciful God. He read Stanza 10 as the "key stanza" where the theme is set out: "With an anvil-ding / And with fire in him forge thy will / Make mercy in all of us, out of us all / Mastery, but be adored, but be adored King." Mackay Brown stood with Hopkins from his own experience of this terrible power, but observed Hopkins to be "safe in sanctuary, not out in the storm."[37] Mackay Brown was clear that "Reading this poem, we must hold in our minds 3 separate images: GMH at the altar, celebrating or assisting Mass, the Incarnation and the nuns on board the *Deutschland* praying."[38] Mackay Brown knew the Latin Mass well enough to see "references to Mass throughout."[39] For example, the Sursum Corda[40] in "And fled with a fling of the heart to the heart of the Host" (Stanza 3). Mackay Brown made the interpretation that this is "the command in the midst in all our troubles, sins, perils to lift up our hearts to God."[41] Again, with the Veni Sanctificator and its "Invocation of the Holy Spirit" he sees the dove and Father Hopkins's heart rising to meet God, likewise dove-winged and tongued with fire, as he prays "cleanse my lips with a live coal" crossing the altar from Epistle side to read the Gospel."[42] You get a strong impression of Mackay Brown having a close intimate relationship that wove in and out of the liturgy as he tracked the priest, Father Hopkins, according to the classical frame of the pre-Vatican II Latin Mass.

Mackay Brown takes a different approach to most studies of the "Wreck of the Deutschland" by a strong focus on the connection of the poem to the Mass. For Mackay Brown, Hopkins

---

37 Ibid.   38 Ibid.   39 Ibid.
40 Latin: "Lift up your hearts" or literally, "Lifted hearts" is the opening dialogue to the Preface of the Eucharistic Prayer or Anaphora in the liturgies of the Christian Church, dating back at least to the third century and the Anaphora of the Apostolic Tradition. The Anaphora is that part of the Eucharist that contains the consecration, anamnesis, and communion.
41 Mackay Brown, *Notes on "The Wreck of the Deutschland," 17 manuscript pages on 20 leaves each 33 × 20.5, signed GM Brown Feb 1963*, NLS.
42 Ibid.

was primarily the priest at the altar. Mackay Brown admired the priest-poet Hopkins and the clarity of his Catholicism. It was clear for all to see. Mackay Brown had to understate his Catholicism in a Calvinistic and eventually secular Orkney. Nevertheless both poets employed every ounce of their creativity in their literary work immersed and shaped by Catholic epistemology radiant in visionary sensations. Of course, these *Essays and Notes* on Hopkins are only emerging now fifty-six years later. Whether there is interest in understanding how this collection of *Essays and Notes* fits into Mackay Brown's development remains to be seen. To date there has not been a strong research impetus to come to terms with his Catholicism other than various stereotypical presentations accompanied by an accommodation to the various cultural stances of the day. One could go further and assert that there has been a strong suppression of what was the central core of his being as person and poet. The audience had wanted Mackay Brown to line up within their own concerns. Mackay Brown, although not formally Catholic at the time of his study, swam against the tide of his times as many converts have done as they try to integrate and be taken seriously in the literary world and the arts in general. Mackay Brown resonated with Hopkins from beginning to end, but was always careful not to overplay his "pen" in this respect, seeing the artistic merit of work as critical to his "place" in the literary canon.

His study of the "Wreck of the Deutschland" is not groundbreaking, but it does give an elevation of the liturgical frame in Mackay Brown's development. He notes that Part I is about Hopkins and that the dominant symbol is fire, whereas Part II is about five nuns, and the dominant symbol is water. The destructive nature of these elements as symbols form a dramatic narrative "in fact divinely sent for our salvation" and "unless we recognize GMH at the altar much of poem's meaning is lost."[43] It was as a priest in his re-presentation of Christ that Hopkins offers himself as total gift, "I kiss my hand / To the stars, lovely asunder Starlight" and through the priesthood "His mystery must be instressed, stressed"[44] (Stanza 5). Mackay Brown takes Hopkins's penetrating study of nature as "itself a veil that hides God from us." The priest Father Hopkins daily

---

43 Ibid. 44 Ibid.

enacted the Passion in the Mass with "a lingering-out sweet skill." Hopkins's "Reverend play with the Word" resides in his inspired use of language that harbors the Logos, the instress of the mystery that God's nature is. Hopkins unites prophecy and poetry as he draws deeply from the Logos, the instressed Christ-Word. Hopkins had hidden his own word (his gift of poetry) in the Word with all truth, beauty, and holiness. And Mackay Brown does the same to the furthest bounds of his being. Both poets reached for the stars, from this world to the "other," from the natural world to the supernatural.

Mackay Brown always took the opportunity to exhibit his fascination with christianized Pythagorean number theory which, although annoying to some, gave an analytic thrust to his composition as he placed himself squarely within the classical literary canon. "The number 5 is given a mystical meaning in the poem." Although "5 seems to the modern mind a quite arbitrary number," Mackay Brown held that the number is "God-devised" and has "a mystical meaning beyond its merely utilitarian function in mathematics."[45] In fact, Mackay Brown reconnected with the late Middle Ages ethos in his native tradition of Orkney. The Foundation Document for St. Magnus Cathedral by Bishop Reid in 1544 evidences the popular liturgical trends and the quick transfer of popular devotions from Europe with a prescription for the "Mass of the Five Wounds."[46] The cipher of the number five illustrates the ascendancy of the liturgical frame in Mackay Brown's algorithmic harp with its poetic infrastructure singing its symmetry "all exquisite and soaring as violin music, that rise clear above his own dilemmas and difficulties."[47]

The mystical significance of five is not lost on Hopkins: "Five! The finding and sake / And cipher of suffering Christ."[48] Mackay Brown does not err on the side of caution in his response knowing the need for the modern mind to re-connect itself with

---

45 Ibid.
46 Clouston, "Foundation and Election of Certain Offices in the Cathedral Church of Orkney for the Service of God, by Robert Reid, Bishop of Orkney." *Records of the Earldom of Orkney*, 1299–1614. Scottish History Society, Edinburgh, 1914, 363–71. GMB had his own copy of this book as part of his personal library. See: Peterson, MacInnes Collection, Mackay Brown Personal Library.
47 Mackay Brown, *For the Islands I Sing*, 51.
48 Mackay Brown, Notes on *"The Wreck of the Deutschland,"* 17 manuscript pages on 20 leaves each 33 × 20.5, signed GM Brown Feb 1963, NLS.

classical learning, "Better to see too much in it than nothing at all."⁴⁹ Hopkins's announcement of the number five with "a trumpet call" enthralled Mackay Brown who proceeded to find his own form and flow within this cipher for the Passion of Christ. What came to be a much-loved characteristic Hopkinsesque juxtaposition is easily understood and experienced by Mackay Brown: "So that beauty and truth flash from those opposites."⁵⁰ Hopkins's "artistic dappling" was never muted, whether by word or number. "A quality, a situation, a flavor do not exist in themselves alone; to GMH they immediately suggest their opposite, their complement, their longed-for fulfilment."⁵¹ The ciphers of the five and the seven are scattered singly and in multiples throughout the poem. Numbers function as symbols of a higher reality from which the modern mind has detached itself.

In Stanza 22 Mackay Brown cites Hopkins, "Stigma, signal, cinquefoil⁵² token / For lettering of the lamb's fleece, ruddying of the rose-flake." Stigma, the mark of disgrace corresponded to the five wounds of Christ left on his body by the crucifixion. These "5 sacrificial wounds" are ciphered through the five Franciscan nuns who carried their impress by virtue of St Francis of Assisi, the founder of their religious order, who bore the stigmata. The mark of disgrace, the sacrificial wounds, signal the inscape of the cinquefoil, the plant of the rose family configured with five leaves of five leaflets and five-petalled yellow flowers. The five nuns went to their death by a ferocious drowning, "come quickly." This is the "lettering of the lamb's fleece, ruddying of the rose-flake." This brings to mind Mackay Brown's exposition of the "lamb of God" in his short story "A Time to Keep": "Two of my lambs had been born dead that morning. They lay, red bits of rag, under the wall. Would bury them afterwards."⁵³ This is a Mackay Brown cipher for the Passion of Christ presented in his early composition, before and after his studies of Hopkins, in parallel with the before, during and after, of his conversion to Catholicism.

Mackay Brown posed the question: "is it coincidental?" that there are "5 × 7 stanzas." He elaborated that seven is the cipher

---

49 Ibid.   50 Ibid.   51 Ibid.
52 A common herbaceous plant of the rose family, with compound leaves of five leaflets and five-petalled yellow flowers.
53 Mackay Brown, *A Time to Keep and Other Stories*, 41.

for "creation-time" and the "number of cardinal virtues and deadly sins," "the spectrum span," "number of loaves and fishes" (5 + 2) with which Christ fed the multitude." The five was clearly "a significant number...5 × 40 souls on the *Deutschland* (40 probably favorite number in holy writ) 5 × 10 drowned or rather 5 × 5 × 2...2 is another important number in the poem, redeeming the unit from solitariness, necessary for balancing, contrast, 'dappling,' that is the art and soul of nature. 5 words in the title, 5 letters in the Holy Name. At mass priest utters 5 words so that bread may become the body of Christ Hoc est enim corpus meum."[54] Mackay Brown analyzed that this was a matter of technique and for Hopkins, "dappling" was key as he inscaped the beauty of creation, the natural world seamlessly instressed on phenomena and the human person.

THE VOYAGE TO LINGUISTIC REALITY

Mackay Brown was familiar with Hopkins's seamless dappling technique. It was technically easier for him to cipher the Passion of Christ than the more abstract doctrine of the Incarnation. When he wrote, the inscape of concrete crucifixion events resonated historically, if not spiritually, with the modern mind. The Incarnation as a natural and supernatural event was shrouded in abstraction and incredulity, but Mackay Brown did not hesitate to capitalize on its silent witness to Christ as Son of God inscaped into creation by the nature of the divine instress. He may not be a priest, but as he observed in Stanza 6, "The incarnation clothes all our lives with meaning." Hopkins had written: "Stroke and stress that stars and storms deliver, that guilt is hushed by, hearts flushed by and melt—but it rides time like riding a river (And here the faithful waver, the faithless fable and miss)." Mackay Brown was again remarkably familiar with the native tradition, the Orkney fable, "And as for pagans, they constructed an elaborate mythology which is ultimately beside the point."[55] Hopkins and Mackay Brown give a divine ordering of the world to their poetry. The christianization of the North Atlantic for Mackay Brown re-ordered the pagan world through

---

54 Mackay Brown, *Notes on "The Wreck of the Deutschland*," *17 manuscript pages on 20 leaves each 33 × 20.5, signed GM Brown Feb 1963, NLS.*
55 Ibid.

"Christ's life and ministry...[and] was so compelling, so real, so vivid that the hungry heart is perfectly satisfied with all it implies, just as the taste-buds and palate are flushed when a ripe sloe is crushed in the mouth."[56] Hopkins developed the old firmament, breached by the Reformation, but none the less inherited and took contemporary minds, age by age, on a voyage of re-discovery through his dappling language, his dancing metrics, re-engaging the mind and heart in the fullness of Christian teaching with the origins and ends the pagans could only guess at. It is as though readers could once again share through the instressed-inscape the whole fullness of God through Christ. Here the grime and dark of human transgressions could be seen for what they were, through his death on the Cross. Hope, forgiveness, and redemption radiate from the language of these passion poets whose authenticity was forged in their spiritual combat.

The distinctiveness of Mackay Brown was always prominent throughout his musings and insights into Hopkins. His Orkney poetics and grounding in Edwin Muir was never far from view. As he writes in his autobiography, "Occasionally a poem would appear in the *Listener*; I found them, in spite of a visionary light, difficult. Edwin Muir is one of those poets to whose 'realm of gold' a key must be found. In 1946 his book of poems *The Voyage* appeared. The key had been in my hand all the time—I read *The Voyage* with delight."[57] He found Muir "difficult" and Hopkins "difficult," surely signposts in his own voyage. He writes in his *Essays and Notes* on "The Wreck of the Deutschland": "The end of every voyage, every life, is God, however much we confuse ourselves with other aims and errands." He contextualizes the "Hopelessness of late 19th century Europe (the Europe that has exiled the Franciscan nuns) with its commerce and materialism and free-thinking."[58] The key for Mackay Brown is the juxtaposition of the "ancient and modern" and the balancing of the violent drama "against natural imperceptible growth." The violent drama of the storm through the eyes of Hopkins the priest is juxtaposed with its sub-narrative of the five Franciscan nuns with "a lingering-out sweet skill" (Stanza 10). Here is the cipher

---

56 Ibid.   57 Mackay Brown, *For the Islands I Sing*, 64.
58 Mackay Brown, *Notes on "The Wreck of the Deutschland,"* 17 manuscript pages on 20 leaves each 33 × 20.5, signed GM Brown Feb 1963, NLS.

of the Incarnation. Stanza 10 opens "With an anvil ding" as good as, Mackay Brown says, "The first line is real GMH novel and daring. The next might have come from a 1000yr old Northern Saga... And with fire in him forge thy will."[59]

The medieval literature of Orkney already at Mackay Brown's disposal and his studies of Old and Middle English were now being flushed with the enduring influence of his poetic and spiritual kinsman, Hopkins. The flight and plight of the nuns is the Reformation legacy, "Gertrude,[60] lily and Luther are 2 of a town." Mackay Brown avoids a harsh stereotypical stance that characterizes Reformation polarizations. His method is analytic and technical as he digs into the artistic sense: "This is the couple-colour that gives significance to the whole."[61] Hopkins's "sweet-lingering-out skill" give Mackay Brown confidence to develop his own version of dappling and couple-colour. Mackay Brown writes: "(a very typical piece of its 'dappling' technique; the sensuous and the spiritual laid on the canvas together in a 'couple-colour' compared with a phrase from one of his letters: 'This life [as a Jesuit] though it is hard is God's will for me, which is more than violets knee-deep).'"[62]

Mackay Brown had a keen eye for the "pure narrative"[63] and the inscapes of "short intricate webs of alliteration and kennings."[64] As he writes, "I write as I must,"[65] and adds in *For the Islands* "with deep feeling for the importance of pure shape."[66] This is the art of aureation rather than a benign decoration. Mackay Brown's strong allegiance to Hopkins's technique and spirituality brought him to the pure Passion narrative: "Christ, then, who came among men in the ripeness of time, thrilled the whole waiting world with His being. Before his Incarnation he had given hints of himself; his work is still not finished, it is 'in high flood yet.' Meantime we owe him, 'hero of Calvary,' our allegiance."[67] Mackay Brown describes Stanzas 12-17 as "A

---

59 Ibid.
60 St. Gertrude (1256-c. 1302), Benedictine nun and mystic and Martin Luther (1483-1546), founder of Protestantism, were both born in Eisleben, Germany.
61 Mackay Brown, *Notes on "The Wreck of the Deutschland," 17 manuscript pages on 20 leaves each 33 × 20.5, signed GM Brown Feb 1963*, NLS.
62 Ibid.   63 Ibid.   64 Ibid.   65 Ibid.
66 Mackay Brown, *For the Islands I Sing*, 65.
67 Mackay Brown, *Notes on "The Wreck of the Deutschland," 17 manuscript pages on 20 leaves each 33 × 20.5, signed GM Brown Feb 1963*, NLS.

superb sea piece, probably most impressive part of the poem." Hopkins's "fine use of close repetition" inscaped the instress of "the heart's panic-stricken search for comfort." Extremely familiar with Hopkins's "hurtle of hell" (Stanza 3) and the color-coupling, the "sweet lingering out skill," the "dovewinged heart" is soothed in purgatory (always very prominent in Mackay Brown's thinking) "To flash from the flame to the flame then, tower from grace to grace." Then again, in the last line in Stanza 3, "From the fire of self love to the fire of divine love, the majestic ascent of the mount of purgatory."[68]

Mackay Brown was not given to systematically working through the poem in an orderly sequence. His mind was attracted to certain features in the "pure narrative" as he "voyaged" according to the Passion of Christ ciphered for him by Hopkins. Finding Hopkins "difficult" he pointed out "Some faults in the poem." The nun, for example, is not a convincing figure...too statuesque, too remote "a kind of sea-going Edith Sitwell...symbolical figure, but she disrupts the naturalistic framework. It is difficult to render holiness in literature, especially this kind of heroic holiness."[69] This is quite a telling statement about what was the stereotypical image of a nun. Something about Hopkins's contrast between the natural force of the storm and the forced drama of the unnaturally uniformed nuns did not sit right with Mackay Brown. Sitwell, who herself became a Catholic in 1955, was observed by some to be a bit of a dramatic poseur of her class and literary circle. I do not know if Mackay Brown had read her book *Aspects of Modern Poetry*[70] and her astute discussion of Hopkins,[71] but he was uncomfortable with "writers as a species...they are not interesting people, in themselves."[72] In these *Essays and Notes* Mackay Brown never shows warmth towards the life and writings of women. Hopkins's fascination with the religious writings of Marie Lataste or his caricature of an Edith Sitwell-type nun were not to Mackay Brown's taste. Hopkins the priest-poet was central to his appreciation, rather than the feminine secondary sources that influenced him. He swam in the tide of the traditional male literary canon (Chaucer, Spenser, Milton, Shakespeare, Blake, Hopkins) with a timely foray into

---

68 Ibid.   69 Ibid.   70 Sitwell, *Aspects of Modern Poetry*.
71 Ibid.   72 Fergusson, *George Mackay Brown: The Life*, 146.

the Edinburgh chorus of his contemporaries during his studies.

Mackay Brown's "final impression" of "The Wreck of the Deutschland" is one of "confusion, a rag-bag with fine things spilling out all over the place. It has not that sure clean shape that one looks for in the very best poetry."[73] Mackay Brown set as the bar the English ballad, "Sir Patrick Spens."[74] Mackay Brown's native tradition is the foreground of his work and here the emphasis is the cut and swirl of the ballad as form and repository of sea lore specifically drawing upon the resonance with the Orcadian Island of Papa Stronsay. Tradition has it that this was the site of Sir Patrick Spens's grave in the Earls Knowe, the longest chambered cairn in the United Kingdom. There is conjecture (somewhat forced) that the shipwreck took place off the coast of the islands.[75] Nevertheless, Mackay Brown brings the attention back to Hopkins's firmament within which he can draw upon all the troubling discordances and dissonances, both public and private. Here he finds rest in an epistemology that gives meaning to his inner world. He is able to interpret his personal obsessions and anxieties as poetic angles and irregularities in the making of a new symmetry. Voyage and shipwreck gave him a sense of Muir's poem "Succession": "We through the generations came / Here by a way we do not know... and our songs and legends call /The hazard and the danger good; for our fathers understood that danger was by hope begot /And hazard by revolving chance since first we drew the enormous lot."[76]

Mackay Brown surrendered to Hopkins's embrace of the divine even though it ran counter to a reading of the poem: "God is not mentioned once." Yet one is left with the impression "that whole action is being worked out in eternity as well as in time: far more so than here, where we are being nagged all the time."[77] There is no doubt Hopkins was a disruptor of poetic convention and that he was passionate about it. Mackay Brown had "the impression that Hopkins, in his exuberant return to the writing of poetry, recklessly threw in all his broodings and theories that he had been pondering in the silent years, without discrimination

---

73 Ibid. 74 Ibid.
75 Papa Stronsay is now the home to Golgotha Monastery.
76 Muir, "Succession," in *Collected Poems*, 222.
77 Mackay Brown, Notes on *"The Wreck of the Deutschland,"* 17 manuscript pages on 20 leaves each 33 × 20.5, signed GM Brown Feb 1963, NLS.

or regard."[78] Yet one can also see in Mackay Brown various stages of his own development of "broodings and theories." The "lack of internal balance," a "good deal of dislocation violent jolting from one mood to another," and "transitions often odd and arbitrary" challenge the reader, but as Mackay Brown had written earlier about Hopkins's "Henry Purcell" sonnet: "The imagery is strange too, almost surrealistic. The great stormfowl of the sestet incongruous; I remember the bird jarred on me for a long time." And, as he adds, "Rich and strange as this poem is, I confess there are elements in it that I find disturbing."[79] "I am thinking of the sculpture of Henry Moore, some of the music of Stravinsky, the early painting of Graham Sutherland, the prose of Joyce (parts of Ulysses for example). Perhaps it remains an early symptom of a new 20th century kind of art—a simultaneous development in painting, music, sculpture, literature, the dance—which attempts to unite the sophisticated and the primitive, so that what has become over delicate and subtle and civilized may draw strength from the savage roots that lie deep in the earth and the unconscious."[80] The pure narrative he applauded was jolted and jarred in a technique reminiscent of impressionistic painting. Hopkins had heralded a new development with his dynamic energy that fired up the old firmament with his language making all things new and Mackay Brown came to a deeper awareness of it. He was experiencing Hopkins the priest-poet, not as Abraham the old Chaldean wanderer but "cruising above him like a star that is in love with distances" as Muir gives voice in his poem, "Succession."[81]

Mackay Brown held Hopkins responsible for dragging "the deity into his art too readily, not only here but in the fine nature sonnets that followed the *Deutschland*: as if he suspected some kind of paganism in pure narrative or pure description and wished to have his poems properly underwritten and guaranteed."[82] Mackay Brown's early champion, Ernest Marwick, had

---

78 Ibid.
79 Mackay Brown, *The Henry Purcell Sonnet of Gerard Manley Hopkins*, 10 manuscript pages each 20.5 × 25 cm, signed George M Brown, NLS.
80 Mackay Brown, *The Windhover* 11MS pp on 6 leaves each 33 × 20.5cm signed George M Brown March 1964 in another ink, NLS.
81 Muir, *Collected Poems*, 221.
82 Mackay Brown, Notes on *"The Wreck of the Deutschland,"* 17 manuscript pages on 20 leaves each 33 × 20.5, signed GM Brown Feb 1963, NLS.

been a constant source of mentoring with regard to just such a feature in some of Mackay Brown's poems. He had cautioned Mackay Brown often about the reception of his "public." Being explicitly religious was seen as a fatal flaw, and Mackay Brown took a different approach to let loose the naturalistic framework of the Greenfields Kirk in an Orkney poetics. Mackay Brown was not the priest, but he was the poet with an expansive field of play, and he worked hard to not look as though "the deity is tacked on" in an obvious arbitrary fashion. Where he saw the *Deutschland* "hung and festooned with references to the Trinity" to have the effect of blurring the imagery "it is difficult to know sometimes which person of the Trinity is being spoken of."[83]

But Mackay Brown did know and fully appreciate the mysterious nature of the Trinity as three persons in One God. He chose to let numbers do the talking as his own technique couple-colored, dappled, and compressed where Hopkins expanded. But there is no doubt Mackay Brown was extremely familiar with the God "who sometimes, in order to stir us out of our lethargy and faithlessness, darkens our lives with annunciations of terror; sometimes he steals through us secretly and sweetly, like sap in a tree."[84] Mackay Brown had many "annunciations of terror," but the secret and sweet sap or life force stemmed and instressed in him a serenity that always came to the surface and to my mind evidenced the univocity of being that implied there was no real distinction between essence and existence. Hopkins and Mackay Brown forged their linguistic reality within this seamlessness of essence and existence, but in doing so Mackay Brown had opened himself up to a critique that undermined his originality.

THE NATIVE TRADITION OF THE MARITIME TRIBE

The storms and shipwrecks that Mackay Brown grew up with were fibered into his being. As an Orcadian child he and his peers imbibed the popular fireside "Legend of the Mester Ship,"[85] that on one level was pure fantasy and, on many others, an empirically-based composition of all the ships that ever, and would ever, sail the Orkney waters to destinations near and far.

---

83 Ibid.   84 Ibid.
85 Mackay Brown, "The Ship That Struck the Moon" in *Northern Lights: A Poet's Sources*, 173–75.

Mackay Brown thrived in the "communal imagination" as it worked "allegorically... and saw the whole world as a ship sailing bravely among comets and stars, over many centuries, to some cosmic destination."[86] The features of his thought and composition took form and shape on a literary trajectory of origins and ends from his earliest beginnings. From the Greenfields Kirk with its biblical and natural understanding of Creation, to the fetching out of its individuated inscape and instress, his purposeful heptahedral design can be discerned. He was able to compress the stall and stem in stars and stations making what appeared as his particular irregularity into a symmetrical regularity as he embedded it in the universal. He elicited an ever-emerging "control" over the hurrahing-harvest of symbols that swarmed, from which the stunning view of man, woman, and child as poetic subjects arose, their uniqueness seamlessly oscillating in the "trembling stations"[87] of universality and particularity. The dynamic interplay of the voyage from origins to ends gathered momentum with a strong abiding interplay between the world of Hopkins with the world of Mackay Brown.

Simon Hall broaches this subject with a view that "Brown's later verse, are a world apart from the rhetorical Hopkinsean gusto of earlier pieces."[88] By "earlier pieces" he means the poems "Storm," or "Prologue," in the collection *The Storm and Other Poems*.[89] Hall takes the view that these early poems compare with Hopkins's "The Wreck of the Deutschland" and "Hurrahing in Harvest" in terms of "early poetic impulse" but that the "mature verse arrives" with Mackay Brown's 1965 collection *The Year of the Whale*. He cites the critic Dunn: "By then Brown had succeeded in sorting the excessively rhetorical to an idiom closer to linguistic reality."[90] I agree that there was change and development, but is it true that the later poems are more of a "linguistic reality" than the earlier? That first collection contains a series of deep, impassioned, and masterful poems that share the world of Hopkins and his technique that Mackay Brown had absorbed and refined according to the uniqueness that made him

---

86 Ibid.
87 Mackay Brown, "Everyman." Unpublished Ms. OLA, EWM Collection.
88 Hall, *The History of Orkney Literature*, 149.
89 Mackay Brown, *Collected Poems of George Mackay Brown*, 3.
90 Hall, *The History of Orkney Literature*, 150.

a great poet rather than an imitator. The universal firmament of Hopkins and Mackay Brown is made so by their emphasis on the particularities of the native tradition.

Mackay Brown's "The Storm" is not half-baked nor does it lend itself to a "pastiche"[91] of Hopkins. Mackay Brown, founded and formed in Orkney, had a greater knowledge and experience of storms than Hopkins. The opening lines, "What blinding storm there was! How it / Flashed with a leap and lance of nails, / Lurching, O suddenly / Over the lambing hills" actually runs in parallel with those of "The Sea from Four Elegies."[92] "The word 'sea' is small and easily uttered. / They utter it lightly who know least about it. / A vast ancient terror is locked in the name / Like energy in an atom." The natural world of the sea storm is inscaped and instressed with such convincing particularity that it speaks for and to those who have experienced it: "Sailors, explorers, fishermen know this. / Women who stand on headlands, they know it. / The maritime tribes knew it well."[93] Mackay Brown mastered a linguistic reality like no other.

The firmament he shared with Hopkins was never far from view. The Christ cipher of lance of nails and lambing hills was more than an impulse in the weave of the poetic tapestry. Christ, ciphered in under-tones, emerged as an over-tone in the coupled-color and word play. Mackay Brown, like Hopkins, technically executed the tones—under and over—working at it in stages, preparing the ground stitch-by-stitch, each a jarring confrontation with a new reality until the realization that the surface image deepened into the instressed-inscape, and had been there "from the beginning."[94] The "realization" was an accommodation or "harvest" in the reader's mind of the swarm of symbols, ever on the move, "on the quiver,"[95] in their "trembling stations"[96] transposing the natural world with the supernatural. This was the sensational vision working across the senses giving sound,

---

91 Murray, R&B, *Interrogation of Silence: The Writings of George Mackay Brown*, 149.
92 Mackay Brown, *Collected Poems of George Mackay Brown*, 168.
93 Ibid.
94 Mackay Brown, *The Henry Purcell Sonnet of Gerard Manley Hopkins, 10 manuscript pages each 20.5 × 25 cm, signed George M Brown, NLS.*
95 Hopkins, *The Letters of Gerard Manley Hopkins to Robert Bridges*, 188.
96 Mackay Brown, "Everyman." Unpublished Ms. OLA, EWM Collection.

sight, touch, smell, and taste to what Mackay Brown would call his "salt mathematics."[97]

The crisis of the existential or psychological storm pressed the emotions hard, "Hounding me" towards "kirk and ale-house,"[98] but it was the visionary sensation of "the thousand candles / Of gorse round my mother's yard"[99] that evidenced the greatness of Mackay Brown and what he saw, experienced, and compressed into his technique. His linguistic reality was strikingly individual, as it should be for a great poet within the classical literary canon. He was not an outlier poet; he was firmly placing himself within the canon of strong writers and strong poets. And he knew it. Hopkins did not intimidate him. The "sweet clear spirit,"[100] "the call of the curlew,"[101] the moral imperative drove his linguistic reality. He was in a "clear imaginative space"[102] working with vigor, suppleness, dexterity, and grace. He was rich, harmonious, various, and precise. He understood the power of language and cultivated it further to the point where the public and private mind, the universal and the particular, expressed unity-in-difference and difference-in-unity, simultaneously. The early work of Mackay Brown reveals a living voice that cannot be destroyed or reversed. But it is true that after the postgraduate study of Hopkins he concealed his firmament so the secular reader could bask in his achievements without having to agree with his religion. And the same could be said for Hopkins. What Mackay Brown articulated as his "salt mathematics"[103] was primarily the Pythagorean number theory in its christianized form practiced by Catholic literary elites from the time of the early Church Fathers. To be able to immortalize storms and shipwrecks was his contribution to a longstanding tradition with which both Hopkins and Mackay Brown aligned themselves. They both came out of a rich, densely textured literary and theological history, and emerged as passion poets whose piety was their forge.

---

97 Mackay Brown, "Sara," in *The Seventh Ghost Book*, 32.
98 Mackay Brown, "The Storm" in *The Collected Poems of George Mackay Brown*, 3. 99 Ibid.
100 Mackay Brown letter to Jeanette Marwick, 12 October 1962. OLA, EWM Collection.
101 Heaney, "Republic of Conscience."
102 Bloom, *The Anxiety of Influence: A Theory of Poetry*, 5.
103 Mackay Brown, "Sara," in *The Seventh Ghost Book*, 32.

Here in this forge, they hammered out their language giving to it the vigor of the sea and its mariners: "down the sand shot out my skiff / Into the long green jaws"[104] color-coupled and chimed in the heat "deep / In summer's sultry throat" and the stammer of "Dry thunder." Mackay Brown captures the force, the speed, the "snarl," the "scudding" dissolved into the "heraldic clouds," "Rampant all around." But it is in the wailing miserere of "The sea—organ and harps—"[105] that is for one reader "rhetorical gusto,"[106] and to another, the music of the sea written with passion and truth. Mackay Brown captures the swing and sway of movement and the fluency of the look of a valley, coupled with peaks that are hard ice, yet yielding. The hard and the soft are punctuated with the hissing spume in the face of the island of Rousay. Mackay Brown localizes the particularity of Orkney storms based on his own experience and that of others (myself included): "What evil joy the storm / Seized us! plunged and spun! / And flung us, skiff and man (wave-crossed, God-lost)."[107] The reader cannot deny the holy isle of Eynhallow in "On a rasp of rock!" with its "shore breakers," but will the reader make the journey in Mackay Brown's clear imaginative space to the "Stained chancel lights. / Cluster of mellow bells, / Crossed hands, scent of holy water?" Mackay Brown creates a great oneness, seamless between the physical sea storm and the existential storm that "danced over all that night, / Loud with demons."[108] The conflation is superb and true to the terrain of the interlaced worlds of nature and human nature. Whether the timeless spiritual space of a monastery on Eynhallow is anything more than historical is for the reader to decide, but Mackay Brown at the very least was "Safe in Brother Colm's cell."[109] Mackay Brown had won this battle for a peaceful and personal safe space he could retreat into by this stage in his life. That battle would never abate across his life, but he had many mornings "in tranced sunshine" where the calm after the storm reassured him. The corn may have lay "squashed on every hill," but nevertheless "trance" and "Tang and tern" were

---

[104] Mackay Brown, "The Storm," in *The Collected Poems of George Mackay Brown*, 3.
[105] Ibid. [106] Hall, *The History of Orkney Literature*, 149.
[107] Mackay Brown, "The Storm" in *The Collected Poems of George Mackay Brown*, 3. [108] Ibid. [109] Ibid.

a visionary sensation of the "high pastures" and the five-sensed inner voice that commanded his attention: "I tell you this, my son: after / That Godsent storm, I find peace here."[110]

Mackay Brown is the definitive artist at work "on the quiver" in the interplay between "Loom" and "Harp with a thousand voices" as he opens up the visionary sensation of the Orkney maritime: She has many "beautiful names": "Great Sweet Mother," "Swan's Path," "Whale's Acre," "Garden of White Roses," "Keeper of Horses," "Giver of Salt and Pearls."[111] The annunciations of "terror" are framed in a poetic beauty enshrined in the "feminine" and a love-hate relationship, as "The Vikings, her closest children" knew only too well, their lives (according to the Mackay Brown vision) called by the "Widow Maker" to a reckoning as their "cold mouths" were "summoned...twice a year, from plough and lovebed."[112] The collection of "The Storm" was never a rhetorical pastiche of Hopkins. It was the founding and defining "prologue" of the Mackay Brown literary corpus. And it is unique, it is of such "thisness" because here was a great poet, evidencing a technique so versatile as he compressed down into the Nordic corridor and beheld the sea in all her magnificence without ever losing sight of being true to nature, and to Orkney. The Fisherman[113] sailing out to the "west flushed" in the seal of the night, at peace in the air, the sea the "quiet scattering of stars" spoke to genuine experience. Mackay Brown was not intimidated by Hopkins or nature. As the world turned in the "gentlest of motion," "washing through the pebbles," the music of nature framed the fisherman tending his creels "on their weeded ledges" and in the "no moon" night there was "Not a sound." And as Mackay Brown carved the runes and kept silent, the sound waves traveled far with the quivering "yelp of a tinker's dog." Silence frames our lives in the face of death by drowning in the blaze of a storm the life of "Jock Halcrow among his lobsters" and gathered in all its pathos in that pathetic yelping. The "no moon night" coupled with "the lighted valley" holds the profound sense of loss to the

---

110 Ibid.
111 Mackay Brown, "The Sea," *The Collected Poems of George Mackay Brown*, 168.   112 Ibid.
113 Mackay Brown, "Fisherman," *The Collected Poems of George Mackay Brown*, 10.

community "in that one dark croft where the light has gone out."

Hall recognizes what was "Brown's entirely"[114] in his technical execution of the "repeated and continual oscillation between the earthly and the heavenly"[115] and marks specific features, "opposites of land and sea, of departure and arrival...strange Biblical/Saga synthesis."[116] The "technical execution" is rooted deep in the firmament that Hopkins and Mackay Brown shared. The christianization of the North Atlantic was especially dear to Mackay Brown, his "Nordic corridor," his "voyage" into the origins and ends by means of a distinctive Orkney poetics. Hall examines Mackay Brown's Orkney with what he sees as four aspects: Orcadian folklore, Norse Orkney, Orkney in relation to the writer's Roman Catholicism, and Orkney under threat from external pressures.[117] But, in fact, the visionary sensation of the firmament that Hopkins and Mackay Brown found themselves aligned in and committed themselves to, drew each of these aspects into the universal and the particular that does not lend itself to separation.

Christianization of the pagan world, to the Catholic mind, was not something that stopped and started. It subsumed pagan myth and folklore, christianizing their forms and content in a kind of metamorphosis that did not deny them but was able to fulfill their aspirant nature and potentiality. Hopkins's affinity with the classical world was deep and intimate and learnèd. Mackay Brown was a classicist, but his particularity pursued synthesis in an Orkney tapestry energized by Christianity and specifically by its catalyst, the Earl Magnus. The Earl was the first Orcadian of note to bear witness through his martyrdom to the christianization of the human person over and beyond the political character imposed upon him. Somehow St. Magnus was more alive than dead in Mackay Brown in the intricacies of his inner nature that over time became increasingly acknowledged in his life and writings in an adoring poetical praise. "This sweet compulsion of art, the pattern"[118] was deeply enriched by Christianity when it came, adding immeasurably to the well-pool of symbols.

---

114 Hall, *The History of Orkney Literature*, 150.
115 Ibid. 116 Ibid. 117 Ibid., 127.
118 Mackay Brown, "Shetland: A Search For Symbols" in *Northern Lights: A Poet's Sources*, 270-71.

The technicalities of Mackay Brown's craft can be found in surprising places across his development. In his short story "Sara"[119] he describes a "salt mathematics" as a process where "the movement of the verse was to be like the sea itself, with short lines and wavering lines, and a variety of rhythms."[120] Hopkins had tracked the sprung organic rhythms of human cognition as it processed the raw materials of sense data flushed with "feeling" as he composed his verse, and Mackay Brown followed him. He emphasized his distinctive native tradition to which he had dedicated himself. This tradition was anonymous and communal in his "dance of words" as the "ballad-men" before him "uttered their great stories" from a recognition of "themselves and their neighbors in their passions and exchanges that bound them together in a community."[121] Mackay Brown saw the shapes and patterns, the instressed-inscapes in the "wave-hierarchies" from "merest ripple to "monstrous comber" that could down many a boat and ship around Orkney. Distinctively, Mackay Brown accepted a simple "theoretical" model for the mechanics of waves in inshore waters as organized in "groups of sevens, building up occasionally to a large wave, seven squared."[122] Then he moved at pace to the "mystical number" seven that "rules everywhere," so much so that in the mid-Atlantic there was an expectation that a "wave-emperor" will arise, "a seventh wave built up to a sixth or seventh power."[123] On this basis he wrote:

> Every canto in my poem, in imitation of the sea, was to have seven sections: of one line, two lines, three lines, four lines, five lines, seven lines, but all mixed and random, for the sea exhibits no regularity in its patterns of sevens. Every seven cantos were to form a group by itself, moving out from the groundswell into deeper movements and rhythms.[124]

His artistic aim was to be a net that hauled and heaved in the experience of "the vast ocean pulse."

---

119 Mackay Brown, "Sara," in *The Seventh Ghost Book*, 25-49.
120 Ibid., 32.   121 Ibid.
122 A group will "modulate" the wave amplitude; it is like another long wave on top. So, the first wave in a group is tiny, the next one is bigger and so on until you get the biggest one in the middle of the group. Then they get smaller again. The last one is tiny, so the biggest wave in the group is in the middle, and if there are 14 waves in a group, the seventh wave is the biggest.
123 Mackay Brown, "Sara," in *The Seventh Ghost Book*, 32.
124 Ibid.

Mackay Brown saw the "manmarks"[125] that were suffocating the age-old co-inherency of the symbolic nature of common everyday objects. For example, the word "fish" had the power to release a plethora of interwoven associations, such as "keel-laying, line-baiting, drowning, salt, moon-drawn waters, hunger, sea harvest, debts and dues"—all stored in the communal memory of a whole way of life. The word "bread" flooded consciousness with plough, harrow, scarecrow, scythe, flail, millstone, oven, and ale-kiln. It was for the artist to live deep and dig deep as "this way of looking at things is over now" and recognize "an origin for music and all the arts that has nothing to do with concert halls, art galleries, and salons set about with tapestries and jars."[126] Mackay Brown was forthright in his direction to align the "primitive atavistic urge" that lay deep in human nature "to unite ourselves with the power that moves the stars, by the offering of our best skills and gifts, so that we may share and celebrate what providence has to give in the way of food, clothing, fire as well as the loveliness we are dowered with from birth to death."[127] Like Hopkins before him, he gave "beauty back, beauty, beauty, beauty, back to God, Beauty's self and beauty's giver."[128]

I do not recognize in Mackay Brown a "romantic longing for the past" or see him as the "despairing antiquarian."[129] Even the notion of "lone tradition bearer" seems to me a heavy weight to carry. The "strange synthesis of the Christian and the pagan" is exactly what christianization is about. Mackay Brown was clear from the start that Christianity is a living and breathing spiritual force and way of life that is true to human nature in all its phases of development. He was a realist of the best kind. "He sees nothing incongruous in having a subterranean, pagan earth creature give a warning against venal sin the like of which we might expect from a Christian God."[130] The dark and the light, the scared and the profane, released a resilience that was a fore-runner of the Resurrection. Mackay Brown's Christianity

---

125 Mackay Brown, *Notebook Two, That Nature is a Heraclitean Fire and the Comfort of the Resurrection*, NLS.
126 Mackay Brown, "Sara," in *The Seventh Ghost Book*, 32.
127 Mackay Brown, "Shetland: A Search For Symbols" in *Northern Lights A Poet's Sources*, 270–71.
128 Hopkins, "The Leaden Echo and the Golden Echo" in *Gerard Manley Hopkins: Poems and Prose*, 52.
129 Hall, *The History of Orkney Literature*, 150.   130 Ibid., 128.

resonated within a firmament always vulnerable "under threat from external pressures,"[131] and he found in Hopkins a way to hone his technique to withstand breach and tensions with his distinctive harmony.

Hall seems surprised that Mackay Brown read Orkney folklore as having "profound and intellectual meaning,"[132] and little did Mackay Brown's Orcadian audience know or understand the exposure to the nature of the Catholic intellectual philosophical tradition that drew from a common epistemology resonating with the past, present, and future, in fact was within and beyond time all at once. But, as Mackay Brown stood "tall" in Orkney and in the literary canon, his merit as the poet was not dependent on his religion. Such a tribute would not please him. Yes, he would like his Catholicism to be accepted, rather than adopted, for its weave and warp in his tapestry of life and work. Nevertheless, the dominance of the heptahedron in the mind and heart of Mackay Brown was made seamless by the instressed, seven-fold inscapes that were held within it, oscillating, on the quiver[133] in an ever-expanding compression. And it worked.

COLLABORATIVE FUSION IN THE REAL PRESENCE

Mackay Brown thrived on his passion partners most notably St. Magnus and Gerard Manley Hopkins. There came a point in his development when he felt able to collaborate with his contemporaries, most notably the photographer Gunni Moberg and the composer Peter Maxwell Davies. The seminal nature of his exposition of an Orkney poetics exerted a powerful attraction in certain quarters for those artists exploring all things Orkney. Mackay Brown from his beginnings was formed as "The ocean heaved, sang, was bitter, was cold, through all my senses."[134] He could compress down "to a hidden musical thread"[135] and Maxwell Davies knew exactly what Mackay Brown meant and, more significantly, how to give voice to the musical technicalities of such an experience. A critical reflection upon the gravitas of their collaboration is worth noting: "When the modern history of artistic collaborations gets written, the chapter on words and

---

[131] Ibid., 127.
[132] Ibid., 129.
[133] Hopkins, *The Letters of Gerard Manley Hopkins to Robert Bridges*, 188.
[134] Mackay Brown, "Sara" in *The Seventh Ghost Book*, 30.
[135] Ibid.

music will need to give some space to George Mackay Brown and Peter Maxwell Davies who, over the past 20 years, have made a poet-and-composer partnership less glamorous than Hofmannsthal and Strauss, less dazzling than Auden and Britten, but of stature and—from all the indications—durability."[136] The appreciation by many of their St. Magnus Festival audiences was well-established for its appeal to the simultaneous universal and particular in that distinctive "taste" of pushing the boundaries together having been "Blown together by the winds and tides and sense of place of Orkney.[137] Their audiences came to sense and relish their "body of work which seems to have been carved, verbally and musically, out of the landscape: hard-grained, massive and austere."[138]

However, there is a perception that both artists were "dreaming dreams of the ancient past which Brown (preoccupied with Nordic and early Christian mythic history) and Davies (compositionally steeped in plainsong) brandished like an amulet against everything they didn't care for in the 20th century."[139] This perception has intensified going forward to the point where the "ancient harps" and richness of the classical traditions have been put aside in favor for the ascendancy of what Muir had identified as "the never-ending sentence" without "origins or ends," whether it be in literature or music or a fusion of the two. Hopkins's genius was to reinvigorate the firmament, giving technical competency and rationale to the point of a divine ordering of his raw materials and making whole again in a new way that accommodated the "times" through which successive generations lived. Hopkins's layering of the sacred and the profane does not insist on the primacy of one at the expense of the other. The collaboration between Mackay Brown and Maxwell Davies is testament to this dimensional layering as it dove-tails into a meaningful fusion.

There is a beautiful articulation of this collaborative fusion between Peter Maxwell Davies in dialogue with Mackay Brown in the 1982 short film, *Valley by the Sea*.[140] Maxwell Davies and Mackay Brown describe how they met and then collaborated,

---

[136] White, "The Aldeburgh of the North: How the Egos Ended up in Orcadia." [137] Ibid. [138] Ibid. [139] Ibid.
[140] BBC Radio Scotland, 1982, *Valley by the Sea*.

sharing in the sights, sounds, and textures of Orkney. The fine tools Mackay Brown often refers to are learned according to the rhythms of the Orkney Poetics that Maxwell Davies absorbed so thoroughly from his time at Rackwick on the island of Hoy. In their mutual sharing, Mackay Brown and Maxwell Davies honed the "sea voices," as, for example, in the "bright sand that sings under your feet."[141] Maxwell Davies articulates the processing of sound with great precision, as Hopkins was able to do with his musical background. To the composer, the organic nature of his art takes up the particular sound of water against rock and wind, where pounding against the high cliffs functions as a resonator of a deep natural frequency below the threshold of hearing. This acts as rhythmic impulse forming overtones and harmonies that are carried about in the wind depending on the direction of its coming. The various points of contact on the cliffs also partition sound into distinct groups of high frequencies that are amplified by the shape of Rackwick Bay. The cumulative nature of these sounds from living in Orkney manifest as a consistent body of knowledge of weather, so much so that the direction of the wind could be identified as it "thrummed" through the house.

Maxwell Davies and Mackay Brown were able to work within a deep harvest in sound and symbol as though they were in command of a whole universe flooded with polyphonic harmonies. The Orkney air was vibrant with "subliminal sound" with its every sound having a "colored edge." Truly they speak to the "sensational vision" that is Orkney. The light from the sun runs in parallel with the reflected light from the sea. This "double light effect" functioned as a "rainbow shimmer" and Maxwell Davies noticed this effect on the spectrum of sound. The exciting vibrancy of their mutually shared sensational vision chimes deeply with Hopkins and the organic perceptions that powered his verse. Maxwell Davies evidenced what became "second nature" to live on the edge of one's sound capacity. Firstly it is experienced unconsciously and then gradually consciousness takes over with the awareness that ears can be used in that way intentionally. He said as a musical composer one can't use that sound "raw," but that, as he was at work composing the very urban and secular score for *The Boyfriend*, he

---

141 Ibid.

let it go in favor of his organic rapport with the natural world around him at Rackwick. It was then he took up composition for Mackay Brown's "Stations of the Cross: From Stone to Thorn," followed by "Hymn to St Magnus." The plethora of Rackwick sounds oozed into his work. He received validation of his own processes and composition from critical points fed back from his musicians, Fires of London.[142] They asked him if they should play their part as a "sea-birds cry...water smashing against rocks and crashing on the shore." It is worth taking note of this articulation, the musicians validating the art of the composition: "it works."[143]

This was the Orkney poetics nurtured in Mackay Brown across his life from birth. Mackay Brown, by candle and fire light, also savored within his own creative silence the sound "shapes" within Maxwell Davies compositions, *Mirror of Whitening Light*[144] and *Dark Angel*[145] with their Orcadian provenance. The reinvigorated firmament of Hopkins schooled him in the art of synthesis where the "Pied Beauty" of "All things counter, original, spare, strange"[146] could find rest in his art. He was able to open a door for the creative genius of Maxwell Davies that was always more than just an exposition of Orkney heritage. Their collaboration became an organic seamless fusion with Maxwell Davies giving a distinctive emphasis to the pitched heart-song of Orkney. Maxwell Davies during his time in Orkney came to a new awareness of "own time-scale," what he called a psychological time that "fluctuated," "accelerated," "retarded," pushing him into a "richness of space" possessed of its own dimensions and perspectives. Here he was drawn into the rising and setting of the sun, and moon, and tides, consciously arriving in the world of Mackay Brown's poetry with its rituals that related to large perennial time cycles. Mackay Brown witnessed this turn of Maxwell Davies's existence and the fact that he could survive the apprenticeship of the cruel wildness and wet of an Orkney winter.

---

[142] The Fires of London, founded as the Pierrot Players, was a British chamber music ensemble that was active from 1965 to 1987. Maxwell Davies took over as sole director, renaming the group the Fires of London. It was disbanded after its 20th anniversary concert in 1987. Maxwell Davies subsequently endorsed a new group Psappha.   [143] Ibid.
[144] Maxwell Davies, *A Mirror of Whitening Light for Orchestra*.
[145] Maxwell Davies, *Dark Angels*.
[146] Hopkins, "Pied Beauty," in *Gerard Manley Hopkins: Poems and Prose*, 30.

The "hidden musical thread" is the spirituality of Mackay Brown with its new lines of development within the Hopkins firmament. It was not a looking back to the medieval world. Once again, the creativity of an artist could look and live within such a firmament with its seamless balance between earth and sea. Through this articulation by Maxwell Davies with his scholastic musical temperament was the convincing evidence of the artists, Maxwell Davies, Mackay Brown, and Gerard Manley Hopkins pitched within the workings of the reinvigorated firmament. Their composition worked from that taste of self, the heart-song, the storm of mind and heart, inscaped and instressed, their consolations and desolations for all to see, hear, smell, taste, and touch: an Orkney poetics, a salt-mathematics, a sensational vision that all at once is "swift, slow; sweet, sour; adazzle, dim."[147] The artistic sense at play across the mutually shared fusion of poetry and music took place in the act of composition from raw materials. The process was an act of contemplation where spiritual activity bubbled below the level of rational thought. In classical Greek terms, this is the pneuma acting upon the psyche, gathering into a oneness below consciousness. Hopkins gave voice to feeling, experienced as a knot of energy, the divine impulse, the instress capable of collapse, slack, and suspension into a nightmarish sense of God's absence. Hopkins felt its fullness as a dead weight and a crushing sudden force. This was the dark night of the soul carrying tension on the very fibers of existence. The emphasis of the native tradition was as personal as it was universal. The *instress,* the divine impulse, was stored in the unconscious in the well of memory below understanding. At a critical moment there was an uncontrolled emotional release or voluntary choice controlled by reason that navigated the borderline between conscious and unconscious that Hopkins described as "on the quiver"[148] and Mackay Brown as "trembling stations."[149] Strong impressions gave rise to mysterious feelings, calling up creative possibilities, made real by the artist. Sensations flowed between stress and slack in the direction of feeling and feelings thronged into stresses in a seamless fusion of associations working below consciousness,

---

147 Ibid.
148 Hopkins, *The Letters of Gerard Manley Hopkins to Robert Bridges,* 188.
149 Mackay Brown, "Everyman." Unpublished MS OLA, EWM Collection.

emerging as poetry and music embedded in their raw materials.

Scotus identified sensation as a spiritual sense linked to innate memory rising and falling with a strong trust in primitive levels of feeling, sensation, memory, and unconscious unknowing.[150] His theory of knowledge was able to process the patterns, form, and shape of the inscape to reveal their complex mechanics, whether it be of water freezing into icicles, evaporating into steam, or the pulsing movement of the sea as sequence of swarming shapes as waves upon wave they break in specific particularity, shaped to their coastline and then falling back to oneness. The unity of being in "on the quiver"[151] or as "trembling stations"[152] were stalled (fixed in position) long enough for the complexity of a whole sequence to be tracked through its changing behavior by the unity of inscape. In this way nature or creation was experienced and understood to be a system of scales with many pitched levels reaching down to a creative power. Hopkins's formation through St. Ignatius's *Spiritual Exercises* gave his experience of sensation the direct intensity of this creative power as the potent touch of God's finger that sustains the universe. Here is the reality of the supernatural, the Godhead, according to Duns Scotus, Hopkins, Mackay Brown and perhaps the agnostic Maxwell Davies. Mackay Brown and Maxwell Davies could look to the Northern Lights as a stringed force of being just as Scotus and Hopkins had articulated. Nature is a living whole, a real entity because it originates as an idea or type in God's mind prior to his will giving it individuated existence. Hopkins had mastered the art of giving this creative entity, human and divine, with complete expression. From grain and mold, seed and wheat come the Eucharist. God's attributes flash forth in creation in clouds as His eyelids, ashsprays as His eyelashes, mountains His shoulders, glaciers His limbs and feet, waterfalls His beard, snowdrifts His taperlit face. Hopkins saw all that beauty coming home in the starlit night. He saw the bluebell as an altar light standing for the Real Presence of Christ.

So, the Mackay Brown story is the faith journey, voyaging towards the Real Presence as he had come to experience it in a

---

150 Heuser, *The Shaping Vision of Gerard Manley Hopkins*, 32.
151 Hopkins, *The Letters of Gerard Manley Hopkins to Robert Bridges*, 188.
152 Mackay Brown, "Everyman." Unpublished MS OLA, EWM Collection.

very precise way. Storms and shipwrecks operate on many levels and are forged and subsequently immortalized in the liturgical form and tone of his writing. Like Hopkins, Christ's "continual presence was a kind of reassurance" for Mackay Brown where "the old beauty and grace would never be completely trodden down into uniform greyness."[153] Getting close to Christ, the Real Presence, is eucharistic in a sacramental universe. This was their firmament. Hopkins and Mackay Brown had Christ in their sight, as they did throughout their poetry, one way or another. Like Hopkins, Mackay Brown lived intensely on the borderline between this world and the "other," ready, and sure-footed, in spite of their "annunciations of terror" to "Drop my harp through a green wave, off Yesnaby, / Next time you row to the lobsters."[154] In the chimed and color-coupled heartsong of the Mackay Brown harp lived the dark night of the soul through the terrain of terror, storm, and shipwreck, holding its form and shape in the liturgical frame that rediscovered in the life voyage a fresh linguistic reality, a collaborative fusion, and the Real Presence. Chapter Seven gathers up Mackay Brown's theological blades of the Real Presence that moved so convincingly to remove him from what had become a literary stasis around him. Hopkins had deemed the one-directional analogical view of the sacramental universe unfit and unable to give the fullest linguistic expression to its natural and supernatural dimensions with the bi-directional blend between the two. Mackay Brown steeped himself in the things he knew best driven as he was by the moral imperative to do so. Artistically he word-gamed his harp with every fiber of his being because it was the only thing he could do "as long as I am the way I am."[155]

---

[153] Mackay Brown, *Two Landscape Poems, a 10pp manuscript essay signed George M Brown 1964, each leaf 25.5 × 20cm*, NLS.
[154] Mackay Brown, "The Five Voyages of Arnor," in *Collected Poems of George Mackay Brown*, 63–64.
[155] Mackay Brown, "Good Morning Scotland"(1 January 1974), BBC transcript, preparatory comment for recording, dated 24 December 1973, OLA, EWM Collection.

CHAPTER SEVEN

Theological Blades

"Everything winds and unwinds like thread on complementary spools—darkness and light, joy and pain, life and death. As one spool empties the others fills. Life is duality—the two flocks, the two folds of the sheep and the goats, black, white; right; wrong. This duality, balance, is all we know for certain. At the moment the thread of the poet's being is running and uncoiling swiftly into the darkness of the self without God."[1]

THROUGHOUT THIS STUDY I HAVE endeavored to demonstrate the consistent movement shared by Hopkins and Mackay Brown from origins to ends driven by the moral imperative. They both drew upon their perceptions of the array of contingent poetic inscapes that came and went in existence given substance and proportion by the stem of the instress. Through form, shape, pattern, and design, whether it was by number, meter, or music, their harmonization of irregularity extended and developed what had become a cliché for many, making it able to carry the heavy weight of the reality of the human person within the world in which they found themselves. Hopkins and Mackay Brown created a poetic algorithm that gathered up things at source and ordered them with epistemic authority. Things at source behaved in predictable ways and evidenced the presence of a creative process that was their cause—First, Prime, and Final—and contextualized them according to what Mackay Brown called "theological blades."[2] Both poets worked on the basis that they had cognition of what was true—and what was not—with an important level of certainty because they were able to draw upon scientific knowledge and other types of knowledge found by believing and feeling. Newman imbued both Hopkins and Mackay Brown with his understanding of the "illative"

---

1 Mackay Brown, *Notes on Spelt From Sibyl's Leaves May 1963*, NLS.
2 Mackay Brown, *Notebook Two*, NLS.

sense[3] which released them from any quiver of indecisiveness in their choice of religion or their poetic responses. Birds in flight or song whether it be curlews or kestrels, or larks created in them what Heaney recognized as the "republic of the conscience."

Mackay Brown referred to his creative processes: "very occasionally . . . one's own directing will is hushed and laid asleep, and then words, images, rhythms, appear on the page that the writer knows with joy beyond his own capacities."[4] This was just one of many observations he made on his own creative powers, and, as Delmaire suggests, "He knew that a poem was stirring inside him, feeling—though blind and inarticulate still its dazzling way through the darkness: a rhythm, an uncertain pulsing, like a late migrant bird lost now and bewildered for a moment, yet on the true course, unerring. It would find its way."[5] Here were the inner processes of the poet's illative sense at work through a transcendent logic that was native to Mackay Brown and Hopkins. "The light grew a little, there was an image: the farm, horses, a harvest-field"[6] and all the irregularities, the cognitive dissonance, were ciphered by means of Mackay Brown's "heptahedron" into the warp and weave of the reinvigorated firmament. Delmaire articulates further:

> This description of the poem in the making could equally apply to the texture of the finished poem, where signification appears hesitant, tentative, retarded—limping, and occasionally suspended, between accretions and setbacks, seeming to mature rather than to unfold, yet strangely bent on "seeking the silence" between, or beneath, words

---

3 Newman, *An Essay in Aid of a Grammar of Assent*. The illative sense refers to a process of judgment that weaves backwards and forwards with depth and breadth to bridge the gaps between objective and subjective knowledge. According to Newman it was integral to the transcendent logic of Catholicism as he developed its Aristotelian credentials (phronesis or practical wisdom) to encompass an energetic test of truth and error. Within the natural state of belief, the illative sense played an essential role as it is modulated and directed by conscience. It is important to take note of the inclusive ethos of the Oxford Movement with Butler's argument from analogy, Keble's moral dimension, Froude's assessment of how opinionated character can embrace orthodox doctrine. Each of these Anglican thinkers influenced Newman and his conversion to Catholicism through his "systems" approach. His journey to assent has become a classic philosophical work both within Catholic and secular thought.

4 Mackay Brown, cited in Delmaire, "Indirection and Meaning in the Poems of George Mackay Brown."   5 Ibid.   6 Ibid.

instead of moving forward. Syntax (hyperbaton, apposition, dislocation, etc) and rhythm conspire against the teleological progression of meaning in George Mackay Brown's poetry.[7]

The teleological argument for the existence of God, popular as it was in the nineteenth century through Paley's version of it, hovered around the Victorian thinkers and poets but was not enough for Newman or Hopkins. Their disruptive legacy has influenced many and continues to this day and beyond. Mackay Brown found teleology and much more in this ethos and, as Delmaire concludes, "What is encouraged instead is a contemplative stasis which lets new, unexpected layers of signification gradually emerge from that welcomed in-betweenness."[8] The poetic accommodation of these "unexpected layers of signification" were marks of Newman's systems approach and most notably the illative sense in the innovative processes of a great poetic mind at work.

AN AMBITIOUS PROJECT

Mackay Brown diligently, thoughtfully, and independently, resonated with Hopkins to the end. In the *Essays and Notes* he was quite ambitious as he tried to encompass Hopkins's poetry within the liturgical frame of the Mass.

> The whole body of GMH's poetry is a kind of reflection of several facets of the Mass; and this is hardly surprising when we consider how important the Mass was to him. It was the most important action that any man could participate in. It was the quintessence of all history, in particular it commemorated the life, death and resurrection both recorded and to come. It was a channel for the release of man's finest energies—praise, gratitude, prayer.[9]

Mackay Brown struggled with this project trying to conceptualize Hopkins's poems within the eucharistic liturgical frame. He got as far as an incomplete diagram where he tried to match up Hopkins's poems and his intuitions of those poems with each liturgical phase of the Mass.

It seems the most relevant stage in the *Essays and Notes*, and this study, to address Mackay Brown's understanding of a

---

7 Ibid.   8 Ibid.
9 Mackay Brown, *Notebook Three*, "Gerard Manley Hopkins and the Mass," NLS.

sacramental view of the universe and, more to the point, what he wrote about the sacramental nature of poetry. It seems a literary convention for certain authors to assert and base their understanding of the religious nature of poetry as part of a sacramental world view where analogical language takes precedence to explain the mystery of an infinite God beyond human cognition and the finite nature of human language. In relation to Mackay Brown, Schmid[10] and Bicket[11] take this view and it goes a long way towards how Hopkins and Mackay Brown may have understood how God took form in the world. In their minds the power of symbols verge on the sacramental while going far beyond it.

Analogical language was an important part of the process of articulating the nature of God, yet Hopkins, and then Mackay Brown, did something different as they increasingly used language univocally. This was the "theological phenomenon"[12] that Hopkins brought to his poetry. Newman had flushed out the cognition of assent that stirred the Jesuit Hopkins to articulate the intelligent design of the inscape stemmed in the divine energy of the instress. Hopkins realized that poetic form and content stand or fall together to give the most complete expression of Christ descending and ascending, penetrating all levels of being. Hopkins followed the natural processes in nature and the human person. Schmid and Bicket touch on the idea that sacramental grace breaks out in the poetry of Hopkins and Mackay Brown, bringing a sense or radiance, if not cosmic rapture, as well as an analogical reasoned articulation of it. The literary method, to use analogical language, explores God's nature with human thinking, using what we do know to give insight into what we do not. But is this the whole story?

Hopkins built capacity into language by the paradigm of inscape and instress that pivoted on an experience of intelligent design in the natural world and the human person. The capacity, the room to expand and align language with nature, was built on the katalogical, difference-in-unity and unity-in-difference,

---

10 Schmid, *Keeping the Sources Pure: The Making of George Mackay Brown.*
11 Bicket, *George Mackay Brown and the Scottish Catholic Imagination.*
12 Balthasar, *The Glory of the Lord: A Theological Aesthetics III, Studies in Theological Style: Lay Styles*, 392.

and understanding of a Trinitarian God, at once descending and ascending. Hopkins epitomized the one-ness of this rising and falling in "The Windhover" with its Christ-bird. His renewed firmament became a literary paradigm that was seminal in its irresistible outreach to the poets that came after him and, as Mackay Brown exemplified in his writing, was "beautifully shaped for survival."[13] To conceptually position Hopkins or Mackay Brown in a sacramental view of the universe is not the whole story. The technicalities of what they achieved in their poetic craft were sourced in a creative unity that they were inheritors of precisely because they aligned themselves within a tradition that stretched back to the Church Fathers, re-opened through the Oxford Movement, and was guided by Newman. Both Hopkins and Mackay Brown escaped the "isms" of their times as they marked out their own literary positioning, making sure it was well documented from beyond their graves. The sacramental world view contained within itself sign and symbol, as they pressed forward to go beyond the likeness they contained as a series of images. Inevitably, analogical language could only go so far, whereas to move into the realm of univocity, as Hopkins did, gave a new field of poetic play where he so convincingly displayed "the unprecedented character of... language" identified by Balthasar as "a theological phenomenon."[14] The glory of the Lord that defined the Balthasarian theological project gave coherency and continuity throughout the twentieth century and beyond, drawing together the Catholic ethos within a world pushing it to the margins. Mackay Brown's self-understanding was positioned in this coherency and continuity through Newman and Hopkins, and his poetic craft is unashamedly dedicated to the glory project through the exposition of his native tradition. Orkney was his theophany, and it was here he found his gifted poetic self so fully. It was no random accident, and he was fully conscious of the truth of his hard-won inner purpose.

In the *Essays and Notes*, Mackay Brown confidently asserts his view of poetical language as he draws upon, and takes issue with, the scholar and literary critic John Pick: "After the writing

---

[13] Bold, *George Mackay Brown*, 113.
[14] Balthasar, *The Glory of the Lord: A Theological Aesthetics III, Studies in Theological Style: Lay Styles*, 392.

of the 'Deutschland' H [Hopkins] saw his poetry as part of that everlasting Gloria (it is not sacramental poetry as Pick says: how can any words be 'sacramental' except the words of the sacraments themselves, and then only if united to the sacramental actions; a sacrament—at least to a Catholic—being one of the seven channels of divine grace, and he was never so arrogant as to claim sacramental power for his poetry)."[15] Mackay Brown spoke with authority on his notions of language and he did so with the greatest respect for John Pick's views. Pick's book[16] was well thumbed by Mackay Brown and its influence is clearly visible in the *Essays and Notes*.

The Catholic Church defines sacramentals as sacred signs that signify effects, particularly of a spiritual nature, and that are obtained through the intercession of the Church. Sacramentals do not confer the grace of the Holy Spirit in the way that the sacraments do, but by the Church's prayer they prepare one to receive grace and dispose a person to cooperate with it. The Catholic attitude is one where the liturgy of the sacraments and sacramentals sanctifies every event of a life of faith with the divine grace that flows from the Paschal mystery of the Passion, Death, and Resurrection of Christ. From this source all sacraments and sacramentals draw their power. Theological or doctrinal "blades" aside, with their religious under- and overtones, Mackay Brown was constantly at pains for any assessment of Hopkins, to be judged upon his artistry rather than for his piety. This increasingly became the guiding principle for his own work, and it was singularly liberating for him to do as Hopkins had done. He could work within Catholicism as an adherent without seeking to be identified as a religious poet. This was important to him and the only way to proceed.

The *Catechism of the Catholic Church* lists three types of sacramentals: blessings, consecrations/dedications, and exorcisms. These are clearly absent from Hopkins's poetry, as well as Mackay Brown's. The Sign of the Cross is a sacramental and Mackay Brown explored that as a frame for his non-liturgical prayerèd verse in the Stations of the Cross and his poetic litanies. In my experience of Mackay Brown, I never saw him with rosary

---

15 Mackay Brown, *Notebook Three "Gerard Manley Hopkins and the Mass,"* NLS.   16 Pick, *Gerard Manley Hopkins: Priest and Poet*.

beads, scapulars, medals, or other devotional articles. It just was not his style to be seen with these items (and to my knowledge these items never surfaced after his death). Of course, Mackay Brown was deeply conscious of the sacraments and sacramentals, but he was not the priest who administered them. There was, I think, a Hopkins/Mackay Brown convergence when it came to the thought and feeling of their shared sensational vision being a real and vibrant actual expression of popular piety. This was their sprung rhythm of life and language. The palpable core of the Incarnation was Scotian, and it carried all aspects of their writing. Poets may draw deeply from liturgy, but poetry was never in itself a sacrament or a sacramental, even though some commentators read it as such. Both Hopkins and Mackay Brown were sensitized to this as they knew an assessment would invariably be made by their literary audience and critics who would struggle and discount the religious nature of their works. The true test of great poetry is the artistry of the craft that can equally withstand the critique of the sacred and profane.

"The Wreck of the Deutschland" set the tone for what Mackay Brown termed as Hopkins's theological blades. Its ecstatic energy disrupts the conventions and expectations of the reader. Mackay Brown endeavored to do two things simultaneously. Firstly, he interlinked each part of "The Wreck of the Deutschland" and, secondly, each of Hopkins's other poems with parts of the Mass. But the project fell short of completion because, although it may have been Mackay Brown's intention, it was not Hopkins's intended craft. Mackay Brown tried to see an overall all-embracing series of patterns in Hopkins's work which may be present there partially, but not fully. It is at this point he might have tried to implement the sacramental world view, but it did not work to look at Hopkins's poems in that way; and the failure to complete the diagram proved it. Nevertheless, this does give an insight into Mackay Brown's perceptions of the Mass and the different energies and cognitions that he himself experienced during his experience of liturgical worship (given that he had not yet been received "officially" into the Catholic Church).

Mackay Brown was formed in the Latin liturgy of the pre-Vatican II Mass and as such began at the Judica Me. The Mass ordinarily began with the recitation of a short part from this

Theological Blades

beautiful psalm (42) from the Old Testament. Mackay Brown makes the point that the Dark Sonnets have the character of the psalm with its emotional distress. The Judica Me—"Have mercy on me O Lord," from David's prayer of distress—is a space for intense introspection. He also placed in parallel "The Bugler, Margaret, Brothers, D/land, Henry Purcell."[17] As Mackay Brown explains, "Right at the start we are convinced of the Fall and of the need for repentance and purification,"[18] adding that the Judica Me redirects within the religious experience of the liturgy as the heart and mind is lifted in the "Hope in God" towards making things new once sin is resolved. Clearly, the universality of the Catholic penitent wounded by original sin and subsequent acts of "self-wise self-will"[19] came to the "Lord of the Eucharist"[20] where "the hell-rooks sally to molest him"[21] but "How it does my heart good, visiting at that bleak hill."[22] Mackay Brown saw the "divine doom"[23] as matched by the uplift of the Judica Me the "sweetest sendings,"[24] the "tufts of consolation"[25] punctuated with the "backwheels though bound home."[26]

Mackay Brown observed in Hopkins a concern for the "innocence of young people" and that the priest saw them as easy prey for the "filth brought in by the Fall, which comes in ever-new-disguises."[27] His notes on "The Bugler's First Communion"[28] express the universal predicament and its particular character in the "child" of the bugler about to receive the Eucharist for the first time:

> The conflict in his soul is a reflection of the great outer war. Christ is the King; he is heir to the boy's soul and to the whole universe; in fact, at this present moment, he reigns absolutely in the first, since the bugler is in a state of grace. By using 'martial images' 'backwheels' suggests an army repulsed and in rout, the great guns reeling back through rut and carnage.[29]

---

17 Mackay Brown, *Notebook Three, Gerard Manley Hopkins and the Mass*, NLS.
18 Ibid.
19 Hopkins, "The Bugler's First Communion" in *Gerard Manley Hopkins Poems and Prose*, 42.   20 Ibid.   21 Ibid.
22 Ibid.   23 Ibid.   24 Ibid.   25 Ibid.   26 Ibid.
27 Mackay Brown, *Notebook Three*, "Gerard Manley Hopkins and the Mass," NLS.
28 Mackay Brown, *Notes on "The Bugler's First Communion,"* 7 manuscript pp on 4 leaves each 33 × 20.5 signed GMB March-April 1964 in pencil, NLS.
29 Ibid.

But darkness never has the last word in Hopkins or Mackay Brown: "The last lines 'Forward-like' suggests advance and victory. But the poet does not disguise his anxiety—'but however' it falls out, it is likely enough heaven in its goodwill and charity to men, their prayers are mine."[30] Mackay Brown noticed the anxiety, the trembling nature of salvation in the eyes of the poets not knowing for certain how they stood before God in all the messy details of their lives. But, as Mackay Brown writes, "we should not forget that it is part of the bugler's duty to sound advance and retreat."[31] Mackay Brown knew the struggle well: the battle between good and evil, innocence and experience oscillates, quivers, trembles, as "the doubt provokes a faith even greater."[32] For Mackay Brown, "The poem is a kind of expanding, a growing upward and outward like a tree."[33] This was poetic convention: "Most English poets follow this pattern."[34]

Again, Mackay Brown notes Hopkins's concern for the "innocence of young people" in his notes on the poem "Spring and Fall (*to a young child*)."[35] He saw its sprung rhythm conveying the inevitability of the cycle of life where "you will weep and know why" countered by "fresh thoughts"[36] that are pressed down hard. Nevertheless, the innocence of a young child stood as a measure and beacon of redemption. Mackay Brown caught "a fleeting glimpse of a young girl watching the branches being stripped by autumn" and the "invocation a whisper of her name Margaret,"[37] but as Hopkins moves the poem to "high metaphysical speculation" in "worlds of wanmeal leafmeal lie" to the "blight man was born for."[38] But one senses Mackay Brown losing interest and he writes, "it is hardly fair to call Margaret one of GMH's people [any more than Marcus Hare[39] or Duns Scotus]."[40] Hopkins's grappling with theodicy is a preoccupation for Mackay Brown as well, and he gives the problem of evil close attention in his later novels, *Magnus* and, more extensively, *Vinland*.

---

30 Ibid.   31 Ibid.   32 Ibid.   33 Ibid.   34 Ibid.
35 Mackay Brown, *Gerard Manley Hopkins People*, 16 manuscript pages each 20.5 × 25 cm, signed George M Brown 1962, NLS.
36 Ibid.   37 Ibid.   38 Ibid.
39 Marcus Hare was the captain who went down with his ship in Hopkins poem "The Loss of the Eurydice" written three years after "The Wreck of the Deutschland."
40 Mackay Brown, *Gerard Manley Hopkins People*, 16 manuscript pages each 20.5 × 25 cm, signed George M Brown 1962, NLS.

Hopkins's poem "Brothers"[41] pays tribute to the beauty of the innocence of youth that so moved Hopkins and Mackay Brown. Furthermore, Fr. Hopkins brings a new sympathy and tenderness in this poem, of the priest moving among his people. Mackay Brown experienced this deep warmth himself from his own Jesuit priests in Orkney. This sympathy and tenderness were palpable in his harp-songs for his people, his audience, drawing them into the native tradition that has endeared him to so many. Mackay Brown's notes on Hopkins's poem "Henry Purcell" convey a certain painful perplexity: "Rich and strange as this poem is, I confess there are elements in it that I find disturbing: words like '(spirit) heaves in HP' and it is 'the forged feature finds me,' 'the rehearsal of own, of abrupt self.'"[42] Mackay Brown resonated with the particularities of the struggles of Hopkins's character and dilemmas and how he could work his own versions of these *inscapes* into the universality of the *instress* through the practice of repentance in this phase of the Mass.

Mackay Brown then sketched out the liturgical phases of the Absolutio, Misearatur, Kyrie, and Gloria, that were unaccompanied by any poem entries. Then, beside the Offertorio, he entered Hopkins's poem "Midday Morning and Evening Sacrifice." In spite of "what hell stalks towards the snatch of" the offering persists "with despatch, of all beauty and freshness blooming and fuming, all thought, and strength were to be held for 'Christ's employment.'" The pattern of movement for Hopkins and Mackay Brown is the theological drama where "Everything winds and unwinds like thread on complementary spools—darkness and light, joy and pain, life and death."[43] It had origins and ends, and the journey between them was one of faith, whether in the refining processes of the liturgy or in life. These poems assigned to the Judica Me demonstrate their mutual pietas in its "honest to God" struggle in the examination of conscience, their examen portrayed in the Ignatian Spiritual Exercises. The pattern of movement in the Mass, the theological drama, carries their personal and particular narrative within the liturgy that "winds and unwinds" in the presence of the compassionate flow of a merciful God.

---

41 Ibid.
42 Mackay Brown, The Henry Purcell Sonnet of Gerard Manley Hopkins, *10 manuscript pages each 20.5 × 25 cm, signed George M Brown, NLS.*
43 Mackay Brown, *Notebook One, Notes on "Spelt from Sibyl's Leaves" May 1963, NLS.*

His ambition to classify and categorize Hopkins in this way is only partially "doable." Inevitably, Mackay Brown was drawn back into the reinvigorated firmament spear-headed in "The Wreck of the Deutschland"[44] that gave frame and trajectory to Mackay Brown's craft and a way to restore loss in language so marked in the post-Reformation world. Doctrines and theology come to life through the Eucharist, the Mass, that Mackay Brown observed in play as the Fr. Hopkins stood at his altar. But at the Veni, Sanctificator (the invocation "Come, Holy Spirit") Mackay Brown is able to cite: "The dove that flies through the storm in the D/Land."[45] At the Lavabo (the first word of that portion of Ps. XXV said by the celebrant at Mass while he washes his hands after the Offertory, from which word the whole ceremony is named). Mackay Brown sees "The purity and brightness of GMH's verse."[46] Mackay Brown cites this "purity and freshness" all his life as a sort of mission statement for Hopkins. "This is what he strove for through all his complex and difficult maze."[47] Mackay Brown, using the translation of the Douay-Rheims Bible,[48] quotes: "That I may hear the word of praise and tell of all thy wondrous works."[49] He continued his liturgical listing with "Innocents,"[50] but left it blank. This allusion to the Holy Innocents evidences thought and feeling not only for the Latin Mass but for the visionary Blake and Mackay Brown's instruction to read and study his writing and painting of "The Last Judgement."[51]

---

[44] Mackay Brown, *Notebook Three. Gerard Manley Hopkins and the Mass*, NLS.
[45] Ibid.   [46] Ibid.   [47] Ibid.
[48] The Douay-Rheims Bible is a translation of the Bible from the Latin Vulgate into English. It was the first officially authorized Catholic Bible translation in English and has formed the basis of some later Roman Catholic Bibles in English. It includes the seven Deutero-Canonical books (also known as the Apocrypha).
[49] Mackay Brown, *Notebook Three. Gerard Manley Hopkins and the Mass*, NLS.
[50] *Holy Innocents*, the children mentioned in Matthew 2:16-18: "Herod perceiving that he was deluded by the wise men, was exceeding angry; and sending men killed the children that were in Bethlehem, and in all the borders thereof, from two years old and under, according to the time which he had diligently inquired of the wise men. Then was fulfilled that which was spoken by Jeremias the prophet, saying: A voice in Rama was heard, lamentation and great mourning; Rachel bewailing her children, and would not be comforted, because they are not." Holy Innocents | Catholic Answers.
[51] Mackay Brown, unpublished Ts. "A Fiddler at the Fair (A Parable)." Sept. 1945. OLA, EWM Collection.

Alongside the listing Sursum Corda (Lift up your hearts) phase of the Mass Mackay Brown included the poems, "Hurrahing in the Harvest" and "The Starlight Night" wherein "the rapture" "the beauty and holiness" open the heart to "praise."[52] Alongside Vere Dignum Est (It is truly meet and just), he bracketed a comparison, "(cf James Joyce Ulysses)." Clearly, James Joyce was a significant figure in the liberation of Mackay Brown as a poet and writer. Leaving Ireland, Joyce exiled himself from his native country, yet went on to write about nothing but Dublin. Joyce rejected the Irish Church, but nevertheless found himself at home in Catholic categories instressed into him by his Jesuit education and formation. Similarly (and conversely) Mackay Brown "bodily" left Orkney to study in Edinburgh, but, in terms of his writing, did he ever truly leave? Hopkins, Joyce, and Mackay Brown shared common ground and divergence as their literary trajectories intertwined in the creative energy of Catholic categories.

Nye later observed Mackay Brown to have, "found the necessary authority to translate remoter states of mind and feeling into the strong unclouded fabric of his own vision."[53] According to Nye, "Everything he touches becomes Orkney and Orkney becomes him."[54] For Hopkins, Joyce, and Mackay Brown the Catholic categories were so intellectually and spiritually liberating that these literary men expressed their uniqueness without being encumbered by the worldly face of the institution. But Mackay Brown was not an inch anti-Catholic. What Nye observed to be, "health in this process which cannot be prized too highly"[55] is a recognition of Mackay Brown's artistry rising over and above his chosen Catholicism. Gifford described Mackay Brown: "Like his books, he seems to belong to a world of longer perspectives: a visionary without feyness."[56] These critics recognized in Mackay Brown the largesse of his creativity and worldview as well its inherent particularities. But the seamless integration between the universal and the particular and its realm of Catholic categories remained an "unknown" to them.

---

52 Mackay Brown, *Two Night Poems and manuscript pp on 4 leaves each 33 × 20.5 in blue and black ink, signed George M Brown 1963*, NLS.
53 Nye, "Turning Fable Into Life," *Scotsman Weekend*, 7.
54 Ibid.   55 Ibid.
56 Gifford, "Splendid Isolation," *Spectrum Review*, 32.

The Jesuit frame, "to arrange things in such a way that they became easy to survey and judge,"[57] was also instilled in Hopkins and Mackay Brown as a creative wellspring. Joyce had divided *Ulysses* into eighteen episodes, each an approximation of the episodes in Homer's *Odyssey*. Similarly, one could say that Mackay Brown tried to survey, judge, and categorize Hopkins's poems within the liturgy of the Mass, phase by phase. But this was not where synthesis was found for Mackay Brown's poetic vision. Mackay Brown's rebellion was against Scottish Calvinism, and gradually his allegiance, assent, and loyalty were to Catholic categories as the world hurtled headlong into an abandonment of classicism, Christianity, and the native tradition that he sought to make his life-long literary project.

Mackay Brown was attentive to a finely tuned liturgical structure and frame wherein he sensed the swarm of symbols had found anchorage. Then he listed and made notes: "*The Bread* A universal and yet X's (Christian), *The Wine* as 'Blood the sign of suffering the sign of joy.'"[58] The "Body and Blood of Xt (Christ) separated in depth. The fraction of the host, the dropping of the particle in the chalice signs Resurrection."[59] The "Bread of Heaven" brought to his mind Hopkins's "The Starlight Night," "this piece-bright paling."[60] Everything came back to the re-presentation of the Passion of Christ in the Eucharist. The "Consecration" was "a moment hallowed, mentioned, merely hinted at."[61] Mackay Brown was opening his own personal interaction within the Mass with the priest Hopkins at the altar. The priest re-presented Christ through the sacraments. This re-presentation through the priest never had "the last word."[62] The Eucharist was held in the silence of the rite and ritual, as well as in the silence of the eucharistic community. The smallest particular thing, "the particle in the chalice," that the priest dropped in from the "host," the Body of Christ, "this piece-bright paling" takes its force into the eucharistic community as they emerge out into the world.

57 Joyce, "You ought to allude to me as a Jesuit," *Irish Times*.
58 Mackay Brown, *Notebook Three. Gerard Manley Hopkins and the Mass*, NLS.
59 Ibid.   60 Ibid.   61 Ibid.
62 Mackay Brown, *Comments on The Starlight Night in Two Night Poems and manuscript pp on 4 leaves each 33 × 20.5 in blue and black ink, signed George M Brown 1963, NLS.*.

Mackay Brown converged with Hopkins in position and attitude: "The Mass is the most important action that anyone can participate in, the pure source of all goodness, truth and beauty."[63] Although he fell short in his project to inscribe each liturgical phase with an accompanying Hopkins poem, he confidently affirmed that, "GMH's total output was a kind of imitation of the Mass, a secondary spring where made of poetry, Catholic and non-Catholic might refresh themselves."[64] Mackay Brown's sketch of the Mass was numbered with theological blades:

> 1. God the Father, 2. Invocation of the Holy Spirit, 3. Benedictus qui venit (the blessing who comes): God the Son is about to become the Bread of Life. The fervid time pattern of the Mass: for of course the Trinity is always there. It is the story of Man's Life on earth, the pure quintessence of all history both past and to come; the symbols are the key.[65]

The fervid time pattern was glowing and burning in Mackay Brown with the fiery passion of Christ on the eucharistic altar and in a eucharistic Greenfields Kirk.

This sketch of the Mass and its phases conjoined with Hopkins's poems was perhaps Mackay Brown trying to formulate an original proposal for some sort of postgraduate topic for his thesis. But this was not his path, and certainly not his nature. It was the poet in him, not the scholar (although he was scholarly) that always burst forth with an intensity that he himself later articulated "As long as I am the way I am"[66] that drove him to hone his craft with a marked authenticity that made him different alongside his literary peers. The moral imperative, the call of the curlew, his sensational vision could not be compressed into a thesis on Hopkins. The art of compression, though, is a mark of his writing and specifically his poetry. Synthesis, in Mackay Brown's mind, is a poetic vision that moves into the realm of univocity with its seamless difference-in-unity and unity-in-difference.

After ranking Mackay Brown alongside Ian Crichton Smith and Edwin Morgan as one of the great modern Scottish poets, Gifford makes the point that "the criticism would be that he's

---

63 Mackay Brown, *Notebook Three, Gerard Manley Hopkins and the Mass*, NLS.
64 Ibid. 65 Ibid.
66 Mackay Brown, "The Poet Speaks," British Council, 2.

tied to a very curious marriage of folklore and pagan ritual: he tends to repeat that a bit, nevertheless the achievement within it is astonishing. I keep thinking of him as like Gerard Manley Hopkins, who worked in a very strange and personal almost obsessive, mythology but nevertheless made great poetry out of it."[67] Nye similarly observes of Mackay Brown: "it might seem that he had no choice but to write in a certain way, and it is assuredly to his great credit that he has learned to perfect that way."[68] Mackay Brown received faint praise from his critics, but it was inevitably offset with what they did not like. The negative criticism loomed large in Mackay Brown's mind with its sense of literary damnation. Nye continues that "mastery of his own mastery allows him to manipulate it" and "can deteriorate into mannerism." Furthermore, for the critics, there is a "conspicuous absence of lightening in Mackay Brown's work" and "I like him least where he uses his Roman Catholicism to do his thinking for him, and where he goes in for counting things (sheep, shadows, herrings whatever)." This "poetical arithmetic is not so much precise as precious. He is a species of Georgianism,[69] though Brown makes it look hard edged by invoking the sagas and ballads as authority for it."[70] Scammell, also in the chorus of critics pithily writes, "Archaism is something of a problem."[71]

This was a healthy critical chorus that had the effect of an endorsement of the ranking of Mackay Brown as a poet of importance. His literary craft, his artistic sense, firmly and unashamedly stood upon its difference from that of his literary peers. Mackay Brown defied the traditional literary canon with the various "isms" he encountered across his lifetime. These "isms" or ideological phases of popular culture continue to influence how his literary works are received and ranked. The sacramental world view was too conventional for Mackay Brown with its serialization of images

---

67 Gifford, "Splendid Isolation," *Spectrum Review*, 32.
68 Nye, "Turning Fable into Life," *Scotsman Weekend*, 7.
69 Poetry Foundation: A poetic movement in England during the reign of George V (1910-1936), promoted in the anthology series *Georgian Poetry*. Its ranks included Rupert Brooke, Siegfried Sassoon, Walter de la Mare, Robert Graves, A. E. Housman, and D. H. Lawrence. The aesthetic principles of Georgianism included a respect for formalism as well as bucolic and romantic subject matter. The devastation of World War I, along with the rise of modernism, signaled the retreat of Georgianism as an influential school of poetry.
70 Nye, "Turning Fable into Life," *Scotsman Weekend*, 7.
71 Scammell, "Hard as Granite, Sweet as Grass," *Books and Poetry*.

as sign and symbol. Schmid gives partial weight[72] to the analogical use of language that superimposed a liturgical narrative as an explanation of why and how Hopkins's and Mackay Brown's work is so radiantly illumined. Bicket left the relationship between Hopkins and Mackay Brown to Schmid[73] while positioning Mackay Brown in a reconstructed "Scottish Catholic imagination" on the basis that such a conceptualization exists in reality. This study has endeavored to move the relationship between Hopkins and Mackay Brown to a more radical positioning based on what these passion poets said, wrote, and believed themselves, rather than what others have said about them.

THE SEAMLESS MOVEMENT OF THE SACRED AND THE PROFANE

Theological blades rather than theological phenomena were more Mackay Brown's style. He had seen Hopkins's intent in "The Windhover" wherein he read that Hopkins "meant to disturb cultured readers."[74] Hopkins had his poetic quest and mission to build in capacity to poetic language, and it was his nature to challenge those who had no ear and heart for his poetic vision finely tuned in the processes of the natural world and the human person. What was disruptive in Hopkins became serene in Mackay Brown. As both passion poets moved within the sacred and the profane, their language and craft were surely blessed by the Eucharist which could not be contained within the strictures of "isms." The Mass and the priesthood were central to Hopkins and to Mackay Brown: "a priest must be awed every morning by the fact that Christ is in the circle of bread on the altar and that he is holding the creator of the universe in his hands."[75] Although Mackay Brown like Hopkins, "believed, in the words of the Mass, that it was only 'through Him' [Christ] that God creates,"[76] he strikingly added "it is not the priest

---

72 Schmid, *Keeping the Sources Pure: The Making of George Mackay Brown*, 155.
73 Bicket, *George Mackay Brown and the Scottish Catholic Imagination*, 45, N144.
74 Mackay Brown, *The Windhover 11 MS pp on 6 leaves each 33 × 20.5cm signed George M Brown March 1964 in another ink*. NLS.
75 Mackay Brown, *Gerard Manley Hopkins and His Public*, 12 manuscript pp on 4 leaves each 33 × 20.5cm signed George M Brown November 1963, NLS.
76 Mackay Brown, *Comments on The Starlight Night in Two Night Poems and manuscript pp on 4 leaves each 33 × 20.5 in blue and black ink, signed George M Brown 1963*, NLS.

who has the last word, though it might appear so; rather the silence after the end of the poem holds a sweet and perfect resolution."[77] The priest is the re-presentation of Christ at the altar who, through the Eucharist, the re-enactment of the Last Supper, brings through the liturgy a place and space of silence. "Silence" is a word that Mackay Brown uses often through the *Essays and Notes* collection. It is this silence through which "Christ himself, the Bread of Life, source of all nourishment and insight and true delight, the power and the glory"[78] is to be contemplated and consumed.

Mackay Brown believed "That Nature is a Heraclitean Fire and the Comfort of the Resurrection"[79] to have a seamless movement between the Greek philosopher who maintained that strife and change were the natural conditions of the universe and the passion Hopkins had for his understanding of the natural world. Intuitively, Mackay Brown absorbed the excited clamor of the metrics, but he adopted a slower rhythm when he wrote: "Slowly and surely today's wind is drying out the marks of yesterday's rainstorm—the impression of horses' hooves and ploughmen's boots and all the wandering feet (arcumambient) of the country folk."[80] Knowing country folk well, one feels here at this point that Mackay Brown was in "Orkney now," with its liturgy of wind and rainstorm through which the "hooves" and "boots" and "wandering feet" give praise at the "plough." What may appear to be "their treadmill" and a life of toil and futility are actually footprints and marks "hiding man's one true direction" towards heaven. As Mackay Brown observes, "Slowly theology is beginning to insert its blade into the poem. We begin to see connections—the storm beaten earth labourers are being compared to the bright heaven-wanderers, the clouds, the roysterers, gay gangs."[81] Mackay Brown emphasizes Hopkins's new perceptions of the particularity of clouds by citing Chaucer, Spenser, Milton, and Wordsworth as poets giving voice to the general nature of clouds. Likewise, Hopkins was guiding readers by his own perceptions when he introduced "cloud-puffballs, torn tufts, tossed pillows." This was a new and exact way of

---

77 Ibid. 78 Ibid.
79 Mackay Brown, *Notebook Two. Notes on That Nature is a Heraclitean Fire*, NLS.
80 Ibid. 81 Ibid.

looking at things. Hopkins was a "poet who wished to see the particular and not the general"[82] and for Mackay Brown, "such extravagance suggests a certain exhaustion of language."[83] Hopkins could craft particularity into language with singularity and originality. The vibrant freshness of clouds became for him an experience of their distinctive and unique nature. The curtain of appearances swept back to reveal the universal that becomes palpable for the reader. Hopkins guides his readers into the hidden reality where they too might connect to the ecstatic unison of the three persons of the Trinity.

Mackay Brown is at one with Hopkins's classical position when he writes, "Nature dies and renews itself. The clouds dissolve and re-form. The elm drops to seed the earth [before withering]. The drenched trampled grass grows, falls again in wind and sun. Pools come and go in the hollows of the earth. Hopkins is celebrating his great theme: the freshness of nature, as he often is."[84] Mackay Brown had engaged all his life with the sacred and the profane, the vestiges of which are in the particularities layered across and at depth in the Orkney Islands. Hopkins, the great classicist, carried his knowledge and learning seamlessly into the Christian attitude of observing the sacred and the profane in all things pagan. Mackay Brown writes, "We can imagine him (Hopkins) with pan pipes far, far back, never having heard of the Trinity and the Church." But nature is not the "crown,"—"man is the crown of nature, the finest work, but when he dies, there is no renewal, he is simply snuffed out, forgotten, a piece of darkness."[85] Mackay Brown accepted Hopkins's "theme" again drawing upon "The pagan poets were (and are) enormously perturbed about this—not only Theocritus and Virgil but DH Lawrence and AE Housman."[86]

Whether there is life after death, and if so, what form it takes, as "all go into the dark" had already been confronted by Hopkins and Mackay Brown. In life and verse they thrived on "diurnal movement, beginning with morning light and cloud, movement and wind and heeling over slowly into twilight and darkness."[87] The confused stance of the pagan and its mix of the sacred and the profane only worked to increase, the "manshape"

82 Ibid.   83 Ibid.   84 Ibid.   85 Ibid.
86 Ibid.   87 Ibid.

shining out in the dark, broken off or dissevered, like a star until "death blots black out."[88] Mackay Brown labored hard to understand the process: "'Disseveral' emphasizes I suppose the unique difference between man and man, even more unique that the difference between cloud and cloud, elm and elm, blue bell and blue bell, to which he [Hopkins] is so sensitive."[89] Mackay Brown did not appear to be entirely convinced: "But there is something wrong with the images—darkness does not blot out a star, it enhances its sharpness and clarity."[90] So, too, then, the darkness of paganism and despair. Yet, as Mackay Brown writes, "without the clarity of pagan art" that is "the romantic cornucopia poured out in fine confusion"[91] we would not truly know the good. This was Mackay Brown's *via negativa:* to know the good by what is not good, to know the light by its opposite, the perturbing confusion of darkness.

The diurnal tide swept through this poem, "it is suddenly dawn again" that startled Mackay Brown "alas, for my taste, too suddenly."[92] Mackay Brown was always looking for the negatives. The poet in him always wanted to exert independence, but, inevitably, he could not resist Hopkins's Christian attitude: "A new and brighter morning, Christ breaks on the old pagan world of delight and despair."[93] This was how it was to the early Christians: "There is no death; man, by means of the Resurrection, renews himself like clouds and trees and grass, but in an eternal day."[94] Mackay Brown sensed the process and worked hard to articulate how and what Hopkins was moving his readers towards: "To convince us of this, it pours out the romantic cornucopia in fine confusion. Night and the star are at odds with each other."[95] Mackay Brown knew the dark shroud of depression, as did Hopkins. They both knew the dark but "in a few lines a trumpet blast, a shipwreck," Mackay Brown had gone deep into "The Wreck of the Deutschland" the Dark Sonnets and "That Nature is a Heraclitean Fire and the Comfort of the Resurrection," all at once: "(Across my floundering deck shone)—very like the 'Deutschland' a dying fire, light, another trumpet blast, a scarecrow, a piece of valuable jewelry: all this thrown at us to batter you into acceptance of a belief in the

---

88 Ibid.   89 Ibid.   90 Ibid.   91 Ibid.
92 Ibid.   93 Ibid.   94 Ibid.   95 Ibid.

Resurrection." "I am all at once what XT [Christ] is since he was what I am. This is theological mathematics that proves men will also be resurrected; but according to the mathematics of XT [Christ]. It will not do."[96]

Mackay Brown then concedes, "What will do are the isolated bits of magnificence." Mackay Brown makes the point that such "bits" are a kind of pastiche of Webster.[97] The "Flesh fade, and mortal trash Fall to the residuary worm" sounded to Mackay Brown like "and This Jack, joke, poor potsherd."[98] Mackay Brown came to Hopkins and this poem as a Christian, not by proof, but by faith. He had fought his fight with the dark and found the light. He made a strong statement of his credo: "The Resurrection (which the poem is trying to prove, though somehow the mathematics of it goes wrong) is not what impresses us—though personally I am bound to believe it and I do believe it."[99] At his core, Mackay Brown stood firm in the Resurrection. That was his ground, yet he was swayed by Hopkins's conceptual development of the firmament: "But what is moving in the poem is to think that Christ's footprints were among the manmarks that it released from the treadmills, that he (Christ) too saw the trees, and the clouds, felt delightfully the bright wind boisterous, and like all of us, feared the hour of his passion and death."[100] Simply put, Mackay Brown stood in the footprints or "manmarks" of Christ, as a unique human person, absorbed in his own (and that of others) treadmill, but the trees, the clouds, the wind, in all their Orkney moods and particularities held his fears and hopes in the Christ Passion, Death, and Resurrection.

THE CREDIBILITY OF SPIRITUAL COMBAT

Hopkins's Dark Sonnets give huge credibility to his experience of depression, both in terms of pathology and as spiritual combat. The battle between the light and the dark with its day-after-day sapping grind of negativity was as frightening as it

---

96 Ibid.
97 John Webster (c. 1580–c.1634) was an English Jacobean dramatist best known for his tragedies *The White Devil* and *The Duchess of Malfi*, that are often regarded as masterpieces of the early 17th-century English stage. His life and career overlapped William Shakespeare's.
98 Mackay Brown, *Notebook Two. Notes on That Nature is a Heraclitean Fire*, NLS. 99 Ibid. 100 Ibid.

was pure courage in the face of Hopkins's honest acknowledgement of his totally relatable human condition. The theological frame conceptualized depression as the dark night of the soul, that gateway to the majestic bursts of light, as the resilient and knowing self finds the strength to continue. Mackay Brown took note: "Slowly theology is beginning to insert its blade into the poem"[101] and these "theological blades" found a new vigor in his mind as he set off afresh in Hopkins's firmament, never for one minute stepping aside from the Christian consciousness of existence and its dark night. "'My own heart let me have pity on' (46), one of the greatest of the dark sonnets; the pathos of the octet melts into the tender half-amused cajolery of the sestet, and ends in a brilliant natural image of mountains and clear sky, like a sudden smile 'Betweenpie mountains lights a lovely mile.'"[102] A Christian can give a conceptual frame to depression with the dark night of the soul formulated by St. John of the Cross and St. Teresa of Avila to whom Mackay Brown alluded a little in these *Essays and Notes*. He was not a great reader of the treatises of the saints and mystics, but he was certainly aware of them. He characterized Hopkins as the psalmist and purveyed the Dark Sonnets as composed by a poet who knew cries of praise, entreaty, and thanksgiving, wrung from the events of his own times and by his own first-hand experiences. In doing so, Hopkins gave what was personal and particular to him, a universality, expressing the attitudes that every human being should have towards God. Hopkins's inmost nature, and Mackay Brown's, was at home in the psalter, the prayer of the Church, with the full range of human experience, including the profound pathos of tragedy and suffering expressed lyrically and musically. Hopkins did not superimpose a liturgical frame, but Mackay Brown did, consciously finding in his art the power to compress the full range of emotions in a set narrative that used the frames of Litany and Stations. Sickness and pain were all too familiar to these poets, but like the biblical psalmists the historical dynamic is interwoven within their compositions.

However, Mackay Brown was already very conscious in himself that:

---

101 Ibid.
102 Mackay Brown, *Notebook Two. Notes on the Dark Sonnets, NLS*.

> It is vain perhaps to probe into the spiritual state of the poet; but nobody has ever suggested that he was a saint. The 'dark night' is (it seems) incommunicable but these sonnets express only too vividly the occasional misery of all men who try to [be a]...saint...in this world...whereas St Teresa of Avila's attempt to convey the 'dark night' to ordinary people leaves us cold and puzzled. The words of St John of the Cross are perhaps the best key to the somber sonnets of GMH. He was all his life too much in love with created things and the world of Christ's absence.[103]

Fergusson, in her brief foray into the *Essays and Notes*, notices the stark contrast in Mackay Brown's mind between Hopkins and St. Teresa in any experience of the dark night of the soul: "Is this a dark night of the soul? Not quite."[104] Mackay Brown was, I think, more in the masculine experience than the feminine when it came to his own spirituality. The rawness of Hopkins's classic everyday "misery" was very relatable to him. He had no energy for Hopkins's interest in the mystical writings of Marie Lataste or St. Teresa of Avila. Hopkins was all-absorbing for him, as was St. Magnus. Their emotional terrain was a better fit. Yet, again, we can look to Hopkins for breaking out of the stereotypical experience of the Dark Night and bringing it into the realm of what Newman accredited as an existential crisis that shapes a poet to become an interpreter[105] of his or her times.

It can be said with greater confidence that Mackay Brown was absorbed in poetry, and especially the poetry of Hopkins. But it was also true to say that the interplay between knowing and believing is not unique to the religious sphere of life. Blaise Pascal sums it up: "The heart has its reasons that reason knows not."[106] Mackay Brown had a consciousness that his heart was that faculty where knowledge was accumulating by intuition. It was an immediate experience intricately connected to the body and its processes. The emotional sweep of everything we understand by instinct, intuition, and the senses has its own cognition or "reasons that reason knows not." Whether the

---

103 ibid
104 Fergusson, "The Praise Singers: Poets George Mackay Brown and Gerard Manley Hopkins," *The Tablet*.
105 Newman, "English Catholic Literature" in *The Idea of a University*, 187.
106 Pascal, Blaise. *Pensées* 4, no. 277.

experience of depression by Hopkins as expressed in his Dark Sonnets was biologically and chemically caused is not exactly known, but it was clear Hopkins himself gave the existential crisis a frame that has touched and resonated with many who suffered from depression in its various forms. I found Mackay Brown did not like to talk about these sonnets in conversation. He would shake his head whilst acknowledging their greatness as he steered towards his preoccupation with "Inversnaid." I always had the impression it was too painful, but equally it could be said he acknowledged their greatness as literary works and a profound expression of suffering and pain. The dark was home to the "pastiche" of those "isolated bits of magnificence" he writes about in "That Nature is a Heraclitean Fire and the Comfort of the Resurrection."[107]

Looking at the sonnets as a distinct group, he writes, "The feeling in all these sonnets of being shut in claustrophobia: an arena, a labyrinth, a prison, a place of exile, a grave."[108] These aspects were all themes in the literary works of Mackay Brown, and much of his early unpublished writings, which he called his half-baked stuff, track his psychological anguish and how he came to understand this as a "crisis." Battling for sanity during ill health was a crisis. But it was here that he personally found Christ, specifically through the martyr Earl Magnus. Like Robert Bridges, he held the view that Hopkins was not "hypocritical and insincere in his religion. No-one can doubt his joy in Christ and Our Lady and the Church and the Saints. But Robert Bridges was right, GMH was a divided man, and his poetry does show 'the naked encounter of the sensualist and the ascetic.'"[109] It was a conventional view of Hopkins, the priest-poet: "On the evidence of these sonnets he did not know just how difficult it would be to become a true priest, pontifex, bridge builder."[110] He was on surer ground, I think, when he wrote: "Those sonnets express the aridity of the soul between two worlds, and [one] not dead but dying with difficulty, the other struggling to be born."[111]

---

[107] Mackay Brown, *Notebook Two. Notes on That Nature is a Heraclitean Fire*, NLS.
[108] Mackay Brown, *Notes on the Dark Sonnets of Gerard Manley Hopkins* 12MS pp on 12 leaves each 25.5 × 20.5 cm signed George M Brown 1962, NLS.
[109] Ibid. [110] Ibid. [111] Ibid.

Theological Blades

Mackay Brown's study of the sonnet "Carrion Comfort" reveals a light touch and confounded Winifred Maynard who disagreed with his understated impressions that tended to veer away from the pain and towards the grains of hope that emerge in the roll and ride of the poem, "No. I don't think this poem has exploded for you yet."[112] Mackay Brown accepted the conventional interpretative frame of the "punishing beast" as "an animal feeding on various carcasses: sensuality, despair" but quickly superimposed the "hero, Christ" and "the soul" as "some kind of malicious dragon with low degraded appetites."[113] Mackay Brown selectively emphasized the positivity of the "struggle." Theological blades to the fore, he took the view that the struggle was terrible, but in appearance only. The struggle was the beginning of a deeper process that turned out to be a "glorious...epical...encounter" that has a "chivalric gaiety."[114] The expansive Hopkins in each of "the 6-stress lines" is able to "give an effect of largeness, spaciousness to the encounter." The struggle is a ritual, a "fight" without which "man could not rise to his full stature as a redeemed creature of God.... There is a hint at the end of what every Christian strives for, the beatific vision"[115] and Mackay Brown includes the quote,[116] "That night, that year of now done darkness I wretch lay wrestling with (my God!) my God."

Mackay Brown puts distance between the experience of depression, even the suicidal thoughts, and Hopkins when he writes, "The 'I' in the poem is more Everyman than GMH."[117] The universalizing of the particular experience, the "thisness" of depression, is in line with the inscape, that inner multi-faceted mental health condition that we have learned to speak more freely about in our times. Hopkins played his part in unearthing and articulating his own dark pit of despair. In "Sonnet 42" Hopkins is very "personal" in "No worst, there is none!" Mackay Brown thought this the "Most terrible of these sonnets" and the "Comfort offered so small."[118] While Winifred Maynard suggests a greater rigor is needed when she writes, "What is it then? Needs more pondering,"[119] Mackay Brown veers away from the pain to remark, "This

---

112 Maynard, in Notes *on the Dark Sonnets of Gerard Manley Hopkins*, 12 MS pp on 12 leaves each 25.5 × 20.5 cm signed George M Brown 1962, NLS.
113 Ibid. 114 Ibid. 115 Ibid.
116 Ibid., from "Carrion Comfort." 117 Ibid.
118 Ibid. 119 Ibid.

strikes me as a good sonnet. The tone is consciously theatrical."[120] Mackay Brown frames the dark pit as a state in which "the poet's uneasiness is betrayed by some shaky transitions from image to image and by two of the worst lines he ever wrote: Fury has shrieked 'No lingering! Let me be fell: force I must be brief.'"[121] My understanding here is that Mackay Brown is speaking from his own experience that depression was never far away; it did in fact linger and its "fell" and "force" was never brief.

The anguish, the lament, the cries for relief, can be identified very clearly in Mackay Brown's early unpublished notes and writings from the 1940s to 1950s. A good place to start is "Man into Oak."[122] It was a recovery position for Mackay Brown to be able to distance himself from his health crisis through his development in writing. It was his literary way out of the labyrinth and dark pit of torment. His own sorrows became immersed in a world sorrow. Both Hopkins and Mackay Brown knew that but found little comfort in it other than being able to see it as a "dark night of the soul" beyond which they had faith that they would come through the combat to the afterlife. It was their personal passion, christianized through the hero Christ. Hopkins was formed in the *Spiritual Exercises of St. Ignatius* and Mackay Brown in the *Orkneyinga Saga*. The heroic and masculine sanctity of St. Ignatius and St. Magnus worked their individual mental health into a spiritual combat that was at once universal, particular, and redemptive.

Mackay Brown concluded with some observations of "Sonnet 43," "To seem the stranger lies "my lot." Hopkins was "in Ireland now" and his plight of separation from England "wife to my creating thought" resonated with Mackay Brown in Edinburgh separated from Orkney "wife to his creating thought." Being the "stranger" was also something he knew a lot about, in Edinburgh and even more intensely in Orkney where his life was under a scrutiny that intensified his Calvinistic depression. Of "Sonnet 44" he wrote, "Now we know what are his symptoms, though not perhaps the root of his sickness."[123] The symptoms of

---

120 Ibid.   121 Ibid.
122 Mackay Brown, "Man into Oak: A Prose Poem." June 1946. OLA, EWM Collection. Cited in *George Mackay Brown: No Separation*, 72–76.
123 Mackay Brown, *Notes on the Dark Sonnets of Gerard Manley Hopkins*, 12 MS pp on 12 leaves each 25.5 × 20.5 cm signed George M Brown 1962, NLS.

depression, the insomnia, the disrupted sleep, the anxiety, and mental agitation, the "black hours" that were all-consuming, the dead emotions of "dull dough sours" the clammy sweats, only scrape the surface of what was much "worse," the damnation that pushed towards a point of no return. Yet, Hopkins strikes back: "I am gall, heartburn," "which GMH found the most thrilling thing in existence."[124] Mackay Brown observed Hopkins to have another angle of vision to find a way out of the labyrinth where negativity is seen as a feature of the "distinctiveness informing all the objects and forms of nature too, but meaningless unless his own lips drank from the tankard."[125] Intellectual distance could be created between the pain and its purpose. Mackay Brown identified and resonated with what "can be the greatest curse, if emphasized in the wrong way."[126] The particular life and the universal are held in unison to witness "the amazing variety of life" that "is ignored for the single existence"[127] if one were left to drown in one's sorrows. No matter the tragic lament of world and personal sorrow, they are one and "like Christ in Gethsemane he accepted 'God's most deep decree.' The 'beast' of 'one's own fallen self' could be and 'is overcome.'"[128]

Hopkins and Mackay Brown did not "continue in the labyrinth forever" where "the damned" are lost to their "sweating selves" tangled in a meaningless combat that never ends.[129] Mackay Brown used Hopkins's poetic phrasing as if it were his own. Clearly, it seems to me he saw no separation between Hopkins's depression and his own, and its shape and form was spiritual combat, not metaphorically but really. Mackay Brown understood the "symptoms." The "root cause" was "the fallen self,"[130] where original sin holds its persuasion of despair. Looking back over his 1940s notes and unpublished writings, one can see Mackay Brown's own symptoms speak in macabre images: "The kitten endured the first weeks of life in a dark forest piled with spider infested boxes and bric a brac."[131] But from his earliest days, Mackay Brown turned from "single life," the particularity, to the "amazing variety of life" by means of the "way of literature." "Sometimes it seems that we in this world may be living in

---

[124] Ibid.   [125] Ibid.   [126] Ibid.   [127] Ibid.
[128] Ibid.   [129] Ibid.   [130] Ibid.
[131] Mackay Brown, *The Commonplace Book*, NLS.

such a confined and loathsome hole—'the sterile promontory' of Hamlet." And it was equally clear the literary way was accompanied by a spirituality that rose up on the backs of "God's most deep decree" and in suffering found resolution to "have patience, if we are supple and yielding to what delightful meadows and perilous seas might we have access?"[132]

The early persona of Mazurin who "loved books but hated reading" discovered that

> the best thing was words that made images that sang and drew fluent lines and gave birth to significant shapes. The best of all was poetry... Mazurin... felt that he was 3 parts dead already—a rather disgusting rag blown about on the winds of life. One evening the good angel spoke to him. Though he could not participate in the gay physical life he would enjoy watching it through his eyes... he came on wells rather oftener than his fellows, and they were sweeter and cooler, even though for him the desert hills quaked at with appalling menace.[133]

Those formative early years wrapped his depression, "his gall and heartburn,"[134] in a kind of dream poem (as I argue in my previous book) where he became a "passion partner" with St. Magnus. "The disease germ came like a lover and leeched to my man's fibers... My buried body curled round an acorn, which fed on its decay like the germ of a dream."[135] Mackay Brown faced "God's most deep decree" and stood before his God and Hopkins's sonnets with the symptoms but also the meaning and purpose of it—as he understood it.

The Jackself is Mazurin, and in Hopkins's "Sonnet 46," Mackay Brown also embraced the virtues to be kind to himself because he had learned how to do that without detracting from the bitter suffering. Here he resonates in Hopkins's particular heart, "My own heart let me have pity on" in a kind of small drama, a morality, with two characters and (perhaps) Jackself's guardian angel who now proceeds to "scatter the hell-rook ranks sally to molest him." The "violence" is "rather with tenderness and cajolery, as one might bribe a hurt child to leave off gathering

---

132 Ibid.
133 Ibid.
134 Hopkins, "Sonnet 44," in *Gerard Manley Hopkins Poems and Prose*, 62.
135 Mackay Brown, "Man into Oak." In Gray, *George Mackay Brown No Separation*, 74.

thorns."[136] And there was much in Hopkins's surging surprise that rose with "suddenly poor Jackself is delivered out of his prison into a lovely world of mountains and light,"[137] as if Mackay Brown were transported to Rackwick "like a choked dry root released leaf and petal to the spring wind."[138] And he could say with Hopkins the psalmist in Sonnet 51, "Thou art indeed just, Lord." This is the "Most austere of the dark sonnets."[139]

How was Mackay Brown using the word "austere" to wrap around Hopkins's verse? It was a word well chosen for its moral stance. At his core, Hopkins practiced what he preached in that he valued self-denial and self-abnegation. His life bore the marks of a man who demonstrated temperance, self-restraint, self-discipline, asceticism, self-sacrifice, abstinence, celibacy, and chastity. Fr. Hopkins, the Catholic priest, would be expected to treasure these values and live them as best he could, and every aspect of his verse was marked with this moral character. Many have explored his temptations; but, nevertheless, his life fulfilled his moral purpose in its formation and the "fight" he put up in the process. This fight or spiritual combat does not take away from the reality of clinical depression, and it is not exactly clear how much his mental health was a blend of being between body and soul. One can say the same about Mackay Brown. The fact that they both took whatever form of depression they experienced (so intensely) and framed it with their Catholic spirituality as some sort of "dark night of the soul" needs to be given closer scrutiny.

As a concept the dark night of the soul is attributed to St. John of the Cross, one of the foremost Spanish poets. The *Spiritual Canticle* and the *Dark Night of the Soul*, are widely considered masterpieces of Spanish poetry, both for their formal style and their rich symbolism and imagery. He also wrote theological commentaries on his poems. His writings and those of St. Teresa of Avila are the most important mystical works in Spanish and have deeply influenced later spiritual writers across the world, such as Salvadore Dali, T. S. Eliot, John Paul II (and many more). The "Dark Night," from which the phrase, "Dark

---

[136] Mackay Brown, *Notes on the Dark Sonnets of Gerard Manley Hopkins*, 12 MS pp on 12 leaves each 25.5 × 20.5 cm signed George M Brown 1962, NLS.
[137] Ibid. [138] Ibid. [139] Ibid.

Night of the Soul" takes its name, narrates the journey of the soul from its bodily home to union with God. It happens during the dark, that represents the hardships and difficulties met in detachment from the world and reaching the light of the union with the Creator. The main idea behind the poem is the painful experience required to attain spiritual maturity and union with God. Hopkins as a Jesuit took his formation from St. Ignatius Loyola, also a Spanish Counter-Reformation spiritual father.

Many have said that Hopkins was never temperamentally suited to the Jesuit religious life, and that this contributed to what they see as his deep unhappiness. But Hopkins himself was truly clear about his vocation, and it was everything to him. Unhappiness or the difficult suffering of the dark night is the essence of the Catholic spiritual interpretation. The Gethsemane crisis for Christ runs in parallel with the concept of the dark night as an existential crisis and as a practical reality. It is also important to take the sources of the dark night as reaching not only to Jesus Christ himself but also to the Bible, the Neo-Platonic tradition of mystical experiences, the pseudo-Dionysian tradition, medieval mysticism, and cross-cultural influences of Islam and secular poetry.

In *Essays and Notes*, Mackay Brown clearly notices the various intellectual positions held by Hopkins, but they are never explored in detail. He was very wary of those interpreting his own writing as mystical (and that includes myself). He was very self-effacing; and, although his depression was all-consuming, he was very guarded about any spiritual interpretation. It did his literary persona no favors amongst a Protestant and secular Orkney or Scotland. Nevertheless, he is appreciated within the Catholic literary world, such as it is. His spiritual mentors were St. Magnus, St. John Henry Newman, and Gerard Manley Hopkins along with the affinity he felt with the medieval monastic tradition of Bede and the literary anchorites such as Julian of Norwich. The particular blend of poet and mystic found a uniqueness in the twentieth century Orcadian poet George Mackay Brown. He soaked up his forbears and contemporaries and was able to find his distinctive literary way whilst embracing the traditional literary canon. He never spurned it for a moment, unpopular as that may be now. The call of the curlew, the moral impetus, the austerity against all the obvious temptations kept him at his writing desk in a very particular and universal way.

A NEW DARK STRENGTH

The most interesting of Mackay Brown's responses to the poetry of Hopkins in the *Essays and Notes* is towards "Spelt from Sibyl's Leaves." Mackay Brown brought his theological blades full circle with this caudal sonnet, remarkable in its "shapelessness" and absorption in "a new dark strength that does not yet know how to direct and embody itself."[140] It was completed in 1886, although there appears to be a debate[141] about this date and whether this sonnet was composed before or after the six dark sonnets, which were written during Hopkins's Dublin years. I have the impression Mackay Brown took the view it was composed after, rather than before. Having explored the Dark Sonnets, Mackay Brown did not allow himself to get too immersed in their dark, desolate moods with the profound terror and pain of the combat with negative forces. He was more open to Hopkins's expansive movement into an expressive and rhythmic metric that authenticated an emergent singing freedom that was beyond the dark experience in a singing "speeding up and then slowing down."[142] Mackay Brown adjudicated on what he saw as the "shapelessness"[143] of the new form. Here he observed the "new dark strength"[144] that needed an expansion of form to accommodate the *inscape* and *instress* of this experience in

---

140 Mackay Brown, *Notebook One. Notes on Spelt From Sibyl's Leaves*, Nov 1963, NLS.

141 Pick, *Gerard Manley Hopkins: Priest and Poet*, 141, 143. Mackay Brown read Pick and quoted him in the *Essays and Notes* collection. He clearly does not agree with Pick on a number of points. In this instance Pick writes of the poem and its publication date, "serves as a direct introduction to the sonnets of 1884-5." Pick cites Robert Bridges" judgment (in the edition of Hopkins's poems) that the poem was written in 1881 as "improbable" as it appears in draft form in Hopkins's "Dublin Note-Book" of 1884-5 thereby bringing it into "proximity" to the experience that inspired the Dark Sonnets during the Dublin period. Pick goes on to critique the poem as prior preparation for the Dark Sonnets that he assumes were composed in 1885. F. R. Leavis, in *New Bearings in English Poetry* (London 1932), also examined the poem in advance of the Dark Sonnets. The critical "convention" appears to be that "Spelt from Sibyl's Leaves" is prior rather than after in terms of the Dark Sonnets. Mackay Brown's *Essays and Notes* appears to support the latter position.

142 Mackay Brown, *Notebook One. Notes on Spelt from Sibyl's Leaves*, Nov 1963, NLS.   143 Ibid.   144 Ibid.

the cordal sonnet. In the standard fourteen lines, he lengthened each line to eight stresses rather than the usual five.—Hopkins called it "the longest sonnet ever made."[145] As Mackay Brown observes of Hopkins, "it is interesting to see, [he] dropped all the experiments which he had done on the sonnet form and returned to a plain classical form."[146]

Mackay Brown read with the eye and the ear, sensing his way through what Hopkins intended as a song "most carefully timed in tempo rubato."[147] True to his classical and pagan sources—and his experience—Hopkins conjured the Cumaean Sibyl, a prophetess in ancient Rome who wrote her warnings on the leaves of oak trees. The Sibyl was a guardian of and guide to the underworld, and her darkness is christianized by Hopkins and Mackay Brown to reveal the under- and over-tones of Hell. Hopkins the Jesuit, immersed and formed in the Spiritual Exercises of St, Ignatius Loyola, meditated periodically on Hell and the "days of wrath" that shall be inflicted on the guilty by the Divine Judgment of a merciful God. The point is that for all the disorder in the world, God's own order appeared by means of Divine Judgment. To judge, in the biblical sense of the term, means to bring into the light, to throw into sharp relief. Divine Judgement acts to clarify and separate the intermingling confusion of good and evil. The personal Creator God is also judge, and by His very nature, and scripture, documents his every word and gesture in the biblical narrative. Christ, Son of God, is the light of the world and brings a harsh exposure to what prefers to remain in the dark. By His presence, the truth can be known by the presence of what is not the truth. Evil, the dark, the false, that is, is known by its opposites, the good, the light, and the truth. Mackay Brown accepted Hopkins's stance, with theological blades where he found a deep resonance in the "dapple" that "for Hopkins meant beauty, harmony, balance, life itself."[148]

---

145 Hopkins, Letter to Robert Bridges 11 December 1886. *The Letters of Gerard Manley Hopkins to Robert Bridges*, 246.
146 Mackay Brown, *Notebook One. Notes on Spelt from Sibyl's Leaves*, Nov 1963, NLS.
147 Hopkins, Letter to Robert Bridges 11 December 1886. *The Letters of Gerard Manley Hopkins to Robert Bridges*, 246.
148 Mackay Brown, *Notebook One. Notes on Spelt from Sibyl's Leaves*, Nov 1963, NLS.

Theological Blades

It is important to note here that Hopkins and Mackay Brown understood and used memory as "a storehouse of unconscious material collective, racial, spiritual) containing pagan myth as allegory or mirror imagery in a primitive world of 'forepitch' where dwelt the types, exemplars, or mothering forms in God's mind prior to actual existence."[149] Their understanding of the unconscious was Platonic, not Freudian.[150] The great Idea of Creation (Mackay Brown's Greenfields Kirk) and Redemption through Christ is projected through nature and the primitive world. Mackay Brown, already an accomplished poet, thereby brought his sources to a conscious state in his writing. Mackay Brown analyzed the unconscious materials that lay in the storehouse: "Earth has lost her memory of these things: a kind of pathetic fallacy which science and philosophy in a sense verify, since how can there be color when there is no light, how can natural objects exist when there is no eye to see them?"[151] He was reflecting on the poem's lines: "her dapple is at an end, astray or aswarm, all throughther,[152] in throngs; 'self in self steepèd and páshed—quite Disremembering, dismembering' all now."[153] The thronging clusters of good and evil made apparent by the contrast of light and dark lent themselves well to the Scottish image and word derivation of combing or "cairding" of tufts of fleecy wool in preparation for the spinning process.

Through an Orcadian poetics, Mackay Brown marshaled the swarm of symbols along the lines Hopkins had brought to the old firmament, seamlessly christianizing the mythical pagan world and the post-Reformation deconstruction. What once was for the pagans an act of projecting human feelings onto the things in nature, the inanimate world of phenomena, and animals,

---

149 Heuser, *The Shaping Vision of Gerard Manley Hopkins*, 75–76.
150 Mackay Brown was not a "Freudian" in any form. He was very aware of Freudian theory and its influence, but he placed his intellectual weight elsewhere. He would get irritated by those who espoused Freudian theory and its stereotypes.
151 Mackay Brown, *Notebook One. Notes on Spelt from Sibyl's Leaves*, Nov 1963, NLS.
152 "Throuither *adv., adj., n.*." *Dictionary of the Scots Language*. As a phr., orig. of two words: mingled one with another, without distinction or discrimination, promiscuously, blended throughout. Gen.Sc., obsol. *To caird throuither*, tr. to comb (tufts of wool) into one mass; intr. and fig., to mix well, harmonise.
153 Hopkins, "Spelt from Sibyl's Leaves," in *Gerard Manley Hopkins Poems and Prose*, 59.

as a "pathetic fallacy,"[154] was now a sensational vision of an angelic procession to the eucharistic sacrifice of Christ through the Virgin Mary and the Incarnation. As remote as this may sound to the modern deconstructed secular mind, this was the universal vision of Christian typology scored or inscaped on the minds of Hopkins and Mackay Brown in their own way. It was not a constraining and inhibiting process. Here they had a new freedom and this sonnet verged on its doorstep with a "new dark strength"[155] to glory in the godhead. The universal myth of creation and redemption in all its particularities through time—pre-Christian and post-Christian—were seamlessly absorbed into the Trinitarian Godhead where the earthly outward display was the Eucharist. Hopkins had launched his vision in "The Wreck of the Deutschland" and subsequent poems. Mackay Brown had launched his vision in his first collection of poems "The Storm" and subsequent literary writings. What he called his unpublished "half-baked stuff" stands as evidence of preparation in its documentation of the processes he went through in his early development.

It was here in this sonnet that Mackay Brown is most fully one with Hopkins. All his youthful turmoil and the literary path he had walked along covered a lot of ground. This was his particular way from the Calvinistic God, his early nurture in Bunyan, his indwelling fascination with Blake, through an Orkney Poetics accompanied by St. Magnus, the *Orkneyinga Saga*, John Henry Newman and Gerard Manley Hopkins as well as his poetic contemporaries both local, national, and international. He came to a poet's knowledge: "Now the poet turns fearfully from the cosmos and applies what he has observed to himself and the life of man in general."[156] As "Our evening is over us; our night whelms, whelms, and will end us,"[157] Mackay Brown discerned:

> Even while he begins to compare the earth light to the life of man, the light continues to ebb, the only natural objects remaining in sight are full of menace, (beak-leaved boughs dragonish) blacker than the approaching night

---

154 Mackay Brown, *Notebook One. Notes on Spelt from Sibyl's Leaves*, Nov 1963, NLS.   155 Ibid.   156 Ibid.
157 Hopkins, "Spelt from Sibyl's Leaves," *in Gerard Manley Hopkins Poems and Prose*, 59.

itself, like some sinister shape (perhaps the medieval demon that used to carry off the souls of the dead) forged and tooled by the last light.[158]

Mackay Brown invested in the "particular" story, its inscape and instress as he quoted: "Our tale, O our oracle!"[159] "Here is the story, here is the inner significance, this is what the Sybil really means."[160] Mackay Brown spoke authoritatively for Hopkins and for himself: "Everything winds and unwinds like thread on complementary spools—darkness and light, joy and pain, life and death."[161] This was the dualistic dilemma that may hold the pagan or secular mind, but not the Christian: "As one spool empties the others fills. Life is duality—the two flocks, the two folds of the sheep and the goats 'black, white; right, wrong.'"[162] And at this point Mackay Brown introduced the parallel of the "Parable of the Last Judgment"[163] that was not commonly employed by literary critics. On this basis, it can be clearly seen that the mind of Mackay Brown was alert to the documented biblical means to bring us into the light from the darkness. The contrast between light and its absence (dark) mirrors that between good and its absence (evil). Any confusion of the intermingling between the two was clarified by Divine Judgment: "When the Son of Man comes in glory, escorted by all the angels, then he will take his seat on the throne of glory."[164] All nations and peoples will assemble before the Son of Man and the separation of sheep and goats signifies the blessing of God and his wrath. The sheep (the upright) go to eternal life for their acts of faith and the goats to eternal punishment for their neglect of the acts of faith. Feeding the hungry, giving drinks to the thirsty, clothing the naked, visiting the sick and those in prison, and welcoming strangers are the ultimate criteria for a life of truth. Hopkins wrote of the "two flocks" "right and wrong" "black and white" on the "rack" of life

---

[158] Mackay Brown, *Notebook One. Notes on Spelt from Sibyl's Leaves*, Nov 1963, NLS.
[159] Hopkins, Gerard Manley. "Spelt from Sibyl's Leaves," in *Gerard Manley Hopkins Poems and Prose*, 59.
[160] Mackay Brown, *Notebook One. Notes on Spelt from Sibyl's Leaves*, Nov 1963, NLS.
[161] Ibid.   [162] Ibid.   [163] Matthew 25:31-46. Ibid.
[164] Ibid.

"Where, selfwrung, selfstrung, sheathe- and shelterless, thoughts against thoughts in groans grind."[165]

But Mackay Brown was unbowed. He was not a victim of the dark. He had in life a great composure; a serenity, and I sense it here in his notes on this poem. He was not stuck in a duality, as he wrote with a marked confidence: "This duality, balance, is all we know for certain."[166] He found a point of balance between good and evil, light, and dark, and although his early and life-long formation was in a Calvinistic wrathful God, he had found his composure and serenity elsewhere in Catholicism. Mackay Brown understood that the trembling stations and oscillation of the Orkney tapestry were between the "tale" and the "oracle," as the weave of the loom exemplifies: "At the moment the thread of the poet's being is running and uncoiling swiftly into the darkness of the self without God. In that sense it is a dark sonnet like the six others. He does not say that the skein will, when the black spool is packed full, inevitably unwind the other way, into brightness. But the implication of returning light runs through the sonnet, so that 'Spelt from Sibyl's Leaves' cannot really be included among those sonnets where it seems that the darkness is down forever."[167] The light of Christ had already triumphed for Mackay Brown, no longer "Man into Oak" as in the unpublished prose poem and in the bleak grey leaves of the 1940s sheaf of notes. Sickness did not break him. Mackay Brown's reading was a convincing argument for this sonnet being composed after the six Dark Sonnets. Hopkins remained unbowed and unbroken despite what he perceived as his many failures. Mackay Brown's interpretation of this sonnet had the feel of composition after the six Dark Sonnets. There is an emerging spirituality where the darkness "in the grotto of the heart"[168] is "down forever."[169] The "cosmological vision of 'Sibyl's Leaves' is of heaven and earth as a sign of the last things."[170] The Catholic minds of Hopkins and Mackay Brown

---

165 Hopkins, "Spelt from Sibyl's Leaves," in *Gerard Manley Hopkins Poems and Prose*.
166 Mackay Brown, *Notebook One. Notes on Spelt from Sibyl's Leaves*, Nov 1963, NLS.   167 Ibid.
168 Heuser, *The Shaping Vision of Gerard Manley Hopkins*, 77.
169 Mackay Brown, *Notebook One. Notes on Spelt from Sibyl's Leaves*, Nov 1963, NLS.
170 Heuser, *The Shaping Vision of Gerard Manley Hopkins*, 77.

Theological Blades

gives voice and measure to Death, Judgment, Heaven, and Hell.

Mackay Brown, versed in the elements of an Orkney poetics, accepted the localized mythology and wove it into the seamless procession of sacrifice, battle, songs of creation and redemption in an unfolding of past, present, and future. Angels and devils, woman and child, dragon and champion were partially recoverable in the Orcadian heritage as shadows that became true types in his vision (as they had for Hopkins). There he found an anticipation of Christ and in medieval Orkney, the champion Earl Magnus crystallized in the type of Christ. The great cosmic battle between good and evil became, then, a prophetic life force for the universe and for Orkney. The sensational vision and its christianization "all throughther, in throngs"[171] of myth and legend, was music to the ears and eyes echoing through the ages towards Divine Judgment at the Second Coming, at the end of time. This is profoundly witnessed in the poem read at Mackay Brown's Requiem Mass on St. Magnus Day April 16th, 1996 — "The Harrowing of Hell."[172] First and last things, first and last poem collections, traced the old firmament and its innovations, in the poetic mind of Mackay Brown. The great Orcadian drama of his native tradition was marked with Mackay Brown's theological blades from first to last in a succession of harp-songs as they "wind and unwind... like thread on complementary spools — darkness and light, joy and pain, life and death."[173] The thread of the poet's being ran and uncoiled swiftly into the darkness of the self without God to emerge from the "harrowing" of spiritual combat with a new dark strength.[174]

---

171 Hopkins, "Spelt from Sibyl's Leaves," in *Gerard Manley Hopkins: Poems and Prose*, 59.
172 Mackay Brown, "The Harrowing of Hell," *Collected Poems of George Mackay Brown*, 400. Read from the *Tablet* by Bishop Mario Conti (Archbishop Emeritus of Glasgow).
173 Mackay Brown, *Notes on Spelt from Sibyl's Leaves, May 1963*, NLS.
174 Ibid.

CONCLUSION

"So, the Catholic Church sees itself and knows itself as a living organism to which the divine truth is being gradually revealed through the Apostles as...each of us can bear a new infusion moving through time we become ever more likely clothed in garments of spirit of Evil and Good, until in the end nothing of the divine is seen in us. But in Eternity we lay aside as outworn coverings, Evil and Good, and as naked souls breathe the pure Essence of Innocence."[1]

THERE IS ONE THING WE CAN BE SURE OF about Mackay Brown—we will always have his writings, and they are many and varied. Sifting through his texts, whether it be word by word, line by line, manuscript by manuscript, genre by genre, published and unpublished, there is a strong level of cohesion as the instressed magnetic power of his primary sources springs to life in clusters of inscaped patterns that hold their own artistic workings. The strong level of cohesion must be worked at using all the senses. Mackay Brown's direction of travel from origins to ends needs a "map," especially so when one endeavors to lead, signal, and develop the discourse between these two poets as they sit together in the reader's mind.

The unfolding of that map through the argumentative terrain of this book holds within itself the two poets sitting together accompanied by their texts both directly and indirectly exploring their poetic core as well as their radial offshoots that were never random. Whatever the Catholicism Mackay Brown espoused, we can be sure it was "a living organism"[2] within his writings from first to last. The art of the living organism is one that "sees itself and knows itself"[3] because both Mackay Brown and Hopkins believed in "the divine truth" that was "gradually revealed through the Apostles."[4] Mackay Brown asserted for himself, as Hopkins had done before him, that "each of us can bear a new infusion."[5] Then, more tentatively, Mackay Brown accepted the life-long task to move "through time"[6] to "become,"[7] under the

---

1 Mackay Brown, *"The Roman Catholic Church" March 1947, NLS.*
2 Ibid.   3 Ibid.   4 Ibid.   5 Ibid.
6 Ibid.   7 Ibid.

promptings of the moral imperative and the call of the curlew, a person and poet. To "become"[8] was expressed in 1947 as a process that held within itself the act of being "clothed in garments of spirit of Evil and Good."[9] Mackay Brown was never dogmatic about it. He held his position at the "trembling stations"[10] where he was led to believe that Divine truth is "ever more likely."[11] At the very least he had an accumulative knowledge that heightened the probability of certainty on his personal faith journey. He had sight of the end to which he was drawn: "until in the end nothing of the divine is seen in us."[12] His meaning was based on his observation and experience of "Evil and Good"[13] blended to the point where they completely masked what lay at the core of the human person. After death, "Evil and Good"[14] are laid aside in Eternity as "outworn coverings,"[15] whereupon "naked souls"[16] are released to "breathe the pure Essence of Innocence."[17] Enthralled, Mackay Brown had borne the inscape of Hopkins's poem "The Caged Skylark"[18] from beginning to end. He was the "dare-gale skylark in a dull cage"[19] and his "mounting spirit in his bone-house"[20] found "that bird beyond remembering his free fells."[21] Like Hopkins, he had his own particular Christ-birds that defied the "drudgery, day-labouring-out life's age."[22]

What writer has there been that so seamlessly crafted his or her art to accept the Orcadian narrative, the native tradition, not only for the sake of Orcadians but for the dignity and truth of the human person? Mackay Brown cleared an imaginative space for himself where, unintimidated and uninhibited, he could continue the work of his predecessors.[23] Chapter by chapter, this book has elevated his voice through its sources alongside Hopkins. In their artistic sense, they converge and differ with no separation because they spoke in one epistemic voice. From the intelligent design of Creation in the Greenfields Kirk to its Eucharistic pulse and rhythms, its textual workings held within

---

[8] Ibid. [9] Ibid.
[10] Mackay Brown, "Everyman." Unpublished MS Orkney Archives, EWM Collection.
[11] Mackay Brown, *The Roman Catholic Church,* 1947 NLS.
[12] Ibid. [13] Ibid. [14] Ibid. [15] Ibid.
[16] Ibid. [17] Ibid.
[18] Hopkins, "The Caged Skylark," *Gerard Manley Hopkins: Poems and Prose,* 31.
[19] Ibid. [20] Ibid. [21] Ibid. [22] Ibid.
[23] Bloom, *The Anxiety of Influence: A Theory of Poetry,* 5.

the *instressed-inscapes* by means of highly sensed elements of verse. The protagonist of this theo-drama was the human person as poetic subject where the inner life of these Passion Partners was so forcefully formed from their experience of terror and anxiety. Their dark night forged the theological blades of their poetic vision. Theology was their sanity. Faith and reason gave warp and weave in a fiery light of praise.

Yes, the poetic vision is cryptic because of the high degree of mystery, and it is right to keep that close. But it is just this mystery that gave rise to the drive towards *univocity* overtaking the literary conventions of one-directional analogical language. Hopkins, and then Mackay Brown, went over and beyond literary devices, not metaphorically but really, to give the fullest expression of what they experienced and believed. They both were formed by Newman and the Oxford Movement ethos, and it is equally important to keep this ethos close to get an authentic understanding of their persons and craft. They both understood the sacramental view of the world, but were able to give it a new vibrancy as they assumed a bi-directional katalogical perspective. There is no doubt that both poets created a space for interpretation and especially so because they knew the critical value of the artistic sense as the criterion by which they would be judged.

Mackay Brown was able to develop his use of language according to the incessant demand of the literary market for a "succession of skillful artists."[24] This artistic succession ensured that language worked "up to its proper perfection."[25] Mackay Brown, like Hopkins, gave his readers a knowledge of his poetry that "leaves their minds swinging; poised, but on the quiver."[26] Here is the mastery of this Orkney poet, able to hone in layer by seamless layer on Orcadian men and women whose "characters are just human beings who happen to live in Hoy or Stromness or Sandwick."[27]

Exactly what or where is George Mackay Brown's place among the poets? How far do these *Essays and Notes* on Gerard Manley Hopkins support his own place within the literary classics and

---

24 Newman, "English Catholic Literature," *The Idea of a University*, 193.
25 Ibid.
26 Hopkins, *The Letters of Gerard Manley Hopkins to Robert Bridges*, 188.
27 Mackay Brown in conversation with E. W. Marwick. *An Orkney Anthology: Selected Works of Ernest Walker Marwick. Vol. 2*, 239.

Conclusion

canon? Mackay Brown worked within a time when some would say that there was a model for the literary canon that does not apply now. But he was very conscious about the "stream" of literature to the point that it was his "way" and all that he wrote swarmed within that stream. The 2020 Christmas edition of the *Orcadian* newspaper nodded towards an answer to those questions with the publication of "Boat and Croft,"[28] a previously unpublished version of "Unlucky Boat."[29] This was a poem he had revised many times. The narrative sparks with the fishing boat "The Skarf" fitted out for hunting the scad or Atlantic horse mackerel with "thwarts" and its range of meanings closely aligned. Firstly, with its noun sense of struts placed crosswise (left/right) in a ship or boat, to brace it crosswise and able to be used as a seat for the rower. Secondly, its adjective sense as "unhappy," "sullen" and "sulky" derived from the Germanic roots of the English language. Mackay Brown runs the word senses in unison, passing them through the audience's mind in a poetry reading forged in a dancing metrical energy, a power-pulsing-wave with a bright fist of symbols. The fisherman and his boat "nail" the particularities of their lives within the "meltings of silver" that is the "Burra Sound" "under the moon" moving stitch by stitch towards "the other place"[30] as the kenning "uncles of Scad" timelessly place-named all those food-gatherers across the ages past, present and future that sustain their communities. The North Atlantic Horse Mackerels shoal in heraldic swarms as "The Skarf" carries the fishing-tackle-come-"wands" that target cuithe and sillock. But the boat dips, floundering on the rocks ushering Tam (or is it Mansie[31] who was Mackay Brown's Everyman?), "to the hall of cold green angels" at the very moment the crofter "Angus of Scad" "Whose neck fluent with drink from the cattle-mart / Snapped like a barley stalk" to be "quarry-dragged" before their time to an ignominious death. "The Skarf," that "unhappy boat," lay "an outcast tree with tins old boots smashed bottles." Enshrined to the end "warped in a web of seedless stone" its

---

28 Mackay Brown, "The Boat and the Croft" published in *Orcadian*, 24 December 2020, 26. Reproduced with permission of the George Mackay Brown Literary estate, see Appendix.
29 Mackay Brown, "Unlucky Boat," *Collected Poems of George Mackay Brown*, 467.
30 Muir, *An Autobiography*, 71.   31 Mansie is a diminutive for Magnus.

shipwrecked legacy was a winter famine as the food-gatherers were diminished by their own ignorance.

So, who or what is "The Skarf"[32] really? That "unhappy boat," that "connecting joint," was drawn deep from the Old Norse skarfr, "nail for fastening a joint; diagonally cut end of a board, or from the "Old English sceorfan to gnaw, bite." And of course, a "connecting joint" also came in the form of Francis Scarfe[33] who exposed Mackay Brown to an early development of his intellectual and technical ability in all things poetic. Scarfe had noted Mackay Brown's "matter-of-factness and imagination,"[34] surely a mark of his prowess in the saga tradition. Mackay Brown flushed out the art of the symbol through an invigoration of the language he had at his disposal. He carried his "infusion"[35] of the memory through word derivation and it became a series of echoes through the successive *inscapes*. "The Skarf" enshrined in his novel *Greenvoe*[36] hovered in Mackay Brown's mind as chronicler, historian, failed fisherman nailing the connection, fastening the joints, as they infused fiery *inscapes* with successive waves of linguistic connectivity. Shape and pattern sent pulsating diagonals that gnawed and bit through to the "opening sky" of the sensational vision "Ignorant sweet in stardark, from swiftstorm, a

---

[32] "connecting joint," late 13c., probably from a Scandinavian source (such as Old Norse skarfr "nail for fastening a joint; diagonally cut end of a board," Swedish skarf, Norwegian skarv), from Proto-Germanic *skarfaz (source also of Dutch scherf), from PIE root *sker- (1) "to cut." Also used as a verb. Or from a dialectal survival of Old English sceorfan "to gnaw, bite."
[33] Scarfe, Frances. "(1911-1986) was an English poet, critic and novelist, who became an academic, translator and Director of the British Institute in Paris. He was born in South Shields; he was brought up from a young age at the Royal Merchant Seaman's Orphanage. He was educated at Armstrong College in Newcastle, which was then part of Durham University, where he earned a Bachelor of Arts degree in 1933. He also studied at Fitzwilliam College, Cambridge and at the Sorbonne. While in Paris he wrote surrealist verse, and dabbled in communism, from which he then retreated. He taught at the University of Glasgow briefly before the outbreak of World War II, in which he worked in the Army's Education Corps. He was posted to Orkney, and the Faroe Islands. While in Orkney he lodged with the family of the young George Mackay Brown, on whom he was a major influence. His book from 1942 was one of the first to engage critically with the Auden Group, if superficially; he returned to Auden in a post-war book of greater depth. After the war he held a number of academic positions." Francis Scarfe — Wikipedia.
[34] Scarfe to Mackay Brown, 11 December 1981, NLS. Cited in Maggie Fergusson *George Mackay Brown: The Life*, 64.
[35] Mackay Brown, *"The Roman Catholic Church," 1947*, NLS.
[36] Mackay Brown, *Greenvoe*.

tryst, A throb among barren curves." The text holds its workings within it with "fissures" that cut deep but carried in "a drift of seapinks" to the seamless "seaward" movement of "herrings in shoals." This movement was a summoning to the other place before the Creator who calls the unborn to true life. "The Skarf" was uprooted, shipwrecked, then "probed" and "fireblown" with Divine Judgement to be "patched, puttied, painted" to carry its load, more soul-journeys from this world to the other. "A boy climbed with his haddocks (And half turned back)" but the "old looms" the firmament "unfolded" by Mackay Brown as he worked alongside Hopkins to "patch, putty and paint," to reinvigorate the language. They "plowed" the native tradition for the sense of the sacred like the twelfth century Icelandic Pingèyrar monks and their associates for whom "the application of Christian learning, especially biblical typology and symbolic thought, was not an intellectual game."[37] The poets made space for "the fold of light" to sweep back into a fallen world. Is that "boy" Mackay Brown himself, turning back to "Scad" but under the moral imperative, the republic of conscience where he heard the call of the curlew, that "new cold cry"? Has he done enough for him to merit "that name they gave him" "keeper of plows" where he works "like melted wax"[38] with a new sensitivity to "The mystery found in the scriptures" as "a many-sided and involved thing; and it takes first one form, then another."[39]

Whether it is acknowledged or not, Mackay Brown was a poet who wrote within a central pool of ideas (a Catholic epistemology) that became increasingly clear to him. This clarity can be seen in his Hopkins studies, represented by these *Essays and Notes*. He saw his origins in the Logos, the Word that was with God and was the Creator God of the Greenfields Kirk. All his writings came through God and were flushed with his grace. Like Hopkins, his work stands as an intricate illumination in the darkness, and even though the darkness at times takes the appearance of overcoming the light, it is not able to do so. In fact, they both knew that the darkness was a necessary part of their life and work that elicited from them an interlaced and illuminated sensational vision. Many

---

[37] Antonsson, "Salvation and Early Saga Writing in Iceland: Aspects of the Work of the Pingèyrar Monks and Their Associates," 130.
[38] Ibid., Joachim of Fiore, *Liber figurarum*, cited in Antonsson, 71.
[39] Ibid.

would say that it was an appealing model that is not able to match reality. Even to aspire to a place in the traditional canon is not that helpful because it reduces "the landscape to a very few peaks, glimpsed above impenetrable clouds."[40]

Mackay Brown was aware of Hopkins's historical context and to an extent he explained what the substance of Hopkins meant as he unraveled his text. Mackay Brown, like Hopkins, aligned himself and his work within a literary model that was epistemological. Poetry of substance was given the warp and weave of ideas that concentrated themselves within the swarm of symbols. Here Mackay Brown moved in his own orbit with an ever-increasing confidence as he attentively articulated his native tradition. He drew from his predecessors, both in and out of Orkney, as he seamlessly earthed and elevated his readers in his sensational vision. The beating heart of the vision is the Word of God, the Logos, who took to himself a human nature and became Christ thereby elevating all of matter and making it a sacrament of the divine presence, not metaphorically but really, in the Eucharist. Mackay Brown and Hopkins were passion partners distinctively working in epistemological unison, witnessed by their word-craft. Yet both knew and understood the artistic sense that was the ultimate criterion of any literary credibility. Hopkins already has a now undisputed literary elevation, but does Mackay Brown pass the test? Had he done enough to merit literary elevation? For Edwin Muir, Seamus Heaney, and Alan Bold and their time-influenced critiques of Mackay Brown it would seem an open question with an uncertain answer. Bold struck a strong tone for a credible artistic sense when he described Mackay Brown's enigmatic literary project as "beautifully shaped for survival."[41]

Mackay Brown began in the "ancient smelters and smiths of poetry,"[42] where the Greenfields Kirk was his smithy and forge. Here he was prompted in his search for the source of Hopkins's "sweet clear spirit."[43] The call of the curlew was to him that peculiar experience of conscience that took the form of an inscape

---

[40] Hensher, "Harold Bloom Finally Betrays How Little He Really Understood Literature," *Spectator*.
[41] Bold, *George Mackay Brown*, 113.   [42] Ibid., 150.
[43] Mackay Brown, Letter to Jeanette Marwick, 12 October 1962. Orkney Archive. EWM Collection.

or voice of the Divine presence deep within the human person. Heaney had articulated the conscience as a republic because he knew the experience was both particular and universal all at once. The "republic" was as private as it was public, and it was arrived at through emotion and reason, with modulated sensations and free will choices. It was an experience that took poets to "holier places than Libraries and Reading-rooms."[44] Mackay Brown fully acknowledged his early development was marked by a lot of "half-baked stuff"[45] as he had tried to find his voice. He went from a position in his writing ensnaring the inscapes of Orkney to being able to infuse them with their instress as he moved increasingly into the epistemic center that he found in the ethos of the medieval period all around him in Orkney, its heart pulsing with the enigmatic St. Magnus.

As his creative and technical ability grew in more defined and weighted ways he assimilated his Greenfields Kirk, the Temple, and its Blind Fiddler into the "Liturgy of April" in celebration of the martyrdom of St. Magnus. Here he found a place to commit with passion to Christ, "giving life and form to writing in the English language"[46] within his times. Mackay Brown saw sky, land, and sea as a natural liturgy able to seamlessly embrace the sacred and the profane. This was to him a liturgical frame that concealed a eucharistic core. He believed the Eucharist to be the heart of the universe. St. Magnus gave him a personal level of intense conviction that stood with him throughout his life and work. This conviction or passion led him to challenge literary conventions where "literature had left the high road and smithy and market-place for the salon and the university and grown anaemic."[47] He saw his craft as a work "in the spirit of the living English language"[48] to advance into the realms of etymons, roots, stems, and derivations to conjure the true sense as he inscribed the *inscapes* as they came to his powers of observation and perception. As words exhibit changes in form and meaning he could dig deep into older texts where meaning might show dialectical variations in earlier history. Poetical

---

44 Newman, "The Tamworth Reading Room," letters to *The Times* 1841.
45 MacInnes, "Finding a Voice in the Forties," *New Shetlander*, 30–33, 36.
46 Newman, "English Catholic Literature," *The Idea of a University*, 193.
47 Mackay Brown, *For the Islands I Sing*, 150.
48 Leavis, "Doughty and Hopkins," *Scrutiny*, 316–17.

word-gaming led in and out of a common ancestral language, its borrowings enabling semantic shift and change that ran parallel to the processing of contemporary linguistic currency.

Muir, Heaney, and Bold could see in Mackay Brown the art of his craft "beautifully shaped for survival";[49] though, as beautiful as shape or inscape can be, it will not survive if it is unable to have the warp and weave of ideas, an epistemic core, to give it as Newman had observed, "outstanding examples of a particular style" that "have lasting worth with a timeless quality."[50] Mackay Brown was able to instress language with his chosen inscapes to the degree that evidence "flexibility in expression of a variety of thoughts and feelings accompanied by a penetrating discernment."[51] His clarity of vision and intellect provided a deep understanding and insight. He added vocabulary and a grace, and harmony underpinned his lexicon. His style as an artist "henceforth becomes a property of the language itself that hitherto did not exist."[52]

There in the reinvigorated firmament, Mackay Brown learned to swim in Hopkins's seminal tide through the "thousand candles of gorse"[53] into the liturgy of Spring, where those darling daffodil "Heads skewered with grief"[54] tremble in the quiver of inscapes. Poem by poem, station by station, Mackay Brown turns repeatedly to the "fisher priest" his offering of "spindrift bread,"[55] spraying in particular radiations that are gale-force-blown from its cresting waves. Mackay Brown saw the eucharistic bread-spray as it "drifts" in the direction of the gale with speed and force to find "the hooked hands" to receive "the harrowed heart of Love."[56] His narrative turns round by round in the stations of his craft as he gives artistic sense to the prayerèd voices of the natural world wherein the monastery stands timelessly in the numbered counterpoint of the "bell" and the "seven sounds of the sea," the "eight times chant of the murmuring psalms in that deep pasture."[57] He wraps the "gentle silken-voiced"[58] Orcadian

---

49 Bold, *George Mackay Brown*, 113.
50 Newman, "English Catholic Literature," *The Idea of a University*, 193.
51 Ibid. 52 Ibid.
53 Mackay Brown, "The Storm," *Collected Poems of George Mackay Brown*, 3.
54 Ibid., "Daffodils," 35.
55 Ibid., "Chapel Between Cornfield and Shore," 35. 56 Ibid.
57 Ibid., "Horseman and Seals, Birsay," 41.
58 Mackay Brown, *An Orkney Tapestry*, 15.

farmer with the "ancient harp" of the sea in "a heraldic stillness and a hoarded symbolism,"[59] flushing sight and sound in "the sheer sensuous relish of utterance."[60] The high tide floods in "with a sound like harps" the seal-prayèred-men are elevated in grace, "one-by-one" to the "new water"[61] of Eternal Life. His barn-church and Bethlehems and Nazareths arose from the "Greenfields Kirk" inscaped and instressed in the human person as "all hallows"[62] in the communion of saints. The "native tradition" in a natural fusion of Orcadian history, culture and folklore and its seamless layers of Icelandic and Celtic analogues was majestically inscaped into a distinctive Orkney poetics that was more Fornaldarsǫgur[63] than a Christian hagiography that caged its sainted skylarks in an unnatural literary stereotype.

Mackay Brown cast his nets "abroad in a seeking wave"[64] that was able to bring life to such as Thorfinn "from the creaking rowlocks of time"[65] as his little-soul-boat fired into the flood to be "flung a glad ghost on a wingless shore."[66] Unmistakably, Mackay Brown, poem by poem, crafted his own distinctive and timeless signature moving from the "Everyman"[67] such as Thorfinn, to the Earl Magnus, inscaped and instressed with Christ: "a bird Winged with fivers" "smothered him in flowers."[68] "Across the April hill," the "liturgy of April"[69] swept with "The Magnustide long swords of rain."[70] The native tradition, the Orcadian Fornaldarsǫgur of the St. Magnus Way, liturgically "in Birsay they move in their furrows... Here Magnus was born, here they laid his bones."[71]

The vigor of the sea and its mariners, who knew only too well its "long green jaws"[72] as they color-couple and chime in

---

59 Ibid., 19.   60 Ibid., 22.
61 Mackay Brown, "Horseman and Seals, Birsay," *Collected Poems of George Mackay Brown*, 41.
62 Mackay Brown, *Two Night Poems and manuscript pp on 4 leaves each 33 × 20.5 in blue and black ink, signed George M Brown 1963*, NLS.
63 (Old Norse: "sagas of antiquity") class of Icelandic sagas dealing with the ancient myths and hero legends of Germania, with the adventures of Vikings, or with other exotic adventures in foreign lands.
64 Mackay Brown, "Thorfinn," *Collected Poems of George Mackay Brown*, 20.
65 Ibid.   66 Ibid.
67 Mackay Brown, "Everyman." Unpublished MS OA: EWM Collection. *Hopkins and His Metric a 12pp manuscript essay signed George M Brown 1964, each leaf 25.5 × 20.5cm*, NLS. Ecclesiastes 13/7/89, in *Rockpools and Daffodils*, 214.
68 Mackay Brown, "The Death Bird," *Collected Poems of George Mackay Brown*, 26.   69 Ibid., "Elegy" 32.   70 Ibid.
71 Ibid., "Places to Visit," 60.   72 Ibid., "The Storm," 3.

the heat "deep / In summer's sultry throat" with the stammer of "Dry thunder." Mackay Brown captured the force, the speed, the "snarl," the "scudding" dissolved into the "heraldic clouds," "Rampant all around." But it was in the wailing *miserere* that the music of the sea was written with passion and truth, "The sea—organ and harps"[73] gave proof that "the old beauty and grace would never be completely trodden down into uniform greyness."[74] Getting their readers close to Christ, the Real Presence, was the Hopkins and Mackay Brown eucharistic journey, in a sacramental universe interwoven with the natural world. This was the Mackay Brown métier—to forge at his kitchen table smithy in the reinvigorated firmament that Hopkins gifted to literature. Hopkins and Mackay Brown have Christ in their sight, whatever they did, throughout their poetry, one way or another. Like Hopkins, Mackay Brown lived intensely on the borderline between this world and the "other," ready, and sure-footed, accompanied as they both were by "annunciations of terror."[75]

Mackay Brown consciously worked from within a certain stream of Christian thinking that was as penetrating as it was original. To embrace the entirety of his writing is a discourse on the deepest questions, the discussion of which is never censored. He beheld the world and gazed on its truth as a ferment of images that in themselves "crave double interpretation."[76] He was driven to locate the point of reference behind the images, and it was there in the company of Hopkins he found their essence behind the appearance. Images challenged his thought, and he learnt the art of expressing words laden with the conceptual and the sensory. The art of the instressed-inscape was practiced as he sat at his kitchen table every morning where his thought and sensory spheres resonated in human language with its vowels, consonants, sound patterns, syntactical forms all oscillating in a pendulum movement that he pushed further and further with theological blades[77] towards fullness of expression. And let us

---

73 Ibid.
74 Mackay Brown, *GMH Two Landscape Poems*, a 10pp manuscript essay signed George M Brown 1964, each leaf 25.5 × 20cm, NLS.
75 Mackay Brown, *Notes on "The Wreck of the Deutschland,"* 17 manuscript pages on 20 leaves each 33 × 20.5, signed GM Brown Feb 1963, NLS.
76 Balthasar, *Theo-Logic I: Truth of the World*, 157.
77 Mackay Brown, *Notebook Two*, NLS.

not forget his attentiveness to Pythagorean number theory[78] and its "theological mathematics."[79]

Like Hopkins, he discovered as you move further into the darkness: "Everything winds and unwinds like thread on complementary spools."[80] Here the poet weaves: "darkness and light, joy and pain, life and death. As one spool empties the others fills."[81] Mackay Brown acknowledged that "Life is duality"[82] but he was always looking for that point of reference behind the array of images[83] so he could freight his words with it. Unity at its very root was that place where he discovered faith and reason in their workings. It demanded of him an integrity of ethics, evidence, and decision.[84] He arrived at the position of "the two flocks, the two folds."[85] Here "the sheep and the goats "black, white; right. Wrong." This duality, balance, is all we know for certain."[86] Here he shows the influence on his thought of Newman and Hopkins both of whom were absorbed into Balthasar. But his life was always on a "thread" that he came to understand as one in which "the poet's being is running and uncoiling swiftly into the darkness of the self without God"[87] to emerge with his texts sparking with light. This is the Mackay Brown voice as strong as I have come across it. Over and over again he stitched his Orkney tapestry, on that poetic journey into the inner darkness of his own personal labyrinth, where the ever-increasing light only intensified the experience of the darkness.

In his poem "Watchman: Night Sea" Mackay Brown turned his gaze to "Waves came on, hooded."[88] Was the hooded an inscape of the curvature of water in its visually pulsing mathematical patterns flushed with sound or was it the hooded heads of serpents interchanging seamlessly with the prayèred heads

---

78 Mackay Brown, Notes on *"The Wreck of the Deutschland," 17 manuscript pages on 20 leaves each 33 × 20.5*, signed GM Brown Feb 1963, NLS, For the Islands I Sing, 168–69.
79 Mackay Brown, *Notebook Two*, NLS.
80 Mackay Brown, *Notes on Spelt From Sibyl's Leaves May 1963*, NLS.
81 Ibid.   82 Ibid.
83 Balthasar, *Theo-Logic I: Truth of the World*, 157.   84 Ibid., 29.
85 Mackay Brown, *Notes on Spelt From Sibyl's Leaves May 1963*, NLS.
86 Ibid.   87 Ibid.
88 Mackay Brown, "Watchman: Night Sea," *The Sea and the Tower*. Reproduced by permission of the George Mackay Brown Literary Estate. See Appendix.

of monastic brothers? How did Mackay Brown achieve that? It was because that was what his mind was processing and the writing of it was an act of artistic mastery. Into time they "streamed, unbodied" in his sensational vision "Like souls in surge from a sacked city." The souls carry "half hid" the life-image heraldically casting their successive inscapes "A gray falcon at fist," "fingered careful coins," "a cherished bronze comb," "a broken shield," "a flung (hooded) harp at the hull." These are images of the "tattered keenings" woven "Into one web of pure dark threnody" of their lament for the passage out of this world into the next. "The wailing between two shores" is held in the "harp" of the poet's mind until the "loom of light / Would clothe me in a silver sea-smock." But the "Watchman" wakens those left in their cold "spit" and "shiver," their faces "flushed" calling them to their "keel" laid "On a hundred labouring shoulders" still making the this-world-journey. And as Heaney adjudicated: "His sense of the world and his way with words are powerfully at one with each other. His vision has something of the skaldic poet's consciousness of inevitable ordeal, something of the haiku master's susceptibility to the delicate and the momentary, and since the beginning of his career he has added uniquely and steadfastly to the riches of poetry in English."[89]

Gerard Manley Hopkins and Mackay Brown are passion partners to the end and beyond. Both poets were on a faith journey. Their passion and piety was an adventure of epic proportions emotionally and intellectually. They knew they would be held to account by the artistic sense. This close reading of Mackay Brown's *Essays and Notes* in manuscript form interwoven as they are with his published and unpublished writings, raises more answers than questions about the closeness of these poets as they worked within a shared firmament. Their common ground elicited in each their particularity, their universality, and the distinctive artistic sense of their literary prowess and achievement. The dancing metrics, the salt mathematics, the heptahedron, the deliberately slow assimilation of the discordant irregularities of his modern times concealed Mackay Brown's seminal sensational vision that was his legacy. His "Song: "I am undone else" is

---

89 Heaney, inside book cover of *The Sea and the Tower*.

Conclusion

an unpublished poem[90] that holds within it that profound self-awareness he concealed so well from those around him. The firmament became for him "my storied halls" that echo with "music and ballade." Before his God he sent out the prayer "Whisper me now" and he awaits absolution "Absolvo te."[91] Is it "The Skarf" that "Unhappy Boat" once again setting sail with its "spread of crimson"?[92] Mackay Brown was called to his station to "Put richness on the gales" and "In sackcloth let me go forth."[93] With echoes of "Corn" and "aureate harvests" he "Surged against those walls" driven by the moral imperative in his republic of conscience "I crave viaticum at the door." Echoes of "Silk and wine, sundials, roses" try to fend off the death tide as it ebbed and flowed with its power of saturation "steeped in sensual oils." But Mackay Brown had early knowledge that there is "other balm" to "ease soul from flesh." And with each of the four three lined verses he intoned "I am undone else."[94] It seems fitting to finish with those words as Mackay Brown worked from the King James Bible translation of Isaiah 6:5.[95]

This very polished poem brings forth the Temple vision and the various personas Mackay Brown assumed for his imperfect self: Mazurin, the Blind Fiddler, the dirty rag, the Skarf, to name but a few. His annunciations of terror that were his life-long depressive afflictions, could not repress the prophetic nature of his literary adventures tinged as they were with his spiritual quest. Keeled by his theological blades, he powered on with deft strokes. He elevated the native tradition he felt called to and compelled by. The unpopularity, the irreverence or even sedition of his vision was just as it should be for the artistry of one working within the fiery glory of the universe and its

---

[90] Mackay Brown, "Song: "I am undone else." 1976. Handwritten MS, EUL, Special Collections. Reproduced by permission of the George Mackay Brown Literary Estate. See Appendix.   [91] Ibid.
[92] Mackay Brown, "The Boat and the Croft" published in *Orcadian*, 26. Reproduced with permission of the George Mackay Brown Literary estate. See Appendix.
[93] Mackay Brown, "Song: 'I am undone else.'" 1976. Handwritten MS, EUL, Special Collections. Reproduced by permission of the George Mackay Brown Literary Estate. See Appendix.   [94] Ibid.
[95] "Then said I, Woe is me! for I am undone; because I am a man of unclean lips, and I dwell in the midst of a people of unclean lips: for mine eyes have seen the King, the LORD of hosts." The Catholic New Jerusalem translation uses "I am lost" rather than "I am undone."

element of theophany. He went against the conventions of his times, "cleansing his lips," so he did not obstruct his commission to proclaim what his eyes saw as he journeyed deep into the North Atlantic Fornaldarsǫgur[96] infusing a map of the artistic sense of his literary Way for others to follow.

---

[96] (Old Norse: "sagas of antiquity") class of Icelandic sagas dealing with the ancient myths and hero legends of Germania, with the adventures of Vikings, or with other exotic adventures in foreign lands.

APPENDIX

BOAT AND CROFT

The *Skarf* nearly did for Scad.
    Fitting thwarts
Rob got a nail in his thumb. He died in the croft
    Bunged to the eyes with rust and penicillin.
One night when Burra Sound was meltings of silver
Under the noon, and the uncles of Scad with wands
    Enchanted cuithe and sillock, she dipped a bow.
    She ushered Tam, his pipe still in his teeth
To the hall of cold green angels. They hauled her up
    Among the rocks, in the track of Angus of Scad
Whose neck fluent with drink from the cattle mart,
Snapped like a barley stalk. Quarry-dragged then,
An outcast tree with tins old boots smashed bottles
She warped, in a web of seedless stone, a winter.

Ignorant, sweet, in stardark, from swiftstorm, a tryst,
    A throb among barren curves.
    The opening sky. Fissures. A drift of seapinks.
    Seaward, the herring in shoals.
    (Is summoned from unborn hosts one hungerer).
    The *Scarf* was uprooted.
She was probed, fireblown, patched, puttied, painted.

    A boy climbed with his haddocks
(And half turned back) to Scad, and a new cold cry.
And (from old looms) unfolded, the fold of light.
Ward, "keeper of plows." That name they gave him.

WATCHMAN: NIGHT SEA

Waves came on, hooded. They streamed, unbodied
    From, it seemed, sundered deaths,
    Like souls in surge from a sacked city.

Each seemed to bear, half hid, an image
    Of what, living, it most had affected.
    One bore a gray falcon at fist.
    One fingered careful coins, all tarnish.

    One cherished a bronze comb
    Wherewith some woman
Still, it might be, stretched yellow hair at a lam.

One reeled under a broken shield—All with
bitterest lamentation paused and passed.

One flung (hooded) a harp at the hull.

I charted the trek of those thousands
And pitied somewhat their pain.
I considered at last
How time might take their tattered keenings
Into one web of dark blue threnody
(My ear assoiled
From snores and scattered night-sighs under the thwarts.)

Only the honey of the boy's sleep
Made true response to the wailing between two shores.

The harp had drenched me, beard to shinbone.
There soon, the loom of light
Would clothe me in a silver sea-smock.
A sailor woke. He shivered. He spat.
His face flushed...Well went the keel
On a hundred labouring shoulders.

SONG: "I AM UNDONE ELSE"

With music and ballade
Echoed my storied halls.
Whisper me now "absolve te."
I am undone else.

My sail, a spread of crimson
Put richness on the gales.
I am sackcloth let me now go forth.
I am undone else.

Corn, aureate harvests
Surged against those walls.
I crave viaticum at the door.
I am undone else.

Silk and wine, sundials, roses—
I steeped on sensual oils.
With other balm ease soul from flesh.
I am undone else.

WORKS CITED

Manuscript Collections

**NATIONAL LIBRARY OF SCOTLAND,
GEORGE MACKAY BROWN ARCHIVE**
By permission of the Literary Estate of George Mackay Brown

Gerard [sic] Manley Hopkins: Two Landscape Poems, a 10-page manuscript essay signed by George Mackay Brown, 1964.

Hopkins and his Metric, a 12-page manuscript essay signed by George Mackay Brown, 1964.

Notes on the Bugler's First Communion, a 7-page manuscript signed by George Mackay Brown, March–April 1964.

Gerard Manley Hopkins and His Public, a 12-page manuscript signed by George Mackay Brown, December 1963–January 1964.

The Windhover, an 11-page manuscript signed by George Mackay Brown, March 1964.

George Manley Hopkins: Two Night Poems, an 8-page manuscript signed by George Mackay Brown, November 1963.

The Two Mary Poems of Gerard Manley Hopkins, a 10-page manuscript signed by George Mackay Brown, October 1963.

Notes on "The Wreck of Deutschland," a 17-page manuscript signed by George Mackay Brown, February 1963.

Notes on the Dark Sonnets of Gerard Manley Hopkins, a 12-page manuscript signed by George Mackay Brown.

The Henry Purcell Sonnet of Gerard Manley Hopkins, a 10-page manuscript signed by George Mackay Brown, 3 December 1962.

Gerard Manley Hopkins's People, a 16-page manuscript signed by George Mackay Brown, November 1962.

Three student notebooks containing notes in George Mackay Brown's hand regarding Hopkins. *Notebook One, Notebook Two, Notebook Three*

(All of the above writings are held under Accession Number 13909).

23 other pages of notes 1947–48, also known as *The Commonplace Book*, includes two quotes "Mazurin...," four quotes that relate to the nature of the poet, time, art, the nature of God, a prayer to cover much of life, and comment on lines from T. S. Eliot *"The Family Reunion."* (Accession Number 13911).

The complete 1947 piece of writing about the nature of the *Roman Catholic Church* (69–74) (Accession Number 13911).

"The Poet Speaks." Peter Orr of the British Council, 14 October 1964 (National Sound Archive). NLS. George Mackay Brown Collection, D124/2//21, 2.

EDINBURGH UNIVERSITY LIBRARY
Song: "I am undone else." 1976. Handwritten MS in "Handlist of manuscripts" H50. George Mackay Brown, 23, MS 3115.
A note held in Edinburgh University Library, Special Collections, George Mackay Brown, MS 2846.1.

ORKNEY LIBRARY ARCHIVE
Ernest Walker Marwick Orkney Archive D31/30/2 and D31/30/4 are drawn upon:
Mackay Brown "The Fiddler At the Fair" 1945.
Mackay Brown "Swan's Way" 1946.
Mackay Brown "Journey to Avilon" 1946.
Mackay Brown Letter to Ernest Marwick 24 October 1946.
Mackay Brown Letter to Jeanette Marwick (wife of Ernest Marwick), 12 October 1962.
Mackay Brown Letter Poem "Ernest, today our sky is lowering" 19 January 1954, from Eastbank Hospital.
Mackay Brown "Saint Magnus Cathedral" Easter 1944. Unpublished Ms.
Mackay Brown "The Story of Scotland. Edwin Muir," 21 November 1988
Mackay Brown "Everyman."
Mackay Brown "Christ Poem." July 1944.

Published Works

The Orcadian Poet George Mackay Brown Reads His Poems and a Story, Internet Archive: Claddagh Records, 1971.
For the Islands I Sing. A collection of poems and short stories. CD. Published by Orkney Aye, 2006. A Young Enterprise Scotland Company.
"Pen Mightier than the Predicament." *Weekend Scotsman*. 22 Feb 1986.
"The End of a Sinister Year," in *Island Diary, Orkney Herald*. December 28th, 1954, 5.
"The 'Immortal Tongue' of Ann Scott-Moncrieff," *Orkney Herald*, 12 November 1953, 3.
"Sara," in *The Seventh Ghost Book*, Barrie & Jenkins, 1971.
The Sun's Net, Stories by George Mackay Brown, Quartet Books, 1978.
"The Boat and the Croft," published in *Orcadian*, 24 December 2020, 26.
A Spell for Green Corn, Hogarth Press, 1970.
A Time to Keep and Other Stories, Polygon, 2006.
An Orkney Tapestry, Quartet Books, 1974.
For the Islands I Sing, John Murray, 1997.
Greenvoe, Polygon, 1972.

Magnus, Canongate Classics, 1998.
"My Scotland: 'Orkney and Scotland,'" in *The Scottish Review: Arts and Environment*, 36, 1984.
Northern Lights: A Poet's Sources, John Murray, 1999.
Rockpools and Daffodils, Gordon Wright Publishing, 1992.
The Collected Poems of George Mackay Brown, ed. A Bevan & B Murray. John Murray, 2005.
The Sea and the Tower, Bayeux, 1994.

SECONDARY WORKS

Abbott, C. C. ed. *The Correspondence of Gerard Manley Hopkins and Richard Watson Dixon*, OUP, 1935.
Antonsson, Haki. "Salvation and Early Saga Writing in Iceland: Aspects of the Work of the Pingèyrar Monks and Their Associates," *Viking and Medieval Scandinavia*. 8, 2012.
Ascherson, Neil. *Seven Poets: Hugh MacDiarmid, Norman MacCaig, Iain Crichton Smith, George Mackay Brown, Robert Garioch, Sorley Maclean, Edwin Morgan*, Third Eye Centre, 1981.
Balthasar, Hans Urs von. *The Glory of the Lord. A Theological Aesthetics. I: Seeing the Form*, Ignatius Press, 1982.
Balthasar, Hans Urs von. *Theo-Logic I: The Truth of the World*, Ignatius Press, 2000.
Barnes, William. *One Hundred Poems*, Dorset Bookshop, 1971.
BBC Radio Scotland, 1982, *Valley by the Sea*, https://www.orkneyology.com/george-mackay-brown.html.
BBC Scotland, "George Mackay Brown 70th Birthday," *One Star in the West*, Broadcast April 1996.
Bicket, Linden, *George Mackay Brown and the Scottish Catholic Imagination* (Scottish Religious Cultures), Edinburgh University Press, 2017.
Blake, William, "The Last Judgement." *Life of William Blake (1880) Vol 2. Prose Writings*, https://en.wikisource.org/wiki/Life_of_William_Blake_(1880).
Bloom, Harold, *The Anxiety of Influence: A Theory of Poetry*, Oxford University Press, 1973, 1997.
Bold, Alan, *George Mackay Brown (Modern Writers Series)*, Oliver & Boyd, 1978.
Brand, John. *Brand's Description of Orkney*, 1721.
Brig o' Waithe, Orkney.com.
Bunyan, John. *Pilgrim's Progress*. W.R. Owens, ed., Oxford University Press, 2003.
Cairns, Craig, ed., *The History of Scottish Literature. Vol. 4: Twentieth Century*, Aberdeen University Press, 1987.

Cambridge, Gerry. "'A Thread Too Bright for the Eye': An Appreciation of George Mackay Brown." *Chapman*, no. 84 (1996).
Campbell, David, "Carried Along by the Rhythms of Childhood," in *The Scotsman*, Saturday 13 October 1990.
Campbell-Johnston, Rachel, "Turmoil and Trauma: Artists in an Age of Anxiety," *The Times*, January 17, 2020.
Catholic Encyclopedia-Catholic Online
Chaucer, Geoffrey, *The Complete Poetical Works*, 1894, https://www.bartleby.com/258/47.html
Close, Ajay, "Splendid Isolation," *Spectrum Review* June 2, 1991.
Clouston, J. Storer, "Foundation and Election of Certain Offices in the Cathedral Church of Orkney for the Service of God, by Robert Reid, Bishop of Orkney," *Records of the Earldom of Orkney*, 1299-1614. Scottish History Society, 1914.
Corcoran, Neil in Vinson, James, and D.L. Kirkpatrick, eds., *Contemporary Poets.*, 4th ed., St. Martin's Press, 1985.
Davis, Graeme. *The Early English Settlement of Orkney and Shetland*, John Donald, 2007.
Davies, Peter Maxwell, *A Mirror of Whitening Light for Orchestra (1976-77)*, YouTube.
Davies, Peter Maxwell, *Dark Angels by Sir Peter Maxwell Davies*, YouTube.
Delmaire, Dominique, "Indirection and Meaning in the Poems of George Mackay Brown." Abstract of a paper delivered at the Congrès de la SAES, atelier Poets and Poetry, May 2011
Derrida, Jacques, *Of Grammatology*, Johns Hopkins University Press, 1997, corrected edition, trans. Gayatri Chakravorty Spivak.
Devlin, Christopher, S.J,, ed., *The Sermons and Devotional Writings of Gerard Manley Hopkins*, Oxford University Press, 1959.
Dictionary of the Scots Language. 2004. Scottish Language Dictionaries, Ltd. <https://www.dsl.ac.uk/entry/snd/throuither>.
Dictionary of the Scots Language:: SND :: sweem (dsl.ac.uk).
Douay-Rheims Catholic Bible Online, Search Study Verses (drbo.org).
Duffy, Eamon, *The Stripping of the Altars*, Yale University Press, 1992.
Duns Scotus. https://en.wikipedia.org/wiki/Dunce.
Fengler, Maria. "Aspects of Catholic Spirituality in the Poetry of George Mackay Brown," in Ioana Zirra and Madeline Potter, eds., *The Literary Avatars of Christian Sacramentality, Theology and Practical Life in Recent Modernity*, Peter Lang Editions, 2016.
Ferguson, R., *George Mackay Brown: The Wound and the Gift*, Saint Andrew Press, 2011.
Fergusson, Maggie, *George Mackay Brown: The Life*, John Murray, 2006.
Fergusson, Maggie, "The Praise Singers: Poets George Mackay Brown and Gerard Manley Hopkins," *The Tablet*, 13th August 2020.

Frye, Northrop, *Fearful Symmetry: A Study of William Blake*, Princeton University Press, 1947.

Gardner, W. H., "The Religious Problem in G.M. Hopkins," *Scrutiny*, June 1937.

Gardner, W. H. ed., *Gerard Manley Hopkins: Poems and Prose*, Penguin, 1971.

Gibbon, Sarah Jane, and James More, "Storyways: Visualising Saintly Impact in a North Atlantic Maritime Landscape," *Open Archaeology* 2019; 5: 235–62.

Gifford, Douglas, "Splendid Isolation," *Spectrum Review*, June 2, 1991.

Gooding, Mel, *Sylvia Wishart: A Study*, The Pier Arts Centre, 2012.

Gray, Alison, *Circle of Light: The Catholic Church in Orkney Since 1560*, John Donald, 2000.

Gray, Alison, *George Mackay Brown: No Separation*, Gracewing, 2016.

Greeley, Andrew, *The Catholic Imagination*, University of California Press, 2001.

Hall, Simon W., *The History of Orkney Literature*, John Donald, 2010.

Hames, Scott, *The Literary Politics of Scottish Devolution*, Edinburgh University Press, 2019.

Hardy, Dom Benedict OSB, *An Introduction to Gregorian Chant*, Pluscarden Abbey https://www.pluscardenabbey.org/.

Heaney, Seamus, *From the Republic of Conscience*, Dublin Amnesty International, 1985.

Hensher, Philip, "Harold Bloom Finally Betrays How Little He Really Understood Literature," *The Spectator* 21 November 2020.

Hopkins, Gerard Manley, *The Letters of Gerard Manley Hopkins to Robert Bridges*, ed., C. C. Abbott, Oxford University Press, 1955 (24 October 1883).

Ignatius of Loyola. *The Spiritual Exercises (1548)*, limovia.net, 2012.

The Spiritual Exercises of St. Ignatius Loyola, Loyola Jesuit Centre.

Jakobsson, H., "Centre and Periphery in Icelandic Medieval Discourse," *Preprint Papers: The 14th International Saga Conference*, Uppsala, 9th–15th August 2009, Vol. 2, https://www.academia.edu/1396953/.

Joachim of Fiore, *Liber figurarum*, Reeves, M. E., *Medieval and Renaissance Studies*, 1950.

Joyce, James, *Ulysses*, Alma Classics, 2017.

Joyce, James, "You ought to allude to me as a Jesuit," *Irish Times*, Jun 14, 2004.

Ker, Ian, *The Catholic Revival in English Literature, 1845–1961: Newman, Hopkins, Belloc, Chesterton, Greene, Waugh*, Gracewing, 2003.

Leavis, F. R., "Doughty and Hopkins," *Scrutiny*, Dec. 1935.

Leslie, Helen, "Border Crossings Landscape and the Other World in the Fornaldarsǫgur," *Preprint Papers: The 14th International Saga*

Conference, Uppsala, 9th–15th August 2009, Vol. 2, https://www.academia.edu/1396953/.

MacBeath, Stuart, "Under Equality's Sun: George Mackay Brown and Socialism from the Margins of Society," M.Phil. thesis, University of Glasgow, 2017.

MacDiarmud, Hugh, "Scotland," from *Complete Poems*, edited by Michael Grieve and W. R. Aitken, Carcanet Press, 2 vols., 1993-94.

MacInnes, Morag. "Finding a Voice in the Forties," *New Shetlander n.s. no. 221*, Hairst, 2002.

McBrien, Richard, *Catholicism*, Harper Collins, 1994.

Maritain, Jacques, *Art And Scholasticism With Other Essays*, Sheed & Ward, 1947.

Maxwell, Jamie, "Review: *The Literary Politics of Scottish Devolution: Voice, Class, Nation* by Scott Hames," *The Herald*, 18th January 2019.

Milton, John, *Areopagitica* (1644), 12–13, http://spenserians.cath.vt.edu/TextRecord.php?&textsid=33429.

Mitchell, Peta, *Cartographic Strategies of Postmodernity: The Figure of the Map in Contemporary Theory and Fiction*, Routledge, 2007.

Muir, Edwin, "The Decline of the Novel," *Essays on Literature and Society*, Hogarth Press, 1949.

Muir, Edwin, "The Political View of Literature," in *Essays on Literature and Society*, Hogarth Press, 1949.

Muir, Edwin, *An Autobiography*, Hogarth Press, 1954.

Muir, Edwin, *Collected Poems*, Faber & Faber, 1984.

Muir, Edwin, *Essays on Literature and Society*, Hogarth Press, 1949.

Murphy, Rosalie, ed., *Contemporary Poets of the English Language*, St. James Press, 1970.

Murray, Rowena, and Brian Murray, *Interrogation of Silence: The Writings of George Mackay Brown*, John Murray, 2004, revised ed., Steve Savage, 2008.

Murray, Rowena, "The Influence of Norse Literature on the Twentieth Century Writer George Mackay Brown," in Strauss, Dietrich, and H. W. Drescher, eds. *Scottish Language and Literature, Medieval and Renaissance*, Proceedings of the Fourth International Conference, 1986.

New Jerusalem Bible, The, Study Edition, Darton Longman & Todd, 1994.

Newman, J. H., *The Idea of a University*, ed. F. M. Turner, Yale University Press, 1996.

Newman, J. H., "The Tamworth Reading Room," letters to *The Times* 1841. http://newmanreader.org/works/arguments/tamworth/section1.html.

Newman, J. H., *An Essay in Aid of a Grammar of Assent*, Clarendon Press, 2000.

Nye, Robert, "Turning Fable into Life," in *The Scotsman Weekend*, 15 June 1991.
"Will George Brown Rank with Edwin Muir?" *Orkney Herald*, 10 January 1950.
Orkney Dictionary, https://orkneydictionary.scot/dictionary/pronunciation/.
Pálsson, Hermann and Paul Edwards, eds., *The Orkneyinga Saga: The History of the Earls of Orkney*, Penguin Books, 1978.
Pascal, Blaise. *Pensées* (1670), ed., L. Brunschvicg, 1909.
Peters, W. A. M., *Gerard Manley Hopkins: A Critical Essay Towards the Understanding of His Poetry*. Oxford University Press, 1948.
Peterson, William S., *George Mackay Brown: A Bibliographical Study of a Twentieth-Century Orkney Writer* (wordpress.com).
Peterson, William S., https://gmbbibliography.wordpress.com/gmbs-personal-library/.
Pick, John, *Gerard Manley Hopkins: Priest and Poet*, Oxford University Press, 1966.
Plato, *The Symposium*, trans. W. A. Hamilton, Penguin, 1951.
Poetry Foundation, https://www.poetryfoundation.org/learn/glossary-terms/georgianism.
Power, Colum, *James Joyce's Catholic Categories*, Wiseblood Books, 2023.
Rahner, Hugo, S.J., *Greek Myths and Christian Mystery*, Burns & Oates, 1963.
Roberts, Gerald, *Gerard Manley Hopkins: The Critical Heritage*, Routledge & Keegan Paul, 2013.
Robertson, J.D.M., J.M. Irvine, and M. Sutherland, *An Orkney Anthology: Selected Works of Ernest Walker Marwick. Vol. 2*. The Orcadian Press, 2012.
Ross, M. M., *Poetry and Dogma: The Transfiguration of Eucharistic Symbols in Seventeenth Century Poetry*, Octagon Books, 1969.
Sarkissian, Adele, "George Mackay Brown," in *Contemporary Authors: Autobiographical Series*, Vol. 6., Gale Research Company, 1988.
Scammell, William, "Hard as Granite, Sweet as Grass," *The Scotsman Weekend: Books & Poetry*, 1991.
Schmid, Sabine, *Keeping the Sources Pure: The Making of George Mackay Brown*, Peter Lang Murray, 2000.
Scott, Alexander, "George Mackay Brown," in Murphy, Rosalie, ed. *Contemporary Poets of the English Language*, St. James Press, 1970.
Scott, Alexander, "Scottish Poetry in the Seventies," *Akros*, Vol 10, No. 28, August 1975.
Scott-Moncrieff, Ann, *The Brig o' Waithe*. Originally published in Ernest Marwick, *Anthology of Orkney Verse*, Kirkwall Press, 1949.
Sillem, Edward, *The Philosophical Notebook, Vol I*, Humanities Press, 1973.
Sitwell, Edith, *Aspects of Modern Poetry*, Duckworth, 1934.

Spenser, Edmund, *A View of the Present State of Ireland* https://alchetron.com/Edmund-Spenser.

Steiner, George, *Tolstoy or Dostoevsky: An Essay in the Old Criticism*, University of Chicago Press, reprint edition, 1985.

Thomas Aquinas, Summa Theologica Summa Theologica Index (sacred-texts.com).

Tracey, David, *The Analogical Imagination: Christian Theology and the Culture of Pluralism*, Crossroad, 1981.

Vinson, James, D.L. Kirkpatrick, eds., *Contemporary Poets*, 4th ed., St. Martin's Press, 1985.

Ward, Bernadette Waterman, "Philosophy and Inscape: Hopkins and the *Formalitas* of Duns Scotus," in *Texas Studies in Literature and Language*, Vol. 32. No. 2., Summer 1990.

Ward, Bernadette Waterman, *World As Word: Philosophical Theology in Gerard Manley Hopkins*, The Catholic University of America Press, 2001.

Warner, Marina. *Alone of All Her Sex: The Myth and Cult of the Virgin Mary*, Pan Books, 1985.

White, Michael, "The Aldeburgh of the North: How the Egos Ended up in Orcadia," *Independent*, 30 June 1996.

Wittig, Kurt, *The Scottish Tradition in Literature*, Oliver & Boyd, 1958.

INDEX

Alliteration, 150, 159, 167, 224
Analogical Imagination, 3, 34, 65
Analogy, 5, 22, 65, 67, 98, 180, 245
Anglo Saxon, 15
Annunciations of terror, 27, 210, 212–13, 216–17, 228, 243, 290, 293
Aquinas, Thomas, 78, 102
Aristotle, 70, 80–81
Arnold, Matthew, 127
Artistic sense, 6, 10, 27–29, 48, 52, 62, 69, 105, 110, 112, 157, 174, 199, 209, 224, 241, 258, 281–82, 286–88, 292, 294
Assonance, 150, 159, 167
Asyndeton, 159, 167–68
Auden, 163, 236, 284
Audience, 6, 37–38, 51, 63, 91, 97, 99, 111–12, 125, 132–33, 136, 151, 166, 170, 176–78, 180, 184, 196, 199, 203–5, 211, 219, 237–38, 250, 253, 283
Augustine, 38–39, 43, 153–55,
Aureation, 216, 224

Balthasar, Hans Urs von, 2–4, 6–10, 13, 23, 28, 34, 44, 66–67, 69, 113–14, 156, 247–48, 290–91
Barnes, William, 125
BBC, 20, 33, 49, 160, 164, 173, 238, 243
Beauty, 5, 7, 31, 35, 42–43, 47, 51, 61, 68–69, 74, 79–81, 91, 93–95, 97, 100, 107–10, 112, 116, 119–23, 129, 135, 137–38, 141, 143–44, 146, 149, 158, 162, 165–66, 177–79, 185, 193, 197, 204, 208, 220–22, 233, 236, 240, 242–43, 253–54, 257, 274, 290
Bi-directional, 6, 8, 23, 28–29, 35, 39, 56, 66–69, 98, 155, 243, 282
Birsay, 168, 208, 288–89
Blake, William, 37, 55–58, 70–72, 130, 138, 225, 276, 299, 300–1

Bloom, Harold, 1, 12, 64, 133, 231, 281, 286
Brand, John, 104
Bridges, Robert, 7, 11, 18, 21–20, 51, 71, 115, 160, 165, 190, 192, 196, 230, 237, 241–42, 266, 273–74, 282
Brinkies Brae, 32, 131
Browning, Robert, 147
Bunyan, John, 37, 54, 61, 71, 276, 299
Burns, Robert, 142

Cairns, Father Frances, S.J., 75
Calvin, John, 59, 97
Campion, Edmund, 189
Catholic:
    Aristotelian, 33, 43, 71, 89, 245
    categories, 33, 40–41, 55, 60, 67, 71, 73–75, 78, 88, 98, 255–56
    imagination, 3–4, 7, 10, 12–13, 18, 21, 30, 34, 44, 49, 53, 65–66, 68, 82, 146, 151–52, 169, 206, 213, 229, 247, 259, 284
    literary elites, 12, 23, 113, 231
    mind and heart, 2, 24, 31, 63, 98, 125, 139, 194, 200, 223, 237, 241
    structure of mind, 75–76
Catholicism, 3–5, 10, 12, 14, 16–17, 44, 60, 63, 74–76, 78, 80, 84, 111, 157, 161, 176, 192, 194, 199, 219, 221, 234, 245, 249, 255, 258, 278, 280
Chaucer, Geoffrey, 70, 99, 142, 162–63, 216, 225, 260
Chesterton, G. K., 73, 301
Christbirds, 126
Christian illumination, 26–27, 139, 144–45, 174
Christian mystery, 85, 88, 95–96, 98
Christianization, 57, 121, 194, 201, 213, 222, 234, 236, 279

Church Fathers, 5, 23, 34, 44, 67, 85, 157, 231, 248, 280
Clement, 157
Co-inherent, 146, 178
Conservative, 186, 191
Copleston, Frederick, 33, 75
Cosmological Argument, 33
Curvature of sound, 145-46, 152, 174, 181, 189

Dante, Alighieri, 62, 128
Dark Angels, 240
Depression, 27, 46, 51, 92, 108, 262-64, 266-72
Difference-in-unity, unity-in-difference, 8-9, 23, 29, 35, 67, 105-6, 108, 119, 126, 158, 164, 167, 206, 213, 231, 247, 257
Diphthongs, 172
Dixon Canon, Richard Watson, 39, 52, 70-71, 196, 200
Donne, John, 133, 160, 163
Douay-Rheims Bible, 254
Dryden, John, 72-73, 147
Dunbar, William, 90, 141-42, 216
Duns Scotus, 4-5, 23, 34, 38, 77, 137, 143-44, 180, 197, 242, 252
Dynamic systems approach, 4, 8-9, 245-46

Edinburgh University, 2, 11, 20, 35, 44, 51
Eliot, T. S., 47-48, 56, 62, 110, 127, 147-49, 161, 164-65, 199, 271
English language, 13-15, 21, 61, 72, 135, 146-47, 173, 181, 199, 283, 287
Epistemology, 2, 7, 17, 20-22, 24, 26, 39, 113, 122, 156, 219, 226, 237, 285
Essay in Aid of a Grammar of Assent, An, 2-4, 14, 22, 115-16, 140, 245
Etymology, 144, 151, 185, 215
Eucharist, 25-28, 33, 53, 57, 59-60, 62, 64, 67, 77-78, 86, 90, 96-99, 124, 131, 168, 177, 179, 182-84, 218, 242-43, 246, 251, 254, 256-57, 259-60, 276, 281, 286-90
Eucharistic Christ, 25, 33
Eynhallow, 232

Ferguson, James, 147
Fibres of being, 118
Fires of London, 239-40
Folklore, 88, 96, 206, 234, 237, 258, 289
Formalitas, 77, 81
Fornaldarsǫgur, 29, 205, 208, 289, 294, 301
Fra Angelico, 97, 138

Gardner, W. H., 12, 56
Giotto, 97, 138
Greek myths, 95-96, 98
Gregorian chant, 170

haeccitas or *thisness,* 38, 159
Half-baked stuff, 51-52, 77, 118, 165-66, 175-76, 188, 199, 266, 276, 287
Heaney, Seamus, 1-2, 5, 18, 67, 231, 245, 286-88, 292
Henryson, Robert, 90, 141
Heptahedron, 28, 155, 157, 164, 171, 174, 208, 210, 237, 245, 292
Herbert, George, 217
Heuser, Alan, 86, 105, 114-15, 119, 154, 166, 171, 173, 242, 275, 278
Hopkins, Gerard Manley:
"As Kingfishers Catch Fire," 108
"Brothers," 251, 253
"Bugler's First Communion, The," 251
"Carrion Comfort," 267
(Dark) Sonnets: 42-46, 93, 52, 251, 262-64, 266-68, 271, 273, 278
"Duns Scotus Oxford," 138, 143-44
"Felix Randal," 165, 200-1

Index

"God's Grandeur," 85, 92–93
"Habit of Perfection," 168–69, 136
"Harry Ploughman," 181, 183, 186
"Henry Purcell," 165–67, 169, 227, 230, 251, 253
"In honour of St Alphonsus Rodriguez Lay brother of the Society of Jesus," 27, 202–4
"Inversnaid," 11, 76, 78, 137, 139, 141–42, 266
"Loss of Eurydice," 142
"That Nature is a Heraclitean Fire and the Comfort of the Resurrection," 101, 103, 110, 180, 186, 236, 260, 262, 266
"Pied Beauty," 94–95, 97, 165, 240
"Sea and the Skylark, The," 77
"Spelt From Sibyl's Leaves," 244, 253, 273–79, 291
"Spring and Fall (*to a young child*)," 252
"Starlight Night, The," 108, 122–23, 137, 177–78, 255–56, 259
"Tom's Garland: Upon the Unemployed," 51, 108, 181, 186–89, 194
"Windhover, The," 96, 107, 126–28, 131–34, 136, 155, 176, 182, 185, 196, 227, 248, 259
"Wreck of the Deutschland, The," 153, 155, 210, 212–13, 217–20, 222–24, 226–27, 229, 250, 252, 254, 262, 276, 290–91

Housman, A. E., 258
Hoy, 19, 32, 94, 101, 208, 239, 282
Humming, 117, 173

Icelandic Pingèyrar monks, 144, 176, 285
Illative Sense, 2, 4, 7–8, 29, 66, 245–46
Individuation, 38, 43, 46, 81, 211
Inscape, 5, 8, 19, 23, 25–26, 30, 32–33, 35, 38, 43, 65, 67, 76–81, 86–98, 99–110, 112, 117–27, 130–31, 135–37, 140–45, 164, 167–74, 211–18, 221–25, 229–30, 235–37, 241–42, 244, 247, 253, 267, 273, 276–77, 280–92
Instress, 5, 19, 23–26, 30–33, 38, 43, 78–79, 85–86, 88–99, 101, 104–7, 110, 112, 114–21, 123–26, 130–31, 135, 137, 140, 143–44, 151, 154, 158, 164, 167, 169, 176–78, 180, 184, 186, 191, 196–97, 204–5, 208, 211–12, 214, 217–23, 225, 228–30, 235, 237, 241, 244, 247, 253, 255, 273, 277, 280, 282, 287–90
Intelligent design, 5, 24–25, 27, 29, 31, 43, 60, 102, 107, 137, 177, 247, 281

Jesuit, 22, 30, 33–34, 40, 43, 70, 75, 78, 80, 84, 88–89, 113, 117, 189, 203–4, 212–13, 224, 247, 253, 255–56, 272, 274
Joyce, James, 55–56, 75–79, 85, 139, 199, 227, 255–56
Julian of Norwich, 272

Katalogical, 8, 23, 29, 35, 56, 66, 106, 155–56, 247
Keats, John, 47, 72, 127, 133, 162, 202
King James Bible, 37–38, 190, 293
Kingdom of God, 30, 131
Kirkwall, 73, 208

Lammas Market, 53
Lataste, Maria, 80, 225, 265
Latin Mass, 218, 254
Lawrence, D. H., 127, 163, 258, 261
Letters, 7, 11, 16, 18, 20–21, 39, 51, 58, 71, 80, 128, 160, 165, 190, 192, 194, 196, 224, 230
Linguistic reality, 27, 222, 228–31, 243

Literary Canon, 12, 50, 61, 67, 69, 71–72, 130, 175, 197, 199, 202, 211, 215–16, 219–20, 225, 231, 258, 272
Literary litanies, 25, 62
Literary Politics, 12, 21
Liturgy of Hours, 170
Lowell, Robert, 163

MacDiarmid, Hugh, 62, 76–79, 139, 165
MacInnes, Ian, 51, 77, 215, 220, 287
MacInnes Collection, 215, 220
Mackay Brown, George: works
 "Abbot, The," 103
 "Big Wind, The," 131
 "Boat and the Croft, The," 283, 293, 295, 298
 "Chapel Between Cornfield and Shore," 167, 169, 288
 "Christ Poem," July 1944, 126, 188, 298
 Commonplace Book (notebook), 11, 18
 "Country Girl," 205
 "Creator," 92
 "Daffodils," 120, 288
 "Death Bird, The," 208, 289
 "December Day, Hoy Sound," 208
 "Doctor," 27, 197–98
 "Elegy," 75, 208, 289
 "The end of a sinister year" (essay), 298
 "Everyman," 7, 27, 62, 158, 175–76, 180, 184, 191, 195, 206–7, 229–30, 241–42, 267, 281, 283, 289, 298
 "Farm Labourer," 201–2
 The Fiddler At the Fair (A Parable), 52
 "Fisherman," 124, 197, 205, 233
 Fishermen with Ploughs (collection), 94, 130–31
 "Five Voyages of Arnor, The," 210, 243

Greenvoe (novel), 284
"Harrowing of Hell, The," 279
"Horseman and Seals Birsay," 170
"In Search of a Green Valley," 32
"Island Diary" (essay), 101
"Island Epiphanies," 131
"letter-poem," 165
"Lifeboatman," 27, 197–98
"Liturgy of April," 75, 157, 287, 289
Loaves and Fishes (collection), 35, 120, 124, 130
"Lodging, The," 125
"Magnificat," 188
Man Into Oak (prose poem), 268, 270
"Masque of Bread," 182
"New Child, A: ECL 11 June 1993," 209
"Night in Troy, The," 103
"The Old Women," 198
"Orkney and Scotland" (essay), 193, 299
"Pen Mightier than the Predicament" (essay), 91, 95, 298
"Places to Visit," 208, 289
"Poet, The," 168
"Prologue," 197, 229, 233
"Rackwick," 93
"Rackwick Stations of the Cross: From Stone to Thorn," 75
"Road Home, The," 208
"The Roman Catholic Church" (essay) March 1947, 20, 40–41, 59–61, 280–81, 284, 297
"Saint Magnus Cathedral" Easter 1944, 175, 183, 298
"Sara" (story), 231, 235–37
"Sea From Four Elegies, The," 230
"Shining Ones, The," 125
"Ship That Struck the Moon, The" (essay), 228
"A Sky-Scape in March" (1951) (essay), 101

Index

"Song: "I am undone else," 292-93, 296, 298
Spell for Green Corn, A (play), 18
"Stars," 125
"Stations of the Cross," 240
"Storm, The," 97, 124, 230-33, 276
"Summer Day," 37, 105, 124
"Sunday in Selskay Isle," 32
"Thorfinn," 205-6, 289
"Unlucky Boat," 283
"Watchman: Night Sea," 291, 295-96
Winterfold (collection), 89, 92
The Year of the Whale (collection), 229
"manmarks," 180, 236, 263
Maritain, Jacques, 48, 79-81, 113
Marwick, Ernest, 19, 22, 30, 53, 74, 148, 203, 227, 282, 298
Marwick, Jeanette, 2, 11, 134, 164, 166, 231, 286, 298
Mass, 53, 61, 64, 77-78, 154, 189, 195-96, 217-18, 220, 222, 246, 249-59, 275, 279
Maxwell Davies, Peter, 1, 130, 237-42
Maynard, Winifred, 128, 130, 139, 267
Metanarrative, 205, 207
Metaphysics, 19, 37-39, 77, 110, 144, 197
Metrics, 1-2, 6, 8, 20-22, 65, 147, 153, 157, 164, 179
Milton, John, 16, 56, 61-62, 71-73, 99, 160, 197, 225, 260
Mirror Of Whitening Light For Orchestra, A, 240
Modernism, 20, 28, 30, 50, 78, 148, 186, 258
Moore, Henry, 55, 77, 227
Moral Argument, 5, 33, 42
Morris, William, 127
Muir, Edwin, 12, 19-20, 22, 35-37, 47, 53, 62-63, 88, 90, 129-30, 141, 146, 163, 198-99, 207, 209, 223, 226-27, 238, 283, 286, 288
Mystical body, 126

National literature, 13, 15-16, 182
Native tradition, 2, 6, 25-26, 29-32, 48, 62, 131-32, 142, 145, 149, 164, 167-68, 173-76, 184, 201, 205, 207-8, 214-16, 220, 222, 226, 228, 230, 235, 241, 248, 253, 256, 279, 281, 285-86, 289, 293
Newman, John Henry, 2-9, 13-17, 20-23, 28-30, 34, 44-45, 47, 49, 52, 63-67, 71, 74-75, 83-84, 114-17, 134-35, 140, 156-57, 182, 192, 213, 244-48, 265, 272, 276, 282, 287-88, 291
Nordic corridor, 217, 233-34
Norn, 15-16, 172
North Atlantic, 29, 57, 83, 194, 201, 204, 207-8, 213, 215, 222, 234, 283, 294

Old Norse, 16, 172, 205-6, 214-15, 284, 289, 294
Onomatopoeia, 76, 78, 139
"on the quiver," 7, 233, 241-42
Orcadian Catholicism, 76, 78
Orcadian rhythm, 152, 217
Origen, 157
Orkney fable, 19, 56, 222
Orkney Herald, 35, 101, 215
Orkney literature, 12, 14, 130, 229, 232, 234, 236
Orkney poetics, 9, 18, 20, 22, 33-36, 71, 74, 109, 112, 130-32, 137, 152, 158, 160, 165, 180, 206, 208, 223, 228, 234, 237-41, 276, 279, 289
Orkneyinga Saga: The History of the Earls of Orkney, 209
Orphir, 101, 131
Oscillation, 7, 26, 29, 158, 233, 278
Oxford Movement, 3, 5, 7, 14, 17, 22, 43, 65, 67, 82-85, 114-15, 148, 157, 192, 195, 245, 248, 282

Pagan, 96, 152, 167, 201, 222–23, 227, 234, 236, 258, 261–62, 274–75, 277
Palimpsest, 204, 209
Papa Stronsay, 226
Papal Hierarchy, 73
Parable, 52–54, 57–61, 73–74, 125, 129, 157, 179, 254, 277
Parnassian poetry, 159
Particularities, 25, 34, 39, 115, 119, 121, 138, 141, 144, 177, 195, 199, 205, 212, 230, 253, 255, 261, 263, 276, 283
Pascal, Blaise, 265
Patmore, Coventry, 71
Personal library, 109, 125, 215, 220
Peters, W. A. M., 75, 80–88, 107, 122, 172
Pick, John, 52, 80, 107–8, 122–23, 248–49, 273
Piers Plowman, 127, 149
Pilgrimage, 57, 158
Plainsong, 238
Plato, 51, 70, 89, 109, 115, 153–57, 171–72, 175, 181, 197, 272, 275
Poetic vision, 6, 10, 14–15, 18, 21, 24, 28, 31, 31–36, 48, 56, 60, 67–68, 76, 116, 124–25, 144, 156, 182, 256–57, 259, 282
Politics, 12, 21, 35, 82, 185–90, 192–95
Pope, Alexander, 72, 147
Post-Modernism, 30
Pound, Ezra, 56, 147, 163
Prayer, 41–42, 46, 54, 62, 64, 74–75, 77, 129, 141, 170, 174, 178, 188, 203, 207, 218, 246, 249, 251–52, 264, 288–89, 291, 293
Pre-Raphaelites, 84, 115
Pre-theologic, 2–3, 5–6, 9, 22, 25, 29, 66, 68–69, 113, 116, 164
Priesthood, 69
Principle of Foundation, 41–42, 129
Principle of Sufficient Reason, 33–34
Private Judgement, 58

Protestant, 13–14, 16, 38–39, 60–65, 68, 71, 73, 78–80, 82, 144, 161, 192, 224
Pythagorean number theory, 26, 152, 155, 181, 220, 231, 291

Rackwick, 32, 45, 239–40, 271
Real Presence, 23, 27, 30, 119, 126, 128, 135, 237, 242–43, 290
Reformation, 3–5, 16, 21–22, 25, 30, 39, 53, 56, 58–59, 61, 64–65, 68–76, 78, 85, 90, 98–99, 102, 104, 115, 119, 122, 133, 143, 148, 167, 192, 195–96, 207, 212–13, 223–34, 254, 272, 275
Religious sense, 10, 52, 69
Rendall, Robert, 36, 132–33
"Republic of Conscience," 1–2, 96, 231, 285, 293
Romanticism, 3, 7, 83, 195
Rossetti, Gabriel, 127
Rousay, 232
Ruskin, John, 84, 115
Russell, Bertrand, 33

Sacramental, 8, 10, 24–26, 30, 34, 65–69, 95, 98, 157, 187, 204, 243, 247–50, 258, 282, 290
Sacraments, 25, 66–67, 86, 96, 200, 249–50, 256
sacred and the profane, 6, 21, 28, 35, 52–53, 57, 76, 101, 238, 258, 261, 287
Salt mathematics, 231, 235, 292
Scapa Flow, 213–14
Scarfe, Francis, 284
Scotism, 44
Scots, 91, 142, 193, 275
Scottish Catholic Imagination, 3, 10, 21, 34, 44, 65, 68, 247, 259
Scott-Moncrief, Ann, 214, 298, 303
Seamless garment, 35, 60, 62–63, 115
Sermons, 14, 116, 128
Shakespeare, 62, 127, 139, 156–60, 162–63, 225, 263

Shelleyan socialist, 72
Silence, 1, 40, 53, 94, 96, 99, 146, 168–69, 174, 183, 198, 202, 216, 233, 240, 245, 256, 260
Sir Robert Peel, 16
Sitwell, Edith, 190, 225
Socialism, 187, 190–91, 194, 199
Spenser, Edmund, 61, 71–73, 99, 133, 147, 225, 260
Spiritual combat, 28, 167, 210, 223, 263, 268–69, 271, 279
Sprung rhythm, 26–27, 33, 110, 125, 139, 144–45, 149, 158–60, 163, 165–67, 172, 174, 178, 182, 193, 201–2, 216, 250, 252
St Ignatius Loyola, 31, 40, 42–43, 45, 80–81, 129, 242, 268, 272, 274
St John of the Cross, 80, 264–65, 271
St Magnus, 18, 36, 38, 61–62, 76, 96, 118, 126, 133, 165, 174–75, 180, 183–85, 196, 201–2, 204–8, 212, 220, 234, 237–8, 240, 252, 265–66, 268, 270, 272, 276, 279, 283, 287, 289
St Magnus Cathedral, 175, 220
St Magnus Festival, 1, 238
St Magnus Way, 208, 289
St Teresa of Avila, 80, 264–65, 271
Stabat Mater, 4
Stalling, 26, 130, 135–37, 145, 151, 163, 181
Stemming, 26, 120, 130, 135–37, 145, 151, 163
Stravinsky, Igor, 55, 77, 227
Stromness, 19, 32, 37, 53, 97, 101, 142, 149, 214, 282
Sutherland, Graham, 49, 55, 77, 227
Swarm of symbols, 22, 26, 29, 36–37, 50, 62, 88, 104, 130, 157, 164, 176, 193, 195, 230, 256, 275, 286
Sydney, Philip, 147
Symmetry, 5, 26, 70–71, 76, 158, 164, 174, 181–82, 185, 210, 213, 216, 220, 226

Tamworth Reading Room, 14, 16, 287
Tapestry, 24, 26, 29, 31–32, 35–36, 48, 50, 76, 110–11, 115, 120, 123–24, 132, 144, 172, 184, 208, 213–14, 216, 230, 234, 237, 278, 288, 291
Teleological Argument, 102, 246
Tennyson, Alfred, 72, 127, 133, 147
The Dark Night of the Soul, 27, 30, 210, 241, 243, 264–65, 268, 271
"the number seven," 25, 67, 100, 155–56, 171, 173, 221, 235, 248
"the number five," 103–4, 151, 155, 208, 210, 212, 219–223, 233, 235, 243, 273, 289
Theocritus, 261
Theological aesthetics, 2, 4, 66, 247
Theological blades, 28, 93, 207, 243–44, 250, 257, 259, 266–67, 273–74, 279, 282, 290, 293
Theophany, 28, 30, 248, 294
Theories of Prosody, 150, 155
Thisness, 38, 135, 159, 166, 180, 196, 210–11, 233, 267
Thomas, Dylan, 163
Thompson, Francis, 136
Tractarians, 157
"trembling stations," 229–30, 242, 279
Trinity, 64, 66, 120, 154, 174, 228, 257, 261
Trochee and dactyl, 162

Unconscious cerebration, 117
Univocity, 5, 17, 22–23, 26, 28, 30, 34–35, 56, 65–68, 79, 94, 99, 106, 108, 124, 135, 152, 155, 164, 180, 211–12, 228, 248, 257, 282

Valley by the Sea, 238, 299
Van Gogh, Vincent, 138–39
Vatican II, 59, 67, 218, 250
Via negativa, 99, 263
Virgil, 261

Virgin Mary, 104, 116, 143, 188, 276
Vowelling, 171–73

Wave-hierarchies, 235
Weather, 101-2, 216-17, 239
Webster, John, 99, 263
Wishart, Sylvia, 44–45

Wittig, Kurt, 142, 216
Wordsworth, William, 72, 99, 156, 163, 260
workshop of looms, 150–51

Yeats, W. B., 62, 146, 163
Yesnaby, 210, 243

ABOUT THE AUTHOR

ALISON GRAY knew George Mackay Brown personally; hence her deep interest in his work and in the theme of Christianization of the North Atlantic. She received her doctorate on John Henry Newman and taught for many years in Catholic education in London. She has previously published *Circle of Light: The Catholic Church in Orkney Since 1560* and *George Mackay Brown: No Separation*. Originally from New Zealand, she lives in Orkney and is a Benedictine Oblate attached to Pluscarden Abbey in Morayshire.

www.ingramcontent.com/pod-product-compliance
Lightning Source LLC
Chambersburg PA
CBHW020324170426
43200CB00006B/264